THE ROYAL NAVY AND
POLAR EXPLORATION
Vol 2: from Franklin to Scott

THE ROYAL NAVY AND
POLAR EXPLORATION
Vol 2: from Franklin to Scott

E.C. COLEMAN

TEMPUS

First published 2007

Tempus Publishing Limited
The Mill, Brimscombe Port,
Stroud, Gloucestershire, GL5 2QG
www.tempus-publishing.com

British Library Cataloguing in Publication Data.
A catalogue record for this book is available from the British Library.

ISBN 978 0 7524 4207 5

Typesetting and origination by Tempus Publishing Limited
Printed in Great Britain

CONTENTS

Emerging from the smoke of a Boy Scout's campfire, Captain Scott leads General Gordon and Admiral Nelson as examples of courage in the face of adversity.

INTRODUCTION

With the stunning victories of the war against Napoleon behind it, the Royal Navy looked for gainful employment for its now much reduced fleet and the men who served it. With the eager support and encouragement of John Barrow, the Second Secretary to the Admiralty, it was decided that there could be no better deployment of ships, men, and materials than in the search for the Northwest Passage, and the attainment of the highest latitudes – both north and south. Indeed, why not reach out for the very Poles themselves?

The men and ships chosen for the task would be following in the wake of celebrated forebears. As far back as Tudor times, Frobisher had probed the north-east coast of North America in search of a passage to Cathay. Davis, Baffin and Hudson stretched the horizons both north and west and had left their names indelibly printed on the map. Edmund Halley had been stunned by the sight of massive, flat-topped 'ice islands' far to the south, and 'Foul Weather Jack' Byron, defeated by storms, had decided to head for warmer climes. Samuel Hearn discovered open waters on the Arctic Sea after travelling overland from Hudson's Bay. James Cook breached Bering's Straits and risked being crushed by the ice to reach Icy Cape on the northern edge of North America. He then circumnavigated the supposed continent of Antarctica before falling to the spears and clubs of the inhabitants of a Pacific island. Cook's midshipman, George Vancouver, investigated in astonishing detail every cove, bay and inlet of the north-west coast of America in an attempt to find a passage. His reward was to have his achievements ignored by a nation at war with the French.

Now under the highly critical eye of the Second Secretary to the Admiralty, it was the turn of men like John and James Ross, Buchan, Franklin, Parry, Back and Richardson.

John Ross all but destroyed his career by turning back in Lancaster Sound in the face of non-existent mountains. Buchan and Franklin failed in their effort to sail to the North Pole, Parry surged through the Arctic Archipelago to reach his Winter Harbour on Melville Island as Franklin, Back and Richardson avoided death through starvation by the narrowest of margins as they followed Hearn's path to the Arctic Sea. Before long, they had returned to extend their discoveries as Parry scoured the northern basin of Hudson's Bay. John and James Ross entered the fray once again to discover the north magnetic pole and to endure an unprecedented four winters in the Arctic as Back was sent to descend his Great Fish River to try and reach them. Undeterred, James Ross then joined Parry in an attempt to walk to the North Pole hauling boats on sledges as Back survived against terrible odds whilst testing himself against the ice of Hudson's Bay. Finally, turning about 180 degrees, James Ross, in company with Crozier, penetrated the Antarctic pack ice and discovered, not only a live volcano, but an astonishing wall of ice that towered above his mast tops; a barrier behind which a seemingly endless plain of shimmering ice reached towards the most southerly horizon humans had ever seen.

Barrow (by now, Sir John), had much to be proud of in the achievements of his protégés. They had borne their standards through the icy reaches of the Arctic and seen them reflected in the south's glistening ice barrier. They had taken their country's flag further towards the Poles than any other nation. But, as those other nations flexed their own maritime ambitions, they represented a challenge to Great Britain with its Empire upon the seas.

With the Poles seemingly out of reach for the time being, there still remained the problem of the Northwest Passage. So much had been done, and so little remained – so little in fact, that a foreign nation might be persuaded to attempt its completion. Something had to be done – and soon.

CHAPTER ONE

'BETTER FELLOWS NEVER BREATHED'

In 1818, the map of Northern America recorded just three points on its northern coast – Icy Cape, and the mouths of the MacKenzie and Coppermine Rivers. Twenty-six years later the map would show the results of Parry's high latitude voyage through Lancaster Sound and Barrow's Straits to reach Longitude 114 degrees West on Melville Island. To the south, along the continent's coast, the passage had been explored from Bering's Straits to Back's Chantry Inlet. The final missing pieces to the south had been filled in by expeditions sent out by the Hudson's Bay Company. Thomas Simpson and Warren Dease (Dease had been with Franklin on his second overland expedition) who had, in 1837, completed the 160-mile gap that remained between Franklin's 1826 furthest west and the waiting boats of the *Blossom*. Over the following two years, the same team had surveyed the coasts to the north and south between Point Turnagain and Back's Great Fish River. In the survey of 'Simpson's Strait' no isthmus connecting King William Land to Felix Boothia had been encountered and charts were already being produced suggesting King William Land to be an island. The same charts showed that the westward course of Parry's voyage and the easterly passage to Back's Great Fish River overlapped each other by 20 degrees of longitude – and the two were separated by less than 300 miles of unknown territory. Not surprisingly, the eighty-two-year-old Sir John Barrow who, with one brief break, had been at the Admiralty for forty years – and who had been instrumental in sending out the nineteenth-century searches for the Northwest Passage – was keen to exploit the re-awakened interest in polar exploration caused by the return of James Ross. Just one final heave could see the problem solved.

Barrow consulted Beaufort, Parry, Richardson and Sabine before sending a proposal to the First Lord of the Admiralty. In it he wrote:

> There is a feeling generally entertained in the several scientific societies, and also among officers of the Navy, that the discovery, or rather the completion of the discovery, of a passage from the Atlantic to the Pacific, round the northern coast of North America, ought not to be abandoned, after so much has been done and so little remains to be done. If the completion of the passage be left to be performed by some other power, England by her neglect of it, after having opened the East and West doors, would be laughed at by all the world for having hesitated to cross the threshold.

Sir John Barrow, Second Secretary to the Admiralty.

To a friend he wrote:

> The Admiralty having done so much, it would be most mortifying, and not very creditable, to let another Naval Power complete what we have begun.

Their Lordships, persuaded that such an expedition would be considerably cheaper than Ross's work in the Antarctic, and that two ships, the *Erebus* and the *Terror*, were available, gave their approval. But who was to be the leader?

Sir John Ross, apart from being in his seventies, had long been out of favour at the Admiralty. His nephew, Sir James Ross, had recently married and had given his word to his new father-in-law that he would not embark upon further polar exploration. Sir William Parry was serving as the Navy's Controller of Steam Machinery and showed no inclination to leave the post. Sir George Back, now working at the Admiralty, likewise showed no interest. Francis Crozier, who may have been favoured to lead by the First Lord, wrote to James Ross saying that he was 'not equal to the leadership'. Sir John Barrow was keen that Commander James Fitzjames should be placed in command. Fitzjames had seen action in China and had taken part in the 1835–1838 Euphrates Expedition, which attempted to establish a mail route to India by crossing Syria and sailing in steamships down the Euphrates River. The expedition had failed, but through no fault of Fitzjames.

Captain Sir James Ross.

He had, however, no polar experience. Only one name remained on the list – Sir John Franklin, currently serving in the Colonies.

Despite introducing elementary education for all, founding a scientific society, and proving to be immensely popular with the general public, much of Franklin's time as Lieutenant-Governor in Van Dieman's Land had been soured by a conflict with the civil authorities. Unable to accept corruption or incompetence, Franklin had dismissed the island's Director of Public Works, the Police Magistrate, and, finally, the Colonial Secretary. When the Secretary of State for the Colonies learned of the latter's removal from office, he not only supported him against Franklin, but sent out a totally unexpected replacement for the Lieutenant-Governor. Franklin was publicly humiliated. The public, however, was not content to leave matters as indicated by the Colonial Office. On the day that he left the island, Franklin departed to 'the enthusiastic cheers which burst forth from the assembled multitude … a loyal and generous people paying a heartfelt tribute of affection to a truly good man.'

Brushing aside suggestions that, at fifty-eight, he might be too old for the task, and with John Richardson's testimony that he was in perfect health, Franklin accepted the offer of command and his appointment to the *Erebus* with great delight. He was returning 'to his profession as a better field for the ability and devotion he had wasted on a thankless office.'

Captain Sir John Franklin.

Captain R.F.M. Crozier.

Commander James Fitzjames.

Above left: Lieutenant Graham Gore.

Above right: Lieutenant James Fairholme.

Lieutenant Henry le Vesconte.

John Reid – Ice Master.

HM Ships *Erebus* and *Terror*.

For his second-in-command, and to be captain of the *Terror*, Franklin chose Crozier who, since his return from the Antarctic, had been touring Europe on half-pay. Fitzjames, sponsored no doubt by Barrow, was appointed to the *Erebus*. The first lieutenant of the *Erebus* was to be Graham Gore (who had served in the *Terror* under Back), the others being Henry le Vesconte and James Fairholme. Edward Little was appointed as first lieutenant of the *Terror* along with Lieutenants George Hodgson and John Irving. Thomas Blanky (who had spent four Arctic winters with John Ross in the *Victory*) and John Reid were appointed as Ice-Masters. Only Franklin, Crozier, Gore, and the Ice-Masters had substantial experience in polar waters although the assistant surgeon of the *Terror*, Alexander Macdonald, had seen service in a whaler and Charles Osmer, the *Erebus*'s purser, had served in the *Blossom* with Beechey.

Despite their recent adventures among Antarctic icebergs, the *Erebus* and *Terror* were in good condition and needed little repair work at Woolwich Dockyard to bring them up to standard for the forthcoming voyage. Twenty feet on each side of the bows were sheathed in sheet iron and their bottoms were coppered to cope with the intended return voyage through the Pacific. The holds of both ships were strengthened to take the greatest innovation of all – two 15-ton former railway engines fitted to provide auxiliary power. The engines, with wheels removed, were placed athwartships, and the propeller shaft connected to the driving axle. The seven-foot screw-propellers were capable of being lifted via a stern well in order to keep them clear of any ice. Hot water from the engine's boilers could be used to heat the ship through pipes fitted beneath the accommodation and cabin deck.

Great care was taken in the provision of supplies and equipment. Victualling stores included over 136,000lbs of flour, almost 6,500lbs of salt meat (fresh water for soaking and cooking not being in short supply in the Arctic), 3,200lbs of canned meat, and nearly 2,400lbs of canned vegetables. 9,300lbs of lemon-juice were taken along with over 20,000 pints of concentrated soup, 9,450lbs of chocolate and 200lbs of pepper. Although it was thought by some that the voyage through the ice would be over in a matter of months, Franklin was prepared to spend at least three winters in the Arctic. The bulk of the canned meat was supplied by Stephen Goldner, a contractor with factories in London and Moldavia. Some of the canned meat – possibly for the private use of the officers – was provided by other suppliers.

Numerous scientific instruments were taken onboard for research into magnetism, wild life, botany, hydrography, refraction and geology. A comprehensive library was supplied, with each vessel having over 1,000 books, including accounts of earlier voyages into the region and bound volumes of *Punch*. Bibles and religious tracts were supplied by organisations interested in the men's moral welfare. Slates and slate pencils were included for the schools Franklin intended to set up during the long winter months. Ample warm clothing and wolf-skin blankets were provided for protection against the expected low temperatures.

The enormous amount of stores, when combined and stowed away, would have placed the ships at risk in an Atlantic crossing. To avoid this, only part of the stores were loaded into *Erebus* and *Terror*. The remainder went into the *Barreto Junior*, a storeship commanded by Lieutenant Edward Griffiths.

Franklin's instructions, written by himself, Barrow and Ross, began in terms that left no doubt as to the expedition's purpose:

> The object of the voyage is the discovery of a Northwest Passage, only a small part of which is still unknown.

He was not:

> ...to examine any channels leading northwards or southwards from Barrow Strait but is to sail through the latter along the latitude of approximately 74 degrees 15' north, until he reaches the longitude (about 98 degrees West) of Cape Walker. Thence he is to steer to the southward and westward towards Bering Strait in as straight a line as is permitted by ice or any unknown land.

If he was prevented by ice from passing south-westward of Cape Walker he was:

> To consider the alternative of passing between Cornwallis Island and North Devon if the strait between them (Wellington Channel) is open.

Once through the Bering Strait he was to call at the Sandwich Islands and Panama in order to send an officer home with the details of the voyage whilst he continued around Cape Horn, regarding indigenous peoples:

The *Eerebus* in the ice.

Any Eskimos or Indians whom he may meet are to be treated as friends and given presents, but he is to be on his guard against any attack.

Once 65 degrees North had been passed, copper cylinders or bottles containing details of their position and the date were to be 'frequently' thrown overboard.

A reception at the Admiralty was held by the First Lord on the evening of 8 May gathering together Franklin, Crozier, Fitzjames, Barrow, James Ross, Parry, Back and Sabine. Ten days later Franklin read Divine Service in the *Erebus*. At the forefront of the congregation were Jane, Lady Franklin; his daughter, Eleanor; and Sophia Cracroft (ardently pursued by Crozier, but without success). At half-past ten the following morning, 19 May 1845, the two ships, smartly painted with black hulls, yellow upper works and white masts, were towed down the Thames by HMS *Rattler*. They left to the cheers of a nation determined in its belief that the mystery of the Northwest Passage was at last about to be unlocked – and by men and ships of the greatest navy the world had ever known.

Only two critics voiced their doubts. John Ross personally expressed his opinion to Franklin that the ships were too big and carried too many men (134 on leaving England). He urged Franklin to leave caches of supplies along his route in case he had to retreat and told him that, if nothing had been heard from the expedition by January 1847, he would volunteer to lead a search expedition. Doctor Richard King – Back's companion on his expedition down the Great Fish River – used every occasion to tell anyone who would listen that waterborne attempts to breach the Arctic would be futile. Only an overland expedition down

Back's River offered any hope of success – a message he would repeat many times, only to be ignored just as often.

Water and four bullocks (bringing the number of live animals up to ten) were obtained at Stromness and Franklin sailed into the Atlantic to the cheers of men manning the rigging of HMS *Rattler* and HMS *Blazer* (the latter commanded by Captain Owen Stanley, one of Back's lieutenants in the *Terror*). The voyage was uneventful and Cape Farewell was rounded without difficulty. Greenland was seen on 25 June and the ships brought to anchor at the Whalefish Island just over a week later. The stores were transferred from the *Barretto Junior* and the last letters home handed over. Fitzjames was in almost a frenzy of excitement. 'I say we shall get through the Northwest Passage *this* year', he wrote to his friend John Barrow, Sir John's son. Franklin had proved to be 'delightful, active, and energetic, and evidently even now, persevering', his mess was 'happy' and the men were 'most agreeable'. To another friend he wrote:

> Don't care is the order of the day; I mean, don't care for difficulties or stoppages; go ahead is the wish. We hear this is a remarkably clear season, but clear, or not, we must 'go ahead' as the Yankees have it; and if we don't get through, it won't be our fault.

Fairholme noted that Franklin 'really looks ten years younger'. The expedition's commander himself ended his last letter to his wife with the words:

> To the Almighty's care I commit you and dear Eleanor. I trust He will shield you under His wings and grant the continual aid of His Holy Spirit. Again, that God may bless and support you both is and will be the constant prayer of your most affectionate husband.

The letters were handed over to Lieutenant Griffith who noted:

> I felt quite low-spirited on leaving Sir John and his officers – better fellows never breathed. They were all in the highest possible spirits, and determined on succeeding if success were possible. I have very great hopes, knowing their capabilities, having witnessed their arrangements, and the spirit by which they are actuated – a set of more undaunted fellows never were got together, or officers better selected.

Griffiths sailed south from Whalefish Island on 12 July, taking with him four invalids from Franklin's ships (one man had earlier been transferred to the *Rattler* – leaving a total of 129). He was followed a few hours later by the *Erebus* and *Terror*, their bows turning to the north. Some ten days later, held up by the ice of northern Baffin Bay, Franklin came across two whaling ships, the *Enterprise* and the *Prince of Wales*. Courtesies were exchanged and Captain Martin of the *Enterprise* went onboard the *Erebus* where he learned from Franklin that he believed the expedition had enough food for five years. If necessary, the supplies could be extended to seven years with the addition of game hunted down during the course of the voyage (Griffiths thought the supplies were only intended to last for three years). Birds were already being shot and salted down as Martin talked to Franklin.

After a return visit by some of the officers to the *Enterprise*, the whalers sailed on 29 July. The last sight they had of the expedition was the *Erebus* and *Terror* moored to an ice-floe, waiting for a chance to continue to the west.

CHAPTER TWO

'NOT OF MUCH USE'

Eighteen months after Franklin and his ships had last been seen, Captain Beechey submitted to the Admiralty a plan for the relief of the expedition. He had not been the first. John Ross had written to the Admiralty in the autumn of the previous year and King continued to press on with his idea of taking an expedition down Back's River – now as an aid to Franklin. Both were politely ignored by the Admiralty. Beechey suggested a combination of a Back River expedition and a voyage to Cape Walker. Lieutenant Griffiths of the *Barretto Junior* wrote to his friend John Barrow imploring him 'to use all your influence in sending three reliefs, as it is perfectly impossible to say which way circumstances may have obliged them to pursue their course.' Whilst the Admiralty considered its response, an Aberdeen whaling Captain, William Penny, with his season coming to an end, tried to enter Lancaster Sound in search of Franklin. The weather conditions, however, forced him back and he never got further than the entrance. Three months later, the Admiralty finally began to turn its mind to thoughts of rescue.

It was decided that the attempt to find Franklin would be done from three directions – two ships would look into Bering's Strait, the western exit of the passage; an overland party would approach from the south; and two ships would follow Franklin's route through Lancaster Sound to Cape Walker.

The western expedition left first. HMS *Plover*, under the leadership of Commander Thomas Moore, who, as a mate in the *Terror*, had served under Crozier on Ross's Antarctic expedition. In January 1845, as a lieutenant, he took the hired barque HMS *Pagoda* across the Antarctic Circle in an attempt to complete the magnetic survey started by Ross. The voyage was plagued by adverse winds and the constant threat of icebergs, but he still achieved much of what he had been sent out to do. The *Pagoda* was to be the last ship dependent on sails alone to cruise the Antarctic waters. Moore was ordered to take the *Plover* as far north as he could 'consistent with the certainty of preventing the ships being beset by the ice.' A harbour was then to be found. With a safe anchorage secured, two of the ship's boats were to try to make their way along the Arctic coast in the attempt to find Franklin, or to meet up with the land expedition. HMS *Herald*, then surveying in the Pacific under the command of Captain Henry Kellett, was to join the *Plover* at Bering's Strait. Kellett had lived a charmed life. He was serving as a lieutenant in HMS *Eden* when a plague hit the ship.

With no surgeon on board, only three officers remained fit with forty-six of the ship's company ill. He was first lieutenant in the *Aetna* when the captain was murdered, and was commanding the *Starling* when she was struck by lightning and dismasted. During the war with China, he had served with such reckless daring that he was promoted to captain and appointed a Commander of the Bath.

Franklin's old friend and companion, the sixty-year-old Sir John Richardson was appointed to lead the overland expedition. Richardson had been knighted in 1846 for his work as Inspector (i.e. chief medical officer) of Haslar Royal Naval Hospital, especially for his introduction of general anaesthesia. His second-in-command was to be the Orkney-born surgeon and Hudson's Bay Company Chief Factor, Dr John Rae. Rae was an obvious, yet unfortunate, choice. A sledge-traveller of extraordinary ability, he had absorbed much of the native skills for land travel and survival. He had wintered on the shore of Repulse Bay in 1846-47 and had travelled 1,200 miles on foot around the coast of 'Committee Bay' – the southern extension of the Gulf of Boothia. However, his superior was Sir George Simpson, a man noted for his dismissive attitude towards the Royal Navy and those of its men who insisted on travelling through his territory. Franklin had been sneered at as someone for whom tea was indispensable, liked his food, and who could not walk more than eight miles a day. George Back was castigated for his 'impertinent interference'. Rae was deeply loyal to the Company and eager to take Simpson's dislike of the Royal Navy to extreme lengths – an attitude that was soon heartily returned.

The remainder of Richardson's team was made up of five seamen and fifteen soldiers from the Corps of Sappers and Miners (Lady Franklin had volunteered to go, but was refused on the grounds that 'disagreeable situations' might arise). Special boats capable of use both on the sea and on rivers were built and a portable, inflatable boat designed by Lieutenant Peter Halkett, obtained. Pemmican was provided by the Royal Clarence Victualling Yard. The men, supplies and boats were sent on a Hudson's Bay Company ship with orders to make their way towards the Mackenzie River from York Factory under the command of John Bell, a Hudson Bay Company Chief Trader.

Richardson and Rae set off on 25 March 1848 and caught up with the seamen and sappers three months later at Methy Portage. Within days Rae was writing to Simpson and other Company officials that the men were trying hard, but were 'a set of the most ragged and dirty looking fellows I have ever seen', and the seamen were 'the worst carriers'. On reaching the Great Slave Lake the party divided, with Bell taking sixteen voyageurs to the Great Bear Lake with orders to build a winter base ('Fort Confidence'), as Richardson, Rae, their men and an Eskimo interpreter, 'Albert One-eye', set off for the mouth of the Mackenzie.

Supplies were left at Fort Good Hope, in case any men from the *Plover* managed to get that far, and the sea was reached on 4 August. More supplies were deposited at Point Separation before a band of 300 Eskimos were met and asked if any sign of Franklin's ships had been seen. None had, so the expedition headed off eastwards along the coast helped by a westerly wind. After passing Cape Parry,

Surgeon Sir John Richardson.

and on approaching Dolphin and Union Strait, the ice began to close in with the shore, bringing with it snow and a marked drop in temperature. Any chance of crossing the strait to Victoria Land had now gone and, before long, the expedition was forced to resort to hauling the boats over the ice and taking advantage of the few open lanes of water that remained available. One of the boats and a supply of pemmican was left at Cape Krusenstern before the remaining two boats – by then badly damaged by the ice – were abandoned near Cape Kendall. The supplies and equipment were shared out by lot and the party set out on snowshoes for Fort Confidence. A new river was found and named the 'Rae' – its crossing achieved with help from a tribe of nearby Eskimos. Richardson River, however, had to be crossed using Halkett's portable boat, powered by dinner plates used as paddles. Thirteen days after setting out from Cape Kendall, Richardson arrived at Fort Confidence. He had learned, both from the Eskimos and by his own endeavours, that it was extremely unlikely that Franklin had passed along the coast between the Mackenzie and the Coppermine. Richardson's own belief was now that the missing expedition would be found somewhere in one of the passages believed to exist 'between Victoria, Banks, and Wollaston's Lands'.

Fort Confidence had been well built by Bell, and the party settled down to a winter of scientific observation with the occasional party enlivened by fiddle music. Richardson spent much of his time reading the scriptures whilst Rae wrote disparagingly about his leader, the soldiers and the seamen. The latter group were described as 'the most awkward, lazy and careless set I ever had anything to do with.' Richardson was considered as 'not of much use'. With his self-acknowledged frequent displays of bad temper Rae may have let his feelings out. This, in turn, could have led to the surprising decision by Richardson that he and his men would return to England the following spring, leaving Rae and his voyageurs to return to the Arctic coast in an attempt to cross the Dolphin and Union Strait and continue the search.

Richardson, Bell, the seamen and soldiers set off from Fort Confidence at the beginning of May 1849 after Rae had been given his instructions for the return to the north. The seamen and sappers were sent to York Factory to await transport in a Hudson's Bay vessel whilst Richardson made his way to Montreal before taking the mail steamer from Boston.

Rae and his voyageurs set out on 9 June and reached the sea half-way through the following month. Closely packed ice and fog held them on the southern coast of Dolphin and Union Strait until mid-August when Rae gave up and started back for Fort Simpson on the Mackenzie. On passage up the Coppermine River, the Eskimo – Albert One-eye – was drowned at Bloody Falls. Despite this failure, and Rae's continued despising of all things to do with the Royal Navy, Richardson never spoke of him in less than courteous terms.

CHAPTER THREE

'AT THE JUNCTION OF FOUR GREAT CHANNELS'

On his return to England, Richardson learned of the death of Sir John Barrow. The tireless and well-respected Admiralty Secretary, who had been behind all naval expeditions since 1818, had died in November the previous year. But, even if the Admiralty had lost its leading polar lobbyist, the torch was snatched with a vengeance by Franklin's wife, Jane, Lady Franklin. A formidable and courageous woman, she had responded to the slow start of the expeditions in search of her husband by issuing posters to the whaling fleet offering up to £2,000 for any information regarding her husband (the Admiralty was offering 100 guineas). She had also begun firing letters across the Atlantic in search of American assistance. At her suggestion James Ross was approached to see if he would lead the eastern expedition. Ross agreed (despite having earlier promised his wife and his father-in-law that he would not do so) and was appointed to the newly purchased HMS *Enterprise*. A second ship – HMS *Investigator* – was also bought from her builders and, at Ross's request, was given to Captain Edward Bird who had served with him in the *Erebus*. Both ships were strengthened for Arctic waters and given supplies for a three-year voyage. A novel addition to the equipment to be taken was the supply of two steam launches. Among those selected by Ross to go on the expedition was Lieutenant Robert McLure who had been with Back in the *Terror* (appointed as the *Enterprise*'s first lieutenant), and his old sledging companion, Thomas Abernethy, who was appointed as one of the expedition's Ice-Masters. The *Enterprise*'s second lieutenant was Francis Leopold McClintock, the son of an Irish dragoon officer.

Ross's orders told him to search the shores of Lancaster Sound, Barrow Strait and Wellington Channel. The *Investigator* was to winter near to Cape Rennell on the northern coast of North Somerset before sending parties out to explore the east and west coasts of North Somerset and Boothia Felix. The *Enterprise* was to winter in Winter Harbour (Parry's old base) on Melville Island, or on the coast of Bank's Land. Sledging parties were then to be sent out to search southwards to try and reach Cape Bathurst (east of the Mackenzie) and, by travelling down the east coast of Banks Island, to attempt to reach Cape Krusenstern (on Dolphin and Union Strait) where they might meet up with Richardson.

The expedition sailed on 12 May 1848, and, after an uneventful Atlantic crossing, reached the Whalefish Islands late the following month. Eight days were

Search parties ashore from Captain James Ross's 1848–49 Search Expedition. From a painting by Lieutenant W. Brown.

spent in carrying out magnetic surveys before the ships continued to the north. At Sanderson's Hope, whalers were seen heading to the south having failed to breach the ice, so Ross worked his way around the inside of a group of islands that held the ice back from the Greenland shore. This act of seamanship brought him to a point where he could force his way through the ice to find open water to the west. Baffin Island was reached at Ponds Bay on 22 August and Ross sailed north and west into Lancaster Sound burning blue lights and firing cannons and rockets in an attempt to attract the attention of either Franklin's men or the local natives who might be able to help his search. Landings were made at Possession Mount and Cape York to leave records and to search for any message from the missing expedition. Neither natives nor messages were apparent. Finding the entrance to Prince Regent Inlet blocked with ice, Ross took his ships north across the eastern end of Barrow Strait and examined the shores of Maxwell Bay before reaching the Wellington Channel where he found that passage choked with ice. Even worse, the ice stretched in a solid barrier right across Barrow Strait to the northern shore of Somerset Island. With falling temperatures, storms and fog, there was no other alternative for Ross than to seek a place to winter and he headed for Port Leopold on the north-east corner of Somerset Island. The ships arrived in the natural harbour on 11 September. It was not a moment too soon. All around them the sea ice was freezing and Ross recorded that the following morning the ice 'completely sealed the mouth of the harbour.' Any plans for separating the ships now had to be abandoned and they began to prepare for the coming season. Following a, by now, well-practiced routine, the topmasts were unshipped and stowed, the upper deck housed over with canvas, and a wall of snow packed against the ship's sides. A school was set up teaching reading, writing, arithmetic, and navigation, and a football competition played on the ice when the weather allowed. Although Ross had failed to find any clues regarding Franklin, and had not got his ships as far to the west as he had hoped, he was not too down-hearted for:

> … being at the junction of the four great channels, of Barrow's Strait, Lancaster Sound, Prince Regent Inlet, and Wellington channel, it was hardly possible for any party, after abandoning their ships, to pass along the shores of any of those inlets without finding indications of the proximity of our Expedition.

During the winter darkness, traps were set to catch arctic foxes. Once caught, the animals were fitted with a copper collar on which was engraved the position of Ross's ships and the depots that had been left on the coasts. It was assumed that any party trying to make its way to safety would shoot the foxes for food and consequently find the collars. The long winter months were also used to prepare for the forthcoming sledge journeys that Ross intended to carry out as soon as the weather and season permitted. Unlike his expeditions under the command of his uncle eighteen years earlier, Ross had no dogs available to him. The sledge-hauling would have to be done by his seamen.

In April and early May 1849, a number of short journeys were made to lay further depots of food and clothing for Franklin's men. With this done, Ross could turn his attention fully to his sledge-journey. He decided to take two sledges with McClintock as his second-in-command along with twelve seamen. The wooden sledges with their canvas and leather hauling traces had been prepared during the winter and were loaded with forty-one days rations (twenty days out, twenty return, with one day spare), tents, clothing, and blankets. Each man's ration was to consist of 1lb of meat, 1lb of biscuit, a pint of chocolate, half a pint of lemon juice, and a quarter pint of rum. With 18 inches of snow underfoot, they set off in the early morning of 15 May to the cheers of the remaining ship's companies. For the first five days they were accompanied by Bird and twenty-nine seamen. Bird had hoped to go further, but Ross told him to return to the ships and get other sledging expeditions under way to look at the coasts around Port Leopold.

The coast of North Somerset trended slightly to the north-west past Cape Rennell before Ross found it began to change direction first westward then south. Once the southward trend had been confirmed, Ross found himself going down the frozen surface of a wide passage ('Peel Sound'), its entrance separated, to the east, by Cape Bunny and, to the west, by Cape Walker. He could have crossed over to the far cape and continued to the west, but he knew that was the route he intended to take later that year, so continued his journey to the south. To their left lay the west coast of North Somerset whilst, far away in the distance to the west, could be seen what appeared to be a series of islands. They could, however, be connected as a single coastline and McClintock was concerned that they might be skirting the edge of a great bay. Numerous indentations were searched and given names as they followed the rising limestone hills of the eastern shore. After twenty-one days, and no evidence that Franklin had passed that way, the party reached a high point named by Ross 'Cape Coulman' after his wife's family. This was their limit both in rations and in endurance.

Several of the men were 'knocked up' and unable to haul the sledges further. Ross called a halt and ordered McClintock to build a cairn on the highest point whilst he and two men pressed on further south for a few hours to see what lay beyond the next most prominent headland. The small party crossed a wide bay ('Four Rivers Bay') and climbed to the top of its southern arm ('Southern Cape'). From their elevated position Ross could see the coast curving away to a large promontory ('Cape Bird') almost forty nautical miles to the south. A further sixty miles from Cape Bird would have brought him to the magnetic pole he had located in 1831. But now he had no choice but to return to his ships.

Rid of the burden of mapping and searching the coast, the return journey was achieved in sixteen days despite, at times, the sledges carrying a sick man and others limping alongside. Although Bird and the rest of the ship's companies were delighted to see their safe return, an air of gloom had descended on Port Leopold with the death of the *Enterprise's* assistant surgeon, twenty-seven-year-old Henry Mathias from a pulmonary disease. Also, in Ross's absence, the captain of the hold

HMS *Investigator* at Port Leopold. The men in the foreground are trapping arctic foxes for tagging with rescue messages.

(a petty officer) of HMS *Investigator* had died, and the surgeon of the *Enterprise*, Dr Robertson, had narrowly escaped death from scurvy.

Bird had sent out sledging parties as Ross had requested. Lieutenant Browne (the expedition's artist) had taken four men and built a cairn on Parry's Peak – a prominent hill on the eastern coast of Prince Regent Inlet. Lieutenant Barnard had searched the northern shore of Barrow Strait, and Lieutenant Robinson had reached down the eastern coast of North Somerset to a point beyond Fury Beach. At this most obvious destination for any party of men trying to escape from the Arctic, Robinson found Parry's stores still in good condition, with no sign that they had been visited since John Ross's stay.

By the end of June, Ross was keen to escape from the harbour and press on to the west in accordance with his original instructions. A large tent was constructed on the shore using the canvas upper-deck housing and twelve months supplies left inside for up to sixty-four people. The *Investigator*'s steam launch (which had performed well during the little use to which it had been put) had its engine taken out and hauled up onto the beach. Much to his concern Ross found that the ice refused to break up, keeping the ships in. Under McClintock's direction sheerlegs were rigged and ice-saws used to cut a channel towards the harbour entrance. Two hundred feet a day were managed despite the ice being up to 5 feet thick. At one stage, the ice cracked of its own accord along the intended route

HMS *North Star* trapped in Wolstenholme Sound.

Wolstenholme Sound with graves of men from HMS *North Star.*

but, by the middle of August, the sea ice was showing no sign of giving way. It was not until the end of the month that the break-up occurred and Ross's ships were able to stand to the north, too late in the season for any practical chance of a voyage to the west.

Twelve miles off the northern shore of Barrow Strait, Ross found himself up against a barrier of old ice. To the west, the ice continued across the strait blocking off any chance of progress in that direction. The ice, however, was breaking up somewhere as a stream of loose pack-ice poured down from the west and trapped Ross's ships in its rigid grip. For a time there was cause for alarm as the ships were nipped in the increasing pressure and both vessels sustained damage. Equally, there was cause for hope. The ice was drifting at a rate of about ten miles a day eastwards towards the entrance to Lancaster Sound. Three weeks after they were beset, the ships were off Pond's Inlet when the ice broke up around them. With no further possibility of continuing the search that year and no desire for a second wintering, Ross signalled to the *Investigator* his intention to return to England. Once clear of a large number of threatening icebergs in northern Baffin's Bay, the ships left the ice behind them on crossing the Arctic Circle and arrived without further incident off Scarborough on 4 November. The following day Ross took the train to London and reported to the Admiralty.

The voyage had failed in its chief objective. Nothing had been learned of the fate of Franklin's expedition. A series of depots had been established along the southern shore of Lancaster Sound which could prove vital to any group of men attempting to escape from the Arctic by that route. 150 miles of new coastline had been explored and meteorological and geological records had been maintained. The first faltering steps in man-hauling sledges had been taken, an experience that McClintock would hone almost to a science (he had already decided that the rations supplied for the journey down Peel Sound were totally inadequate and should be trebled). For many on the expedition, however, the most memorable, and worst aspect, had been the food. The salt beef was frequently found to weigh less than half its contracted weight, and the canned foods often proved to be half-empty. Even those that were acceptable in weight were of such poor quality that one member of the expedition wrote a letter to the press saying, 'We had three sorts of soup – viz., ox cheek, vegetable, and gravy – the latter two were never used for any purpose but to wash the dishes up with, and the former was the most inferior of its kind.'

Unknown to Ross until his return, polar experience had been gained on his behalf by HMS *North Star*. Under the command of James Saunders, the *North Star* had been sent out in May 1849, with supplies for Ross and orders to search Smith and Jones sounds for any traces of Franklin. Trapped by ice in late September on the north-west coast of Greenland, Saunders was forced to winter in Wolstenholme Sound. During his wintering, four of his ship's company died. Able Seamen William Sharp, Richard Baker, and George Deverell; along with William Brisley, a boatswain's Mate. Each man was buried ashore and a tombstone raised to mark the site. The *North Star* did not escape until 1 August the following year. Several harbours were then visited, including Port Leopold, but all were found to be iced up. At the end of the month Saunders decided to return home calling at Navy Board Inlet where a huge cache of supplies were left. Included among the stores deposited on the beach were 124 pairs of carpet (felt) boots, 378 bottles of brandy, 835 bottles of rum, 34 bottles of port, 70 gallons of white wine, 136 pints of preserved milk, and 495lbs of walnuts. The *North Star* arrived at Spithead a month later having lost four men to scurvy.

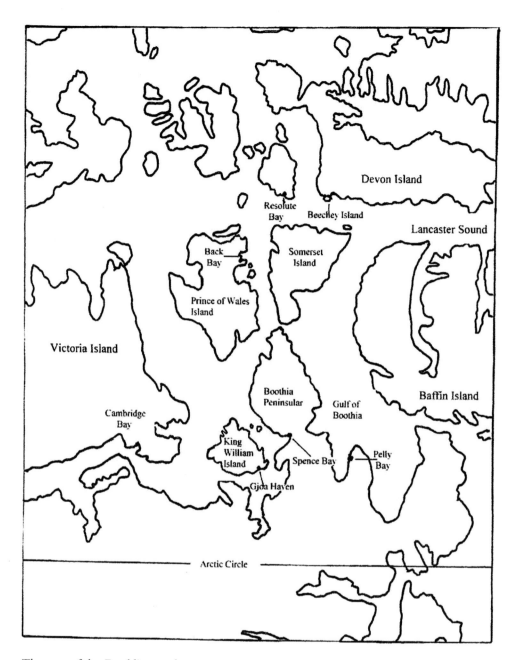

The area of the Franklin searches.

As for James Ross, his voyage with the *Enterprise* and *Investigator* was to be his last. He retired to a quiet life shared with his wife, Anne, and – apart from acting in an advisory capacity – never again became involved with polar activities. He died at Aylesbury in 1862. Later, Ross was to be granted the most spectacular award ever granted to a polar explorer. He had a crater on the moon named in his honour.

CHAPTER FOUR

'AND NO DESPAIRING'

When John Rae returned from his failed attempt to reach Victoria Island, he regained his fur-trading post at Fort Simpson on the Mackenzie River. Much to his surprise, as the winter of 1849 was just about to descend, he found himself having to host Lieutenant William Pullen and two seamen. The strangers had left HMS *Plover* in late July and had made their way up the Mackenzie River to his doorstep.

The *Plover*, built for capacity rather than speed, had failed to join the *Herald* at their Kotzebue Sound rendezvous and had been forced to spend the 1848-49 winter in an anchorage on the mountainous Chukotka (Siberia) coast. Soon frozen in, Commander Moore instigated the usual round of schooling, entertainments, and preparations for the coming season. A stone-built house was constructed for the blacksmith's forge and for the drying of clothes. He was fortunate that the local natives – the Chukchee – proved to be an amiable people who had no difficulty in rubbing along with the newcomers. So great did the trust between the two communities become that, when the local chief's wife gave birth, Moore celebrated with a twenty-one gun salute. At the subsequent christening, rockets were fired in celebration – one of the missiles miss-fired, fizzling along the ground with hordes of gleeful Chukchees in pursuit.

In March 1849, Moore sent the *Plover*'s second master, Henry Martin, acting mate William Hooper, and master's assistant William Moore 100 miles north to East Cape (Cape Dezhnev) to search for signs of Franklin along the coast and, if possible to cross Bering's Straits to Kotzebue Sound. They were to use a dog-sledge, take supplies for twelve days, and be guided by two natives. After getting lost on the sea ice, William Moore's health broke down and he was sent back to the ship under the care of natives from a nearby village. East Cape was reached but the guides refused to go any further as they were frightened of the local natives. Nothing was found of the missing expedition and Hooper and Martin returned safely after six weeks absence.

When the sea ice outside the harbour began to break up, Moore put officers and men to work sawing through the six-foot thick ice which barred his path to the open sea. After twenty-two days they had cut a lane 2,000 yards long and, on 13 June 1849, the ship broke free. The *Plover* immediately set sail across the Bering Strait to Chamisso Island in Kotzebue Sound and was joined a day later by Kellett in the *Herald* – he had wintered at Honolulu. A week after the arrival of the *Herald,* the two ships saw the schooner *Nancy Dawson,* flying the burgee of the Royal Thames Yacht Club and owned by former Royal Navy mate Robert Shedden, sail into the anchorage. Shedden came from a wealthy background and, after serving and being wounded in the Chinese War, chose to spend his time and money cruising around the world. At Hong Kong he learned of the search for Franklin and decided to offer his services and his vessel. Intending to investigate the waters north of Bering's Strait he had met up with the *Herald* at Awachta Bay near Petropavlovsk and Kellet had accepted his offer of help despite his reservations about the yachts crew (mainly American, recently recruited at Hong Kong). On meeting them, Kellett considered the crew of the *Nancy Dawson* to be 'a most disorganised set of men' – he was later to change this to 'a most disaffected set'.

The three vessels sailed on 18 July. Two days later they were off Point Hope in a thick fog keeping company by means of gongs and bells as whales spouted all around them. Where possible, a landing was made and the coast searched. Parties of natives were met ashore whilst others paddled out to the ships. There, the women would trade their clothing 'even to their second pair of breeches' for tobacco and beads. Following the coast as it trended to the north-east, the ships arrived off Wainwright Inlet a week after leaving Chamisso Island. Kellett had intended to use the inlet as his northern rendezvous but, on examination, it was found that the entrance was too shallow. There was, nevertheless, important work to get under way.

The Admiralty had decided that an expedition should be launched from the ships once their furthest point north had been reached. A boat party was to be sent along the southern shore of the Beaufort Sea as far as the mouth of the Mackenzie. The river was then to be ascended and the winter spent at a Hudson's Bay Company fort before the party would return to the ships, or make their own way to England. Kellett chose the first lieutenant of the *Plover* – Lieutenant William Pullen – to command the expedition. Pullen had joined the ship from the *Herald* when they had met in Kotzebue Sound having made his own way from England to Honolulu via Panama. A Devon-born man, the thirty-six-year-old Pullen had entered the navy at the age of fourteen and had spent much of his recent service surveying off the coast of eastern Canada. He was to take four boats with him, a thirty-foot schooner-rigged pinnace named the *Owen*, another half-decked pinnace, and two whalers. Joining Pullen were William Hooper; the second master, Henry Martin; and twenty-two men. With Kellett's approval, Sheddon would accompany Pullen in the *Nancy Dawson* as far into the Beaufort Sea as he could with safety. Seventy days supply of preserved meat were put into the boats along with ten cases of pemmican intended for Franklin's party.

Under full sail the boats took their leave of the ships on 25 July. For five days Pullen examined the coast and questioned those natives he came across after assuring them of his friendship by rubbing noses – 'not a pleasant salutation, I assure you.' One native had an injured hand and asked Pullen to dress it for him.

When the task was completed the Eskimo went away with 'a cleaner hand than I think he ever had before.' On the thirtieth, Pullen was stopped by ice off Point Barrow and anchored his boats to a large ice-floe. It was clear that the *Nancy Dawson* could not get any further and that the two large pinnaces would be unmanageable if the party had to cross ice or land to get to open waters. Pullen decided to send them back with the *Nancy Dawson* under Martin's command. The spot was marked by a twenty-foot cross marked on the shore with the words 'Plover's boats arrived on 2 August. Intelligence, 10 feet N.E.'. The 'intelligence' was a letter buried in a preserved meat tin. In the letter, Pullen recorded his intended journey, the number of men, the provisions he was carrying, and the places of rendezvous for the *Herald* and *Plover*.

Now with thirteen men, the two whalers and a large native vessel (oomiak) he had traded from the Eskimos, Pullen took advantage of narrow lanes through the ice to make his way to the east. He landed at Point Berens to bury a cache of provisions and fell foul of the local Eskimos when they tried to steal a shovel. Returning to their boats, they set off with an increasing number of natives following them along the shore. A further attempt at landing was met by armed Eskimos and, at one point, forty natives approached in boats and loosed a number of arrows without causing injury. With a favourable wind, the natives were left behind but near disaster struck during a night sheltering in the lee of Herschel Island. At half-past-one in the morning, Pullen was woken from his sleep on the ice with the news that a sudden shift of wind had caused the boats to be swamped. The water had soaked everything, the worst damage being caused to the navigational instruments. Pullen found that his sextant and the dip circle – used for magnetic surveys – were beyond repair. After more than six hours of bailing and rescuing what could be saved, the party was ready to press on, 'no one seemed discouraged, but, like sailors, dangers and difficulties over, nothing more is thought of it, and no despairing.' The westerlies, however, continued to help their progress and the mouth of the Mackenzie was gained on 2 September. Misled by an out-of-date chart, Pullen entered the Rat River by mistake and, with snow falling heavily, arrived at Fort McPherson, a Hudson's Bay Post on the Peel River. On finding the Company's officer – Mr Hardisty – welcoming, and with his assurance that he had plenty of provisions, Pullen decided to leave Hooper and five men with one of the whalers at the post with orders to join him on the Great Slave Lake the following spring. This action was taken to prevent the full party of fourteen men arriving unannounced at another post, an event that could have caused strain on both rations and relationships.

Returning down the Peel River to the mouth of the Mackenzie, Pullen arrived at Point Separation and found a despatch from Sir John Richardson in a cache of pemmican. The message ordered him to make his way to Fort Simpson where he would not only find Dr John Rae in charge, but ample provisions brought by Rae from Fort Confidence.

Much of the journey up the Mackenzie required 'tracking' – hauling the heavy boat against the stream with snow falling and the temperature below freezing.

It took three weeks, with brief stops at two Hudson's Bay Company posts (where moccasins were obtained to replace the men's leather boots), before Fort Simpson was reached at 11 a.m. on 3 October.

Rae's welcome was cordial and Pullen sent a despatch to the Admiralty describing his journey so far. In it he enclosed a letter for his wife, Abigail, requesting, 'their Lordships' to excuse his, 'taking the liberty' and asking them if they would, 'be good enough to have it posted'.

The winter months passed without event, but the relationship between Rae and Pullen declined. Where Pullen had been 'a most agreeable man' on his arrival, by the start of the new year Rae was writing that they 'did not pull well together' and that the naval officer 'had a peculiar abruptness of manner and peremptoriness of tone which is not over agreeable to us half savages of the north.' Confidences that Pullen had given to Rae were soon spread as malicious gossip. Before long, the headquarters of the Company were aware that the *Plover's* captain – Commander Moore – had been selling spirits to the natives and had 'kept an Esquimaux girl in his cabin for purposes which were too evident'.

When, in May 1850, Rae travelled down the Mackenzie he met Hooper and the men from Fort McPherson. Rae was horrified to learn that Hooper was collecting material for a book on his experiences. Amongst the stories of murder and starvation among the natives that Hooper had picked up (and intended to publish) were that spring's 'misfortunes at Pelly Banks' where three of the Company's employees had lost their provisions in a fire and had resorted to cannibalism. Furious at this reflection of events in his area, Rae wrote of the two naval officers as being, 'self-sufficient donkeys'.

Ten days after Rae's return to Fort Simpson, and with his party now completed with Hooper's arrival, Pullen set off with Rae and the Mackenzie River Fur-brigade up river towards the Great Slave Lake. Five days later, just as they were about to enter the lake, they met two Indians in a Company canoe bearing despatches. Pullen had a letter from the Admiralty. It informed him that, if 'practicable' he should return to the Arctic coast and continue to search for Franklin 'from Cape Bathurst towards Bank's Land' but:

> With regard to the manner and direction of any search you may make, my Lords would leave it to your judgement and discretion, desiring you to feel assured that should any reasonable objections to such a search present themselves, their Lordships would feel no disappointment, so far as your conduct is concerned, at your determining to return with your party to England.

Any disappointment at this interruption to their homeward journey was tempered with the news that Pullen had been promoted to commander, and Hooper to acting lieutenant.

Rae also had new orders. Ignoring a request from the Admiralty that he 'aid and co-operate with Commander Pullen' the Company instead ordered him to explore the landward side of 'that portion of the Northern Sea lying between Cape

Walker on the east, Melville Island and Banks's Land to the south.' Consequently, a great opportunity for a combined effort was lost as Pullen would have to go down the Mackenzie and reach Cape Bathurst before crossing northwards to Banks's Land as Rae took the Coppermine Route to reach the area Ross had intended to search in the *Enterprise*. Even worse, Rae (supported by Sir George Simpson's sour note that the company search would be 'attended with very serious inconvenience to the business') claimed he could not organise an expedition until the following spring, whereas Pullen was desperate to turn immediately.

Rae may have been further influenced in his reluctance to set off promptly by a letter he received from Lady Franklin. In it she made clear her disappointment in his return from the Arctic coast the previous year after having been sent to the area by Richardson, 'The real fact of your being at the Mackenzie without having even entered, if I understand rightly, that promising passage came upon us like a thunderbolt.' There was more evidence that the Company's territory was liable to suffer yet more naval incursions; 'I am attempting a private Expedition to reach James Ross' Straits (represented as a clear passage in my husbands charts)' and a heavy hint that Rae might like to get involved to the east, 'The scheme is wholly incomplete however unless the bottom of the Gulf of Boothia (your old quarters) and estuary of the Fish River be also examined.' After a request that he return to the search, either in command of, or in combination with, Pullen, he was asked to let the naval officer know the details of the letter. Whether Rae did or did not is unknown, but he certainly showed no enthusiasm for working with Pullen or any other naval officer.

The naval party – minus three invalids who had been exchanged for three Company men – began their journey down the Mackenzie and reached the Arctic sea on 22 July. They found their route to be a mass of broken, drifting ice that could be neither crossed nor sailed through. After an immense struggle, Cape Bathurst was reached by 8 August and Pullen waited for a week on the shore hoping that the ice would clear and give him passage across to Banks' Land. But, with no abatement in the weather, no sign of the ice allowing him through, and with the season well advanced, Pullen decided he could do no more and returned to the Mackenzie. The party wintered once again as guests of the Hudson's Bay Company before returning to England where Pullen was to find the search for Franklin at a new level of activity, and that his part in the search had not ended with his return from Cape Bathurst. Hooper, on the other hand, had been badly affected by the conditions he had endured in the north. In declining health he wrote an account of his time on the coast of Siberia before dying two years after his return.

CHAPTER FIVE

'EVERYTHING SHOULD BE DONE AT ONCE'

Whilst at Whalefish Island in July 1845, Franklin wrote to a friend:

> What I fear most respecting my wife is, that if we do not return at the time she has fixed in her mind, she may become very nervous… In order to prevent too great anxiety either on her part or that of my daughter they should be encouraged not to look for our arrival, earnestly, till our provisions gets short.

Franklin's concerns were not without foundation. Only seventeen months had passed before Lady Franklin was sounding out James Ross; 'And should it please Providence that we should not see them return when we are led to expect them, will you be the man to go in search of them, as you did so nobly for the missing whalers?'. In September 1847, she was ecstatic with the news of the proposed Admiralty effort, 'Richardson one way and Ross another!', only, within two months, to become agitated by the apparent slowness of the preparations, 'If they survive a third winter it will be a sure instance of successful endurance. How can anyone speak of *1849*? Therefore everything should be done *at once.*'

Whilst Ross and Richardson were away looking for her husband, Lady Franklin wrote to the President of the United States for help. The reply was prompt and courteous, 'every proper effort' would be made by the United States Government, but little could be done immediately beyond bringing the matter to the attention of American ships and whalers.

There had been a frisson of hope when the *Chieftain* whaler forwarded to the Admiralty a sketched chart, drawn by an Eskimo and purporting to show the positions of both Franklin's and Ross's expeditions. Parry, however, dampened the excitement by declaring the sketch to be merely the result of the Eskimo's desire to respond to the whalers' frequent enquiries about the lost ships.

As far back as April 1847, the Admiralty had begun formally asking 'Arctic officers' for their opinions on Franklin's probable position and fate. Under the chairmanship of Beaufort (who had turned down promotion to Vice-Admiral in order to remain at his post as Hydrographer) the 'Arctic Council' met rarely but dutifully responded with letters and suggestions for extending the search. With the return of Richardson and Ross, and with nothing arising from Pullen's voyage, the Arctic Council, backed by Lady Franklin, fellow officers, and public opinion, provided enough

LADY FRANKLIN.
(From an early Portrait.)

Left: Jane, Lady Franklin.

Below: The Arctic Council. From left to right: Back, Parry, Bird, James Ross, Beaufort (the hydrographer of the Navy), John Barrow (the son of Sir John), Sabine, Hamilton, Richardson and Beechey. To the rear are portraits of Franklin, Fitzjames and Sir John Barrow.

pressure for the Admiralty to begin examining proposals for a further attempt to find the missing expedition. One further prod to their Lordships was the news that the United States Navy were about to become involved in the search.

Lady Franklin had been in correspondence with an American friend, Silas Burrows, and he had passed her letters on to a New York ship owner, Henry Grinnell. Never slow to put his wealth and influence at the service of a good cause, Grinnell, prevailed upon his Republican Party relations and his friends to urge the support of the Senate and Congress. To further show his commitment, Grinnell wrote to Lady Franklin, 'I shall purchase two small schooners of about 70 tons and take the chance of procuring officers and men. I intend that they shall sail about 1 May.' In the outcome, the two ships proved to be brigantines named *Advance* and *Rescue,* the former of 144 tons, the latter 90. Both ships were specially prepared for service in icy waters with decks insulated with felt and cork and their bows sheathed in iron sheeting. The rudders were capable of being unshipped within three minutes, a double suite of sails and cordage was provided along with provisions for three years absence. The services of naval officers were approved and, after a Lieutenant Roger turned down the offer of command, the opportunity was offered to Lieutenant Edwin De Haven. De Haven had been working on the staff of Lieutenant Matthew Maury, the Superintendent of the Depot of Charts and Instruments. A highly skilled hydrographer, Maury firmly believed in the existence of an open polar sea above the Arctic ice and jumped at the opportunity to get a ship into that part of the world. In De Haven, he knew he had a good man as the thirty-four-year-old seaman had sailed as acting Master with Wilkes on the 1838-42 US Exploring Expedition. Passed Midshipman Samuel Griffin was appointed as second in command of the expedition and given command of the *Rescue* (the title 'Passed' meant that the officer was awaiting a vacancy for promotion). Once a slight difficulty in providing naval men for the ships companies had been surmounted, De Haven received his orders. He was to concentrate his search on the Wellington Channel and, once well up the waterway, to look for 'an open sea to the northward and westward.' This was not merely an attempt by Maury to prove his ideas, but an instruction based upon a well-founded possibility that Franklin might have gone that way. De Haven could split his forces if the situation suggested it, sending one ship to the west and Cape Walker as the other probed Wellington Channel. He was strictly reminded that the vessels belonged to Henry Grinnell and told, 'You will therefore be careful of them, that they may be returned to their owner in good condition.'

The Americans were not the only ones to have private funding stiffened by official backing. Lady Franklin's pressure on the Admiralty resulted in their purchasing two newly built brigs. In effect hiring the ships out without charge, the Admiralty Lords agreed that the *Lady Franklin* and the *Sophia* (the latter named after Franklin's niece and his wife's best friend, Sophia Cracroft) were to be under the overall command of Captain William Penny. An experienced whaling captain with no naval background, Penny (or 'silver Penny' as Lady Franklin called him) had been the first of the whalers to enter Lancaster Sound in

Lieutenant Edwin De Haven USN, commander of the US Grinnel Expedition and captain of the *Advance*.

search of any sign of the vanished expedition. The command of the *Sophia* went to James Stewart – the son of a whaling captain. There was to be no demand for naval men to man the two ships. Lady Franklin agreed with Penny that naval seamen 'are fine fellows for fighting or in a storm at sea, but not for marching on the ice, etc'. The orders Penny received from the Admiralty accepted that they, 'do not deem it advisable to furnish you with minute instructions as to the course you are to pursue.' However, it was their 'desire that a certain strait, known as Alderman Jones Sound, and which would not appear to have as yet examined, should be searched; you are hereby required and directed in the first instance to that Sound…'

Dr King, Back's companion on his journey down the Fish River, continued to be loud in his demands that he should be allowed to lead an expedition down the river to its estuary where, he believed, Franklin's men would be found. Lady Franklin dismissed his protestations out of hand in the belief that it was only by ships that her husband would be rescued – not by a troublesome practitioner of medicine with no knowledge of the seaman's mind. However, she had turned to the idea that Franklin had penetrated to the south, even to the North American coast itself. There was no evidence that he had reached to the west, therefore, he may have encountered difficulties on the lower western coasts of Boothia Felix. She wrote to Sir James Ross suggesting an expedition:

... to the Strait which bears your name, or to the estuary of the Fish River, both of which I have ever thought and think still ought to be examined.

She continued:

Sir James Ross Strait ought to be examined at both ends. I mean that the little isthmus half water, half land, as Rae has represented it, (but which was all water in the charts with which the Erebus sailed) should be crossed either from the E. or from the W. my theory being that if the crews of the Erebus and Terror left their ships, say in 1849 or even 50, somewhere to the W. of the entrance to your strait, they would make for it as a short cut into Regent Inlet and so up to Fury Beach in preference to struggling back around Cape Walker or any other Cape the way they came, and in preference to making for the coast of N. America and the interior Hudson Bay settlements, a course of which Sir John must well know all the dangers and difficulties.

With no sign of Sir James Ross being keen to launch such an expedition, Lady Franklin, using her own funds and money that had been raised by public subscription, purchased the *Prince Albert*, a topsail schooner built on the Isle of Wight and previously engaged in carrying fruit from the Azores. To command her, Lady Franklin appointed Commander Charles Forsyth, a naval officer with experience in surveying, but none in ice navigation. Delighted with his appointment, Forsyth did not challenge Lady Franklin's choice of William Parker Snow as the expedition clerk; or an ex-Hudson's Bay company man, John Smith, as the steward; nor her allowing the rest of the crew to be recruited from whaling men at Aberdeen where the ship was being fitted out for her intended voyage. Smith had never previously served as a steward, but did have the advantage of a smattering of the Eskimo language; Parker Snow was a highly self-opinionated Royal Navy deserter who had cleared the charges against him by saving a man from a shark attack. He was also keen to have the ship manned by 'convicted criminals' who could be relied upon to have 'almost inexhaustible mental resources.' In fact, the crew turned out to be thirteen rather lack-lustre men led by two mutually antagonistic mates. Forsyth, a naval officer and, therefore, a gentleman, was soon to find that he had no-one with whom he could converse, and a crew to whom the concept of naval discipline had but little meaning.

Astonishingly, when the expedition commander is borne in mind, the second of the totally private search expeditions also collected a crew to whom indiscipline came as second nature. When Sir John Ross last saw Franklin he assured him that, if nothing had been heard from the departing expedition by 1847, he would come in search of him. Ross's earlier attempt to get Admiralty approval for a search had been rejected but, by early 1850, having raised money by public subscription, and with help from the Hudson's Bay Company, he was now ready to get involved – with or without their Lordship's support.

Now seventy-three years old, Ross had a 100-ton yacht built for him at an Ayr shipyard. Naming his vessel *Felix* in honour of his old benefactor and gin distiller,

Felix Booth, he had her strengthened for Arctic service. The bows were 'a perfect mass of timber' with double planking and a sheathing of galvanised iron protected the vessel's sides from ice damage. Following the generally accepted principle (except in the case of the *Prince Albert*) that ships heading north should not be unaccompanied, Ross also intended to take out with him the tiny twelve-ton yacht *Mary*. As his second-in-command, Ross chose Commander Charles Phillips who had served as the second lieutenant in the *Terror* under Crozier during Sir James Ross's Antarctic Expedition. The master was the redoubtable – if hard drinking – Thomas Abernathy, who had first entered polar waters under Parry in 1827.

It was, however, not the Americans, the semi-official vessels, nor the private enterprises that were first away in 1850. The Admiralty, stung into action by pressure from Lady Franklin and public opinion, decided that the *Enterprise* and the *Investigator*, recently back from Sir James Ross's expedition, should be used in a further attempt to look at the problem from the west. To command this new initiative they selected Captain Richard Collinson CB, the son of a clergyman and an experienced surveyor who had earned rapid promotion and honours for his work in surveying the Canton and Yang-tse-kiang rivers during the first Chinese War. Command of the *Investigator* went to Commander Robert McClure who, in addition to serving as her first lieutenant under Bird in Ross's search for Franklin, was also with Back in the *Terror*. McClure was promoted from lieutenant to take over the appointment and was to find difficulty in handling his new status when dealing with the *Investigator*'s other officers. Thirty-two-year-old Johann Miertsching was appointed by the missionary Moravian Brotherhood to be the expedition's interpreter. A German, he could speak the language of the natives of Labrador but had no English. He had been intended to take passage in Collinson's ship, but ended up in the *Investigator*.

As it was important to get the ships to the west as quickly as possible, the *Enterprise* and the *Investigator* sailed from Plymouth on 20 January 1850. After separating during the Atlantic passage the ships met up again off Tierra del Fuego only to lose sight of each other once the Pacific had been reached. McClure's voyage had not, so far, been a happy cruise as he had spent much of his time arguing with his other officers. When the first lieutenant, William Haswell, left the upper deck for a few moments during his watch, he returned to find that all three topmasts had been carried away in a squall. McClure exploded in anger – much to the bafflement of Miertsching – and put Haswell under arrest. When the appointed rendezvous – Honolulu – was reached, McClure found that Collinson had sailed less than twenty-four hours earlier. Officers from two other ships approached McClure to plead on Haswell's behalf and found that his mood had changed. With Collinson on his way to the north, another plan was forming in McClure's mind against which problems concerning his first lieutenant paled into insignificance. The *Investigator* sailed on the evening of 4 July but, instead of following in the wake of the *Enterprise* and heading north-west to sail around the western limit of the Aleutian Island chain, McClure decided on a bold and risky

Captain Richard Collinson.

plan – he intended to sail *through* the islands and arrive at the Kotzebue Sound rendezvous ahead of Collinson.

Sixteen days out of Honolulu, whilst feeling his way through banks of fog, McClure managed to nudge his way gently between Amlia and Seguam islands to reach the Bering Sea. His gamble had paid off. Just over a week later, the *Investigator* fired her signal cannons at the entrance to Kotzebue Sound and met up with the *Plover* on the afternoon of 29 July. Trying, with little success, to convince Moore that he believed that Collinson was ahead of him, McClure handed over despatches and set sail for the next appointed rendezvous, Cape Lisburne. There he fell in with Kellett in the *Herald* who was equally unimpressed with McClure's protestations that the *Enterprise* had, somehow, passed through the area without finding either Moore or himself. The situation was made more awkward as Kellett was senior to McClure and could have demanded that the *Investigator* remained there until the arrival of the *Enterprise*. However, McClure could always claim that the interests of the missing expedition must come first and, as it was late in the season, and while the broken ice continued to allow his progress to the north, the search for Franklin remained the priority. Despite his unease, Kellett could not argue with such logic, and gave his reluctant permission for the *Investigator* to carry on. Both ships headed northwards with McClure in the lead, eager to shake off the senior officer. Just as it seemed the ships were about to part company,

Captain Robert McClure
in Arctic clothing.

Kellett came alongside the *Investigator* and signalled 'Had you not better wait
forty-eight hours?' McClure replied with 'Important duty, cannot upon my own
responsibility.' Kellett asked for the reply to be repeated. It was, and Kellett gave
up, merely watching as the *Investigator* disappeared amongst the drifting ice leaving
only a letter to the Admiralty announcing McClure's intention to sail along the
coast of North America to the 130th Meridian unless an opportunity came to
reach the shores of Banks Land.

Two weeks later, the *Enterprise* sailed into Port Clarence where Collinson
found both Kellett and Moore. He had tried to get further north but had been
prevented from doing so by the ice of the Beaufort Sea. Where McClure had
been able to vanish northwards just before the ice closed in, Collinson's voyage

around the western end of the Aleutians had delayed him just long enough to miss the opportunity to follow in the wake of his subordinate. There was no point in the *Enterprise* remaining in the area for the winter, so Collinson left to spend the season at Hong Kong.

When Lieutenant Pullen's boats had separated from the pinnace *Owen* and the *Nancy Dawson* off Point Barrow in early August 1849, the *Plover*'s second master, Henry Martin, received a plea for help from Robert Sheddon. The *Nancy Dawson*'s American seamen were on the verge of mutiny over the allocation of provisions and were refusing to hoist the yacht's launch on board. Martin went over, listened to the men's complaints, and put three of the ring-leaders in irons. Two Royal Marines under the command of a corporal remained on the *Nancy Dawson* and loaded small-arms were given to the increasingly ailing Sheddon as there had been mutterings among his crew that, 'some of them would do for him'. When the *Herald* was sighted, Kellett (returning to the area after discovering 'Herald Island') came onboard the yacht and read the 'ships articles' to the crew, removed the three offenders, and put the *Nancy Dawson* under the command of the *Herald*'s second master with orders to take the yacht to the Mexican port of Mazatlan, there to wait for the arrival of the *Herald*. The yacht had not been long in that port before the 'noble hearted' Robert Sheddon died. The *Nancy Dawson* eventually returned to England, becoming the first yacht to circumnavigate the globe.

Joining the *Plover* at Kotzebue Sound, Kellet found that Moore was away surveying the Buckland River leaving behind a report that natives had been found living inland. Deciding to follow up this report, Kellett set off with a strong party, 'sufficient to ensure respect from these people'. He was to find, however, that the natives were both honest and 'very fine men' who joined in with his seamen as they ran and jumped along the beach for exercise. What most impressed the natives, nevertheless, was the younger officers' skill in shooting birds with their shotguns. Having caught up with Moore, Kellett left his first lieutenant, Rochfort Maguire, to continue upriver with Moore whilst he returned to the ships to supervise the transfer of stores from the *Herald* to the *Plover*, and to check the latter's preparations to face the coming winter.

Moore and the survey party returned safely on 19 September to find the *Plover* already housed in. Only the topmasts remained to be taken down once Moore had decided on his final site for wintering. Ten days later, Kellett sailed for Mazatlan where he arrived on 14 November. Despatches were forwarded to the Admiralty, 'giving their Lordships a detailed account of my proceeding while in the Arctic circle' – nothing had been found of Franklin.

An equal lack of success attended the *Plover*'s parties sent out during the winter to range along the coast in search of any clue to Franklin's expedition. In March of 1850, the splendidly named, Bedford Clapperton Trevelyan Pim, a mate who had been loaned from the *Herald*, set off overland, in pursuit of rumours that ships had been seen off Point Barrow and that white men had been seen in the Alaskan interior. Pim, accompanied by a Russian interpreter named Pavil Bosky, hauled a sledge overland to the Russian fort at Mikhailovskiy (St Michael) on the south coast of Norton Sound. They had taken provisions for fifteen days, but poor weather and sledging conditions had delayed them and they did not reach the Russian post until twenty-six days after their departure. Their survival had depended upon food they had been able to purchase from the natives, or by hunting. At the fort, the rumour of white men in the interior was strengthened, but Pim, without funds to buy extra provisions or the authority to mount a further expedition, returned to the *Plover* on 29 April eager to persuade Moore to set a search in motion. Much to his disappointment, Moore refused, having discounted the rumours, believing the unknown white men to be employees of the Hudson's Bay Company. He was not, however, so dismissive about a rumour of ships being seen off Point Barrow and when the *Herald* returned with supplies in July (and to take Pim back onboard), he took the *Plover* north to Icy Cape. Taking thirteen men in two boats, Moore searched the coast eastwards beyond Point Barrow and interviewed any natives encountered before rejoining the *Plover* off Wainwright Inlet. Nothing had been found of Franklin's party, but a new, safe, anchorage had been discovered east of Point Barrow and named Elson Lagoon. The *Herald* had remained off Cape Lisburne and the two ships joined company on 13 August – two weeks after the *Investigator* had taken her abrupt leave of Kellett. With the season advancing, and with the *Enterprise* expected daily, Kellett ordered both ships to Port Clarence where he had decided the *Plover* would spend the approaching winter. Shortly after their arrival, Collinson sailed in to join them.

Not intending to remain long in the area before leaving to winter in Hong Kong, Collinson decided to call at Mikhailovskiy to drop off Lieutenant John Barnard, Assistant Surgeon Edward Adams, and one seaman, with orders to look further into the rumours initially investigated by Pim. Barnard was an obvious choice having led one of Sir James Ross's sledge expeditions whilst at Port Leopold the previous year. Leaving Adams and the seaman at the fort, Barnard set off with Pim's old companion, Pavil Bosky, and Vaile Deriabin, the manager of the post at Darabin (Nulato) – some 200 miles to the north-east of Mikhailovskiy. The party arrived safely at Darabin on 16 January. A month later, in the early hours of the morning, Deriabin left his native wife to go outside his cabin and found himself confronted by eighty Indians. He was immediately set upon and mortally stabbed before he managed to break free and stagger back into his cabin where his wife barred the door behind him. At this, the natives broke into the neighbouring cabin where Barnard was just rousing himself in response to the commotion. Snatching up his double-barrelled shotgun, he managed to get off two shots before he was overwhelmed by the Indians. Beaten about the head and body with the stock of the gun, Barnard collapsed and was repeatedly stabbed with knives and spears. Three arrows were shot into his body from close range. Bosky, totally unarmed, fended the Indians off with a blanket until he could grab a spear and then drove the Indians from the room, but not before he, also, had received three arrows from the retreating attackers. The Indians then fell upon an adjoining native village killing fifty-six before leaving.

Nine days later Adams was given a message by an Indian. It read:

Dear Adams,

I am dreadfully wounded in the abdomen, my entrails are hanging out. I do not suppose that I shall live long enough to see you. The Cu-u-chuk Indians made the attack whilst we were in our beds. Bosky is badly wounded and Deriabin dead. I think my wound would have been trifling had I medical advice. I am in great pain; nearly all the natives of the village are murdered. Set out for this with all haste.

John Barnard

Adams reached Darabin on 16 March, a month after the attack, having been badly delayed by melting rivers. Barnard was dead, and both his and Deriabin's bodies lay frozen solid where they had died. Bosky was still alive but in a poor condition. The surgeon buried Barnard and Deriabin in the post's graveyard before putting Bosky on his sledge and returning to Mikhailovskiy. The brave interpreter lived just another three weeks before succumbing to his wounds.

For Kellett and the *Herald*, with the end of the 1850 season, the time came to leave Arctic waters. The months spent amidst the ice had not proved profitable, but not for want of trying. The *Plover* had been supplied and assisted for three seasons, and now Collinson was in the area. The *Herald* sailed from Port Clarence in September and arrived in England the following June. Two months after his return, the twenty-five-year-old Pim was made lieutenant and began immediately to agitate for a Franklin search to take place along the north-east coast of Siberia. The Admiralty refused to back his ideas. Support, nevertheless, was available in the shape of Lady Franklin, the Royal Geographical Society, and the Prime Minister – Lord John Russell – who arranged a grant of £500 from the Treasury. All that remained was to obtain Russian approval. Pim arrived at St Petersburg in early December fully equipped with boats, weapons, and the full paraphernalia of an Arctic search and spent the next two weeks kicking his heels whilst waiting for an appointment with the Tsar. When the audience was granted, Pim learned that the Russians had calculated that he would need 1,200 to 1,500 dogs for his sledges. Such a huge amount of animals, the Tsar assured him, would seriously jeopardise the survival of the people living in the area. Such an expedition, therefore, had to be out of the question. Pim – who believed he could do the work with just 200 dogs – argued his case strongly, something the Tsar would not have been used to. Permission, however, was not to be granted – even the British Ambassador to the Imperial Court thought the idea to be 'little short of madness'. Pim could do nothing more but return home and report his failure to Lady Franklin.

Two years earlier, at the end of January 1850, the Admiralty had had the *Plover* wintering at Kotzebue Sound and the *Herald* at Honolulu waiting to go north once again. The *North Star* was trapped in the ice of Wolstenholme Sound and, out in the Atlantic, the *Enterprise* and the *Investigator* were heading towards the Magellan Straits before they also reached northwards towards Bering's Straits. Pullen and his men were spending the winter in forts around the Mackenzie, unaware that they were about to be asked to go back to the Arctic coast. But no-one apart from the occasional whaler – prompted, no doubt, in part, by the newly offered reward of

£20,000 for any information leading to the rescue, or discovery of the fate of, the Franklin Expedition – was looking for the missing expedition from the east. The Admiralty was aware that the Americans were about to join the search; and that Lady Franklin's men, Penny and Forsyth, would soon begin preparations; as would Captain Sir John Ross. The Arctic Council now came up with the suggestion that four Royal Naval ships should be sent through Lancaster Sound.

CHAPTER SIX

'UNTIRING LABOUR AND GOOD FEELING'

In March 1850, it was announced that two 400-ton sailing vessels had been purchased at £13 per ton. They were to be commissioned as HMS *Resolute* and HMS *Assistance* and fitted out under the guidance of James Biggs, Sir James Ross's purser in the *Enterprise*. The ships were similar in design to the *Enterprise* and required little major alteration. Biggs, therefore, was able to concentrate on such matters as the extension of the heating system on the lower deck, the provision of effective bilge pumps, and the supply of a ventilator for the ship's stove. He also arranged for the ship's scuttles (portholes) and deck lights to be made capable of opening to increase ventilation. The boats he provided for the expedition allowed each vessel to have two whalers, one thirty-foot and one twenty-five-foot, 'all sharp at both ends', four twenty-five-foot 'gig cutters', one twelve-foot dingy; one seven-foot punt; and two 'India-rubber or Macintosh boats, inflated by bellows.' So impressed were the officers by Biggs' work that, before they sailed, he was presented with a silver salver as a mark 'of their general esteem'. He may well have had much to do with the selection of provisions for the voyage which, after the complaints from the *Enterprise*, proved to be 'the very best of everything the country could afford.'

To act as tenders to the sailing ships, two 150-foot long, 350-ton merchant screw steamers, rigged as three-masted schooners, were purchased. Originally named *Eider* and *Free Trader* they were commissioned into the Royal Navy as HMS *Pioneer* and HMS *Intrepid*.

To command the expedition and as commander of the *Resolute*, their Lordships appointed Captain Horatio Austin, an officer of long and distinguished service. He had entered the Service under the sponsorship of Captain Sir Thomas Hardy – Nelson's captain of the *Victory* at Trafalgar – and took an active part in the war against America, including the capture of five gunboats, a battle at which one of the lieutenants involved was John Franklin. Austin was the first lieutenant of the *Fury* under Hoppner when she was wrecked on the shores of North Somerset. He had crossed the Panama Isthmus on foot as part of a scientific survey, and led large bodies of marines and soldiers in attacks on castles and towns on the coast of Syria. He had spent much time on royal yachts and in the process become one of the navy's foremost experts on steam-driven ships. At the time of his appointment to the *Resolute*, Austin was the captain of Woolwich Dockyard. He was a popular

The Austin Expedition: HMS *Intrepid* next to the *Assistance, Resolute* and *Pioneer.*

officer of undoubted bravery and leadership, but one who did not take kindly to the rough manners of a whaling captain such as Penny. Relations between the two had not gone well from the time they first met, and one of his officers felt he had to write to Penny explaining that Austin was 'a warm-hearted sailor – blunt of speech perhaps.' Lady Franklin was later to write that Austin 'never liked Penny being employed at all.'

At Austin's request, command of the *Assistance* went to Captain Erasmus Ommanney, the son of the Member of Parliament for Barnstaple. His grandfather and two of his uncles were Admirals, and it was under the patronage of one of his uncles that he entered the Navy in 1826. A year later (aged thirteen) he took part in the Battle of Navarino under Sir Edward Codrington. Promoted to lieutenant in 1835, his first appointment was to the *Cove* under James Ross and, as a result, was brought to the attention of the Admiralty for his conduct in the ice of Baffin's Bay. Ommanney was promoted to captain in 1846, shortly before he was given the job of supervising relief measures during the famine in Ireland. This was followed by a period on half-pay until his appointment under Austin.

The command of the *Pioneer* went to Lieutenant Sherard Osborn, the son of an army officer. He had been given his first command – a tender operating in Malayan waters – at the age of sixteen prior to taking part in the China War and being present at the capture of Woosung. Before his appointment to the *Pioneer,* Osborn had command of the steamer *Dwarf.* He had shown an early eagerness to become involved in the search for Franklin when he had written to the Admiralty from the *Dwarf* at the end of January 1849:

As an unknown officer I feel much diffidence in thus craving your Lordship's sanction to a step attended with so great a responsibility – but the importance of the safety of the Polar Expedition in a Professional and National point of view, will, I trust, be found to justify me, in volunteering my willing aid towards its accomplishment; and if a hearty confidence in my ability to overcome difficulties and a sanguine belief in the success that will attend the undertaking be any proof of my competency to be entrusted with such a duty your Lordships may rest assured that I shall not disappoint your expectations.

The breathless, single-sentence, appeal fell upon deaf ears; the First Lord annotating the request with the words 'Thank and decline'.

The *Intrepid* went to Lieutenant J. Bertie Cator, the thirty-year-old son of a Yorkshire clergyman and close relative of several Admirals. His first command was of a number of junks taken as prizes during the China War and later, under the command of Lieutenant Henry Kellett, help in the capture of a Chinese fort.

Although the commanding officers of the ships held responsibility for their vessels, one aspect of the expedition was to fall squarely upon the shoulders of the first lieutenant of the *Assistance* – Francis McClintock. Following on from his experiences under Sir James Ross in the *Enterprise*, McClintock was placed in charge of the Expedition's sledging stores. He designed a new pattern sledge (the 'runner' sledge), 2 feet longer, wider by 6 inches and with wider metal runners and upturned fronts. Small stanchions supported a rectangular, waterproof, 'trough' which contained the sledge's load and could be used as a boat to cross open leads of ice. Fourteen of these large sledges were provided in addition to twelve smaller 'flat' sledges (i.e. flat-bottomed, without runners) for auxiliary expeditions or for the use of small teams. Waterproof tents with similarly proofed groundsheets and supported by bamboo poles were provided to shelter sledge teams of seven men. Two wolf-skins were provided for each tent for extra warmth and each man was to be issued with a thick blanket bag to sleep in. McClintock also arranged the supply of six Halkett's inflatable boats, forty pairs of Eskimo winter boots (more were later to be purchased from the natives themselves), and thirty balloons to be used as aerial message carriers.

The Society for the Diffusion of Useful Knowledge gave the ships a number of books, the nature of which was reflected in the Society's title, and the Admiralty supplied each ship with a copy of 'O'Byrne's Naval Biography'.

The *Lady Franklin* and the *Sophia*, the first of the fleet intended for Lancaster Sound in 1850, left Aberdeen under William Penny's command on 13 April. He had written to Lady Franklin the previous month saying: 'I shall feel very disappointed if I do not get a fortnight's start of Commodore Austin.' Three weeks later *Resolute* and *Assistance*, towed by their respective tenders, left Greenhithe at seven on the morning of 3 May. Austin's orders from the Admiralty told him that the main object of the expedition was 'for you to use every exertion to reach Melville Island, detaching a portion of your ships to search the shores of Wellington Channel and the coast about Cape Walker'.

On the afternoon of the twenty-second, the *Advance* and the *Rescue* left Brooklyn Navy Yard in company with a pilot boat carrying Henry Grinnell as he waved farewell to the ships he had so nobly funded. His magnanimous gesture had been echoed by the officers and men of the American expedition – they knew of the £20,000 reward offered by the Admiralty, but had all signed a document refusing to accept any reward if they should find the missing expedition. The following day, on the other side of Atlantic, Sir John Ross in the *Felix*, with the *Mary* astern, found being towed out of Loch Ryan by a Stranraer steamer was not to be the straightforward parting he had hoped for. The master, Abernathy, had drunk himself into 'a state of insanity' and Alexander Sivewright – the mate – was 'furious with drink'. The remainder of the crew (which included three more Sivewrights) were also drunk and, at first, had refused to weigh anchor. Then, when the steamer cast off the tow, the crew refused to hoist sail and Ross was put to the embarrassment of having to ask the steamer's crew for help in getting the sails up. Five miles down the loch, off the Cairn Ryan anchorage, some among the crew demanded that the vessels be anchored and force had to be used to prevent the anchor from being slipped. Showing no small amount of courage, Ross, and Commander Phillips kept the yachts on track until enough of the crew had sobered up to take over their duties. The correspondent of the *Shipping Gazette* noted that:

> Mr Abernethy, the master, and several of the crew repented the engagement they had entered upon, and would have detained the vessel had it been in their power. They were particularly anxious to know what security they were to have for their wages when they returned; but this was a point upon which Sir John could give them no satisfaction.

What satisfaction was given by Commander Forsyth to the crew of the *Prince Albert* when he sailed from Aberdeen on 5 July is not known, but they, apparently, did little for him: 'On this voyage I had not a soul that I could associate with.' It was, however, likely to have been a musical vessel as a set of bagpipes, a fiddle, and an accordion were taken on board. Unfortunately, an organ – a gift from Prince Albert – sent, 'to cheer and lighten the labours of those gallant men in their laudable and hazardous enterprise' arrived too late.

For the most part, the different voyages across the Atlantic and through the Davis Strait were without incident. Only the *Pioneer* suffered damage when she was caught between two ice floes and received a dented side and a few broken timbers. Some of her seamen had a narrow escape however, when – armed solely with a shotgun and bird shot – they chased a polar bear across the ice with the intention of capturing it and putting it to work dragging their sledges. At the last minute they had a change of heart and left the animal alone when their feeble firepower failed to bring it to heel.

Austin's ships were stopped by the ice of Melville Bay. Just ahead of them Penny was weaving his way through the many narrow leads until he was stopped at Cape York. To their rear Ross and Forsyth were about to catch up. Whilst off Cape York, Penny landed and questioned a group of Eskimos on whether they had seen anything of Franklin's ships or men. Nothing had been seen, but when Austin's squadron arrived with Ross (Penny having left the previous day), Ross's

Sir John Ross's yacht *Felix* at Loch Ryan.

native interpreter, Adam Beck, was to claim that, during an interview with the same Eskimos that Penny had spoken to, he had heard a different tale. Now, apparently, the natives were full of tales about two ships that had been lost, their men being drowned or murdered by Eskimos. To all except Ross, it was clear that the natives were simply embroidering the information they had picked up whilst being questioned by Penny, or they were exaggerating the events surrounding the nearby wintering of the *North Star* the previous year (Saunders had escaped from the ice only days earlier and would soon be on his way home after having fallen in with Ross and Forsyth). It was even possible that Beck knew of the story before he had joined Ross and was in pursuit of some imaginary benefit to himself. After careful investigation, Beck's account was totally disregarded, and two days had been lost in a fruitless frisson of excitement.

Penny had gone north to check Jones' Sound. Finding it blocked with ice, he then headed towards Lancaster Sound where he fell in with De Haven's ships. With Ross and Forsyth heading for the same waterway, Austin ordered Ommanney to search the northern shores of the sound with the *Assistance* and the *Intrepid* whilst he did the same with his ships on the southern shore.

On the evening of 23 August, Ommanney, taking temporary passage in the *Intrepid*, saw a cairn on Cape Riley – a spit of land jutting out from the south-west corner of Devon Island. Landing to investigate, he found the cairn empty but, nearby, he came across some duck shot, two polished stones with straight lines scratched into them, and some empty Goldner's preserved meat cans. The rectangular outline of a tent, marked by the stones used to hold down its sides, was also found at the site. It was the first evidence of Franklin's passage that way, no other voyage had recorded landing at the site. Another site close by revealed:

…some empty preserved meat tins with Donkin's name, some fragments of towel and clothing, part of the rim of a beaver hat, which had been punched for wadding, pieces of rope and sailcloth with the Dockyard mark, a piece of carpet, glass bottles, fragments of a blue-ware plate, clay pipe with remains of the wad in it, several pieces of other tin vessels, various bits of wood. I also found an iron bar 5ft in length, an ash pole with a cross head, attached to it there were some hooks of bent iron – apparently constructed for fishing.

After exchanging courtesies with the *Rescue*, which had just arrived, and telling them of the finds, Ommanney set off at high speed towards Beechey Island. The *Rescue* then fell in with Penny who had visited Cape Spencer and had also found items abandoned by Franklin's expedition. On learning of Ommanney's visit to the cairn, Penny flew into a towering rage in front of the bemused Americans and accused Ommanney of finding a note from Franklin in the cairn and of keeping the information to himself. When Penny threatened to shoot Ommanney on their next meeting, De Haven fell in with the mood and announced that he would promptly return home if Penny's accusation proved to be the truth. In fact, they did not have long to wait before the matter was cleared up. From off Cape Riley a cairn had been spotted on the high ground of Beechey Island. Ommanney made directly for it, 'in full confidence that some document would be found containing information of the missing Expedition.' To his great disappointment, careful examination revealed nothing. There were, however, many other signs that Franklin had stayed on the island. Penny – soon persuaded of the falsehood of his accusations – joined him, and the island was given a thorough search.

Tucked close into the south-west corner of Devon Island with Barrow's Strait to the south and the entrance to the Wellington Channel to the west, Beechey Island proved to be a bleak horde of Franklin relics. Among them were the remains of a blacksmith's forge, carpenter's workshop, and an observatory. A storehouse had been built and a shooting range (probably for the training of hunters) had been laid out. Even a garden had been dug over. A 'finger post' bearing a black pointing hand on a white background showed the direction to where the ships had been anchored. A pair of gloves had been left behind held down by rocks. Fragments of paper, canvas, and rope lay scattered over much of the island yet, despite a vigorous search being made, and a cairn found on the crest of the island's high ground being torn down, no note or message had been found. This was a wholly unexpected omission. Franklin, known for his usually strict obedience to the letter of his instructions, should have left a message recording his progress thus far, and his future intentions. The absence of such a note could only be explained by assuming that the expedition had been forced to leave the island in a hurry – possibly as a result of the ice breaking up and freeing the ships. This might account for the abandoned gloves, and the fact that the blacksmith's anvil had been taken, but not the block on which it rested.

If there had been any doubts about the time Franklin had been on the island they were soon dispelled by the discovery of three graves. Leading Stoker John

Beechey Island – note the three Franklin Expedition gravestones to the right.

Wellington Channel from Beechey Island.

Torrington of the *Terror* had died on 1 January 1846. Three days later he was joined in death by the *Erebus*'s Able Seaman John Hartnell. From the same ship, Royal Marine Private William Braine had been laid to rest following his death on 3 April. Hartnell's tombstone sternly reminded him, 'Thus saith the Lord of Hosts, consider your ways.' Braine was reminded to 'Choose ye this day whom ye will serve.' Whatever the men from the *Erebus* had done to deserve such sharp reminders of their frailty was not known, but their tombstones told the searchers that Franklin had wintered on Beechey Island during the dark months of 1845–1846.

Another, darkly implied, message was also revealed to the Beechey Island searchers. At some distance from the main centre of activity on the island, Ommanney and the others came across neatly arranged piles of empty food cans. Almost 700 cans were found in the piles in addition to numerous other empty cans found around the island. To Sir John Ross, Ommanney, and later to Sir John Richardson, such a discovery could only mean one thing. That the contents of the cans, be it meat, soup, or vegetables had gone bad. How else could such a large number of cans be accounted for so early in the expedition?

It would not have been the intention of Franklin's expedition to have used the canned provisions until much later in the voyage. Not only had they started out with fresh meat in the shape of ten bullocks, augmented with a large number of birds that had already been killed when they had last been seen by the whaler *Prince of Wales* before entering Lancaster Sound, but the ships also carried a large amount of salt meat – almost double of that carried in cans. In normal sea voyages, the problem presented by salt meat was the copious amount of fresh water needed in its preparation. Where canned food was available in such circumstances it made sense to use it in preference to depleting, un-necessarily, the fresh water stocks. In the Arctic, however, the supply of fresh water was not a problem and the 'preserved' canned food would have been held back as the last resource. There was other evidence that the canned food may have been bad. In 1851 stocks of canned food (made by the same manufacturer that supplied Franklin's ships) held in the Royal Clarence Victualling Yard were found to be in such a bad state that the stench caused complaints by the local populace. An examination revealed that just one in fifteen of the cans had contents that were fit for human consumption. A soap manufacturer who purchased the cans in the hope of extracting fat for his product noted that 'the stench was so dreadful that I was obliged to order it away'. Complaints from ships were commonplace and seamen referred to the product as 'canned carrion'. 9,000 cans had been returned to the victualling yard by ships from the Mediterranean and Far East – their contents 'putrid'. The *Plover* had sailed in 1848 with 'many' cans 'weeping' and when a later survey of all of her 10,000 cans of meat was carried out, *all* were found to have been rotten. A Parliamentary Select Committee of 1852 looked into the problem and noted that there had been 'great condemnations' of Goldner's canned meat from 1844 onwards and that:

> …increasing complaints and subsequent condemnations and rejection under surveys, ordinary and special, on delivery to the store, and on subsequent extraordinary occasions, induced the Admiralty not only to put an end to and cancel the contract deed of 1851, but to prohibit any deliveries under that contract at the Government Yards.

The manufacturer, Stephen Goldner, fled the country, but still supplied pickled goods to the navy and canned meat to London's retailers. (The can produced by Donkin, and found by Ommanney on Cape Riley, prompts the likely suggestion that the officers purchased their own supplies.)

Of the more than 8,000 cans of meat, and of other cans of concentrated soup intended to provide over 20,000 pints, less than 700 empty cans were ever found – the vast bulk of those being on Beechey Island. Some would have been retained onboard as additional mess 'traps' (for well over a century later, metal containers were to be known as 'fannies' from the legend that the murdered and dismembered body of little Fanny Adams was used to fill the cans), but Franklin's ship would have had far more than enough cans for that purpose. It is, however, unlikely that the cans would have been simply thrown overboard. The forge found on Beechey Island could have been used to reclaim the sheet metal. The lead used in the manufacture of the cans could have been used for many purposes including the production of musket-balls for use on the shooting range. The cans left remaining on Beechey Island may have been all that were left when the island was hastily deserted in July or August 1846. Clearly, Sir John Franklin had suffered a serious blow to his stock of provisions.

Austin, with the *Resolute* and the *Pioneer*, arrived on the scene four days after the discoveries on Beechey Island. In the waters between Cape Spencer (to the north of Beechey Island) and the island itself, he found Ross with the *Felix* and the *Mary*, Penny's *Lady Franklin* and *Sophia*, and the American *Rescue*. Just to the north the *Advance* was trapped in the ice – but with search parties ashore – and, from his crow's nest, Austin could see Ommanney's ships across the entrance to the Wellington Channel. His immediate chief aim was to continue as far to the west as he possibly could before being forced to seek shelter for the winter. For the next few days the ice to the west was probed all along its length from Cornwallis Island across Barrow's Strait in the search for an open lane.

Whilst the search for an entrance to the west continued, Dr Elisha Kent Kane, the surgeon in the *Rescue*, visited the *Resolute* and was impressed by the naval discipline, morning prayers, evening quarters, inspections, double pay, and the prospect of promotion for the officers. On a return visit to the American ship, Austin was described as 'the jolliest old Englishman ever seen.' During a call upon Ross, Austin tried to persuade the seventy-three-year-old sailor to return to England with news of the expedition, but Ross, who had already sent homing pigeons on their way, refused. There was, however, another volunteer.

Forsyth and the *Prince Albert* separated from Ross on 17 August and had arrived at Port Leopold three days later. Prince Regent Inlet was entered and Fury Beach reached on the twenty-second. The intended destination was Brentford Bay to the south, but the ice reached across the inlet barring any further progress in that direction. Forsyth consulted his crew and gained the general opinion that, as the known anchorages were expected to be iced up (as Port Leopold had been), there was no other option but to return home. Snow – who had proved constantly argumentative during the voyage – was sent northwards along the east coast of North Somerset to see if any unknown harbour existed. None was found, but Snow began to agitate for the ship finding somewhere to winter in case 'any drooping stragglers (from Franklin's expedition) arrive'. Forsyth was more convinced that Snow wanted to spend the winter living on 'the excellent provisions and earning double pay without doing any earthly service to the cause.'

Prince Regent Inlet was cleared and the *Prince Albert* headed westwards until the ice was met. Forsyth then headed for the north shore of Barrow's Strait where a signal-post was spotted on Cape Riley. From the message near the post, and from De Haven, who had brought the *Advance* close inshore, it was learned that evidence had been found of Franklin's expedition. Forsyth now convinced himself that this news should be taken home at the earliest opportunity. Setting off eastwards he fell in with Saunders and the *North Star*, but said nothing of the discoveries in case Saunders should arrive home first with the news.

Prince Albert in Melville Bay.

The *Prince Albert* reached Aberdeen on the first day of October. Despite bringing home proof that Franklin had got beyond Baffin's Bay, Lady Franklin was less than impressed. She wrote to a friend, 'The *Prince Albert* has returned and done nothing.' Forsyth returned to his naval duties, was appointed to command a ship on the China Station, and promoted to captain in 1857. After further commands he went on the Retired List in 1870 and died three years later. Snow set off to write a colourful account of his time in the north before accepting command of a ship in the service of the Patagonian Missionary Society. Dismissed from his command after clashes with the Society, Snow returned to England where he died almost penniless in 1895.

In the meantime, by 24 September 1850, it was obvious to Austin that no further progress was going to be made that season and, after having failed to make his way to a safe harbour, he ordered his squadron to prepare for a winter in the ice between the southern tip of Cornwallis Island and Griffith Island. Ross and Penny took their vessels into Assistance Bay on the southern shore of Cornwallis Island. The Americans, with no regard for superstition or nautical tradition, had chosen Friday, the thirteenth to return home. The next day saw them trapped in the ice and drifting northwards up the Wellington Channel. Locked into the ice, they drifted further north than any of the search expeditions had managed to reach, before being swept helplessly south and west until they were forced out of Lancaster Sound in early January 1851. The slow drift south continued with the Arctic Circle being passed at the end of April. The ice broke up around them in the first week of June. After visiting the west coast of Greenland, the ships returned to New York on 7 September after a gallant, but fruitless, enterprise. Lieutenant De Haven returned to his position at the Depot of Charts and Instruments, but his health had been seriously impaired. He had suffered from scurvy and had probably damaged his eyes with snow-blindness. Six years after his return his sight had almost completely gone. He died in 1865.

As the top masts were lowered and the upper decks housed in on Austin's vessels, preparations for the 1851 spring search were put in hand. A small sledging party was sent westwards to Somerville and Lowther islands to establish supply cairns, while others were sent further west along the route to Melville Island, and to the coast of Cornwallis Island. Penny arrived from Assistance Bay in his dog sledge (he had thirty-two dogs with him) and it was agreed with Austin that he would undertake the search of Wellington Channel. Austin would concentrate on trying to reach Melville Island whilst searching along the northern shores of Viscount Melville Sound. Other parties would be sent to the south and west from Cape Walker.

To help the winter pass, 'as cheerfully and as healthfully as possible', games and exercises on the ice were arranged, a schoolroom was set up, and entertainments provided. The *Assistance* produced a popular weekly newssheet, the 'Aurora Borealis' which asked questions such as, 'What insect that Noah had with him, were these regions named after?' (Answer 'The Arc tic'). Articles about Arctic birdlife were placed alongside imaginary letters from home – an example being:

The men of the Austin Expedition discovering the problems of having ice underfoot.

Left: A page from the *Illustrated Arctic News* recording winter entertainments.

Below: The Austin Expedition 'Royal Arctic Theatre'.

Opposite: Arctic sledging dress.

My dear Sur, My George which is in this exhibition was always for never in the last, a looking at Aroro Borehamlieo which i am credibitaly hinformed niver shows out a day times. Now who the himpertinent hussi his i should like to know, she cant be no good leastweighs, looking arter married men in those could parts, more in partikler by star lite, in opes you may publish this, that he may know i've my i on him. Sairey.

Another correspondent, observing that there were 'crow's nests' in the Arctic, enquired when the crow shooting season would begin. On 9 November, a theatre was set up on the *Assistance*. Captain Austin arrived in a covered sledge drawn by eight men dressed as footmen with a coachman in charge. The burning of blue lights announced his approach and, on his arrival, he was ushered to his 'state box'.

The effect of the theatre was as perfect as anything could be made onboard a ship, the decorations and chandeliers were tastefully executed, and when lit up were most brilliant, the drop-scene by Lieutenant Browne received much applause, the effect was extraordinary considering he had but three colours to work with, the scenery was all much admired. The Band was composed of *Resolute*'s and our own men.

With the arrival of spring 1851, McClintock began his final preparations for the sledging expeditions. There were to be four types of expedition – 'Extended', 'Limited', 'Auxiliary', and 'Reserve and Hydrographical', the latter being used to carry out scientific work if not needed in support of the others. By the middle of March training had begun with four hours of 'walking excursions' with between five and seven men hauling the fully loaded sledges in temperatures as low as -43 degrees Fahrenheit. Each day, weather permitting, fifteen sledges (six extended, six limited, two auxiliaries, and one reserve) formed two lines and began their procession across the ice. Experiments were carried out bending sails on the sledges and with the use of kites as an aid to hauling.

As a novelty, and to help with morale, the sledges were given names and mottoes. Ommanney's team pulled the *Reliance*; McClintock's the *Perseverance*; and Walter May, a mate in the *Resolute*, commanded the *Excellent*. Some of the mottoes were sharp and to the point, others less so. Osborn's *True Blue* had 'Never Despair'; Frederick Krabbe, the second master of the *Assistance,* had 'One and All' for his sledge, *Success*; whilst Browne's *Enterprise* gloried in 'Gaze where some distant speck a sail implies, with all the thirsting eye of enterprise.'

Another new feature was the use of sledge flags. Ommanney had a white Maltese cross on a red field; the *Resolute*'s surgeon, Abraham Bradford, had a St George's Cross waving over a sledge named after his ship; McClintock had St Patrick's Cross, and the *Assistance*'s Lieutenant Frederick Mecham flew a flag bearing a white raised arm clutching an arrow, its tip piercing a heart, the whole on a red background, for his sledge, *Succour.*

On 11 April, the fully loaded sledges were taken to the corner of Griffith Island. Three days later they were rejoined by their crews and Austin. The captain inspected the sledges, gave a speech, and joined the sledgers for lunch. Shortly afterwards, the sound of cheering from 102 men rolled across the ice as the sledges were urged forward beneath their fluttering banners. The search for Franklin was again underway.

The South Western Division, under the command of Ommanney set off to the south-west. At Cape Walker, a week after they had set out, Ommanney sent Browne in a southerly direction to search the coasts along the western edge of Peel Sound as he and Osborn followed the coast as it trended to the south-west. Robert Aldrich, the first lieutenant of the *Resolute*, commanded the northern detachment. He planned to search the west coast of Bathurst Island. Bradford would explore the east coast of Melville Island as McClintock – the most experienced sledger of them all – would strike out along the island's southern shore.

Above: Captain Austin addressing an exploring party.

Opposite: Practising taking astronomical sights as a polar bear approaches unobserved.

Departure of the South Western Division.

All the sledging parties soon settled down into a similar routine. After eight to ten hours of hauling, with a half-hour break for lunch, the tent was erected and a supper of biscuit, pemmican, and rum served out. Warm clothing was worn in the blanket sleeping bags, only the outer cotton 'duck' jumpers and the carpet boots being taken off. The following morning, after forcing their feet into the, by now, frozen boots, and having stowed the tent on the sledge, a breakfast of chocolate and biscuit was had before the pull commenced at 6 o'clock. The officers hauled with the men except when sextant sightings had to be taken (Henry Webb, a second engineer with the rank of mate, had voluntarily taken one of the men's places at the traces of Osborn's sledge). Any game sighted was tracked down and shot to add to the rations.

Of the extended sledges, the first back to the ships was Browne. He had suffered from continual bad weather on his way down Peel Sound. The coastline along which he had travelled had proved to be continuous and he had turned for home when the coast had taken a westward trend ('Browne Bay'). Browne had been away for forty-four days, had travelled for 375 miles, and brought the news that the sound was frozen solid and was 'rarely, if ever, open to navigation'.

Ommanney and Osborn had discovered that Cape Walker was the north-east corner of an island ('Russell Island') and Mecham was sent to search its southern coast as they set off along the shores of a mainland ('Prince of Wales Land') to the south. Osborn recorded the spirit which animated the men under his command as they hauled the *True Blue*.

On them fell the hard labour, to us (the officers) fell the honours of the enterprise; yet none excelled the men in cheerfulness and sanguine hopefulness of a successful issue to our enterprise. They had their moments of pleasure too – plenty of them in spite of the cold, in spite of fatigue. There was honest congratulation after a good day's work; there

Departure of the Western Division.

was the time after the pemmican had been eaten; and each one, drawing up his blanket-bag around his chin, sat, pannikin in hand, and received from the cook the half gill of grog; and, after drinking it, there was sometimes an hour's conversation, in which there was more hearty merriment, I trow, than in many a palace, – dry witticisms or caustic remarks which made one's sides ache with laughter.

A number of inlets were explored without result as the coast continued in the south-westerly direction until a large bay ('Ommanney Bay') was encountered. Sending Osborn to cross the mouth of the bay, and to see what he could find to the south, Ommanney followed the bay coast as it swung towards the east. Osborn soon reached, what appeared to be, the most westerly point of the land before it began to trend south-eastwards. He pressed on for a few miles before attempting to head out westwards across the frozen sea. When a combination of fog and broken ice prevented any further progress, Osborn turned back towards the ships. He arrived after being away for fifty-eight days having travelled for 506 miles. Two days later, Ommanney turned up safely having walked over 480 miles, the last few of which had been over ice that was breaking up. At one stage he had been forced to use a bridge of boarding pikes to get his sledge across cracks as the ice broke apart beneath him and his team.

Aldrich was next to return. He had been away for sixty-two days and had covered 550 miles, seventy of which had been along unknown shores of eastern Bathurst Island.

Collecting ice for water.

Eighteen days later he was followed by Bradford who, after separating from McClintock, had searched the north-eastern coast of Byam Martin Island, passed along its northern tip and part of the north-western coast, before crossing the ice to the eastern shores of Melville Island. The coast of the island was searched to the south until its south-east corner was reached. In his eighty days away, Bradford and his men had travelled 669 miles. At one stage, early in the expedition, Bradford had badly sprained his ankle. When he suggested to his men that they might have to return to the ships, they lifted him onto the sledge and hauled him sat upon its top rather than turn back too early.

Later, on the same day that Bradford had returned, another sledge was seen approaching the ships. It was McClintock. Some of the men from his team had been badly frostbitten and were replaced – much to their annoyance – by men from the auxiliary sledge which had accompanied them for part of the journey. As McClintock's men pulled their sledge along the southern shore of Melville Island their rations and fuel were increased by the hunting down of two polar bears and a muskox. Parry's Winter Harbour was reached and passed before the high cliffs of Cape Dundas were reached. McClintock climbed to the highest point and saw, far to the west and north-west, nothing but impassable ice, ice that none of Franklin's ships could possibly have breached. With no purpose in continuing to the west, McClintock followed the coastline round into Liddon Gulf, crossing over to Bushnan's Cove where he found the wheels of Parry's cart and the remains of a meal that had been eaten thirty-one years earlier. There was, however, no evidence of Franklin having visited the site, so McClintock headed overland to Winter Harbour where he camped close by the huge, ten-foot tall and twenty-two-foot wide rock on which Parry's surgeon had recorded the presence of *Hecla* and *Griper* in 1819-1820 with a chiselled inscription. Leaving a record of their own visit in a metal cylinder on top of the rock, McClintock turned back to the ships. He arrived thirty-six days after leaving Winter Harbour having been away for eighty days during which he travelled a total of 760 miles. When the days lost due to poor weather are discounted, McClintock's men were covering almost ten miles a day towing behind them, over land and ice, almost a ton in weight. When looking at the achievements of all his sledging parties, Austin noted for the Admiralty's benefit:

> I feel it would be a source of much satisfaction to their Lordships to know that every officer reports the conduct of his men to have been most exemplary, which with their untiring labour and good feeling exhibited towards each other was highly gratifying. And I must not omit to mention, that the crews are reported to have been animated by the example of the junior officers, who were most constantly at the drag ropes.

Although much new coastline had been explored, no evidence of Franklin's expedition had been found. There was, however, from the evidence provided by Brown, a strong suggestion that the ice would have prevented the missing explorer from going south down Peel Sound, or west to Melville Island. This being the case, and according to his orders, Franklin should then have tried the Wellington Channel.

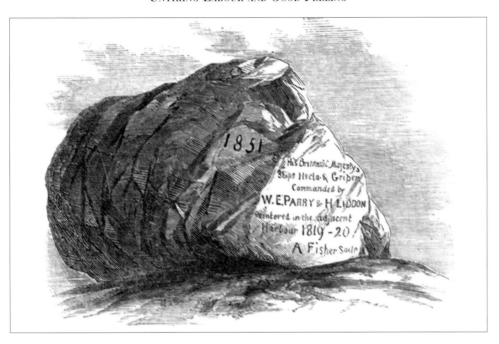

Parry's rock with McClintock's chiselled addition.

The Austin Expedition released balloons which not only released leaflets, but also dropped parachutes containing rescue information.

After a false start brought to an end by gales, Penny had set off up Wellington Channel with six man-hauled sledges and one dog-sledge. Two parties under Stewart and Dr Peter Sutherland were sent to explore the eastern shores of the strait as Penny and Dr R. Anstruther Goodsire (brother of Franklin's assistant surgeon in the *Erebus*) continued along the east coast of Cornwallis Island. As Penny followed his coast in its north-west then westerly trend, he discovered a large island ('Baillie Hamilton Island'). Crossing with some difficulty to the island, and from a high point, Penny looked westwards across open water. Was this the open sea many expected to be found to the north of Parry's archipelago? Penny believed so, and not only that. This, he now believed, was the route taken by Franklin. Dashing back to his ships, Penny – with the aid of Ross's carpenters – built a sledge to carry the *Lady Franklin*'s six-oared whaler. Returning north, Penny came across Sutherland on his way back after searching his section of the eastern shores. Nothing had been found and Stewart had continued following the coastline.

Penny reached open water further south than when he had last seen it, and had to struggle against strong northerly gales and drifting ice in making his way back to Baillie Hamilton Island. Eventually passing along its southern shores, he found his way to the west was blocked by a jam of loose ice. Following the front of the ice to where it met land in the north, a cairn caused a few moments of excitement only to be revealed as having been built by Stewart at his furthest point ('Cape Becher', named after Captain Alexander Becher who worked for the Admiralty Hydrographer). From the land, Penny could see open water ('Penny Strait') across the ice with a 'water sky' suggesting more open water beyond the horizon. Frustrated, and with his provisions low, Penny turned back, abandoning his boat 100 miles from his ship and walking overland until he reached Assistance Bay on 25 July. During their journeys, both Penny and Goodsire had found single pieces of wood, of pine and English elm that could have come from Franklin's ships.

August 10 saw Austin's ships break free of the ice after almost eleven months in its grip. The following afternoon, the squadron arrived off Assistance Bay, where both Penny and Ross were now free of the ice. Penny went onboard the *Resolute* to meet Austin, and Ommanney arrived at the meeting to find Penny, having told Austin of his searches up the Wellington channel, with a 'firm conviction that there was nothing to justify another winter on his part.' The whaling captain then continued 'Expressing a great anxiety to act in concert requesting that one of his ships might accompany a steamer … to make further examination (of Wellington Channel).' Austin, with 'marked courtesy and deference' asked Penny, 'whether it was his opinion that a further examination was required' but could get no answer. Penny, 'labouring under very strong excitement and speaking in a very wild manner making pointed remarks quite uncalled for', refused to give an opinion and departed; 'on leaving the ship Penny's conduct was such as could not be passed unnoticed, hardly deigning to reply as he went over the side'. Austin then wrote a letter to Penny in order to make his request for an opinion official: 'Under the circumstances I now await your reply to my letter transmitted herewith, in order that I may make known to you at the earliest moment the plans for the future movement of this expedition.' Still no reply was forthcoming, so Austin wrote again explicitly, 'to request that you will be pleased to acquaint me, whether you consider that the search of Wellington Strait, made by the expedition under your charge, is so satisfactory as to render a further prosecution in that direction, if practicable, unnecessary.' No reply had been received by that evening, so Austin and Ommanney went onboard the *Lady Franklin* and found Penny, 'disinclined to commit himself to an opinion'. At this, Austin 'remonstrated with Penny on his conduct and pointed out the necessity of being furnished with an opinion.' Penny agreed to do so but, by the following morning, still no answer had been received. Again the two Royal Navy captains went onboard Penny's ship where they found Penny pacing the deck, 'his manner was very peculiar, he made short answers and avoided entering into conversation.' In an effort to help things along, Austin offered Penny any provisions that he might require, 'Penny replied sharply, he did not come to this country on a fool's errand, he knew what he was about when he came out here, people did not come out to this country without knowing what they were about.' Nevertheless, at last a reply appeared, 'Sir, Your question is easily answered. My opinion is, Wellington Channel requires no further search, all has been done in the power of man to accomplish, and no trace can be found. What else can be done?' Penny then set sail without telling Austin, 'what his plans were, or when he was going.'

Penny's ire may have been aroused when he found that Austin, before leaving the Arctic for England at the end of August, intended to direct his search towards Jones Sound, the very area that he had been 'required and directed' to search in the orders given to him by the Admiralty. That he had signally failed to do so, and that Austin was about to do it in his stead, meant only one thing to Penny – he had to get back to England before Austin and put his side of the case.

The *Lady Franklin* and the *Sophia* reached England in early September and Penny lost no time in broadcasting his version of events. Lady Franklin wrote to Grinnell, 'in much agitation and confusion of mind'. Penny, she continued, had 'discovered the passage which there can be scarcely a doubt the ships have taken, since it is the only opening they have found anywhere.' This, however, was the desperate cry of a wife. Even in her distress, she was not completely taken in by her previously 'silver' Penny, describing him as 'an enterprising but unlettered man who … entered a lofty service for which by education and knowledge of the world he was not prepared.' The popular press, on the other hand, had no doubt that Penny had behaved perfectly in every respect; 'It is to be deeply regretted that Captain Austin … although satisfied that Sir John Franklin did not prosecute the object of his mission to the southward and westward of Wellington Strait did not feel himself authorised to prosecute a further search, through that strait to the northward. By this unaccountable decision a golden opportunity of following up first successes has been lost.' The Royal Navy and its allies took a different view. The whaling captain was 'coldly received' at the Admiralty, their Lordships allowing their views to be expressed in a sympathetic publication:

Captain Penny was directed by his orders to examine Jones Sound first, and if possible penetrate by it to the north of the Parry Islands. But he leaves that for Captain Austin to do! What would have been the consequences if any officer of Captain Austin's expedition had treated his orders in this way … How different was the conduct of the American Officers, to their honour be it said. They waited on Captain Austin on his own quarterdeck and applied for orders from the Commodore! And yet we see a portion of the press fretting about what it does not understand, and throwing the blame on Captain Austin because he did not do what he was not asked to do, and because he has done everything which his orders required him to do.

The general view in naval circles was that with no clue to follow to the south and west, and with the Wellington Channel frozen solid, Austin did right in beginning his return home in August – there being no point in remaining in the Arctic for another winter. If necessary, and if thought appropriate, another expedition could be sent the following summer with little or no loss of search time. Austin's only naval detractor was Sherard Osborn who, having failed to gain a recommendation for promotion (as had McClintock and Cator), wrote sourly to Penny saying, 'I am young yet and have room and time enough to win a Post-Captain's commission in spite of Captain Austin or any other Liar in buttons.'

For Penny, it was to be the end of his association with the Royal Navy and with the Franklin search. He had his portrait painted wearing his fur clothing with his right hand clenched and resting on a white ensign bearing the words, 'God aiding us to do our duty'. He returned to whaling, whilst setting up missions to spread Christianity among the Eskimos, and campaigning to keep the Americans away from any claims to Arctic territory. He died in 1892.

Sir John Ross, having been separated from Penny in the latter's dash for home, arrived at Loch Ryan on 25 September. He had hoped that the North Star had left supplies for him at the Greenland port of Godhavn. With these he had intended to winter at Wolstenholme Sound before searching the east coast of Greenland between Whale Sound and Melville Bay. Saunders, however, had not been able to call in at Godhavn and so no provisions were available. The reason Ross was keen to remain in the area was his continued belief in Adam Beck's account of the loss of Franklin's ships:

I am clearly of opinion that the missing ships under the command of Sir John Franklin, having remained at their winter quarters, Beechey Island, until September 1846, and seeing that there could be no possibility of advancing further that season (after which they would have had only one year's provisions) that they had, on their attempt to return home round the north end of the pack, been wrecked on the east coast of Baffin's Bay; and in short, that the report of Adam Beck is in every respect true.

Lady Franklin merely responded to Ross's support of the Adam Beck report with, 'a deep sense of gratitude to Sir John Ross for murdering her husband.'

Captain Sir John Ross.

It was to be Sir John Ross's last visit to the frozen waters of the Arctic. Little
had been achieved by his efforts to search for Franklin. Commander Phillips had
tried to cross Cornwallis Island, but had been driven back by low temperatures
and poor weather. The *Mary* had been left at Beechey Island as a hopeful gesture
that anyone trying to escape from the Arctic might use her, failing which, she
could be of use to any future expeditions. Ross was promoted to Rear-Admiral
on his return and remained active in the astronomical, meteorological, geological
and geographical spheres of influence whilst writing a biography of Admiral
Krusenstern and a paper, 'On Intemperance in the Royal Navy'. He continued
his interest in naval engineering and became involved with the introduction of a
telegraph between Scotland and Ireland. His constant travelling in pursuit of his
many interests may have led to his death in August 1856.

Austin arrived home five days after Ross. His attempt to enter Jones Sound had
been thwarted by the ice and his arrival at Woolwich was met by a tangible air
of disappointment. Penny had already soured the atmosphere and there was little
welcome from the press or the general public. In an effort to shed some light on the
conduct of the expedition the Admiralty convened a committee of enquiry composed
of Rear-Admirals Bowles and Fanshawe, along with captains Parry, Beechey, and
Back. Penny and Stewart were both interviewed and allowed to put their side
of the argument. Opinions were taken from Austin, Ommanney, Sir John Ross,

Richardson, Kellett, and Scoresby. The committee's report was published on 20 November. Penny was found to have repeatedly informed Austin that he did not wish to return up the Wellington Channel and only changed his mind on returning to England:

> We can only account for his subsequent change of language on his arrival in England (as he himself states in his evidence) that 'he found everybody disappointed;' that it had been said, 'more might have been done'; and 'that he therefore wished to have the means of going out again'.

Penny also received a mild rebuke in the report's suggestion that:

> We think that considerable benefit might have arisen, especially with reference to future operations in Wellington Strait, if one of the expeditions had remained near the entrance about a fortnight longer, in order to obtain the latest information of the state of the ice in that direction, and therefore, the practicability of the navigation of this Strait, and we think that this might have been accomplished by Mr Penny without involving any serious risk of being detained during the winter.

The committee felt, based upon the opinion eventually given by Penny, that:

> We do not think Captain Austin would have been justified in commencing a fresh search in a direction, concerning which he naturally considered himself to have received such authentic information.

Finally, the committee proposed that the same ships that had been under Austin's command should be returned to the Arctic and based upon Beechey Island in time for the 1853 searching season, but with the strict orders that:

> In the event of any irreparable disaster to the ships so proceeding, or if they should be too firmly fixed in the ice to be extricated during the summer of 1853, they are to be abandoned and the crews brought down to the depot.

Captain Erasmus Ommanney, the man who first found evidence of Franklin's route, never returned to polar waters. He was appointed Controller-General of the Coast-Guard before – on the outbreak of the Crimean War – being given command of a squadron responsible for blockading Archangel. Having served with distinction throughout the war he then served in the West Indies and the Mediterranean before being appointed as Senior Officer at Gibraltar. Promoted to Rear-Admiral in 1864 and to Vice-Admiral seven years later, Ommanney was placed on the retired list in 1875. He was knighted and advanced to Admiral in 1877. In 1890, according to a custom which had arisen following the Battle of Navarino, Ommanney – being the senior (and then sole) surviving officer from the battle (which had taken place sixty-three years earlier) – received the captured flag of the Turkish commander-in-chief. As the last of the line of officers who took part in the battle, he presented the flag to the King of Greece. Ommanney died at the home of his son – Erasmus Austin Ommanney – in 1904.

On his return, and with the enquiry into his expedition behind him, Captain Horatio Austin was appointed as Superintendent of the Packet Service. In 1854 he was placed in charge of Deptford Dockyard and promoted to flag rank in 1857. Three years later he was advanced to Vice-Admiral and created a Knight Commander of the Bath. Austin was appointed as Admiral Superintendent of Malta Dockyard in 1863 and died in 1865.

The return of the Austin Expedition had not left the eastern Arctic entirely empty of Franklin search ships. When the *Prince Albert* had returned under Forsyth, Lady Franklin determined that the vessel should be sent back to Prince Regent's Inlet with the minimum of delay supported by her own funds and public subscriptions. A large number of volunteers were available to her (including Parker Snow), but her final choice was almost alarming in its contrasts. To command the vessel she appointed William Kennedy, a hard-bitten thirty-seven-year-old mixed-race fur trader whose only experience of the sea was as a passenger on a trans-Atlantic steamship. A religious man of deep Calvinistic piety, Kennedy had heard Franklin preach at Cumberland House in 1819 when he was five years old. The impression the sincere and honest seaman had made on him that Sunday had remained with him down the years, and when the chance came to take part in his rescue, Kennedy left for England. Lady Franklin found him to be 'a remarkable and most favourable specimen of the half-European, half-Indian race'.

As the *Prince Albert*'s second-in-command, Lady Franklin chose Joseph-Rene Bellot, a junior officer (*enseigne-de-vaisseau*) in the French Navy and a fervent Roman Catholic who was skilled in both seamanship and navigation. Despite Kennedy's refusal to allow any form of alcohol onboard the *Prince Albert*, the two men of wildly differing religion, culture, and experience were to work extremely well together.

Bellot was also very impressed with Lady Franklin's choice of third officer for the expedition. Against all common sense, and probably only out of sympathy, she selected the fifty-seven-year-old John Hepburn, the seaman who had been with Franklin in his journey down the Coppermine River in 1821. After commanding a small supply ship, and serving as a warder at Haslar naval hospital, Hepburn had rejoined Franklin and found work in Van Dieman's Land before returning to England in 1850. In inviting him to join the expedition, Lady Franklin had written to him saying, 'you must not attempt to say (for I know you always think humbly of your merits) that you are not competent, for we all believe & know you are'. Hepburn replied that he would, 'readily strain every nerve in my search of my worthy Chief.' John Leask, the Ice-Master of the *North Star* under Saunders, was appointed to the same position on the *Prince Albert*.

The *Prince Albert* sailed from Aberdeen on 22 May 1851. After picking up sledge-dogs from one of the Danish settlements and falling in with De Haven and the American expedition in Melville Bay, Port Leopold was reached only to be found to be choked with ice. Eager not to be delayed, Kennedy pushed on into Prince Regent's Inlet but met ice off Fury Beach which forced him to return to Port Leopold. There, Kennedy – perhaps through his lack of understanding of navigation in ice-bound coastal waters – took a small boat and four men, without supplies, into the harbour to check Sir James Ross's cache and to see if Austin had left a message. He had not long passed the entrance when an easterly wind drove loose ice into the harbour sealing it off. Behind them, the *Prince Albert* was being forced towards the shore by the same wind and Bellot was faced with a dilemma. He could try and hold his ground – but accept the almost certainty of being driven ashore and wrecked – or set sail and escape, leaving Kennedy and his men trapped at Port Leopold. Reluctantly, but inevitably, Bellot chose to save the ship and took her thirty miles to the south where he found Batty Bay open. Behind them the ice closed off the entrance to Prince Regent's Inlet – there would be no sailing back to collect Kennedy.

Once the ship had been secured, Bellot and three of his men set off northwards to reach Port Leopold, only to be driven back by the wind and freshly fallen snow. It was clear that, as the season advanced, a journey along the coast was out of the question. If Kennedy had failed to reach the shore at Port Leopold, he and his men would already be dead. If, however, he managed to make it to the beach he would be able to survive on the supplies left by Ross. Bellot, therefore, could afford to wait until the waters of Prince Regent's Inlet froze over and provided an easier and safer route to the north. Once again, in his eagerness, Bellot set off too early and had to return to his ship after the ice had given way under his party.

Bellot took to the ice for a third time on 17 October, taking with him two seamen and Robert Cowie, the ship's surgeon. His plan had been merely to retrieve some stores that had been abandoned during the last attempt but, on reaching the spot, Bellot decided to make a dash north. They reached Port Leopold the following day – six weeks after the parties had separated – to find their shipmates living in a modest degree of comfort beneath the upturned boat and surviving well on the cache left by Ross. Kennedy's chief complaint was that he did not have a bible with him to help pass the time. The *Prince Albert* was regained on October 26 and preparations made for the rapidly approaching winter.

CHAPTER SEVEN

'SUCH A MAN AS BELCHER IS ON THE TRACK'

Taking the advice of the Committee of Enquiry into the Austin Expedition, the Admiralty decided to recommission the same ships Austin had used for another attempt at rescue through Lancaster Sound. To command the new expedition they appointed Captain Sir Edward Belcher CB, an officer of extraordinary ability and achievement. Entering the Royal Navy at the age of thirteen, Belcher had spent much of his career engaging the enemy at close quarters. Before he was fifteen years old he had taken part in attempts to 'cut-out' a French flagship, and had been present at the bombardment of Algiers. During the Portuguese civil war he saved many lives by taking a boat across to the walls of a fort that was firing on defenceless ships and persuading them to stop. In China, during a break from sinking numerous enemy vessels, he led the storming party that captured forts at Wangtong and Canton and led the army's rocket division in other shore campaigns. In fending off a pirate attack off the coast of Japan he was so badly wounded that the surgeon noted that his injuries were worse than 'the loss of two limbs'. Belcher had hardly recovered from his wounds before he had rescued the crew of a wrecked British merchantman who had fallen into the hands of natives on Borneo. As a lieutenant on anti-slavery patrols he had already captured one slaver, driven a heavily armed one away, and forced another into wrecking itself ashore, before finding himself up against the American slaver, *Mammoth*. With just fifteen men he boarded her in the face of her eight 24-pounder guns and fought the ship's forty-two man crew into surrender. Such were his diplomatic skills that he was awarded a presentation sword by the Dey of Algiers, successfully acted as the intermediary between the opposing Portuguese factions (leaving to the cheers of both sides), and earned the praise of the Spanish for out-negotiating the French in their attempt to secure land in the Philippines. He was constantly in demand from Admirals to be placed on their staffs, and had turned down Parry's offer of an appointment to the *Hecla* in that officer's momentous penetration of Lancaster Sound in 1821, due to having accepted an appointment elsewhere. He had, however, been able to take up Beechey's offer of a position on the *Blossom* during the voyage to Bering's Strait to await Franklin. What, in particular, had attracted both Parry and Beechey, had been Belcher's skills in surveying. This ability had first been noted when, at only fourteen years of age, he had climbed to the masthead of HMS *Abercrombie* and made a survey of the enemy positions in the Basque Roads.

During service at Bermuda he studied the approaches to the harbour to such a high standard that if a ship ran aground he was sent to extricate it and bring it safely to anchor. In all, he saved eleven vessels during his time on the island. Inevitably, he was given command of three surveying vessels. In the first, HMS *Aetna*, he charted the coasts of Lancashire (where he earned the thanks of the Admiralty for putting down a riot), West Africa and Portugal, and insisted on such a high standard of hygiene in the ship that when he returned after three and a half years absence he had not lost a single man. In the *Sulphur*, he was sent out to the Pacific where, when not taking part in the fighting, he became involved in surveying the approaches to Canton whilst under fire. When appointed to the *Samarang* he carried out surveys around Borneo, Japan and the Philippines. His book, *A Treatise on Nautical Surveying*, published in 1835, had become the standard work on the subject. In addition to his fighting and surveying skills, Belcher, was an immensely practical man. Whilst in command of the paddle-steamer HMS *Carron*, he learned that the engineers required four days to carry out a repair. Belcher did the job himself in four hours. He designed, amongst other things, a new rudder, gun-carriage and anchor. For two of his ships, the *Sulphur* and the *Starling*, he practiced a newly developed skill of sail-making by making up two complete suits of sails out of 58,000 yards of canvas.

Unfortunately, possibly as a result of his own abilities and extremely high standards, by the time Belcher was appointed to command the *Assistance*, he had become a rigid authoritarian whose inflexibility allowed no other opinion than his own. One of his biographers, the hostile Sir John Knox Laughton, thought his appointment to lead the 1852 Arctic Expedition an 'unfortunate one; for Belcher, though an able and experienced surveyor, had neither the temper nor the tact necessary for a commanding officer under circumstances of peculiar difficulty. Perhaps no officer of equal ability has ever succeeded in inspiring so much personal dislike'. Belcher's senior lieutenants on the *Assistance* were Walter May and John Cheyne, both had served on the Austin Expedition.

Captain Henry Kellett found he was to return to the north in command of the *Resolute* and as second-in-command of the expedition. His first lieutenant was to be Frederick Mecham; the second, Bedford Pim – both experienced polar travellers. McClintock, now a commander, was appointed to the *Intrepid* (Bertie Cator had also been promoted to commander and had gone to the Coast-Guard). Austin's view of Osborn could not have been all that damning as, much to his delight, he was returned to the command of the *Pioneer*. To serve as a depot ship to the expedition, Belcher was supplied with the *North Star*. Commander William Pullen was appointed to be her captain, keen to be back in the Franklin search after his experiences on the coast of North America. The *North Star's* surgeon also had polar experience. He was Robert McCormick who had first seen Arctic waters as assistant surgeon on the *Hecla* in Parry's 1827 North Pole Expedition. For a short time he had served on the *Beagle* under Commander Robert Fitzroy (where, on leaving, Darwin recorded his departure as 'no loss'), and had been with Ross on his 1840 Antarctic Expedition.

The Belcher Expedition, 1852 – *Assistance* (Belcher), *North Star* (Pullen), *Resolute* (Kellett).

The Belcher Expedition, 1852 – *Intrepid* (McClintock), *Pioneer* (Osborn).

Above left: Captain Sir Edward Belcher.

Above right: Captain Henry Kellett.

A second French naval officer had volunteered his services for the Franklin search. *Enseigne-de-vaisseau* Emile de Bray, the son of a Parisian artist, had corresponded with Bellot and been fired with the idea of joining the searching expeditions. Having gained permission from the Minister for the Navy, de Bray entered HMS *Resolute*, the day prior to sailing. His shipmate, George Nares, with the splendid self-assurance of the times in which he lived, noted that, 'The Frenchman does not seem an Englishman, but I suppose he will improve on acquaintance'.

Just before setting off for Lancaster Sound in mid-April, Belcher learned of a possible Franklin breakthrough from a quite different quarter.

John Rae had left Fort Confidence in April 1851 and, with two men and dog-sledges, crossed over the ice of Dolphin and Union Strait to Victoria Land. After a probe to the east he turned and searched westwards along the southern coast until he had followed it to Prince Albert Sound – thus proving that 'Wollaston Land' was actually part of Victoria Land ('Victoria Island'). Naming his furthest point 'Cape Back' (after Captain Sir George Back, Vice President of the Royal Geographical Society – Rae was keen to be awarded the Society's Gold Medal), Rae returned to the Coppermine where he had arranged to have two boats brought up from Fort Cumberland. Taking his two small vessels across the, now open, waters of Coronation Gulf, Rae reached just to the west of a large protected harbour (Cambridge Bay) seen by Dease and Simpson in 1838. Turning the south-east corner of Victoria Island into a wide channel ('Victoria Strait') Rae

Lieutenant Osborn (*Pioneer*), Mr Allard (master of the *Pioneer*), Commander McClintock (*Intrepid*), Mr Pullen (master of the *North Star*), Commander Richards (*Assistance*).

continued sailing up the north-west trending coast along a gap between the ice and the shore. A large inlet ('Albert Edward Bay') was discovered and searched before a north-east wind drove the ice onto the shore just to the north of the bay, cutting off any further progress with the boats. Rae, with three men, then attempted to get as far north as they could but were prevented from getting beyond a point where the coast began to trend to the west. The rocky limestone terrain proved too much for their native footwear and they were forced to return to their boats. At this point the party was about forty miles from the north-west coast of King William Land and James Ross's Victory Point, but the ice stretching across the strait cut short any proposals to head in that direction.

Rae made his way back along the eastern and southern shores of Victoria Island. As he approached Cambridge Bay, he found part of a pine flagstaff. A line was secured to the piece by copper tacks which bore the broad arrow mark of British Government property. Almost at the same time, he picked up a piece of oak that may have been part of a ship's stanchion. Rae arrived back at Fort Confidence on 10 September and reached Fort Simpson just over two weeks later. There he found he had been granted leave of absence and decided, rather than rushing to England with his discoveries, to take a leisurely journey through the northern part of the USA calling at Chicago, Detroit, and New York. His report of the boat journey, although dated 27 September, did not appear until he reached London on 3 April 1852 – just as Belcher's expedition was about to leave.

Even faced with Rae's two items of wreckage, it was unlikely that Belcher would have been able to have done anything other than return to Beechey Island in an attempt to follow the presumed Franklin route up Wellington Channel. There was no suggestion that Franklin had gone south (although Lady Franklin was beginning to believe that he had) and the items could have come from Collinson's *Enterprise* or McClure's *Investigator*, both of which, by July 1851, had vanished into the ice north-east of Bering's Strait. With his plans unaltered by Rae's arrival, Belcher and his five ships sailed from Woolwich on 15 April 1852.

Following a stormy crossing, the squadron reached Godhavn. Whilst in the process of anchoring, a strong wind blew up and the *Assistance* dragged her anchor, losing part of her false keel. *Pioneer* was pushed against an iceberg and lost part of her mizzen mast and, the following morning, *North Star* ran aground. No serious damage was done, however, and the ships were able to sail within a week. They headed to the north-east to take advantage of the gap between the ice and the shore only to find that the wind was driving the ice down upon them. The *Resolution* was caught between two floes and lost her rudder as the pressure lifted her up and heeled her 35 degrees over to port. To prevent this happening to the other ships, Belcher ordered that docks be cut into the floes to protect them from being equally 'nipped'. Two days later the ice broke up and the squadron continued northwards to Melville Bay where they fell in once more with the ice requiring, yet again, docks to be cut. They were joined by a number of whalers who all cut docks except for the single American vessel – the *McClellan*. Her failure to take such a precaution led to her being nipped, and her crew were forced to take to the ice as the ship was crushed by the great pressure. Under normal circumstances, tradition had it that – once the crew had abandoned the vessel – her stores (especially her stocks of alcohol) were available to be looted by any other ships in the vicinity. The nearby whalers, however, had reckoned without Belcher who, appalled by the prospect of hordes of drunken whaling men reeling around his own vessels, hoisted a white ensign on the wreck, paid her captain for the goods remaining onboard, and sent a guard of Royal Marines across to the stricken ship to prevent anything being removed. The outraged whalers retaliated by chalking 'Teddy Belcher the pirate' on the *McClellan's* side.

After thirty-eight days trapped in the ice, the break-up came and Belcher was able to escape. By 12 August, all his squadron had gathered at Beechey Island. No time was to be wasted for, to the north and west, the waters lay free of ice. A probe by the *Intrepid* up the Wellington Channel revealed clear water for twenty-five miles with wide lanes stretching further still. To the west, broken ice dotted the waters of Barrow's Strait, but with little threat to the iron-shod bows of *Resolution*. In order to carry out the sailing orders given to him by the Admiralty before leaving, Belcher had decided that he would take the *Assistance* and *Pioneer* up Wellington Channel and Kellett would head westwards with the *Resolution* and *Intrepid*. The *North Star* would remain at Beechey Island both as a stores depot, and as a safe refuge in case of disaster.

Commander Edward Inglefield's *Isabel*.

Shortly after his arrival, Belcher, in company with Kellett, Commander Richards, and Lieutenant Cheyne, landed on Beechey Island and gave the whole island a close and detailed search. They dug holes 10 feet north of anything that was clearly man-made and even lined up the headboards of the graves in the hope that they might find a clue to the direction taken by Franklin. Nothing was found. Differing markedly from the opinion expressed by Austin and his officers, Belcher and fellow searchers could only note that they:

> ...arrived at the conviction that no hurry in removing from these winter quarters can be traced. Everything bears the stamp of order and regularity; and although it is a matter of intense surprise and incomprehensible to all, it is my firm conviction that no intention of leaving a record at this position existed.

On the night of the thirteenth Belcher hosted a party on the *Assistance* for the officers of the ships and much champagne was drunk. Only one of the invited guests was missing. Surgeon McCormick, refused permission by Belcher to take a small boat up Wellington Channel, stayed in his cabin onboard the *North Star* in protest. The following morning, all 212 men on the expedition mustered on the ice beneath a fluttering white ensign to hear Belcher wish them well and to hope for a successful outcome. When he had finished, the meeting broke up with rounds of handshaking and bursts of cheering as the men gave each other their own good wishes – perhaps for the last time.

Belcher and his consort sailed that day having given orders to Pullen that he was to organise sledge journeys before the end of that season to make depots of supplies on the east side of Wellington Channel. He was also to ensure that McCormick was put in charge of at least one of the sledges, as he had 'been expressly selected and appropriated for this duty'. Kellett followed Belcher out of Erebus and Terror Bay once his storing had been completed. Left alone, Pullen began to prepare the *North Star* for a lonely winter. Three weeks later he was amazed to see a vessel wearing a British flag haul into sight.

In January 1852, a merchant service officer, Captain Donald Beatson, decided he would enter the Franklin search by taking a vessel through Bering's Strait and search for the missing expedition in the presumed open waters to the north. Nothing came of the idea except for a sum of money that had been raised from public subscription. It was decided that this money should be given to Lady Franklin to use as she wished in the furtherance of the search. With the minimum of delay she purchased a 170-ton, 30 horse-power, steam-assisted schooner named *Isabel,* and placed her under the command of Commander Edward Inglefield. The son of a Rear-Admiral, the thirty-two-year-old Inglefield was aged twelve when he entered the Royal Navy and had seen active service off Syria (where he had been part of the storming party that had captured Sidon) and in the Parana River, Argentina. For two years he had served under Belcher carrying out surveys in the East Indies. In a plan agreed with Lady Franklin, he was to enter Baffin's Bay and try to gain entry into Smith's and Jones' sounds. The return home was to be by the west coast of Baffin's Bay and Labrador – the whole voyage to be completed in a single season. As an added spur, Inglefield was to look into the mysterious sighting by the brig, *Renovation,* somewhere around the middle of April 1851. Two unidentified ships had been seen stranded on an iceberg in the Davies Straits. They had been sketched by the *Renovation*'s Mate, Robert Simpson, but the brig's captain had not immediately disclosed the information and was eventually, 'afraid of the shame which would attend its publicity after so long a time had elapsed.' Nevertheless, when obtained, the report was fraught with possibilities:

> On a nearer approach to the ice, under the water it could be observed shelving out to a considerable distance at the lee side, thus acting like a vane in keeping that part to leeward; on passing as close as prudence would allow, two three-masted vessels were observed close to the berg, but out of the berg; they were regularly housed (i.e. the upper deck covered in for the winter), with their topsail yards and topgallantmasts down. No human being could be seen.

The officer who had obtained this information – James Shore, Second Master in HMS *Sampson* – was of the opinion that:

> Supposing them to be Sir J. Franklin's ships, the fact of no human beings being seen may, I think, be easily accounted for. The catastrophe of an iceberg breaking away from the place where it had formed would, no doubt, be sufficient to cause the crews to rush on

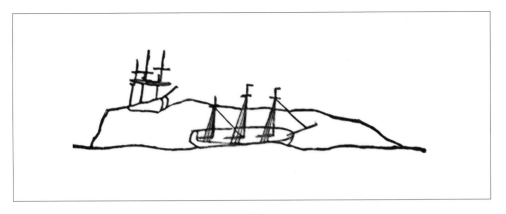

Sketch made by Robert Simpson, mate of the *Renovation*, Spring 1851.

foot to the nearest safe point; the ships driving away with the berg in the interval would leave no means of rejoining them.

So, had Franklin and his men been stranded on the ice?

The Screw Discovery Vessel *Isabel* sailed from Peterhead on 10 July with a, 'jolly, good tempered set' of men, except for Ogston, the third mate, who Inglefield described as a, 'heavy, stupid, half-witted, deaf fellow'. Lady Franklin was informed that, 'No two stones that shall be found as though laid by civilised hands shall be left unturned and I will seek as though it were my brother I would find.'

After picking up sledge dogs at Upernavick, Inglefield crossed Melville Bay before being stopped by the ice. Whilst waiting for a path to open up he landed to meet some Eskimos and question them about Franklin. He believed the natives had never met Europeans before and found that, 'fatter, healthier people I never saw'. They knew nothing of the missing expedition and a subsequent search of the adjacent shore revealed nothing. He felt, therefore, that he could, 'put at rest the foolish story of Adam Beck.' Firing a cannon and launching rockets during the hours of darkness as he continued northwards, Inglefield came across two large openings to the east that offered the possibility of future access to an open Polar Sea. Desperately keen to enter, 'a strait (Murchison Sound) that if pursued might define Greenland as an island', his 'sense of duty' to his search for Franklin made him tack and follow the coastline to the north-west. Steam was used for the next two days to reach the entrance to Smith Sound, 'It was a lovely morning, that of 27 August, when within pistol-shot of Cape Alexander, we beheld before our enchanted gaze open water as far as the eye could reach, and extending between the two extremes of land we beheld for about seven or eight points of the compass'. The elation, however, was to be short-lived. After reaching beyond 78 degrees – the then furthest north of any exploration vessel – a gale blew the *Isabel* out of the sound. The western shore had been closely examined from the ship's deck, but no sign of the passage of any ships could be seen. Inglefield then turned to Jones Sound which he again entered through open waters, but fog, gales, and driving ice forced him out. In searching its shores through telescopes, no place for a winter quarters had been seen and its cliffs seemed to, 'defy the foot of man'. Entering Lancaster Sound, the *North Star,* 'waiting daily for the ice to seal them in for the winter', was reached on the morning of 7 September and Inglefield handed over a welcome bundle of letters and newspaper to Pullen. The *Isabel* waited for twelve hours for the ship's company of the depot ship to write letters for home and, whilst this was being done, Inglefield landed on the snow-covered Beechey Island to visit the site of Franklin's winter camp.

The planned voyage of the *Isabel* down the western shores of Baffin's Bay proved to be impossible due to gales and the encroaching darkness. On 12 October, Inglefield's Ice-Masters suggested that he abandon any further search and turn for home or risk being trapped in the ice. Accordingly, the ship left the coast at Cumberland Bay and arrived at Peterhead during the first days of November. Inglefield was able to reassure Lady Franklin that all was well in the north and, 'that such a man as Belcher is on *the* track.' Nothing, however, had been learned of the *Renovation*'s mystery ships on the iceberg. Nevertheless, his voyage had covered new ground, and Parry considered Inglefield's achievements to have placed him, 'among the most distinguished of our Arctic Navigators' – but his return came under the shadow of the arrival, a month earlier, of Kennedy and the *Prince Albert.*

With the new year but a few weeks old, Kennedy and Bellot had begun sledging journeys south from Batty Bay. They were intent on establishing caches that would help them reach Fury Beach, their intended starting point for the spring sledging expedition to the west. The experience gained on these relatively short journeys convinced Kennedy that they would be unable to carry out Lady Franklin's full instructions and fully trace the western shores of Boothia Felix. Instead, he intended to go no further south than the North Magnetic Pole, a decision prompted in part by an outbreak of scurvy on the ship.

Kennedy set off from Batty Bay for Fury Beach on 24 February with five men and was followed a week later by Bellot with a further seven men, the *Prince Albert* being left in the charge of John Hepburn. On mustering at Fury Beach it was found that supplies were short and Bellot had to return to Batty Bay to obtain more. He also brought more men and a sledge to act as a fatigue party that would help with the launch of the main sledge journey. They eventually set off on 29 March and reached Brentford Bay before sending the fatigue party back.

Following the coast of the bay as it trended to the south-west they were surprised to find a cliff-lined opening leading roughly westwards. Kennedy and his party made their way along the southern shore of North Somerset with – to their south and across the ice-bound passage ('Bellot Strait') – the most northerly coastline of North America. About two miles wide, the strait continued across the peninsula until it opened out into what Kennedy believed to be a large bay curving away to the north and west until its shores lined their western horizon. The presence of land to the north could only mean one thing: Franklin's ships could not have passed down those waters from Barrow's Strait. There was, therefore, no need to examine the western coast of Boothia Felix as far south as the Magnetic North Pole.

Two days were spent in crossing westward over the twenty-five-mile-wide frozen bay until Kennedy, Bellot, and the twelve seamen 'struck a low-lying beach, and pursued our course on it over gentle undulations in a direction due west.' Before them the land flattened out as they continued on to the north-west only to find themselves on the shores of another great bay blocked with ice stretching to the far horizon. Unknown to them, they were at Ommanney Bay. They had been crossing the southern part of Prince of Wales Island and had reached its western coast. The ice before them, jumbled and rearing up in great pressure ridges, clearly indicated that no ships could have passed that way and that a search to the south would have, consequently, been pointless. Kennedy turned to the north-east and re-crossed the island, meeting Peel Sound just south of a modest bay ('Back Bay') that had been traversed by the *Resolute*'s Lieutenant Browne almost exactly a year earlier. The party took their sledges up the north-east coast of the island until they reached Cape Walker. From there they crossed the entrance to the sound (which Kennedy now described as an 'inlet'), continued around the top of North Somerset and into Prince Regent's Inlet, until they reached the *Prince Albert* at Batty Bay on 30 May. They had been away for three months, used dogs to help haul their sledges, and had slept in snow houses (igloos). When the men had to assist the dogs by hauling on the sledge traces, Kennedy noted in his report to the Admiralty that Bellot always took, 'an equal share with the men in dragging the sledge, and ever encouraging them in their arduous labours by his native cheerful disposition.'

The *Prince Albert* was cut free from the ice of Batty Bay on 6 August and Kennedy took her over to Beechey Island where he found Pullen and the *North Star*. He had arrived six weeks after Inglefield had sailed to examine the west coast of Baffin's Bay. With no such directions to delay his passage, Kennedy arrived home almost a month before the *Isabel*. He had little to report apart from the important discovery of Bellot Strait and the confirmation that Lieutenant Browne had been right in his assumption that Franklin could not have gone down Peel Sound. Stones he had picked up at Batty Bay for use as ballast went to Sir Roderick Murchison to be examined for fossil remains. Sir John Richardson saw a dangerous precedent in the manner that Kennedy had carried out his sledging journey and hoped that naval search expeditions would not try to emulate him as, 'Naval men are not yet alive to the advantage of dispensing with tents, building snow houses, and living almost wholly on pemmican on their journeys, hence they require larger parties with much auxiliary assistance from fatigue parties.'

CHAPTER EIGHT

'THE UTMOST ENDURANCE AND MOST ZEALOUS ENERGY'

As the last of Lady Franklin's two private expeditions arrived home, far, far to the north-west, Commander Robert McClure and the ship's company of the *Investigator* found themselves facing a very bleak future. Following his separation from Kellett and the *Herald* at the end of July 1851, McClure had sailed round Barrow Point and, after making contact with a group of Eskimos, ran aground near the Yarborough Inlet. Eleven casks of valuable salt beef were lost as the stores were unloaded to lighten the vessel while ice closed in from the north, threatening to force her against the shore. A fortunate change of wind direction allowed the *Investigator* to break free of the shoals and she continued eastwards through an open channel between the shore and the ice. More natives were met and messages left in the hope that they would reach the nearest Hudson's Bay Company posts. East of Cape Bathurst, Franklin Bay was entered and revealed the unexpected phenomenon of tall plumes of smoke rising from the base of the shore-lining cliffs. McClure sent Lieutenant Samuel Gurney Cresswell away in a whaler accompanied by the surgeon, Anderson, and the ship's interpreter, Johann Miertsching, to discover the cause of the strange sight. On their arrival at the beach the stench of sulphur soon explained the volcanic origins of the smoke.

On rounding the towering cliffs of Cape Parry, the *Investigator* found that further detailed examination of the coast was prevented by a four-mile-wide belt of ice lying close in to the shore. As winter was approaching, McClure had hopes of continuing to the east in search of a safe harbour. The ice, however, clearly barring his approach to the coast, meant that he either had to return to the west, or risk a winter trapped in a floe. Just at that moment, a mist to the north lifted and McClure saw, beyond open water, high ground lining the north-east horizon. This was new land, unmarked on any chart. By the following morning McClure had arrived off the unknown cliffs and, taking a party ashore, claimed the new territory for his Sovereign, naming it 'Baring's Land' after the First Lord of the Admiralty. The soaring headland on which they stood was honoured with the name 'Nelson's Head'.

Following the limestone cliffs as they trended to the north-east, McClure found himself entering what appeared to be a wide inlet with land rising on its eastern shore. Presented with clear water ahead, McClure pressed on in the hope that he might have found a passage through to Melville Sound, now less than 100 miles to the north-east. Two days into the waterway, two islands were encountered and named 'Princess

Left: Commander Robert McClure.

Below: The discovery of the Princess Royal Islands.

Bottom: The ice closing around the *Investigator.*

HMS *Investigator* in the ice of the Beaufort Sea, September 1850.

Royal Islands'. At the same time, ice was seen to be sweeping down the channel. The *Investigator* managed to reach north of the islands to within thirty miles of Melville Sound, but soon found herself in the grip of the ice and under threat of being forced onshore by a driving gale. Fortunately, McClure was able to use ice-anchors to secure the ship to a large floe which grounded before the rocks were reached. With great effort the *Investigator* was eventually warped a mile through the pack and out of immediate danger. But, with the sea freezing around them they were soon locked into the ice and at its mercy as it drifted south towards the Princess Royal Islands. Again, the floe which held them ran aground, saving them from being forced ashore. The ice itself, however, continued to be pressed against the ship and forced her over on to her side as the deck planking cracked and splintered and her main beams groaned under the pressure. The ship's company were mustered on the upper deck in -36 degrees Fahrenheit, ready to take to the ice should the ship finally surrender to the pressure, but some of the seamen, thinking that their last day on earth had arrived, broke into the liquor store and proceeded to get drunk while the ship spun slowly round as the floe was 'coach-wheeled' along the shore once more to the north. By the first week of October, the pressure ceased and the ship was returned, more or less, to an upright position and prepared for winter. With this complete, McClure encouraged his men to erect a stage on which they could dance, sing, or give recitations, most of them had earned the chance for a release to the tension they had been suffering from for the past few weeks.

Investigator trapped in the ice.

After claiming possession of the land to the east ('Prince Albert Land') and the two islands, McClure sledged north up the frozen channel with the ship's second master – Stephen Court (who had been with Ross in the *Enterprise*) – and six seamen. On the morning of 21 October, they left to the cheers of those remaining behind, but Court was back within a few hours to collect a new sledge, the one they had been using had collapsed after just a few miles of being hauled over the piled and broken ice.

Living for the first few meals on a diet of mainly melted snow and frozen pemmican, McClure's party soon picked up enough experience to add oatmeal or chocolate to lukewarm water. Thirst became a problem, however, as the water that lay on the surface of the ice proved to be salt. Nevertheless, five days after they had started from the ship, in the darkness of the late morning, McClure and Court climbed a 600 foot hill on Prince Albert Land and waited for the sun to rise. As it did, they were rewarded by the sight of the coast of the land on which they stood turning, and continuing to turn, to the east. To their north-west, the corner of Baring's Land (Banks' Land) turned westwards, whilst ahead of them a frozen sea lay bare of any land in the direction of Melville Island and Parry's furthest point. A Northwest Passage, dreamt of by generations of adventurers, had been discovered. That night, the sledge haulers were given an extra glass of rum to celebrate.

With the temperatures plummeting and their rations already low, McClure could not stay too long to enjoy his discovery. Once a cairn had been erected, a message placed inside, and the channel up which they had travelled given the name 'Prince of Wales Strait', the party began their journey back to the *Investigator*. About twelve miles from the ship, McClure decided to push on alone to prepare a comfortable reception for his sledge-crew. However, fog descended and he missed the ship, having to spend the night alone in the bitter cold. To add to his concerns, all his ammunition was used up in trying to attract attention, leaving none to defend himself against prowling polar bears. Unable to see anything or anyone that could help him find the ship, McClure curled up on the ice and went to sleep. He was awoken by what he took to be the flash of a rocket but, on looking up, he saw a brilliant display of the aurora-borealis arching across the starlit sky. Unable to return to his sleep, he walked up and down the floe to keep warm until the sun rose and revealed that he was just four miles from the *Investigator*. After less than an hour's walk, McClure clambered onboard his ship and was followed a few hours later by Court and the other men – they had spent the night in their tent seven miles from the vessel rather than risk getting lost in the fog. Good news awaited them that almost matched their sighting of Melville Sound. A shooting party had returned from Prince Albert Land with over 1,000lbs of musk-ox meat. A welcome addition to their stocks to replace the salt-beef that had been lost and a large number of cans of meat that had proved to be rotten.

The winter passed without incident and, by February 1851, the ship's company were out on the ice playing rounders in an effort to get fit for a series of sledge journeys McClure had planned for the spring. A depot was established on the largest of the Princess Royal Islands and a boat was left on the eastern shore of the strait, both to help in case of sledge crews, or even the ship itself, meeting with disaster. Three six-week sledging journeys were planned, each with one officer and six men. The first lieutenant, William Haswell, was to travel down the south-east shore, Cresswell was to trace the shore to the north-west, and a mate, Robert Wynniatt, was ordered to make his way around the shores of Prince Albert Land to the east in a somewhat ambitious attempt to reach Cape Walker. The three expeditions set out on 18 April to the usual cheers, each man's share of the hauling amounting to 200lbs. None could look forward to much comfort in the coming weeks:

> If they should feel cold, they must be patient; for until they return to the ship there will be no fire to warm them. Should their parched tongues cleave to their mouths, they must swallow snow to allay their thirst; for water there is none. Should their health fail, pity is all that their comrades can give them; for the sledge must move on its daily march. If hungry, they must console themselves by looking forward to being better fed when the travelling is over; for the rations are necessarily, in sledge journeys, weighed off to an ounce; in short, from the time they leave the ship until their return to it, the service is ever one of suffering and privation which calls for the utmost endurance and most zealous energy.

Lieutenant Cresswell's sledging party hauling over the broken ice.

Three weeks after setting out, Wynniatt returned saying that, at a distance of 120 miles from the ship, he had fallen and broken his chronometer. McClure was, 'pained beyond measure', not only was there no spare remaining onboard, but considerable time had been lost in returning to the ship. Wynniatt was soon heading north again with his ears considerably warmer from his captain's opinion of his action.

Cresswell emerged from the ice on 20 May, having spent thirty-two days away from the ship. His party had covered 170 miles of the northern and north-eastern coasts and found that it trended to the south, suggesting that Baring's Land was an island. No trace of the Franklin expedition had been seen. Cresswell had hoped to stay out longer, but had been forced to return when two of his men suffered badly from frostbite. McClure, nevertheless, soon found another use for his recently gained experience. A polar bear was shot the day after Cresswell's return which, on its stomach being opened up, was found to contain an extraordinary mixture of raisins, leaf-tobacco, cubed pork, and sticking-plaster. Fearing that such a combination could only have come from Collinson's *Enterprise*, only two days after his return McClure sent Cresswell out once again, with rations for three weeks to search the south-east coast of Baring's Land – the only quarter as yet unvisited. Two days into Cresswell's journey, the real reason for the bear's stomach contents came to light. A preserved meat can, still containing remnants of the same meal the bear had eaten, was found on the ice. Someone from the *Investigator* (possibly from Haswell's party) had used an empty can to store the items and it had probably fallen from a sledge to be found and opened by the hungry bear.

After an absence of forty-seven days, Haswell returned to the ship with no news of Franklin. He had reached a large inlet on Wollaston Land before turning back. Ten days later John Rae was to stand on the opposite shore of the same inlet. Haswell had come across an Eskimo encampment, but had been unable to have any sensible form of conversation with them. Keen to know if they had any news of Franklin, and to see whether they had any knowledge of the geography of the area, McClure and Miertsching, the interpreter, set off to find them. The natives proved to be an amiable people who had no knowledge of the missing expedition and had no contact with any European traders. They knew of a land to the south named 'Nunavaksaraluk' (North America) but had never been there. McClure returned after two days away.

Next to return was Wynniatt. He had failed to reach Cape Walker, not through lack of effort, but as a result of the coastline of Prince Albert Land trending to the south-east (he would also not have wanted to lose sight of land by striking out eastwards across the ice without a checked and working chronometer). Wynniatt had been away for thirty-one days on his second journey, and, although unaware of it, had reached a point opposite to, and less than thirty miles from, that achieved by Osborn on the same day on the west coast of Prince of Wales Island. He was also able to report to McClure that, from his furthest point, he had seen the coastline trending to the north-east. An observation that, not unexpectedly, led his captain to become convinced that Prince Albert Land was connected by an unbroken shore to Cape Walker.

Cresswell returned with no news of the *Enterprise* or of Franklin to the south-west. He had, however, been forced to use his inflatable Halkett boat to cross a number of open lanes of water that stretched across the strait. The ice to the south was on the verge of breaking up.

The *Investigator* was ready by the middle of June to continue her voyage to the northern end of Prince of Wales Strait, but had to wait until the seventh of the following month before open water was seen in the vicinity. A week later, without a sound, the ice around the ship parted and left her floating in a fifty-foot wide pool. An attempt to break through the ice and proceed to the north around the west of the Princess Royal Islands almost led to the ship being forced ashore, but a return to the eastern side of the strait allowed a safer passage until the pack surrounded the vessel once again to the north of the islands. Three weeks were spent drifting at the mercy of the floe which, at one point, took them within twenty-five miles of the northern end of the strait, before the ship could break free with the wind set in the north-east. Unable to press through the ice to the north 'all hopes disappeared' and, at 9 o'clock on the morning of 16 August, with ice already beginning to form on the surface of the open water around the ship, McClure turned about and raced to the south – he did not want to spend another winter in the confines of Prince of Wales Strait.

The *Investigator* off Baring's Land (Banks' Island).

Nelson Head was rounded the following day and the southern shores followed until the land turned northwards around a low spit of land ('Cape Kellett'). At this point McClure had to make a hard decision. The coast of North America was within easy sailing distance over open waters to the south, he had discovered a route for the Northwest Passage (albeit blocked by ice), and had spent a hard winter trapped in the ice. Despite a search of the shores around him, no evidence that Franklin had passed that way had been found. On the other hand, he had not actually *passed* through the Northwest Passage, he had a ship in excellent condition, and men with only minor medical problems. Ahead of him a six-mile-wide lane of open water ran up the western coast of Baring's Land and, if he could double its north-western corner, there might, just might, be an opening to give him passage into Melville Sound. From there, the route home was well-known and glory assured. Not unreasonably, McClure turned his bows to the north.

The next day was spent in an exhilarating dash to the north, the low land to the east beginning to rise and become more rugged. The depth beneath the keel increased markedly and the ice moved in closer to the shore, narrowing the open waters through with they sailed. Suddenly, the situation changed to one of dreadful danger. With cliffs rearing to the starboard and a solid mass of ice-floes

The *Investigator* in great danger as she is lifted by the ice.

rearing up 10 feet out of the water to port, the channel grew more and more narrow. Eventually, the ship's boats were used to tow the *Investigator* forward as she could not be controlled by sail in such a small space. Retreat was out of the questions as any attempt to 'round to' would have caused the loss of the jib-boom against the cliffs. Matters took a turn for the worse beyond a projection of land McClure had named 'Cape Prince Alfred'. The wind, which had been mainly from the south-east, turned westerly and began to drive the pack towards the cliffs. Ahead of him, McClure could see ice already being forced ashore but was fortunate in finding himself alongside 'a small but heavy piece of ice, grounded in twelve fathoms'. The *Investigator* was secured to the floe with the prayer that it was not struck on its seaward side by a larger floe. Such an incident could have seen the complete destruction of the ship. That evening, at 9 o'clock, the floe began to judder alarmingly and the ship was lifted 6 feet out of the water as a tongue of ice beneath her was pressed towards the beach. Their luck held, however, as the floe to which they were secured began to break up on its seaward edge, relieving the pressure. Now they were closer inshore, almost up against ice lining the beach, with their floe even more firmly grounded. For the next nine days, until 29 August, they seemed relatively secure but, on that day a strong westerly drove the pack ice against the shore. A huge floe forced its leading edge beneath the seaward rim of the ice holding the *Investigator* and began to lever the mass of ice upwards. McClure and his ship's company, their ship trapped between the floes, could only watch in horror as the monstrous white mass slowly reared up to a height that matched their masthead. As this was happening, the ship itself began to rise and gained a list to port as its beams groaned and cracked under the mounting pressure. It seemed that the ship would either be crushed beneath the floe as it toppled over on top of her, or would be nipped to destruction as the floes pressed in from either side. Then, just as it seemed as if their fate was to leave their bones on that hostile shore, the floes cracked apart and their frozen moorings fell back into the sea. The effect was to wrench the floe off the seabed and cause it to drift out into the pack pulling the *Investigator* with it. McClure ensured that his ice-anchors held and reinforced his hold onto the floe by means of additional hawsers, 'Our proximity to the shore compelled, as our only hopes of safety, the absolute necessity of holding on to it'. To be adrift on a lee shore with huge masses of ice bearing down would have invited disaster, but the violence of the elements had yet to subside and, once again, the floe was on the move, this time towards a low spit of land that already had floes piling up on its shores. Clearly seeing the danger from a grounded floe right in their path, McClure sent the gunner's mate, John Kerr, across the heaving ice with a charge of gunpowder to see if the floe could be split. With great difficulty Kerr reached the threat, but the charge did little damage and soon the ship was within a few feet of being pounded to a wreck. The first part to receive the blow was the stern post and a, 'heavy grind which shook every mast, and caused beams and decks to complain as she trembled to the violence of the shock, plainly indicated that the struggle would be of short duration'. McClure decided on a last, desperate, measure. Several of the ice-anchors and other cables had parted with the collision and he now gave the order that all the mooring lines were to be cast off. His hope was that, rather than be crushed between the floes, the *Investigator* might drift free onto the shore. There, her hulk could be used as an 'asylum for the winter'. But, before the order could be carried out, the floe against which they were being forced split and the pressure fell away in an instant. That, for the time being was the end of their struggle, 'By midnight the ice was stationary and everything quiet'.

It seemed to all that they had reached the furthest possible point that year. The thermometer was falling and the ice remained fixed at all points off the land. Hunting parties were sent ashore and came back with remarkable tales of a forest of petrified trees being found, a remarkable discovery in an area where only the ground-spreading dwarf willow was known to exist. Other men collected fifty-five tons of rocks from the beach for use as ballast to replace the weight of the used stores.

On 10 September, a change of wind direction to the south brought rain and a rise in the temperature. At mid-day the ice began to move away from the shore taking the *Investigator* with it. Charges of gunpowder had to be used to free the ship before she could reach the safety of another grounded floe. Once again the ice closed in and had to be blasted apart by using a 26 gallon rum barrel packed with 255lbs of gunpowder. For the next two weeks the *Investigator* was sailed, warped, towed and forced up the coast. At one time the gap between the ice and the cliff-lined shore was so narrow that the starboard studding-sail boom had to be hoisted clear in order to avoid damage from striking the sheer rock wall. The north-west corner of 'Baring's Land' (by now accepted by McClure to be actually Banks' Land) was turned and the land began to trend slightly to the south of east. Their course continued eastwards through waters that were icing over as they passed. Two possible harbours were seen, but both proved to be blocked with ice. In the early hours of 24 September, McClure found himself on the western horn of a large bay that was rapidly filling with loose ice blown in from the north. Having checked to see if there was open water ahead, and, finding only solid ice, he decided that this inlet should be the site of his second wintering. By 7.45am the ship was anchored in four and a half fathoms, and by that night, the sea had frozen around them in the haven that McClure named 'Bay of Mercy' (Mercy Bay).

Once the ship had been prepared for the coming winter, McClure sent Court the few miles along the coast to the east to link up with the furthest point reached by Cresswell in the spring. The ship's second master succeeded with little difficulty but brought back unwelcome news. Whilst out on the ice, he had narrowly escaped death when the floe broke away from the land and drifted out to sea. Only by the desperate measure of leaping from one loose piece of ice to another did he and his party eventually reach the safety of the shore. Behind them, the ice cleared for several miles out to sea. If McClure had not locked the *Investigator* into the Bay of Mercy he may have found a passage to take him many miles further to the east, and into Melville Sound.

By now the ship's stocks of supplies were becoming critical and McClure was forced to reduce the rations by a third. He made an exception for Christmas when, following divine service and a walk for exercise on the ice, 'dancing, skylarking, and singing were kept up on the lower deck with unflagging spirit, good humour, cheerfulness, and propriety'. The winter passed to a background of howling wolves and violent snow storms of such ferocity that, at one stage the weight of accumulated snow cracked the ice holding the ship causing her to reel alarmingly until the floe re-froze. There was little of the organised entertainment and schooling that had characterised other expeditions – the chief entertainment being the sight of two ravens continually annoying the ship's dog.

With the arrival of the new year McClure encouraged hunting parties in an attempt to increase the available supplies. One of the parties was led by the popular Sergeant John Woon of the Royal Marines. Also ashore hunting was a black seaman named Charles Anderson, a large powerful man who 'represented himself as a Canadian', but may have been an escaped slave. Anderson, in pursuit of a deer, became lost and was found some time later 'beside himself with excitement and horror' by Woon. The sergeant managed to persuade him by a combination of encouragement and threats to walk for a short distance, but Anderson went into convulsions and collapsed, bleeding at the nose and mouth. Woon, although only 5 feet 7 inches tall, slinging both their muskets over his shoulder, proceeded to drag the inert man towards the ship beneath the dark skies of the Arctic winter. The only time Woon could find to rest was when he had hauled Anderson up to the top of a ridge from where he could roll his burden down the other side, a 'rather severe treatment for an invalid but it had the merit of arousing the man somewhat from his lethargy'. After ten hours of exertion, Woon had dragged Anderson to within a mile of the ship and could see rockets being sent up to guide him home. At this point, however, Woon was overcome with exhaustion and Anderson, unable to move, pleaded 'to be left alone to die'. The sergeant now stumbled on alone only to meet a search party on its way out to look for the two men. Anderson was found frozen almost rigid and it was with great difficulty that his mouth could be forced open and brandy poured down his throat. Once safely onboard, it was discovered that Anderson was severely frostbitten and had to lose parts of both feet, some fingers, and part of his nose. McClure was so impressed by Woon's effort that he had a special silver medal produced which, on the obverse, bore the words 'For Exceptional Bravery and Intrepidity'.

On 11 April 1852, McClure set off to cross Melville Sound to Parry's Winter Harbour on Melville Island to complete the link between his western expedition and those from the east. Due to poor weather, the 150-mile crossing took seventeen days, only to end in deep disappointment. On the top of 'Parry's Rock' McClure found the message left by McClintock the previous June – the first he knew of Austin's expedition. There was no ship as he had hoped, and no depot of supplies. A note was left giving the *Investigator*'s position before the party returned to the ship. There they found that hunting parties had produced over 1000lbs of deer meat. They also found that scurvy had appeared.

Sergeant John Woon of the Royal Marines rescuing a shipmate.

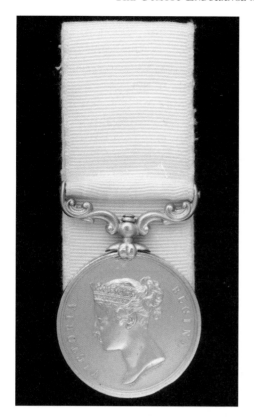

Above left: Sergeant John Woon's bravery medal – obverse.

Above right: Sergeant John Woon's bravery medal – reverse.

Instead of relief from the ice, the summer brought fogs, snow showers, and low temperatures. In June, the ice was found to have actually thickened rather than showing signs of melting. The following month saw the ice retreat from around the edge of the bay, and a few lanes opened up in the straits outside, but no signs of a break up could be seen. The meat supply ran out in the first week of July as shooting parties returned empty-handed. The situation was saved by Sergeant Woon who came across two bull musk-oxen. With only a couple of musket-balls left he brought one down but only injured the other. The wounded animal turned to charge and Woon was forced to fire his musket 'worm' (a cleaning tool) at the enraged beast. When this failed to kill the animal, Woon re-charged his gun and, waiting until the charging bull was within 6 feet of him, fired his iron ramrod, piercing the animal's heart. The two musk-oxen produced 'after deducting offal and hunter's perquisites' a total of 650lbs of meat.

With the arrival of September, it was clear to all that the ship was not to break free that year and that they were faced with yet another winter locked into the ice. The ship's company were mustered and McClure told them of his plans for their future. He had decided that, in the following spring, half the ship's company, thirty officers and men, would be divided into two parties. One would make its way south and attempt to reach the Hudson's Bay posts up the Mackenzie River; the other would head eastwards to Cape Spencer, near Beechey Island, where McClintock's note had informed them that a boat and supplies had been cached. McClure and the remainder of the ship's company would stay with the *Investigator* in the hope that they could break out later in the season. Failing that, they would set off for the cache at Port Leopold. His speech was 'well received' by his men and their spirits remained generally high, despite their rum ration being reduced by a half shortly afterwards. However, at least two men were badly affected by their circumstance. An able-seaman, Mark Bradley, quietly succumbed to the pressure and was reduced to shuffling harmlessly about the ship and talking to himself. The mate, Robert Wynniatt, on the other hand, became loud and aggressive to such a degree that he had to be put in irons for his own and other's safety.

The winter was spent to a background of increasing hunger. Even the officers, with their private stocks long gone, were reduced to a diet of a cup of cocoa for breakfast, a small portion of bread, half a pound of salt meat 'containing a good proportion of bone', and 'just enough vegetable to swear by.' A cup of weak tea was available for the evening. At Christmas, however, caution and rationing was ignored. 'Each mess was gaily illuminated and decorated with original paintings by our lower-deck artists, exhibiting the ship in her perilous positions during the transit of the Polar Sea, along with divers other subjects: but the grand feature of the day was the enormous plum-puddings, some weighing 26lbs., haunches of venison, hares roasted, and soup made of the same, with ptarmigan and sea pies.' Outside, the temperature fell to an unprecedented -65 degrees Fahrenheit.

Much of February 1853 was spent in spreading an 800 yard lane of gravel towards the entrance of the inlet, its heat-retaining properties intended to melt a path for the ship's escape if the heat-reflecting ice refused to show any signs of breaking up. Despite this gesture towards a hoped-for future, on 3 March, McClure listed those who were to be sent home via the Mackenzie or Lancaster Sound. In a change of plan, Lieutenant Haswell would lead thirty men (including the unfortunate Wynniatt) to the east, whilst Lieutenant Cresswell would take ten men south to the Mackenzie. The captain of the forecastle, John Calder, would travel with Cresswell as far as the Princess Royal Islands where he would load a sledge with cases of potato and chocolate and return to the ship. McClure included amongst those to go, all nineteen men on the sick list, explaining that he wished to retain, 'the most effective men in the event of being detained for another winter'. The ship's surgeon, Alexander Armstrong, approached McClure with the suggestion that the plan be abandoned. In his professional opinion, few of those ordered to leave were fit enough for the journey. The captain refused to consider any change to his plans. Twelve days later, all the 'travellers' were put on full rations to prepare them for the journey ahead. McClure had decided that the date for the sledging parties to leave would be 15 April.

The mood was not enhanced when the expedition suffered its first death on 5 April. For reasons known only to himself, one of the seamen went to the sick-bay and drank the remnants contained in a number of medicine bottles with fatal results. McClure had to muster the ship's company and give them an uplifting talk to try and keep their morale as high as possible. The following day, a caribou was hung up in readiness for the preparation of a substantial meal that might help lift the gloom which had descended on the ship. Letters were written home with copies for each of the departing parties. McClure wrote a despatch to the Admiralty in which he remarked upon the 'cheerfulness, propriety, and good conduct' of his officers and men. Strangely, despite the huge number of cans with rotten contents, he also pointedly remarked upon the 'excellence' of Messrs Gamble's preserved meat. To his sister he wrote that the same 'arm that sustained the first ark of Gopherwood as it floated over the waters of an engulphed world, has guided our ark of British oak'.

Later on the sixth, McClure and Haswell were walking on the ice discussing the problem of digging a grave on the frozen shore for the recent fatality when they saw a figure hurrying towards them from the entrance to the bay. At first they thought it was one of their men being chased by a bear but, as he drew closer they saw that his clothing was unlike any they had onboard. Even this was explainable if one of the ship's company had designed himself a new outfit for the coming sledge journey. At about 200 yards the figure began to wave his arms and shout, but any intelligible words were lost in the wind and sounded more like 'a wild screech'.

Lieutenant Bedford Pim greets McClure.

As the strange sight grew closer, McClure could see that he had a face 'as black as ebony' and half considered taking flight from the apparition. As he grew closer still, McClure shouted out 'In the name of God, who are you?' Back came the astounding reply, 'I'm Lieutenant Pim, late of the *Herald*, and now in the *Resolute*. Captain Kellett is in her at Dealy Island!' Unable to speak, McClure reached forward and shook Pim by the hand. Within minutes the upper deck of the *Investigator* was crowded with men eager to see the newcomer. Gone were the depressing thoughts of the approaching sledge journeys: 'We now, God be praised, consider ourselves saved'.

CHAPTER NINE

'FINAL, DECIDED, AND MOST UNMISTAKEABLE ORDERS'

Kellett and the *Resolute* had been towed clear of Beechey Island by the *Intrepid* in the early afternoon of 15 August 1852. Belcher and his consort had already disappeared up the open waters of Wellington Channel. Just off Assistance Harbour, on the south coast of Cornwallis Island, the *Resolute* ran aground in shoaling waters and was forced over on to her port side. She was then struck by an ice floe which sent the ship lurching over to starboard, her masts, 'bent like a reed; you might have sheepshanked the rigging' and 60 feet of false keel was torn away. Towed free by the *Intrepid*, Kellett was soon 'proceeding merrily' westward through loose ice past Griffith and Lowther islands. A barrier of ice was met just to the west of Lowther Island and Kellett returned to its ice-littered shores with the intention of seeking a place to winter but, after landing and climbing a hill with McClintock and Mecham, Kellett saw open water to the north. With the *Intrepid* in the lead, the intervening ice was broken through 'at the expense of some heavy blows' and Kellett found he had a clear run through a succession of heavy snow showers. Byam Martin Island was reached on the thirty-first and Melville Island sighted the following day, the occasion being marked by McClintock running up the signal message 'I wish you joy'.

Carefully making his way along the south of the island, sometimes under sail, at others under tow, Kellett scoured the shore for a suitable place to winter. He intended to get as far to the west as he could, but knew he might have to retreat to a previously agreed harbour. At all costs, a winter spent locked into the open ice had to be avoided. In the early hours of the morning of 7 September, Winter Harbour lay off the starboard side with Parry's Rock some four miles away. But ice filled the inlet, and all that could be done was to leave a small depot for future sledging journeys. The great sandstone rock was not visited – and McClure's message remained undisturbed.

Knowing that he could not, with safety, continue to the west, Kellett came about and returned the twenty miles to Bridport Bay. He had earlier seen that the bay was clear of ice and, on entering, found a secure place to winter by cutting a dock into an old floe that remained fast to the south-eastern side of Dealy Island. 100 yards apart, and less than 1,000 yards from the shore of the island, the two ships were frozen in two days after their arrival.

As Kellett prepared the ships for the winter, McClintock was sent north across Melville Island to establish a depot at Point Nias on Hecla and Griper Bay. It took him three journeys and a total of thirty-six days. In addition to taking a sledge, McClintock used a hand-cart and moved more than a ton of stores and provisions. Kellett noted, 'This was a most arduous piece of work, well and cleverly performed, without accident; his people looking better than when they started.'

Sledging expeditions were sent out to the west on 22 September to establish further depots for the spring travelling. One of these, led by Mecham, had visited Winter Harbour and found McClure's message. Kellett found himself in the position of knowing where the *Investigator* was the previous May – when the message was deposited, but not necessarily where she was four months later. The broken up state of the ice between Melville Island and Bank's Land precluded sledging, young ice prevented boat travel, and there was not enough open water for a ship to get through. No attempt to reach McClure could be made until the following spring.

On 5 November, the Frenchman, de Bray, had his breakfast disturbed by the sound of an alarming commotion out on the ice. Reaching the upper deck he looked towards the *Intrepid* and saw the effigy of Guy Fawkes being carried on a chair, accompanied by men in cocked hats. Loud abuse was hurled at the be-wigged figure and songs were sung in favour of his downfall. That night two effigies were burnt, one from each ship, to a toast of an extra ration of rum. Such behaviour set the light-hearted standard for the winter. Lieutenant Pim had a walking race around Dealy Island against the mate, George Nares (Nares won with 82 minutes against Pim's 85). Theatricals were performed in the *Resolute*, the *Intrepid* providing a 'soiree fantastique', and a magic lantern show. The master and the purser taught reading and writing. McClintock concentrated on the detail of the coming sledge expeditions, his calculations being confused by discovering that the 4lb cans of meat actually contained 4.5lbs. He had also refined the principle of the 'satellite' sledge. At 5 feet long and weighing just 14lb, the satellite carried just fuel, food and blanket bags. It enabled two or three men to make a rapid search of an area whilst leaving the main, heavier, sledge as a depot or to be used elsewhere.

Pim, in company with the surgeon, William Domville, nine men, six dogs, and two sledges, left for the Bay of Mercy on 10 March in the hope that McClure and the *Investigator* were still there. Pim intended to reach Cape Dundas on the south-west coast of Melville Island before crossing the sound to Bank's Land but, just short of the cape, the large, man-hauled, sledge broke. Heavily conscious that time was against him, Pim ordered Domville to take the broken sledge with its stores to Cape Dundas whilst he and two men took the dog-sledge directly across to the Bay of Mercy. On the afternoon of 6 April, the inlet opened up before them and Pim, racing ahead, saw the bare masts of the *Investigator* rising from a huge mound of banked-up snow. To his great relief, figures could be seen moving across the ice and he broke out into a wild run, yelling against a driving wind.

Three weeks after Pim had left, Kellett sent out two sledge expeditions to continue the search for Franklin. Only nine men in the *Resolute* and eight men in the *Intrepid* were to remain behind. With his men mustered on the ice ready to start, and after prayers, Kellett told them that he, 'hoped they would leave little for any one to do coming after us, and that by their exertions they would render the expedition so remarkable, that every person would feel proud in having belonged to it.' With few left behind to give them a farewell cheer, the two parties cheered each other as they set off with fluttering sledge flags adding a splash of colour to the scene. Mecham and Nares crossed the land to Liddon Gulf and then followed the coastline around to the north-west. A stretch of ice (Kellett Strait) was crossed to reach an island (Eglinton Island) which revealed another, much larger, island (Prince Patrick Island) to the north. Having sent Nares and the support sledge back to the ship, Mecham, with his sledge *Discovery* beneath its scarlet flag, landed on the larger island and explored its south and western coasts, finding substantial amounts of petrified wood. With the aid of northerly winds to fill the sails he had hoisted on his sledges Mecham crossed the island and returned to Melville Island, reaching the ship on 6 July. He had been away for ninety-one days, had sledged for 1,173 miles and discovered 785 miles of new coast.

McClintock, his sledge named *Star of the North* and flying a blue flag with a white star, and with de Bray in charge of his support sledge, was joined at the start of his journey by Kellett and Lieutenant Richard Vesey Hamilton, formerly of the *Assistance* under Ommanney. The route to Hecla and Griper Bay proved to be very difficult for the sledges and, on several occasions, all thirty-nine men had to haul on a single sledge to get it across rocky ravines. Kellett, who had no experience of such work wrote:

> I have been a long time at sea, and seen various trying services, but I have never seen such labour, and such misery after. No amount of money is an equivalent ... I should like to see the travelling men get an Arctic medal.

He returned to his ship after giving three and a half days of help and encouragement. Two weeks later Hamilton returned having got McClintock and de Bray onto the ice of Hecla and Griper Bay.

McClintock headed north-west along the northern Melville Island coast until it turned south. At 'Cape de Bray' the French officer was sent back and arrived at the *Resolute* on 17 May towing the corpse of one of his seamen on his sledge – the man had died of a heart problem. McClintock continued south-west down the coast of Melville Island until he reached a deep inlet he named 'Purchase Bay' after the *Intrepid*'s second engineer. There he built a cairn and left a note inside for Mecham who, before long, could be expected to make his way up that coast. From Purchase Bay, McClintock returned northwards before crossing over the ice to a low land mass that had frequently appeared on his north-western horizon. To this land of red sandstone he gave the name 'Prince Patrick Island'. A brief visit was made to another island to the south (Eglinton Island) before he returned to Prince Patrick and searched the shores of 'Intrepid Bay'. The eastern coast of the island was then explored to its northern tip, the party struggling through deep thawing snow in which the sledges sank and they were forced to wade waist deep.

Two small islands to the north were searched before McClintock turned south down the western coast for a few miles and, using his satellite sledge and two men, explored the wide 'Satellite Bay'. Without a tent, and with only their wet blanket bags for warmth, they survived a savage gale only by sheltering in the lee of their tiny sledge. To the west of them, grounded in the shallow waters off the island, enormous blue-white floes lay piled on top of each other, blown there across the frozen Arctic Sea.

McClintock and his party left Prince Patrick Island for a small island that had been seen to the east. McClintock had been so impressed by its covering of moss that he had named it 'Emerald Isle'. The journey over proved to be extremely difficult. Knee-deep snow was in the process of turning to slush and the sledge could only be kept on the move by a series of repeated standing pulls. To make matters even worse, rain had sculpted the ice beneath their feet into 'needle ice', an array of thin, sharp, spikes that severely damaged their feet through their canvas footwear. Two days were spent searching the southern coast of Emerald Isle before they set off for the northern shore of Melville Island. At Point Nias, at the head of Hecla and Griper Bay, one of McClintock's team, a Royal Marine Private who had continued to heave on the traces despite increasing pain, suddenly collapsed. For eighteen hours McClintock nursed the man until he had recovered enough to be placed on the sledge. Any relief the invalid got was, however, to be short-lived. It soon became clear that the sledge could no longer be dragged through the interior of the island with its swathes of boggy ground and steep ravines. McClintock was forced to abandon it along with 550lbs of stores and provisions and start a four-day march to reach their ship off Dealy Island. They arrived limping and exhausted at mid-day on 18 July after having been away for 105 days during which time they had dragged their sledges for 1,408 miles, 768 of which were new discoveries. Now, back on the decks of their ship, they heard some astounding news. The *Investigator* had not only been found, but most of her ship's company were now in the *Resolute* and the *Intrepid*.

On 19 April, a day which Kellett proclaimed would 'be kept as a holiday by my heirs and successors for ever', Pim had returned with McClure. Not long after their meeting at the Bay of Mercy, Pim had handed McClure a letter from Kellett. In it Kellett had asked McClure to provide him with medical evidence that his men were in a fit condition to remain with the *Investigator* for another winter. McClure was not slow to realise what this meant. If it could be shown that the *Investigator*'s men were in no condition to spend another winter at the Bay of Mercy, Kellett would almost certainly order her abandonment, and this time McClure could not fly to the north under full sail to escape Kellett's order.

Once the warm and heartfelt greetings were out of the way, McClure set about trying to convince Kellett that the *Investigator* would break free that summer and that his ship's company would be prepared to stay onboard. But, with the arrival of Cresswell with Miertsching and twenty-four of the *Investigator*'s men, McClure's arguments were exposed as bluff. The men of the *Resolute* and the *Intrepid* were shocked by the sight that met their eyes as they welcomed the rescued invalids.

Their 'tottering gait, attenuated form, and care-worn expression of countenance' easily persuaded Kellett that they had been through a harrowing experience, and could not be allowed – even at their own wish – to remain with the ship. McClure argued that these men were, in fact, the feeblest of his ship's company and that the men remaining onboard were in a much healthier state. His pleas were ignored by Kellett who gave him an order to abandon his ship. Still McClure argued, although out-ranked by Kellett, he was, after all, the captain of his own ship under orders from the Admiralty. Kellett agreed upon a compromise. McClure would return to the *Investigator* taking with him Surgeon Domville (McClure did not trust the opinions of his own surgeon). If McClure could find twenty volunteers who wished to remain with the ships, and they were all passed as fit by Domville, then he would be allowed to remain with the *Investigator*. If he failed to find enough fit volunteers, she would be abandoned.

As McClure returned to his ship, Kellett turned his mind to the problem of the *Investigator's* invalids. It would be better for all concerned, he decided, if they could be sent to Beechey Island. There they could rest in the *North Star* until one of the expected supply ships arrived from England. A travelling party was raised from the few men left in the *Resolute* and *Intrepid* and placed under the command of the mate, Richard 'Paddy' Roche. Kellett ordered him to take Lieutenant Cresswell, the mentally disturbed mate, Wynniatt, and the remainder of the *Investigator's* men across the 300 miles to Beechey Island and into the care of Pullen. The journey was carried out with little difficulty and the *North Star* provided a safe haven until the second week of August when, much to their delight, they were treated to the novel sight of the first iron-built screw steamer to enter the Arctic, HMS *Phoenix*, rounding Cape Riley. She was commanded by Commander Edward Inglefield, late of the *Isabel*, who had eagerly volunteered to get back into the Franklin search. He was accompanied by the storeship, *Breadalbane*, packed to the gunwales with coal, provisions, and rum. The arrival of poor weather proved a hazard in unloading the *Breadalbane* and, eventually, relays of sledges had to be used to transfer her supplies to the *North Star*. On 21 August, ice moving into the bay afforded the *Investigator* men yet another novel sight, but one they could have done without. In the early hours of the morning, Assistant Master William Fawckner – the Government Agent appointed to the *Breadalbane* – was jolted awake by his cabin door springing open. As he hurriedly dressed, a succession of loud bangs and groans of stressed timber told him that the ship was in the grip of the ice. Reaching the upper deck he found men trying to save the ship's boats. Their efforts soon proved to be futile as the pressing ice crushed the boats to matchwood before they could be released. A glance into the ship's hold revealed to Fawckner that the hull was collapsing under the enormous pressure. At this he 'roared like a bull' to anyone within earshot ordering them to get clear of the ship before jumping over the side himself. Standing only in his stockinged feet, 'the cold was little thought of at the exciting moment', he was met by Inglefield who had run across the buckling ice from the nearby *Phoenix*. Ordered back into the ship by the senior officer, Fawckner found 5 foot of water in the hold and the starboard bow collapsing inwards. He returned to the ice just in time. Behind him the ship began to sink very rapidly, 'the time her bowsprit touched the ice, until her mastheads were out of sight, did not occupy above one minute and a half'. From the first nip of the ice to her disappearance beneath its surface, the loss of the *Breadalbane* had taken no more than fifteen minutes.

Inglefield sailed three days later taking with him the crew of the lost ship. He also took Lieutenant Samuel Gurney Cresswell of the *Investigator* – to whom went the honour of being the first man to pass through the Northwest Passage – and Surgeon Robert McCormick. Against Belcher's orders (who had permitted only a sledge journey, but was out of sight up Wellington Channel), McCormick had led a boat expedition up the eastern coast of the Wellington Channel with the hope that a waterway connecting with Jones Sound might be found leading from Baring Bay. He had set off with six men on 19 August and, after a journey of great difficulty, found that no such channel existed. He returned to the *North Star* on 8 September. When, during the following spring, communications had been established with the *Assistance* and *Pioneer* by means of frequent sledge journeys, McCormick proposed to Belcher that he be allowed to take John Ross's old yacht, *Mary*, still aground on Beechey Island, out of Lancaster Sound and up into Smith Sound before returning home in her. Belcher refused to grant such permission and McCormick returned to England in the *Phoenix*.

Inglefield also took back some bitterly sad news. When he had sailed from England, he had brought out with him Lieutenant Joseph-Rene Bellot, the gallant French naval officer who had served in the *Prince Albert* under Kennedy. Desperate to return to the search ('Give me but a plank to lie upon, a corner wherein to put

The *Phoenix* and the *Breadalbane*.

my clothes; I ask no more'), Bellot had obtained leave from the French Navy and, showered with the almost maternal affections of Lady Franklin, had taken passage in the *Phoenix*. On arrival at Beechey Island, he begged to be employed at the earliest opportunity so Pullen sent him and four seamen up Wellington Channel with despatches for Belcher. Eight days later, two of the seamen returned exhausted to Beechey Island with the tragic news that Bellot had been lost. The party had been attempting to land from the ice when the floe on which Bellot and two of the seamen stood on was blown out to sea. They built themselves an igloo in the shelter of a large hummock and settled down to wait for the ice to drift closer to the shore. As they waited Bellot told the men with him that 'nothing made him more happy than to think that he was not on shore, for, knowing his duty as an officer, he would see the last danger, adding that he would rather die here than be on shore to be saved'. On the morning of 18 August, Bellot left the shelter to see how the ice was drifting. He was followed four minutes later by Able Seaman William Johnson (according to Pullen 'a good and moral man') who was unable to find him. All that remained of the missing Bellot was a walking stick seen lying on the far side of a thirty-foot crack in the ice. With little else to go on, it could only be assumed that the French officer had fallen through the ice and had failed to surface. Two days later, Johnson and his companion used a 'piece of ice' as a raft to reach the shore where they joined the other two seamen.

The *Phoenix* arrived back in England in the early days of October and, on the seventh, Cresswell reported to the Admiralty the 'proud intelligence of the achievement of the Northwest Passage'. He was the first man in history to pass along the top of North America from the Pacific to the Atlantic Oceans and to his captain, Robert Le Mesurier McClure, went the laurels for making the first discovery of a passage through the ice-bound islands of the Arctic Archipelago.

But for McClure himself, back at Mercy Bay and onboard the *Investigator* in late May, events did not seem quite so flattering. When he asked for twenty volunteers to remain with the ship for another winter, to his 'surprise and mortification' only four men stepped forward. Even, however, if every man had shown himself as willing, the medical survey carried out by surgeons Armstrong and Domville would have put an end to matters. In their report to Kellett they wrote, regarding the health of the remaining officers and men of the *Investigator*, that, 'their present state of health is such as renders them utterly unfit to undergo the rigour of another winter in this climate, without entertaining the most serious apprehension for the consequence.' For McClure it was the end of his dream of taking his ship through the Northwest Passage. He would have to settle for the honour of leading the first body of men across the top of North America. Reluctantly, he gave the order for the ship to be secured against future gales and a depot established ashore for the use of Collinson in case the *Enterprise* should came that way. Wooden markers were erected over the graves of the three men who had lost their lives in the Bay of Mercy. Finally, on 3 June, the white ensign was run up to the mast-head and the order to abandon the ship was given. Two weeks later they arrived at Dealy Island and were shared out between Kellett's two ships.

Sledge parties abandoning the *Investigator* in the Bay of God's Mercy.

Roche returned from Beechey Island with letters and the latest news after a 600 mile round trip that took him just six weeks. The return of the sledging parties led by Mecham and McClintock were followed by that of Lieutenant Hamilton.

Hamilton had been ordered to the north of Melville Island by making his way up the west coast of the Sabine Peninsula. To the surprise and pleasure of all concerned, as he camped near the northernmost point of the peninsula, Hamilton was approached by a sledging party led by Commander George Richards of the *Assistance*. Richards was on his way to search the west coast of Melville Island but, on hearing that McClintock had 'poached upon his ground' decided, instead, to call upon Kellett at Dealy Island. Only hours before, he had separated from another party led by Sherard Osborn who was now on his way back to the Eastern Division. After giving Richards the route to Dealy Island, Hamilton decided to try and catch up with Osborn in order that Belcher could be informed of the latest situation with Kellett's Western Division. Taking the satellite sledge and two men he set off in pursuit. The following day the sledge was damaged when it capsized over a hummock and Hamilton pressed on alone, reaching Osborn two days later. He was joined shortly afterwards by his own men along with the sledge to which they had carried out temporary repairs. Osborn had his ship's carpenter's mate with him and soon the lightweight sledge was restored to full working order. Following the exchange of information, the parties separated on 28 May and Hamilton returned to his main party after an absence of ten days. Continuing northwards, the tip of the Sabine Peninsula was reached and an island ('Vesey Hamilton Island') seen across the ice to the north-west. It proved to consist of four square miles of low land with a scattering of small peaked hills in the north. The water found on the island tasted strongly of sulphur and reminded Hamilton of the water to be found at Harrogate, the Yorkshire spa town. Even further to the north a smaller island could be seen. Hamilton did not visit it but named it 'Markham Island' after Clemence Markham, his midshipman friend in the *Assistance* under Ommanney. It was now 9 June and Hamilton had completed his orders of surveying the eastern shores of Hecla and Griper Bay. He arrived back at Dealy Island twelve days later having been away for fifty-four days and covering 675 miles – a rate of twelve miles a day. No trace of Franklin had been found.

Kellett had intended to send the *Intrepid* to Beechey Island with McClure and his ship's company, but the total lack of any evidence that the Franklin Expedition had entered the north-west Arctic caused him to change his mind. Instead, both ships would head eastwards with the view of offering Belcher the entire division to be employed in a more fruitful area.

Whilst waiting for the ice to break up, Kellett had a substantial building erected on Dealy Island to act as a supply depot for the use of Collinson or any other 'distressed parties' in need of its supplies. Forty feet long, 14 feet wide, and with walls between 7 and 8 feet high and 4 feet thick, the storehouse required 100 tons of stone for its completion. Enough provisions, clothing, arms and munitions were placed inside to last sixty-six men 210 days. (The building and its valuable contents survived for sixty-four years until it was vandalised and looted in 1917 by a party led by the Canadian explorer, Vilhjalmur Stefansson – a noted critic of the Royal Navy's Arctic exploration.)

Another means of passing the time until the ships were freed was found in sporting activities on the ice. For the seamen there was straightforward racing and wrestling with cash prizes as an incentive. The officers resorted to betting against each other. The Frenchman, de Bray, placed a wager with Kellett that he could give him a twenty-five yard start over 100 yards and still beat him. Kellett accepted the bet and won handsomely as de Bray limped off the course with a strained leg. Kellett then bet Pim £3 that he could beat him over the same distance given a 50-yard start – but whilst carrying McClintock on his back. Pim accepted and lost. The fastest officer of all proved to be Nares who covered 100 yards in 14 seconds and 300 yards in 46 seconds.

On 18 August a gale burst upon them from the north and drove the ice – with the ships still held tight – clear of the shore. The following day the ice broke up and Kellett and his men found themselves afloat and faced with an open lane to the east between Melville Island and the pack ice to the south. But, the wind which cleared the ice from the shore also drove the floes down Byam Martin Channel and Kellett found, once he had reached the south-east corner of Melville Island, that further progress was blocked by the stream of ice pouring down from the north. The succeeding days were spent anxiously watching for a gap in the ice that would allow them to reach across the mouth of the channel to the lee of Bathurst Island where open water could be expected. To Kellett's consternation, however, the wind dropped and the ice remained a solid barrier across his bows. As the frustrating days passed, winter began to approach. Snow fell, the hours of darkness grew longer, and the sea around the ships began to freeze. By 18 September, a month after they had left Dealy Island with such high hopes, Kellett's men began to prepare the ships for their second winter, and McClure's 'Investigators' found themselves facing their fourth season of Arctic darkness. The only encouraging sign came from the ship's hunting parties who came back from Melville Island with so much musk-ox meat that, once it was hung on the ships' rigging, they looked more like 'butchers' stalls than British discovery ships.'

With the ships secured for the winter, thoughts turned to maintaining the men's morale. There was no great eagerness to start up a school, but the *Resolute's* barrel organ was brought up, only to find that its repertoire had been reduced from ten tunes to one, the possibly inappropriate anthem 'There's a good time coming boys'. Preparations were put under way for Guy Fawkes Night and nearly led to an extremely serious incident. Whilst the officers were dining in the *Resolute's* gunroom the men prepared fireworks on the messdeck from a mixture of gunpowder and turpentine. The careless use of a lantern ignited the compound, starting a fire and filling the lower deck with smoke. Fortunately, the blaze was dealt with quickly and the officers informed that the smoke was merely the result of a heater malfunction. Christmas was cheered by songs from the 'Royal Arctic Choral Society' and the 'Ethiopian Serenaders' whilst a grizzled Marine put on a frock and frilly cap to sing an old lady's lament of 'I'm only ninety-five'. The 'Royal Intrepid Saloon' put on a much appreciated performance of 'Box and Cox' and the *Intrepid's* master, Frederick Krabbe (the grandson of a Danish officer captured during the Napoleonic wars), baffled everyone with his 'conjuring and phantasmagorical entertainments'. The most novel enterprise of all, however, came from Lieutenant Hamilton. With the ships only 400 yards apart, he was able to rig a galvanic battery-powered electric telegraph between them, the connecting wire suspended on boat oars thirty yards apart. The first message to be passed was 'How are you off for soap?' Before long, the officers had discovered how long-distance games of chess could be played using the telegraph.

By early March, Kellett was able to send a party over to Beechey Island to make contact with Belcher. Hamilton, Roche, and Court were chosen with two men and nine dogs. The following day Roche was back with the sledge needing repairs. It took two days to mend the damage and Roche set off to rejoin Hamilton and the others who had been left camping on the ice. Twenty-four hours later an exhausted Hamilton returned to the ship to report that a gun, kept loaded on the sledge in case of attack from polar bears, had gone off and shot Roche through the thigh. Nares was sent out as a replacement and the party eventually reached the *North Star* twelve days later.

With Hamilton gone, Kellett sent out two other parties. Krabbe was ordered to return to the Bay of Mercy to check on the condition of the *Investigator* and to bring back the officer's journals. Mecham was to go down Prince of Wales Strait to look for signs of Collinson and the *Enterprise*. Both parties set off on 3 April. A week later, after a speech from Kellett praising their conduct, McClure and the Investigators set out for Beechey Island and the *North Star*. Only one seaman was unable to walk and had to be carried on a dog-sledge.

Just hours after the Investigators had departed, a sledge was seen heading towards the *Resolute*. It proved to be Hamilton returning from Beechey Island with Commander Richards of the *Assistance* carrying letters and dispatches. Amongst the former was a private (i.e. unofficial) letter from Belcher to Kellett. When he opened and read its contents, Kellett was, in turn, baffled and outraged.

One of the letter's paragraphs read:

> Should Captain Collinson fortunately reach you, you will pursue the same course, and not under any consideration risk the detention of another season. These are the views of the Government; and having so far explained myself, I will not hamper you with further instructions than, meet me at Beechey Island, with the crews of all vessels, before 26 August.

What could such words mean? Did they suggest that, if Collinson *failed* to appear, could Kellett 'risk the detention of another season'? Any such idea seemed to be clearly contradicted by Belcher's apparent assumption that Kellett was intending to abandon his ships. However, there was no direct order from Belcher to carry out such abandonment, and Kellett had formed no intention of doing so. Both the *Resolute* and the *Intrepid* were in a good state of repair, there was no shortage of provision, the morale of both ship's companies was high, the ships were ideally placed to take advantage of any break-up of the ice, and no clue had yet been discovered about the fate of Franklin. Furthermore, for Kellett, there was an even darker side. He had already been forced to give the order to abandon one vessel – the *Investigator* – an account of which would have to be settled before a Court-Martial on his return to England. Now it was being suggested *in a private letter* that he abandon two more of Her Majesty's Ships. This was more than Kellett could tolerate. If he was to abandon his ships, he would only do so by a direct order from Belcher, delivered in an official manner.

McClintock – equally incensed by the vague instructions – was sent by Kellett over to the *Assistance* with a letter requesting, 'final, decided, and most unmistakeable orders' and with the authority to put the case against abandonment with as much force as possible. Fifteen days later, McClintock returned with Belcher's answer. Despite arguing, 'most fully and freely' against the senior officer's decision – even to the extent of employing Kellett's own phrase that anyone who ordered abandonment, 'would deserve to have their jackets taken off their backs' (i.e. flogged) – Belcher remained adamant. The ships were to be abandoned, and McClintock was issued with, 'distinct orders for Captain Kellett to abandon both *Resolute* and *Intrepid*'.

Resolute and *Intrepid* are abandoned.

With his fate decided for him, Kellett set about obeying his detested orders. Hamilton was sent on 8 June to Dealy Island to leave a message for Mecham and Krabbe informing them of the new situation. Nares and Roche were sent to establish a depot on Cape Cockburn for the two western expeditions. On the night of the fourteenth, with both ships secured and prepared to be battened down on their departure, the remaining officers held a final dinner in the *Resolute* gun-room. The following day, forty-two officers and men mustered on the ice to give three final cheers to the ships that had been their home for two years and had seen them safely through two Arctic winters. Thirteen days later, the Investigators, already crowded into the *North Star* at Beechey Island, found they had to make room for dozens more of their former shipmates. Mecham, Krabbe, and Hamilton arrived a few days later. Krabbe had found the *Investigator* listing ten degrees to starboard and slowly filling with ice. It was unlikely that she would last for more than a few further seasons. Only one journal – that of the first lieutenant, Haswell – had been found. Mecham had reached the Princess Royal Islands and found a message from Collinson. A second message was found on a small island further to the south. From these messages it was learned that the *Enterprise*'s sledges had visited the south-west coast of Melville Island, and the coasts of Prince Albert Land (Prince Albert Peninsula). In August 1852, Collinson had returned down the Prince of Wales Strait with the intention of passing up the western coast of Bank's Land or of penetrating the channel seen between Wollaston Land and Prince Albert Land (Prince Albert Sound). During his journey, Mecham had been away for seventy days and had sledged for 1,157 miles. His average daily march had been over eighteen miles and, on one occasion, had covered thirty miles in a single day. McClintock, who had held the sledging record before it was beaten by Mecham, described the journey as, 'a most splendid feat'. Such praise, however, was not forthcoming from the expedition commander – Sir Edward Belcher.

The eastern division, comprising the *Assistance* under Belcher himself and the *Pioneer* under the command of Sherard Osborn, had ascended the Wellington Channel on 14 August 1852. Finding open waters, Belcher, 'having already made my mind up not to interfere with any land which could have been seen and named by Captain Penny's people', pushed on past Baillie Hamilton Island and Cape Becher into Penny Strait. In the late afternoon of the sixteenth, the land to the north – Grinnell Land (Grinnell Peninsula) – ended in a 1,000-foot cliff on which Belcher had a large cairn erected. Just in case the American, De Haven, had not named all the peninsula, the land was claimed for the sovereign and given the rather clumsy name of 'Northumberland of North Britain' with an inlet at its base being named 'Northumberland Sound'. The appearance of ice in the offing prompted Belcher to get his ships into the sound for the winter, but the encroaching ice prevented his plans and he had to settle for a smaller inlet three miles to the west. Despite the ice, the sea remained open to the north and Belcher decided to use the time available to him to continue the search for as long as he could. Three sledging parties were arranged. Belcher and Richards were to use boats to thread their way northwards through the coastal ice, whilst Osborn took a party overland to establish a depot in case of a retreat by the other parties. All the sledging parties soon found themselves at the mercy of the Admiralty's policy of buying equipment from the cheapest sources. Instead of being brazed, the spirit stoves and tea kettles had been put together using lead-based solder and, consequently, when heat was applied the stoves fell apart and the spouts fell off the kettles. Osborn noted:

> Doubtless the government paid very handsomely for these inefficient clap-traps, but our blacksmith had enough to do to keep them in repair; indeed we were lucky to obtain him, for the steam-department (engineers and stokers) did not aid us in such matters, beyond helping the blacksmith in tin-work and at the bellows.

On 27 August, at a point where the land turned abruptly eastwards, Belcher ordered Richards to continue along the coast whilst he put to sea northwards. That evening a landing was made on an island which Belcher named 'Exmouth Island' after the Commander-in-Chief at the Battle of Algiers (the day being the anniversary of the battle). To the east a larger island ('Table Island') could be seen, but Belcher was more interested in the land that was revealed between snow showers seventeen miles to the north. After two days spent searching Exmouth Island, Belcher's party set off across the open water (Belcher Channel). A combination of canvas tent-bottoms used as sails and vigorous pulling at the oars saw them stepping on the land's shores after six hours in a boat practically awash with its cargo of sledge, bedding, provisions, and tent. Almost immediately, the ice followed them and sealed their landing place off from open water. Belcher named the land 'North Cornwall' (Cornwall Island) in honour of the Duke of Cornwall, the Queen's eldest son. Taking his telescope to a high point, Belcher searched the seas to the west but could see no sign of any land in that direction. Returning to the landing place, he had the boat hauled eastwards along the beach until he found a point where the ice allowed him to get afloat once more. Continuing to follow the coast as it trended to the south-east, the party reached the south-eastern angle of the island. From there the land vanished northwards into the showers of heavy snow that were now continually falling. A camp was made on the point as Belcher searched the horizon for any sign of land to the east; again there was nothing to be seen. No improvement in the weather seemed imminent, and with ice forming on the surface of the sea, there was no point in putting the party at risk of being trapped. Belcher returned south via Exmouth and Table islands before re-uniting with Richards on the mainland. The lack of signs of any animal life and the absence of land led him to the conclusion that any further searches to the north-west would be a waste of time, 'Our only resource now is the close search of the coast line west and south-westerly, and north and easterly, for any traces of vessels or crews'.

On his return to the ships, Belcher was pleased to see that his first lieutenant, Walter May, had used the experience he gained as a mate under Austin in the *Resolute* to lower the top-masts and house the ship in for the winter. Boats and stores had been landed and an observatory built ashore to house the declination magnetometer used for magnetic observations. With little further for him to do, Belcher decided that there was just time for one more sledge expedition. On 22 September, in company with Richards and Osborn, he set off to search the east coast of Penny Strait. Three days later they were camped on an island when, to their bitter consternation, the ice broke up and drifted from the shore leaving them stranded without a boat. For a week they existed on a walrus they had killed whilst finding themselves in the peculiar position of praying for low temperatures, a prayer, 'uncommon in these cold regions'. It took more than a week for the sea to freeze to a thickness that would take their weight and, even then, their journey across to the mainland proved extremely hazardous with the ice constantly threatening to give way beneath them. With their safe return to the ships there were to be no more expeditions that year.

The ship's companies settled in for the winter. A performance of *Hamlet* was attempted but had to be abandoned due to a gale which rendered the performers inaudible. A second attempt was made and marred only by the fact that a cloud of condensation hovered 3 feet above the floor of the stage so that the audience could only see the actors' legs and lower bodies. Osborn provided a dinner in the *Pioneer* for the officers at which toasts were made to 'bright eyes' and 'polar brothers'. On Christmas day, Belcher was drawn by 'state-sledge' to the *Pioneer* to receive the seasonal hospitality from Osborn's ship's company, and then was returned to the *Assistance* for a second bout of toasts from the officers and seamen of his own ship.

The returning sun was seen for the first time on 18 February 1853, and preparations were immediately set under way for the forthcoming sledge

Assistance and *Pioneer* in their winter quarters.

expeditions. Richards was to set out across Penny Strait accompanied by Osborn, May, fifty-five men, six sledges and two boats. Belcher was to head to the east to see if a passage existed to Jones Sound.

Richards' party left the *Assistance* on 10 April and crossed to the northern shore of Bathurst Island where the two boats were cached on the beach. May remained with the party as it headed westwards until his rations required him to return across the still-frozen Penny Straits. Passing along the northern shores of three islands ('Sherard Osborn', 'Helena', and 'Cameron' islands), Richards and Osborn crossed the northern end of Byam Martin Channel to the eastern coast of the Sabine Peninsula of Melville Island where the parties separated. Osborn – with his sledge *John Barrow* – was to return to the ships with the support sledges whilst Richards and his men, hauling the sledge *Sir Edward*, continued on to the western shores of the island. With only a short distance travelled, Osborn was caught up by Vesey Hamilton and given the information that the *Investigator* had been discovered. He then re-crossed Byam Martin Channel, went north around Cameron Island and passed through the strait between Helena and Sherard Osborn Islands and the north coast of Bathurst Island. On reaching the boats, Osborn had to choose between crossing the (now open) waters to give Belcher the news about McClure and the *Investigator*, of waiting for Richard's party, or of using the open waters and good weather to continue the search. Deciding on the latter, he left a message for Richards and took one of the boats down the eastern coast of Bathurst Island. Unfortunately, his diminishing supplies caused him to turn northwards just beyond the position which would have confirmed that an open channel existed between Bathurst and Cornwallis islands. He arrived back onboard the *Pioneer* on 15 July after having been absent for ninety-seven days.

Three days earlier Belcher had shaken the hand of Richards on his return. After separating from Osborn, Richards had come across the tracks of Hamilton's sledge and followed them to meet up with the *Resolute*'s lieutenant. In addition to learning of the fate of the *Investigator*, Richards also heard that McClintock and Mecham were searching the western coasts of Melville Island. Instead of turning back, he decided to cross 127 miles over the island to pay a call on Kellett's division at Dealy Island and give a first-hand account of the events taking place north of the Wellington Channel. Richards arrived at Dealy Island on 5 June to a warm welcome. Kellett was camped out near Cape Bounty and de Bray was despatched to find him and tell him of Richards' arrival. The two men met on the seventh and Richards was able to leave the following day. He travelled up the east coast of Melville Island, crossed Byam Martin Channel, and passed north around Cameron Island before following Osborn's route along the top of Bathurst Island, arriving at Northumberland Sound on 12 July after a journey of 808 miles.

Belcher had taken his sledge *Londesborough* eastwards on 2 May and, whilst passing along the northern shore of Devon Island, had discovered 'Princess Royal Island'. From its northern high ground ('Britannia Cliff') he saw a 'loom of land' to the north-east and set off in that direction. As he approached, Belcher found himself nearing a number of small islands with, what could have been, a larger island to their rear. Unsure about the possible insularity of the greater land mass he named it 'Graham Land' (Graham Island) and travelled down its western coast before heading south to another large island he named 'Skye Island' (Buckingham Island). Continuing still further south he landed on another island he named 'North Kent' after the recently deceased Duke. The entire group of islands were given the name 'Victoria Archipelago'.

From the south-western shores of North Kent, Belcher was able to look out on the sight that had been his main goal – a channel linking the waters of Jones Sound with those off north-west Devon Island. It was a significant discovery that laid open the possibility that Franklin, after ascending the Wellington Channel, could have rounded Northumberland of North Britain, passed along the coast of north-west Devon Island, and entered Jones Sound from the west. However, Belcher found no evidence to substantiate the possibility. His party arrived back at the *Assistance* on 22 June, having been away for fifty-two days.

When Osborn returned to his ship he found both vessels prepared and already afloat. The off-shore ice had broken up and Belcher lost no time in heading southwards, he did not want to run the risk of Kellett returning home without the news of the discovery of a western entrance to Jones Sound. Ten miles south of Cape Becher, to everyone's surprise, a boat was seen heading in their direction. It turned out to be Commander Pullen who had sailed up the Wellington Channel to seek orders regarding the future of the Investigators and to inform Belcher that the ice in Barrow's Strait showed no signs of breaking up. With the minimum of delay, Pullen was sent back to Beechey Island with orders that, if the *Intrepid* arrived off the island, she was to be ordered to remain, and that the *North Star* should take the Investigators back to England 'at the earliest safe moment'.

In a hurried dispatch to the Admiralty, Belcher noted that, 'a mile gained in this dreaded Strait is a consideration for risking wintering here.' He knew he could have sailed over to the west of Dundas and Baillie Hamilton islands and found open waters on the route used by Pullen but, now he had given orders for the safe return of the Investigators, and made provisions for the *Intrepid* to be at hand in case of emergency, he now felt it was worth the risk of searching the eastern shore of Wellington Channel as they curved around Prince Albert and Baring Bays – the risk involved lay in the great sheet of ice that blocked much of the water ahead.

With the *Pioneer* leading the way the two ships spent the following days passing down the western coast of Devon Island. As they did so, Osborn became more and more agitated over the risk of being frozen in for a third winter and frequently offered to tow the *Assistance* westwards across the channel to where open waters would allow them to escape to Beechey Island. But Belcher, still keen to find evidence that Franklin had passed that way refused to leave the ice. By late August, Osborn's fears were realised. Both ships were frozen in for the winter at the southern end of Baring Bay, fifty miles north of Beechey Island. An event, according to Osborn, caused by Belcher's 'Ignorance of the first rules of navigation in arctic seas'. From that point on, relations between the two officers deteriorated rapidly.

The winter passed with a gloom unequalled in previous naval expeditions. Walter May, the first lieutenant of the *Assistance*, was a fine artist and had proved himself to be a competent sledger, but he lacked the attention to detail required to be a good first lieutenant – especially one serving directly under the pedantic eye of a captain like Belcher. Reports were rendered on paper of the incorrect size, he seemed unaware of the importance of his rank, and he failed to report the shooting of an arctic hare. Belcher, worn down by his age (he was fifty-five years old) and a second winter on a fruitless search, could stand no more. May was relieved of his duties. The second lieutenant, John Cheyne, rallying to the support of his friend May, was also stood down. Matters then grew even worse. When he heard a rumour that his actions were being sneered at onboard the *Pioneer*, Belcher threatened to have all communication between the steamer and his own ship cut off. This brought Osborn across the ice in loud protest, Belcher's response was to have him placed under arrest, and to turn for support to the bottle.

By the middle of February 1854, Belcher had weighed up all the options that were open to him and had come to the conclusion that, if none of the expedition ships could break free of the ice that summer, they would have to be abandoned. To forward his decision on to Kellett, Richards was ordered to take two sledges over the fifty miles of ice to Beechey Island. When the commander suggested that the temperatures were too low for such a journey, Belcher merely commented that the temperatures would, inevitably, get higher as the season advanced. Richards set off on the twenty-second and had not gone far before problems began to set in. In temperatures colder than -70 degrees Fahrenheit, and with the rations (including the rum) frozen solid, his men grew more and more exhausted with every step they took. Frostbite quickly took effect and, even when the rations had been thawed, the men's stomachs promptly rejected the food. After three sleepless nights, and with the men surviving on little more than a ship's biscuit and a tot of rum, Richards had 'serious misgivings' about continuing, but a northerly wind came to their aid and, with sails rigged, the sledges were blown to the south. The men's exhaustion, however, continued to grow until, off Point Innes, some eight miles north of Beechey Island, only Richards and one of the *Assistance*'s mates, Frederick Herbert, were capable of pressing on. As the risks of one of the officers going on alone outweighed that of leaving the men to sleep in the tent, both Richards and Herbert set off for Beechey Island to seek help. Weak from lack of food and debilitated by the extreme cold they collapsed, exhausted, onboard the *North Star* five days after they had set out from the *Assistance*. A search party immediately set out to collect the remainder of the party and, once all had been safely delivered to Pullen's ship, it took a week of care before any regained their health and strength. When writing later, Osborn gave as a reason for the party's desperate determination to continue their journey, their intense desire to get away from Belcher; 'It seemed as if human endurance could go no further; yet they tugged on, for anything was better than returning to the wretchedness they had left onboard their ship'. Three weeks later, Richards joined Hamilton – who had been sent by Kellett to make contact with Belcher – on his return to the *Resolute*, taking the dispatches and the private letter with its ambiguous words suggesting abandonment.

On 17 July, the assembled ship's companies of the *Resolute*, *Investigator* (Pullen had not been able to break free of the ice to take them home), *Intrepid*, and *North Star*, witnessed the arrival of Belcher as, mounted in his sledge-drawn gig, he was towed into the bay by ten seamen. The boat would have been carried as a safety measure and as an aid in crossing open water. Probably to lighten the atmosphere he might encounter on his arrival, Belcher had climbed into the boat in order to arrive as if it was a perfectly normal visit by a senior officer at sea. To complete the traditional greeting, Captain Kellett and Commanders McClure, Pullen, and McClintock 'manned the side' to welcome him.

Pullen had built a depot on Beechey Island to which he had given the name 'Northumberland House'. The building was cleaned out and smartened up for use as accommodation for Belcher. A kitchen area was added and a galley stove, rescued from the whaler *McClellan*, installed. Another item recovered from the whaler was her capstan. This was a ball-mounted octagonal column, and Belcher had it erected close to Northumberland House as a memorial to the thirty-two men who had died on the search for Franklin. Shortly afterwards it was joined by a marble plaque in memory of Bellot, unveiled – appropriately – by his fellow French naval officer, de Bray.

The advance of summer had brought no break up of the ice between Beechey Island and the mainland, and the *North Star* had remained firmly frozen into the floe. There were, however, considerable numbers of men with little to do. Belcher ordered that they be employed in cutting a channel from the ship to the open waters. Within a month they had cut a channel twenty yards wide and almost a mile in length. The *North Star* was then warped forward to the ice edge and readied for the voyage home.

Whilst the ice around Beechey Island had remained rigid, that to the north had begun to move. Belcher was given a report that the *Assistance* and the *Pioneer* had drifted several miles to the south. He decided to return to the ship and asked for volunteers to accompany him. If it was thought the ships might continue their drift, they would remain onboard with a small number of volunteers from the *Assistance*'s ship's company. McClintock; surgeons Lyall (*Assistance*) and Scott (*Resolute*); and Robert Jenkins, a mate on the *North Star*, all offered themselves and set off with Belcher back up the Wellington Channel. However, the twenty-mile barrier of ice that separated the ships from the open waters to the south soon convinced Belcher that the ships were not going to break free, a conviction supported on his arrival where he found that not a single man wanted to volunteer for an extra winter in the Arctic. Finding nothing to change his original idea of abandonment, Belcher gave the order. The ships' hatches were battened down, ensigns were hoisted, and the ships' companies mustered on the ice.

Belcher and the men from the *Assistance* and the *Pioneer* arrived at Beechey Island on 27 August. There was to be no delay in leaving. The *North Star* was actually clear of the ice and relays of boats were used to get the newcomers on board. In all, 263 men were to be crammed into a ship meant for a ship's company of sixty. Commander Richards was just bringing the last boats alongside when a curtain of off-shore fog lifted slightly. Much to everyone's surprise and astonishment, a steam-ship was seen to be rounding Cape Riley. It was Inglefield arriving just in time with the *Phoenix* and, in tow, the *Talbot*. A great cheer rang out across the grey waters. The arrival of Inglefield's ships meant a much more comfortable – and safer – voyage home.

With the situation subject to a sudden change in fortunes, Belcher was obliged to re-assess his priorities. The senior officers were mustered (although, for some reason, Kellett did not attend) and Belcher took great care to explain that the only reason to remain in the Arctic, beyond continuing the Franklin search, was to try and find Collinson and the *Enterprise*. From the message picked up by Mecham at the Princess Royal Islands, it seemed clear that Collinson had returned to the southern coast of Victoria Island, a move that placed him 'in a region free from the perils of arctic ice'. From there, his options were to return via Bering's Strait, or to go overland to one of the Hudson's Bay Company posts. There was even the possibility that Rae might be in the area, a situation that Belcher considered would 'materially alter the face of his difficulties'. Furthermore, Collinson did not get the slightest mention in the orders he had received from the Admiralty. McClintock was unimpressed by the tone of the consultation and felt that Belcher, 'neither wanted our opinion nor intended altering his own.' Osborn, not invited of course, as he was still under arrest, remarked that Belcher had merely shown, 'a crooked state of mind, revealed in crooked language.'

The ships arrived in England on 28 September to a muted welcome. Not only had they failed to find any trace of the missing Franklin Expedition, but the public mind was preoccupied with the war against Russia. Osborn, still seething at his arrest, immediately contacted the Admiralty to demand a Court-Martial. The cooler, wiser, heads of their Lordships, however, refused to grant Osborn his chance to clear his name (and, no doubt, blacken Belcher's). Whatever the circumstances, and despite being coloured with the best motives, Osborn had behaved in an improper manner. A Court-Martial might have found for Belcher, and a talented young officer's career would have been finished. Instead, the Admiralty promoted him to commander and packed him off to take charge of the Coastguard at Norfolk giving him a chance to calm down and recover his health. Within months he was in the Black Sea creating havoc amongst the stores depots intended for the provisioning of Sebastopol, actions which led to his promotion to captain. After distinguished service in China in command of the paddle-wheel frigate *Furious* (in which his sailing master was Stephen Court, late of the *Investigator*), he was put in command of a squadron of six steamers for the suppression of piracy off the Chinese coast. His orders suggested that he would be under the direct control of the Chinese Imperial Government but, on his arrival, he found that a number of petty mandarins were also to dictate his actions. Consequently, he gave up the appointment and returned home with all his fellow officers. Following command of one of the Navy's first turret ships, Osborn accepted the job of agent to the Indian railways, overseeing their reorganisation and improvement until ill-health forced him to take a job as managing director of a telegraph construction company. In 1871 he was given command of HMS *Hercules* as part of the Channel Fleet until his promotion to Rear-Admiral two years later. He died in 1875, having edited McClure's journals and seen their publication under the title *Discovery of the North-West Passage*.

McClintock was promoted to captain on his return and Frederick Mecham was made commander. The latter officer was appointed to the command of HMS *Vixen* with the Pacific Fleet and died of bronchitis four years later at Honolulu aged twenty-nine. Vesey Hamilton had to wait two years before his promotion to commander. In the meantime he commanded a gunboat off China, taking part in the Battle of Fatshan. He was promoted to captain in 1862 and became the Captain Superintendent of Pembroke Dockyard in 1874.

Walter May, Belcher's long-suffering first lieutenant, was rewarded for his removal from office by being promoted to commander. But he had had enough of the Service, and retired to become a professional water-colour artist. He published a series of scenes from the voyage of the *Assistance*. The discoverer of the *Investigator*, Lieutenant Bedford Pim, was soon re-employed in command of a gunboat in the Baltic and was wounded at the bombardment of Sveaborg. Sent to China in 1857 he was again wounded during the operations in the Canton River before being invalided home and promoted to commander. In 1859 Pim was appointed to the Central America station and became an enthusiast for a proposed Nicaraguan

McClintock on his promotion to
captain.

route across the isthmus to the Pacific. He purchased land on the proposed route
(an act which earned him the Admiralty's disapproval) and tried to set up the
Nicaraguan Railway Company, but the enterprise failed. After his promotion to
captain in 1868, Pim turned his talents to the law and entered the Inner Temple as
a student at the age of forty-four. He was called to the bar in 1873 and admitted as
a barrister of Gray's Inn the following month. Most of his subsequent legal work
was in Admiralty cases. He was elected as Member of Parliament for Gravesend
in 1874 and became an active member of the Anthropological Institute. In 1885,
Pim was promoted to Rear-Admiral and died the following year – 'a true-hearted
sailor of the old school – brave, generous, and unselfish.'

Commander William Pullen also saw service in the Baltic before being
promoted to captain in 1856. He supervised the soundings taken for the undersea
telegraph which ran from Suez to Aden before being sent out to undertake a
survey of the Bermuda Islands in 1863. After service with the Coastguard he was
promoted to Rear-Admiral in 1874 and to Vice-Admiral five years later. He died
in 1887.

Following his return from the Arctic, Captain Edward Inglefield was sent out to the Black Sea where he took part in the capture of Kinburn. He was promoted to Rear-Admiral in 1869 and Vice-Admiral in 1875. Knighted in 1877, he was promoted to admiral two years later and made Commander-in-Chief on the North America station. Inglefield married his second wife at the age of seventy-four and died the following year. Well-known for a mind both artistic and inventive he had paintings exhibited at the Royal Academy, invented the hydraulic steering gear, designed a new type of anchor, and is probably best remembered for the 'Inglefield clip' – a swivelling device designed to replace the wooden toggle used to secure a flag to its halliard.

On his return from the Arctic, Sergeant John Woon, the indefatigable Royal Marine who had rescued the seaman, Anderson, was sent out to China as an acting sergeant-major and was mentioned in despatches for his conduct in the assault on the Taku Forts (of the 400 Royal Marines who started the attack, only 150 reached the first barricades – of them, only enough survived to put up a single ladder against the wall of the fort.) When, in 1866, the Queen decided that specially selected men could be drawn from the ranks to become officers, Woon was among the first to be chosen and was promoted to quartermaster-lieutenant the following year. In 1873, he saw his son – also named John – join the Royal Marines as a lieutenant. Woon died whilst still serving in the Corps in 1877. His son, John, survived to become General Sir John Woon, Knight Commander of the Bath.

McClure faced a Court-Martial for the loss of the *Investigator* but was cleared of all fault and received the praise of the court for his conduct. A Parliamentary Committee decided that he had discovered *a* Northwest Passage (Lady Franklin had objected to the prize of *the* Northwest Passage until her husband had been found) and he and his ship's company were awarded the prize of £10,000. Promoted to captain (back-dated to December 1850) and knighted, McClure was appointed to the Pacific Station and ended up commanding a battalion of the naval brigade in the capture of Canton. Promoted to Rear-Admiral in 1867 and Vice-Admiral six years later, McClure died in May 1873. Osborn wrote of him that he, 'was stern, cool and bold in all perils, severe as a disciplinarian, self-reliant, yet modest as became an officer'.

Henry Kellett faced his Court-Martial and also came away fully acquitted on the grounds that he had acted under the orders of Belcher. His sword was returned to him with the comment that he had worn it, 'with honour and credit and service to your country'. Immediate reward was granted in the shape of promotion to commodore and an appointment to the West Indies. He was promoted to Rear-Admiral in 1862 and to Vice-Admiral in 1868. The following year saw him being awarded a knighthood and being appointed as Commander-in-Chief on the China station. He died in 1875.

The Court-Martial of Sir Edward Belcher was, like the others, more of a formality than an attempt to bring his conduct under examination. On several counts he was right in abandoning his ships, but the court needed to look no

Above left: John Woon as a quartermaster-lieutenant.

Above right: HMS *Resolute*, still flying the Stars and Stripes, returns to England, courtesy of the United States of America.

On her return, the *Resolute* is visited by Queen Victoria.

further than his orders. He had been given 'wide discretion' in orders that told him 'We do not … consider it necessary to encumber you with minute instructions for your guidance … we leave it for you to decide'. He had 'decided' against a background of two fruitless years of searching, the deaths of some of his men, and the risk of further deaths. There was no guarantee that any of the ships would have broken free the following summer, and he did not want to risk another expedition being sent out for his relief. His orders had actually stated that, once the ships were placed into his care, 'there is one object which, in the exercise of that care, will naturally engage your constant attention, and that is the safe return of your party to this country'. Furthermore, there were the findings and recommendations of the inquiry into the Austin Expedition. These stated that, 'it should be enjoined with equal strictness that, in the event of any irreparable disaster to the ships so proceeding, or if they should be too firmly fixed in the ice to be extricated during the summer of 1853, they are to be abandoned, and the crews brought down to the depot'. Belcher had done exactly what the Court of Enquiry's 'strictness' had demanded. But in the end, it was the risk of further loss of life that had been the deciding factor, Belcher wrote:

Is the sacrifice of life to be weighed against the loss of timber, which, if returned to England, as all previous experience has shown, is of no further value as a sailing-vessel, but simply to be sold 'to break up'? Finally, I do feel infinite gratification that it pleased God to afford me determination to perform my duty in the precise manner I did, under the circumstances and difficulties by which I found myself surrounded.

As his Court-Martial closed, Belcher's sword was handed back to him in silence, 'without observation'. He had been associated with the loss of five of Her Majesty's Ships combined with failure in his objectives, just as the country was beginning a war and needed examples of success. It was no time to look for excuses, nor to seek praise in the huge areas of the Arctic that had been discovered, or the lives that might have been saved. Belcher became the cause of failure to find Franklin, and the target of his fellow officer's published accounts of the expedition. His courage could never be doubted, but his peremptory attitude, pedantic manner, and inflexibility all worked against him. He was never to be employed by the Navy again and retired to a life of writing and scientific experimentation. He wrote his account of the expedition and a novel which his biographer, following the fashion of Belcher's enemies, described as 'exceedingly stupid'. Belcher was promoted to Rear-Admiral in 1861 and Vice-Admiral five years later. In 1867 he was appointed a Knight Commander of the Bath and made Admiral the following year. He died, unlamented in senior naval circles, in March 1877.

Even Nature herself turned against Belcher. In September 1855, Captain James Buddington of the American whaler *George Henry*, whilst searching for whales in the Davis Strait, saw a three-masted sailing ship in the distance. At first not a lot of notice was taken of the stranger and she remained in sight for the next seven days before Buddington ordered four of his men to take a boat across to her. To

Queen Victoria is received on board the *Resolute* by Captain Hartstene and his officers.

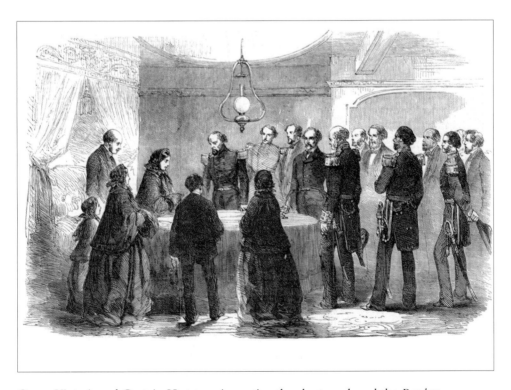

Queen Victoria and Captain Hartstene inspecting the charts on board the *Resolute*.

The *Resolute* desk in the Oval Office of the White House.

their astonishment, they found themselves climbing up the side of HMS *Resolute* – last seen by Kellett and his men fifteen months earlier when they abandoned her 1,000 miles away in Barrow's Strait. The ship, freed from the ice during the summer of 1855, had drifted through Lancaster Sound, down Baffin's Bay, and into Davis Strait. Buddington, with no small difficulty, managed to bring the vessel into the Connecticut port of New London. As soon as Queen Victoria was made aware of what had happened she waived all rights to the ship and left her disposal to Buddington. Learning of this, Congress then purchased the *Resolute*, had her refitted, and sailed across the Atlantic as a gift to the Royal Navy. Such magnanimity could not go unrecognised at the highest level and the Queen herself arrived at Spithead to accept the return of the ship. Her temporary commander, Captain Hartstene, handed the ship over, 'as a token of love, admiration, and respect to Your Majesty personally.' The Royal Navy's embarrassment at this turn of events was not tempered by Captain Buddington's comments, 'that Sir Edward Belcher acted perfectly rightly in abandoning the vessels under the circumstances'. As a show of gratitude to the Americans for their return of the vessel, a large, ornate, desk was made from her timbers and presented to the President. The desk still remains in use in the Oval Office of the White House in the twenty-first century.

CHAPTER TEN

'ONE OF THE MOST CAPABLE AND ENTERPRISING SAILORS'

Belcher's squadron had not been alone in the eastern Arctic. Under the sponsorship of Henry Grinnell and others, the *Advance* had returned to the Franklin search under the command of Elisha Kent Kane, the ship's surgeon during the De Haven expedition of 1850-51. Kane, with little experience of command at sea, or of navigation, and with a crew of mixed ability and temperament, was to use Inglefield's newly published map of the entrance to Smith Sound in an effort to penetrate as far north from Baffin's Bay as he could.

With a Union Jack flying from her main-mast, to declare her intention of searching for Franklin, the *Advance* sailed from New York on 30 May 1853. The entrance to Smith Sound was passed in early August and the ship put into an inlet (Rensselaer Bay) on the coast of Greenland on 10 September. During autumn sledge journeys were made to deposit caches ready for the following spring, and the massive Humboldt Glacier was discovered north of their wintering harbour. An attempt by Kane, at the end of April 1854, to continue northwards by sledge had to be abandoned due to scurvy and frostbite. On 20 May, a party crossed to the west and headed north from Inglefield's Cape Sabine. They returned to the ship after eleven days having reached beyond 79 degrees. A further attempt to reach northwards along the coast of Greenland, passing along the base of the Humboldt Glacier, discovered a new land beyond which was honoured by the name 'Washington' (Northern Greenland), and reached a point where the ice to the west narrowed to a thirty-five mile wide strait ('Kennedy Strait'). A fourth sledging expedition, consisting of William Morton, the ship's Irish steward and the expedition's Eskimo guide and hunter, Hans Hendricks, sledged northwards across the open ice of 'Kane's Sea' (Kane Basin) and surveyed the western coast to 81 degrees, 22'N where their progress was halted by a huge cape towering high above them. The two men climbed the rocky cliff and found below them the half-expected appearance of an open sea 'lashed by heavy surf'. About fifty miles to the north, a truncated peak could be seen. Morton generously named the hill 'Mount Sir Edward Parry' and, to the cliff on which he stood, he gave the name 'Cape Constitution'. The ceremony was completed by the unfurling of the same flag that Wilkes had taken to the far south. If nothing else, Kane's expedition had found 'proof' of the long-held theory that an open sea existed to the north. From that point on, the fortunes of the second Grinnell Expedition rapidly declined.

When it became evident that the ship would not be freed from the grip of the ice, and that a second Arctic winter would have to be faced, Kane tried to reach the ships of Belcher's expedition by taking a boat and five men across to Lancaster Sound. They were forced to return to the ship when confronted by a solid, unbroken, sheet of ice at the entrance to Jones Sound. By August, nine of Kane's men decided that they had had enough and – much against his advice – chose to leave the ship and try to reach the West Greenland settlement of Upernarvik. Four months later, and in very poor condition, they also returned to the *Advance*.

The succeeding winter was passed in miserable conditions. Scurvy became rampant with, at times, just Kane and one other man capable of movement. Three men died, two of tetanus, and one after the amputation of a foot affected by frostbite. Fortunately, contact was made with a local group of Eskimos who were, 'never thoroughly to be trusted; but, by a mixed course of intimidation and kindness, became of essential service'.

The possibility of facing a third winter was unthinkable and, on 17 May 1855, Kane abandoned the *Advance*. With four men so ill that they had to be carried on dog-sledges, the party set off to the south. After thirty-one days of gruelling labour dragging sledges and boats across eighty miles of ice, open water was reached at Cape Alexander, the entrance to Smiths Sound. The party arrived at Upernarvik, 'in excellent health and spirits', twenty days later from the *Advance*. Passage was taken in a Danish vessel to Godhavn where Kane fell in with an American expedition commanded by Lieutenant Hartstene (later to command the *Resolute* on her return to England) with two rescue ships sent to try and find him. The survivors arrived at New York in October having made the important discovery and survey of the Kane Basin and Kennedy Channel, and had looked out across on open polar sea. They had been the first into what became known as 'The American Route to the Pole', but nothing had been seen of the Franklin Expedition.

Five months before Kane sailed into New York, Captain Richard Collinson arrived at Spithead with the *Enterprise*. He had been away for five years and had accomplished one of the most extraordinary and difficult voyages in the history of seamanship.

Following his wintering at Hong Kong, Collinson had returned to the broken ice off Point Barrow in late July 1851. Almost immediately he found himself at odds with his hot-headed second master, Francis Skead. In common with the other officers, Skead was desperately keen to push on into the ice and demanded that the ship's company should be set to work warping and towing the ship forward. Collinson however, no doubt much to the delight of his men, preferred to wait for a favourable wind. Unfortunately, his decision led to the *Enterprise* being caught in the grip of the ice and drifting to the west. It also led to a breakdown in relationships between Collinson and his officers to the extent that Skead spent much of the next three years under arrest, and all the other officers being placed under arrest at one time or another. Collinson had found, to his cost, that by intervening in the personal disputes between his officers in an effort to settle them amicably, he was continually exacerbating them to the extent that he became the target of undisciplined reactions. Nevertheless, he always insisted that he, 'only exercised the power entrusted to me when absolutely necessary'.

The ship did not remain locked in the ice for long and, on 26 August, the southern coast of Banks' Land came into view. That same day, the *Enterprise* entered Prince of Wales Strait ten days after McClure had left it to sail up the western coast of Banks Land. Unknown to him, Collinson was about to embark on a frustrating voyage in the wake of others. On arriving at the Princess Royal Islands a cairn was spotted. Inside a message was found from McClure informing Collinson that he had wintered at the site, and that Viscount Melville Sound had been crossed and Melville Island reached. The *Enterprise* continued on to the top of the strait and, as McClure before him, Collinson was stopped by the ice. With nothing further to detain him, Collinson turned southwards and left the Prince of Wales Strait to double Nelson's Head and reach northwards, once again in McClure's wake. At Point Kellett, another message confirmed that McClure had passed that way. The following day, the ice of the Beaufort Sea could be seen pressing against the western coast of Bank's Island ahead of the ship and more huge floes could be seen in the offing. Even a modest westerly wind could have blown the ice onto the shore, trapping and probably crushing the vessel. Placing prudence before hazard, Collinson turned his bows to the south. Just 100 miles to the north, the *Investigator* groaned and creaked as she was caught in the relentless grip of massive floes.

The *Enterprise* regained the entrance to the Prince of Wales Strait and, on its south-east coast, Collinson entered Walker Bay and found a small harbour ('Winter Cove') in which to winter. By the following April, the second master had become insolent beyond measure and Collinson, unable to tolerate such behaviour any further, placed him under arrest.

With the arrival of spring, 1852, Collinson sent out a number of sledging parties to search for any clues to the missing Franklin Expedition. Lieutenant C.T. Jago headed southwards across Minto Bay to search around Cape Wollaston as Collinson took two sledges back up Prince of Wales Strait. At its northern end Collinson sent the mate, Murray Parks, across to Melville Island whilst he followed Wynniatt's route down the north-east coast of Victoria Land. Parks reached Melville Island only by leaving his sledge and tent marooned on the impassable ice of Viscount Melville Sound. He returned to the sledge after eleven days without shelter and arrived back at the ship after an absence of seventy-four days. Collinson had returned after fifty-one days and Jago after forty-nine.

The *Enterprise* was freed from the ice on 5 August and Collinson took her up Prince Albert's Sound to see if it separated Wollaston and Victoria lands into two islands. Instead, like Rae the year before, he found it to be a deep inlet with no eastern or northern exit. Returning westwards, Collinson rounded Cape Baring and entered the western end of the Dolphin and Union Strait. From there he began one of the most extraordinary voyages undertaken in polar history. Ahead of him lay a labyrinth of islands and shoals as his route passed eastwards between the North American mainland and the southern shores of Victoria Island. Difficult enough under normal circumstances, Collinson faced the challenge of taking a large sailing ship through 300 miles of such waters without the assistance of his second most senior navigator (under arrest) and with his remaining officers surly and unco-operative. All he had to guide him was a rough chart produced by Thomas Simpson after his boat journey of 1837. Using the highest of skills combined with rare ability, and whilst carefully charting his progress, Collinson reached Cambridge Bay safely in time to prepare the ship for the coming winter. In addition to the normal preparations, Collinson had a skittle alley laid out on the compressed snow that insulated the ship's upper deck, and had a billiard table made of snow and ice, with cushions made from stuffed walrus hide and with wooden balls made by the carpenter. Fish were found to be plentiful in the area and contacts with the local Eskimos proved useful for providing caribou meat. Such contacts with the natives, although amicable, were difficult due to the lack of an interpreter. Johann Miertsching had been appointed as the expedition interpreter, but he was, by now, firmly stuck in the ice of Mercy Bay along with the rest of the Investigators. After some prompting, the Eskimos did produce an unreliable chart of the east coast of Victoria Island, and even showed the presence of a vessel (probably Rae's boat from 1851), but the lack of proper communication blocked any substantial help the natives might have been able to offer in the search for Franklin.

HMS *Enterprise* entering Dolphin and Union Strait, September 1852.

The spring of 1853 saw Collinson putting into effect his plans for continuing the search for the missing expedition. With just two large sledges (*Enterprise* and *Victoria*) and one smaller one (*Royal Albert*), he had, at first, considered sending one sledge up the east coast of Victoria Island and the other across the 120 miles of ice to King William Land. But his experience at Walker Bay (and possibly the recalcitrance of his officers – two of whom were under arrest) persuaded him that the two large sledges should be used in support of each other with the smaller one being used as a satellite. As for the route, Collinson decided to search the eastern coast of Victoria Island. He could reasonably believe that the coast would eventually link up with that which he had searched on the north-east of the island, thus forming part of a route that could have been taken by Franklin – and there was always the vessel the Eskimos had suggested on their chart (Collinson knew nothing of Rae having been in the area).

The sledges set off on 12 April and, having rounded the south-east corner of Victoria Island and entered Rae's Victoria Strait, found themselves amongst a mass of tumbled ice. Huge hummocks and pressure ridges made the going extremely difficult and Collinson could congratulate himself on choosing to take all the sledges with him as their combined man-power was frequently needed to haul them forward. After several days of exhausting effort they came across a cairn erected on a small islet. Upon opening it, they found to their disappointment, a note from Rae recording his journey along the coast two years before. If such a note had been found earlier, Collinson might have changed his route to search the western coast of King William Island. But it was too late now and the ice was too rough to cross over to James Ross's Victory Point – forty miles to the east, on the low shores of north-west King William Island. Pressing on until the coastline veered away to the north-west, the party continued northwards to an island which Collinson named 'Gateshead Island'. There they turned back, the expedition arriving at the *Enterprise* on 31 May after forty-nine days and having found nothing but disappointment.

Some weeks later, one of the seamen was roaming along the coast to the south of Cambridge Bay looking for driftwood for fuel when he stumbled across some wooden wreckage. Most of it was unidentifiable, but one piece looked like part of a door or hatch frame. Such an item might just have come from one of Franklin's ships, but gave no clue how it had arrived on the beach. Without such a clue, nor any means of confirming its origin, Collinson could not put at risk the lives of his men with his fuel running low. By 10 August, the *Enterprise* was ready for sea and Collinson took her westwards along the same treacherous passage that had brought him so far to the east. Emerging safely from Dolphin and Union Strait, Collinson found his further progress hampered by ice and snow-bearing westerly gales. Eventually, having struggled to 100 miles west of the mouth of the MacKenzie, and a little short of Franklin's Return Reef, he was forced to haul into Camden Bay on the north Alaskan coast and to prepare for his third winter in the Arctic.

It was to be another year before Collinson could bring the *Enterprise* to Point Barrow where he fell in with the *Plover* on 28 August 1854. The patient supply ship – which had last seen England almost six years earlier – was now under the command of Commander Rochfort Maguire, the former first lieutenant of Kellett's *Herald* (Moore had been replaced, promoted to captain, and was now serving as Governor in the Falkland Islands). On 16 September, both ships sailed from the Arctic. The *Plover* reached San Francisco and, upon examination, was found to be in such a poor condition that she was taken out of service and sold for scrap.

This was to be the last of the Admiralty-sponsored search expeditions, Collinson arrived home in May 1855, to a welcome of weary official indifference. 100 men a day were dying on the battlefields of the Crimea and examples of heroism such as that of the Light Brigade at Balaclava were badly needed, not the leader of a failed mission demanding that his officers be Court-Martialled for insubordination. The trials were denied and Collinson's protestations ignored. To his great embarrassment the offending officers were promoted and went on to complete undistinguished careers, there being no McClinocks, Osborns, or Pims among them. He was awarded the Founder's Gold Medal by the Royal Geographical Society, but was allowed no claim on the prize for finding a Northwest Passage despite being the official leader of the expedition which saw McClure and his men achieve the passage (the Parliamentary Select Committee, however, in referring to both Kellett and Collinson, 'passed the warmest encomiums upon his important services, suggesting, at the same time, that the country would hail with satisfaction any distinction or favour that might be conferred on them' – none was). Outraged by the meagre result of five years effort, Collinson never again applied for a command. He went on to achieve high office with Trinity House, becoming an elder brother and then deputy master. He was promoted to Rear-Admiral in 1862, Vice-Admiral seven years later, and to Admiral in 1875, the same year he was made a Knight Commander of the Bath. Until his death in 1883, Collinson lived with his mother and sisters whilst serving his local community in a wide range of offices. Sadly, he never lived to hear the Norwegian explorer, Roald Amundsen, who, having taken his tiny motor-vessel, *Gjoa*, along the same westward route towards the Bering Straits, correctly described Collinson as, 'one of the most capable and enterprising sailors the world has ever produced.'

Two years after his return, Collinson, and every other officer, petty officer, seaman, and attached civilian, received a special form of recognition for their endeavours amongst the fields of Arctic ice. In 1853, impressed by the effort required in sledge hauling, Kellett had recorded that, 'I should like to see the travelling men get an Arctic medal'. McClure had even gone to the extent of issuing his own, unofficial, medals to Sergeant Woon and others he thought deserving of some special distinction. In May 1855, Richard Sainthill, a medal enthusiast, wrote in an article entitled 'Numismatic Crumbs' that 'reference to honorary medals, conferred for meritorious services, brings forcibly to my thoughts one class of our gallant countrymen, who, as yet, have not in this manner

Above left: The Arctic Medal – obverse.

Above right: The Arctic Medal – reverse.

been ennobled by the favour of the Crown. I refer to the officers and seamen who have so distinguished themselves in our expeditions to discover "the passage by the North Pole", at length successfully achieved'. The article was published in the naval press and interest in the idea began to grow. By July, the *Times* was able to report: 'We hear that medals have been proposed for all who have served in the Arctic region, a proposition which will doubtless give general satisfaction.' Two years after Sainthill's article, the *London Gazette* announced the award of The Arctic Medal 1818-55 to the participants in thirty-five sea-borne Arctic expeditions. One – John Ross's *Victory* expedition of 1829-33 – was included despite not being an Admiralty-backed voyage. None of the land expeditions of Franklin, Back and Richardson were mentioned, nor were the voyages of the *Nancy Dawson*, *Felix*, *Prince Albert*, *Isabel*, *Breadalbane* or the *Talbot*, yet all their participants also received the medal. In November 1857, the award of the medal was extended to expeditions under the command of Lieutenant De Haven USN, Surgeon Kane USN, and Lieutenant Hartstene USN. Eighteen months later, officers and men of the Hudson Bay Company, who had been involved in the naval expeditions and searches, were also awarded the medal.

CHAPTER ELEVEN

'TRUE TO THE INSTINCTS OF MONOPOLY'

For the Admiralty, and for the Government, the business of searching for a Northwest Passage was now at an end. It had been a long and weary matter, carried out at great cost in lives and money. Even the normally supportive *United Services Gazette*, glad that the long haul was over, published a dreary epitaph:

> The question of a North-West Passage has been fairly solved, and Polar expeditions are, we hope, set at rest forever. The intrinsic value of the discovery is, we grant, nothing. The passage will probably never again be attempted, and its existence is of no moment whatever, but it has this negative value, that it will render all such expeditions needless for the future.

But in more than 100 homes throughout the country, the main question had still not been settled. Where were their husbands, fathers, and brothers? The men who had sailed with such high hopes under the command of Sir John Franklin. Their doughty champion was Jane, Lady Franklin, who, despite receiving some of the most savage blows to her valiant spirit, refused to leave the fate of her husband to Government clerks who wished to draw a line under all things to do with the Arctic.

The first blow fell in a letter from the Admiralty Secretary dated 12 January 1854:

> Madam, it is my painful duty to announce to you the decision of the Board of Admiralty, that at the termination of the present financial year, which ends on 5 April next, the names of Sir John Franklin and of the officers of the Erebus and Terror will be removed from the List of the Royal Navy, and that the accumulation of pay, which has hitherto been considered due to those ship's companies, will thenceforth cease.

This had been followed up by an announcement in the *London Gazette* of Friday, 20 January 1854. Signed by the Secretary to the Admiralty, a notice was published, 'By command of the Lords Commissioners of the Admiralty' and read:

> Notice is hereby given that if the intelligence be not received, before the 31st March next, of the officers and crews of Her Majesty's ships Erebus and Terror being alive,

the names of the officers will be removed from the Navy List, and they and the crews of those ships will be considered as having died in Her Majesty's service.

It took some days before Lady Franklin could rally herself to make a response, 'I have to apologise that it has not been in my power sooner to acknowledge your letter of the thirteenth inst. but the shock it inflicted on my already shattered health was such as not to permit me any mental exertion until now.'

Then, in late October 1854, came another hammer blow. Doctor John Rae landed at Deal, Kent on the twenty-second and hurried straight to the Admiralty. The following day the *Times* published a report and letter from the Hudson Bay Company surgeon. The report read:

I have the honour to mention for the information of my Lords Commissioners of the Admiralty that during my journey over the ice and snows this spring with a view to completing the survey of the west shore of Boothia, I met with Esquimaux in Pelly Bay from one of whom I learned that a party of 'white men' (Kabloonans) had perished from want of food some distance to the westward and not far beyond a large river containing many falls and rapids. Subsequently further particulars were received and a number of articles purchased which places the fate of a portion, if not all, of the then survivors of Sir John Franklin's long-lost party beyond a doubt – a fate as terrible as the imagination can conceive.

The substance of the information obtained at various times and from various sources was as follows:

In the spring four winters past (spring 1850) a party of 'white men' amounting to about forty men were seen travelling south-ward over the ice and dragging a boat with them by some Esquimaux who were killing seals near the north shore of King Williams's Land, which is a large island. None of the party could speak the Esquimaux language intelligibly but by signs the natives were made to understand that their ship, or ships, had been crushed by ice and that they were now going to where they expected to find deer to shoot. From the appearance of the men, all of whom except one officer, looked thin, they were supposed to be getting short of provisions, and they purchased a small seal from the natives. At a later date the same season but previous to the breaking up of the ice, the bodies of some thirty persons were discovered on the continent, and five on an island near it, about a day's journey to the north-west of a large stream which can be no other than Back's Great Fish River (called by the Esquimaux – Ooot-ko-hi-ca-lik) as its description and that of the low shore in the neighbourhood of Point Ogle and Montreal Island agree exactly with that of Sir George Back. Some of the bodies had been buried (probably those of the first victims of famine); some were in a tent or tents, others under the boat which had been turned over to form a shelter, and several lay scattered about in different directions. Of those found on the island one was supposed to have been an officer, as he had a telescope strapped over his shoulders, and his double-barrelled gun lay underneath him.

From the mutilated state of many of the corpses and the contents of the kettles it is evident that our wretched countrymen had been driven to the last resource – cannibalism – as a means of prolonging existence.

There appeared to have been an abundant stock of ammunition, as the powder was emptied in a heap on the ground by the natives out of the kegs or cases containing it; and a quantity of ball and shot was found below high-water mark, having probably been left on the ice close to the beach. There must have been a number of watches, compasses, telescopes, guns (several double-barrelled) etc., all of which appear to have been broken up, as I saw pieces of these different articles with the Esquimaux and, together with some silver spoons and forks, purchased as many as I could get. A list of the most important of these, I enclose, with a rough sketch of the crests and initials on the forks and spoons. The articles themselves will be handed over to the secretary of the Honourable Hudson's Bay Company on my arrival in London.

None of the Esquimaux with whom I conversed had seen the 'whites' nor had they ever been at the place where the bodies were found, but had their information from those who had been there and who had seen the party when travelling.

I offer no apology for taking the liberty of addressing you as I do from a belief that their Lordships would be desirous of being put in possession at as early a date as possible of any tiding, however meagre and unexpectedly obtained, regarding this painfully interesting subject.

The same issue of the *Times* carried a letter from Rae in which he listed some of the items he had obtained from the natives. Among them was a small silver plate – such as might be attached to a walking stick – engraved with the words 'Sir John Franklin K.C.B.'. There could be no doubting that Rae had stumbled across the most vital clue yet found in the search for Franklin, but the manner of its presentation, the nature of its contents, and his actions upon making the discovery, were soon to come under the most searching and hostile enquiry.

Rae had applied to the Hudson's Bay Company for permission to lead an expedition to survey the last remaining unexplored part of the North American coastline. The west coast of Boothia Felix between Castor and Pollux River (the furthest point east reached by Dease and Simpson in 1838) and the western end of the Bellot Strait had not been surveyed – and Rae had a particular reason for wanting to do it. When he had last been in the region, during his 1846-47 expedition, he had reached and named Pelly Bay. Pushing on alone, he claimed to have reached John Ross's Lord Mayor's Bay and found that a hoped-for waterway linking Prince Regent's Inlet to Simpson's Strait did not exist – Boothia was, in fact, a peninsula. He then returned to an island in Pelly Bay and carried out a survey of the bay from the island's highest hill. When his report reached the Admiralty their Lordships were less than impressed either with his claim to have surveyed the coast of Pelly Bay, or to have reached Lord Mayor's Bay. Even Richard King, Back's companion on the 1834 Fish River expedition – and no friend of the Admiralty's – wrote that Rae's visit to Ross's site was 'far from evident'. The 'survey' of Pelly Bay from the top of a hill on an island failed to meet the exacting standards required by the chart-makers employed in the Admiralty's Hydrographic Office, a lack of precision compounded by the fact that Rae had broken his chronometer and had tried to estimate his position by a combination of dead reckoning and a length of string. Consequently, on subsequent charts, much of the coast of Pelly Bay was indicated by a dotted line (i.e. an unconfirmed survey). Rae was furious and wrote to Rear-Admiral Sir Francis Beaufort – the Hydrographer of the Navy – complaining that he considered it, 'extremely hard … that my facts should be doubted'. To a friend he wrote that the Admiralty's position had only been taken out of 'spite'. To make things even worse, in 1852, Beaufort, Parry, and Richardson, refused to accept Rae's positioning of Fort Hope – his 1846-47 wintering base at Repulse Bay – as not merely a mistake, but as 'impossible'.

With permission to return to the Pelly Bay area, Rae could not only re-cover the same ground as he had in 1847, but could also ensure that the Hudson's Bay Company could deprive the Royal Navy of the final laurels to be earned from completing the last stretch of unknown coastline. The necessary permission was granted with little difficulty and Rae left York Factory with twelve men and two boats on 24 June 1853. At Churchill he picked up Ooligbuck, an Eskimo interpreter described by Rae as 'one of the greatest rascals unhung', who could

Rear-Admiral Sir Francis Beaufort – the hydrographer of the Navy.

'be relied upon to tell as nearly as possible what was said and no more.' (this native was the son of the Ooligbuck who had accompanied Franklin on his expedition up the Mackenzie). After a false start, some of the party were sent back and Rae decided to spend the winter close to Fort Hope.

He left Repulse Bay with four men and Ooligbuck on 31 March 1854, and arrived at Pelly Bay eighteen days later. Within a few days, Eskimos had been met. Some were old acquaintances, but others, who had never seen white men before, proved to be difficult and became threatening when Rae told them that he wanted to go to the west. Buying them off by purchasing some seal-meat, he pressed on only to find that his interpreter suddenly took flight and was only forced to return to the party, 'after a sharp race of four or five miles.'

They were joined on 21 April by two 'very intelligent' Eskimos who agreed to accompany them for the next two days. From one of these natives – Innookpoozheejook – Rae heard some stunning news. The man:

...had never met whites before but said that a number of Kabloonans, at least thirty five or forty, had starved to death west of a large river a long distance off. Perhaps about ten or twelve days journey. Could not tell the distance, never had been there, and could not accompany us so far. Dead bodies seen beyond two large rivers; did not know the place, could not or would not explain it on a chart.

In support of his story, Innookpoozheejook had with him a gold-lace cap-band such as worn around the caps of naval officers.

In the short space of an interpreted conversation, Rae had found himself with more information about the whereabouts of the missing Franklin Expedition than all the search expeditions of the last six years put together. His response was to disregard it altogether and continue on his way towards Castor and Pollux River. He reached Dease and Simpson's cairn six days later before turning north (away from the entrance to the Back River – the most likely site of the disaster) and continued up the coast of Boothia Felix. From the northern tip of a large bay ('Shepherd Bay') Rae could look across open ice (Rae Strait) to the shores of King William Land. A few miles further up the coast he could see more land to the west which he took to be James Ross's Matty Island. He could now say without any doubt that King William Land was, in fact, King William *Island*. At this point, still many miles short of his stated intention of reaching Bellot Strait, Rae turned and retraced his steps towards Repulse Bay – his back turned upon the possibility of discovering what had happened to Franklin and his men.

At Pelly Bay, more Eskimos were met and Rae began to collect a number of items that not only confirmed they had come from Franklin's Expedition, but also continued to point towards the mouth of Back's River as the site of the tragedy. On his return to Repulse Bay, more natives began turning up with watch cases, engraved silver cutlery, buttons, coins, and – perhaps the most chilling item of all – the neck-badge from Franklin's Guelphic Order of Hanover. The same decoration he had worn when having his photograph taken just before sailing in May 1845.

Rae spent two months at Repulse Bay questioning the bearers of the Franklin artefacts. Again, all the evidence he obtained pointed to the region of Back's River – again, he did nothing apart from prepare to get to England with his story as quickly as possible. After all, not only was there a reward for finding evidence which confirmed the fate of the Franklin Expedition, he now had a glorious opportunity to strike at the gilded reputation of the Royal Navy and its officers.

The act of cannibalism was viewed with particular horror amongst Victorian society. Revulsion had swept across North America when, in 1846 (the second winter of Franklin's Expedition), a wagon train had been stranded for the winter in the Rocky Mountains, and its survivors were found to have resorted to cannibalism. Such feelings, however, had no place in the lives of the Eskimos. Nature caused them to live in a region of great scarcity where survival often depended upon the pragmatic use of whatever sources were available – and if that meant surviving on the bodies of the dead, then, no matter how regrettable it may be, it had to be done. During the two months Rae spent at Repulse Bay in the summer of 1854, he would have found little difficulty in implanting the suggestion that Franklin's men had turned to cannibalism in an attempt to survive. Not only would such an idea make sense to the natives, it might also have been a welcome diversion from what they knew to be the truth.

There was, for Rae, one further exquisite pleasure to be gained in the suggestion of cannibalism. In 1849, a party of three Hudson's Bay men had set out to spend the winter at Pelly Banks, an outpost on the Pelly River and part of Rae's Fort Simpson District. Having established their camp the three men went hunting only to return to find that their base, along with their supplies, had been destroyed by fire. Only one man survived the winter. According to his version of events, whilst he had been away hunting, one of the other men had died and the third man had, 'eaten all or the greater part of his dead companion'. In his report on the matter, Rae buried the fact of cannibalism in a single sentence and the matter was not pursued further. However, much to his mortification, Rae discovered that Lieutenant William Hooper – who along with Pullen had been described by Rae as a 'self-sufficient donkey' – gave a full account of the incident in a book he published on his return to England. To charge Franklin's men with cannibalism would level the score, and assuage the humiliation of the dotted line of Pelly Bay on the Admiralty chart. All that remained to be done was to ensure that the Admiralty could not censor his report on his arrival in England. This was done by the simple expedient of releasing it to the Canadian press before he sailed, thus leaving the Admiralty little choice but to allow it to be published without modification.

When word of cannibalism reached the streets a predictable outrage swept throughout England. Charles Dickens took to his pen and scoured the history of the Royal Navy for examples of the dreaded act. Despite great trials such as Lieutenant Bligh's open boat journey, a similar experience undergone by Captain Edwards of HMS *Pandora*, and Franklin's own experiences on his return up the Coppermine River, Dickens could list but a single example, when men of the wrecked *Nautilus* ate the corpse of one of their shipmates after a mere four days (they were rescued two days later). Apart from the devouring of a midshipman's dog by the men of the *Wager* there was nothing else. Franklin's men could have been depended upon not to have indulged in such a horrible practice through, 'their own firmness, in their fortitude, their lofty sense of duty, their courage, and their religion'. The *Sun* thundered: 'The more we reflect upon the "fate of the Franklin Expedition", the less we are inclined to believe that this noble band of adventurers resorted to cannibalism. No – they never resorted to such horrors. Cannibalism! – the gallant Sir John Franklin a cannibal – such men as Crozier, Fitzjames, Stanley, Goodsire, Cannibals!' The *Times*, six days after it had published Rae's report, began to lift a corner of the dark pall that had fallen across the memory of Franklin – Eskimos, they suggested, were 'Like all savages ... liars' and although they seemed 'a harmless race little given to violence, they might have been tempted by the emaciation and weakness of the white men to attack them.' When Rae spoke at the Royal Geographic Society, the President – lord Ellesmere – was warned that he would have to be a 'good pilot' as 'many jostling seamen' would be present.

If bringing home tales of cannibalism was the worst of the charges levelled against Rae, it was far from being the only one. Why, for example, had he not rushed to the suggested scene of the tragedy – an area that had not been searched and one that was a mere two days march away? It was highly unlikely that there would have been any survivors, but there was every chance that some form of record still remained to explain the disaster. At first Rae claimed that he had decided to return immediately in order, 'to prevent the risk of more valuable lives being sacrificed in a useless search'. This was later changed to:

> The information obtained on my outward journey was not sufficiently clear to enable me to fix with any degree of certainty on the position at which the party were starved, and to have travelled westwards without sufficient knowledge on this point, when the land was covered a foot and a half or more with deep snow would, as I then thought, and still think, have been useless.

This from a man who claimed to have travelled 6,555 miles on foot through the Arctic – 1,100 of them that very spring – a man who was suffering from no injury, and one who had ample supplies and ammunition.

Rae's many critics felt they knew the answer to the question of his speedy return – the £10,000 pound reward. Incredibly, Rae answered this by claiming that he did not know such an award existed. This astonishing claim was made against the fact that the first reward (£20,000 for whoever 'should discover and effectually relieve' the Franklin party) had been announced in 1848 – *before* Rae had set off with Richardson down the Mackenzie River to look for Franklin. The £10,000 reward for 'ascertaining the fate' of Franklin was announced in 1850 since when Rae had been in England for a whole year during which time he had visited the Admiralty and met naval officers engaged in the search. Whether he knew of it or not, Rae wasted no time in applying for the reward, 'that is very surely to be mine.'

The only obvious response to Rae's information was to send an expedition to visit the area as quickly as possible. The Royal Navy, embroiled in the war against Russia, could not spare the men so asked the Hudson's Bay Company for help. The Company's half-hearted response was to send two men, James Anderson and James Stewart, down Back's Great Fish River in canoes ('a paltry expedition'). They returned after three months having reached Montreal Island at the mouth of the river and spending nine days at the site. They had found a few fragments of wood, some rope, chain-hooks, tools, pieces of bunting, and a letter-clip, but had been able to go no further as their canoes were unable to handle the rougher waters to the north. They had met Eskimos, but had been unable to communicate with them as neither of them spoke the native language. Not a single trace of a body was found. Their return was met with scorn by naval officers with Arctic experience. Where were the bones of the dead? 'We hardly suppose that Dr Rae, with all his desire to fasten cannibalism on his countrymen, will contend that they consumed the bones as well as the flesh of their emaciated comrades'. Why were birch bark canoes 'of inferior quality used … all incapable of approaching or venturing upon an open sea, and manned by a party not one of whom was capable of taking a common astronomical observation? Why were no graves found, no clothing, no guns, or ammunition?' Anderson and Stewart's meeting with Eskimos had resulted in nothing more than 'a few meagre driblets of apocryphal information from a camp of Esquimaux women, communicated by signs, and eked out by imagination.' The Hudson's Bay Company had, 'true to the instincts of monopoly', failed to achieve anything.

Despite this, and much to the disgust of naval officers, the Government awarded Rae the £10,000 for 'ascertaining the fate' of the Franklin Expedition. Many felt that Rae, using 'thrice-diluted' information from natives who were 'notoriously addicted to falsehood and deception', had ascertained nothing more than 'the fate of sundry spoons, forks, and other relics'. Furthermore, it was felt that the removal of the reward would dampen down enthusiasm for continuing the search, especially amongst the Americans, where 'the spirit of Arctic enterprise … burns brightly across the Atlantic.' A measure of the naval officers distaste for Rae could be seen in one proposal that, rather than be given to him, the reward should go to the Eskimos of Pelly Bay, 'if they can but free themselves from the charge of murder'. When, later, Rae suggested that naval expeditions should adopt native methods of survival, the Admiralty showed their opinion of him with the superbly disdainful reply:

> The prime consideration of fox-hunting is not the killing of the fox, but the observance of good form during the pursuit and at the kill. The objective of polar explorations is to explore properly and not to evade the hazards of the game through the vulgar subterfuge of going native.

Richard King openly questioned Rae's honesty, 'Although I had always my misgivings of Dr Rae's ability as a traveller … I can only hope that he made the journey to Castor and Pollux River and hence to Cape Porter… The means by which Dr Rae became possessed of the relics of the Franklin expedition will ever be a matter of doubt in my mind.' Lady Franklin, for whom Rae's achievement had brought welcome confirmation that her husband had achieved a Northwest Passage *before* McClure, simply dismissed him as being 'hairy and disagreeable'.

There was to be another shadow which was to haunt Rae. The 'active and intelligent' Thomas Mistegan, one of the men who had been with Rae on his 1853-54 expedition had, on his return from Repulse Bay, gone to visit his local priest, the Reverend Thomas Hurlburt. Mistegan had confessed to the clergyman that, 'one or two of the men may still be alive.' If such a thing was possible, Rae may have turned his back on their only chance of rescue.

Following his award, Rae carried out a survey of proposed telegraph lines between Britain and America and between Toronto and the Pacific before settling down in London. On one of his telegraph surveys he landed on the coast of Greenland and got no more than sixteen miles before being stopped on a glacier by a snowfall. Much to his embarrassment he had to be rescued by a deeply unimpressed Captain Allen Young – a lieutenant in the Royal Naval Reserve. The great Fridtjof Nansen was later to dismiss Rae's effort as merely 'getting a few miles inland'. Nevertheless, Rae spent a large proportion of the following years taking every opportunity to complain about the Royal Navy's role in polar exploration, frequently attending lectures at the Royal Geographical Society to challenge the achievements of naval expeditions. He died in 1893 and was buried in the churchyard of St Magnus Cathedral, Kirkwall. Inside the church, a life-sized reclining statue was placed near the altar as a memorial complete with the words, 'Intrepid discoverer of the fate of Sir John Franklin's last expedition' – a title John Rae was repeatedly forced to defend ever since his return from Pelly Bay.

CHAPTER TWELVE

'TO STRUGGLE MANFULLY FOR LIFE'

With the end of the Crimean War, Lady Franklin, with public support and the backing of senior naval officers and the Royal Society, requested the raising of an expedition, 'to satisfy the honour of our country, and to clear up a mystery which has excited the sympathy of the civilised world'. Her plea was soon strengthened by the return of the *Resolute* fitted out and ready for Arctic service. The Admiralty, however, had no intention of returning to the Arctic. The Secretary wrote to Lady Franklin, 'My Lords have arrived at the conclusion that they would not be justified, for any objects which in their opinion can be attained by an expedition to the Arctic Seas, in exposing the lives of officers and men to the risks inseparable from any such enterprise'.

By the time the official reply had arrived, Lady Franklin had already gained wind of the Admiralty rejection and had embarked on a fund-raising attempt to get up yet another private expedition to continue the search. She sold off her lands in Australia and looked around for a suitable vessel. Her agent – John Rennie – wrote to her in March 1857 with the news that he had found a likely vessel in the shape of the screw yacht *Fox*: 'If you can get the vessel for £2,000 she is a "dead bargain". She has only made one voyage to Norway. I think she cost from £9,000 to £10,000 originally.' By removing the *Fox*'s coppering and brass propeller and selling them, money could be raised to have the yacht's planking doubled and to have a more efficient iron propeller fitted. Taking Rennie's advice, Lady Franklin paid for the *Fox* from the £3,000 that had been contributed by public subscription.

Next came the problem of who was to command the expedition. Lady Franklin had been keen on the American surgeon, Dr Kane, when there had been the possibility of the *Resolute* being made available. Now that the Admiralty had refused to allow the ship to be used, and with Kane's death, she turned to Captain Collinson. He turned her down and recommended Captain Rochfort Maguire (formerly of the *Plover*) but Lady Franklin wanted Maguire in reserve in case there should be a change of mind about the *Resolute*. She then tried Captain George Richards who had been with Belcher, but he had been appointed to the British Columbia Boundary Commission and was not available. Lady Franklin then went to the man who was probably the most fitted of all to command the proposed expedition – Captain Francis Leopold McClintock.

The yacht *Fox*.

Commander Rochfort Maguire,
captain of HMS *Plover* 1852–54.

On his return with the Belcher Expedition in 1854, McClintock had been promoted to captain at the early age of thirty-five. This promotion had effectively removed him from the opportunity of command during the Crimean War. Despite his constantly applying for an appointment, all the earlier commands went to senior captains or had already been promised to other junior captains. Much of McClintock's time whilst waiting for a command had been spent in helping Sherard Osborn in completing his account of McClure's voyage in the *Investigator*, lecturing on Arctic exploration, and studying at the Royal Naval College at Portsmouth. When the call came from Lady Franklin he replied, 'The Honourable Post you offer me, I need not tell you, is most congenial to my feeling, and I at once accept it.' First, however, approval had to be sought from the Admiralty for a leave of absence. There may have been some difficulty in gaining such approval as Their Lordships had shown a marked lack of interest in sponsoring further Arctic exploration, but Lady Franklin dealt with the problem in practiced diplomatic style. The day she received McClintock's letter of acceptance she wrote to Prince Albert to acquaint him of her progress so far in raising a private expedition and mentioning that McClintock had accepted her offer of command: 'there is no name in the Annals of Arctic enterprise which can be considered more eminent'. She further went on to suggest that, if McClintock did not gain the Admiralty's approval she would have no other option but to engage Captain Hartstene of the United States Navy. The very next day Lady Franklin received a letter from the Admiralty stating: 'My Lords have given Captain McClintock 18 months leave of absence'. McClintock was promptly telegraphed with the message, 'Your leave is granted; the *Fox* is mine; the refit will commence immediately'. A delighted Sophia Cracroft – the friend and companion of Lady Franklin – wrote to Henry Grinnell telling him that McClintock was a man who had, 'never lost that equanimity which is his most remarkable characteristic as combined with his other qualities (Capt. Maguire says of him, that his temper is worth £1,000 a year to him)'.

Whilst the *Fox* was being strengthened for Arctic service, McClintock set about raising officers and men. He had hoped that his second-in-command would be Lieutenant Bedford Pim, but Pim was resting after being injured in China. Instead he chose the twenty-six-year-old Lieutenant William Robertson Hobson on the recommendation of Maguire under whom Hobson had served for two winters in the *Plover* at Point Barrow. Since his return Hobson had been employed in the Black Sea and Baltic fleets and was considered by Sophia Cracroft as, 'a first-rate officer, also strong and vigorous, with the merriest face in the world, and ready for anything.'

The ship's sailing master came from a most unusual source. Although only thirty-two years old, Captain Allen ('Alleno') Young had seen long and distinguished service in command of both sail and steam merchant ships and had commanded a troop-ship on the Black Sea. Recommended by Lady Franklin, Young – like McClintock – insisted on serving without pay. He also contributed £500 towards the expedition's expenses. Dr. David Walker (at whose expense Hobson 'makes himself merry')

Captain Francis Leopold
McClintock wearing his
Arctic Medal.

Lieutenant William Hobson.

was appointed as ship's surgeon and photographer. The ship's engineer was George Brand. A last-minute appointment was made to Carl Petersen, a widely experienced Danish Eskimo interpreter who had seen service with both Penny and Kane (on being offered the post Petersen had remarked of McClintock 'I know him – this man I will follow.'). Most of the seamen were 'men-o-war's men' with the senior man being William Harvey who had served as boatswain's mate in the *Resolute* and the *North Star*. Harvey now gloried in the newly introduced rating of 'Chief Petty Officer'. Also in keeping with a practice only recently introduced into the Royal Navy, the men were given a dark blue uniform with the word 'Fox' embroidered in red across their shirt fronts. Altogether the *Fox* would carry a complement of twenty-five officers and men.

The Admiralty's initial reluctance to become involved in further searches for Franklin was overcome to the point where a liberal supply of stores and supplies were made available to McClintock (helped in some measure by the fact that Captain Austin was in command at Deptford). Ice-saws, ice-anchors and ice-claws were supplied along with a canvas housing for the upper deck during winter. Arctic clothing, medicines, charts, library books, navigational and hydrographic instruments were all provided. Lemon juice and 6682lbs of pemmican in 42lb cases were sent from the Victualling Yard. The Board of Ordinance (temporarily responsible for naval armaments) supplied guns, powder, shot, blasting powder, rockets, and a signal-mortar. The Royal Society granted £50 for the purchase of scientific instruments as the *Fox* was likely to operate in the region of the Magnetic Pole. Nevertheless, compared to earlier expeditions, McClintock was sailing with considerably fewer stores and provision. His response was typical: 'the less the means, the more arduous must be the achievement; the greater the risk, the more glorious would be the success, the more honourable even the defeat, if defeat awaits us.'

Days before he was due to depart, McClintock dined with Captain Washington – Beaufort's replacement as Hydrographer of the Navy. Among the other diners were Dr. David Livingstone and the explorer of the Sahara, Dr. Heinrich Barth – the latter giving a considerable contribution to McClintock's forthcoming venture.

Lady Franklin, Sophia Cracroft and Captain Rochfort Maguire travelled to Aberdeen to have lunch onboard the *Fox* on the day of her departure. At McClintock's request, Lady Franklin gave him a set of instructions for the voyage. As might be expected, these were drawn up very loosely to ensure that McClintock should not feel fettered by any rigid commands. The rescue of any of Franklin's men would be 'the noblest result of our efforts.' The obtaining of any documents and personal relics was the next most important aim, followed by confirmation that her husband had achieved the discovery of the Northwest Passage. On completion of the lunch, Lady Franklin and the others left to the cheers of the yacht's crew. That evening, the *Fox* slipped her moorings and, 'entering fully into the spirit of the cruise', promptly ran aground. It was not until high water the following day that she was freed and able to proceed.

Orkney was passed on 2 July and Cape Farewell rounded ten days later. Vast fields of broken ice were met, swept around the cape from Greenland's eastern seaboard and pushed up the western coast. A seaman who had become gravely ill with a lung infection added an urgency to the need to reach Fredrikshaab (the most southerly of the Danish settlements) in the hope of finding a ship to take him home. After a difficult navigation through the ice and fog the harbour was reached safely. Stores were purchased and McClintock stretched his legs in company with the local Government Inspector as approval for the invalid's passage was arranged. Before the *Fox* sailed north for Godhavn to pick up the next home-bound vessel, the Inspector visited the ship to pay a courtesy call. He was rowed out in a large seal-skin oomiak (women's boat) with native 'frisky damsels' pulling at the oars. Godhavn was reached just over a week later and the *Fox* arrived barely in time to get the sick man aboard the departing vessel which was already at sea. He was sent across to the ship supported by bottles of cod-liver oil prepared by his mess-mates in the hope that it would improve his condition – it did, and he survived to see old age.

Ten sledge-dogs were picked up at Godhavn and an Eskimo dog-driver recruited. Twenty-three-year-old Anton Christian was taken down to the messdeck, given a close haircut and a scrub down before being arrayed in seaman's clothing, much to his discomfiture but much to the envy of his native friends. McClintock also came across a marble tablet that had been prepared by Henry Grinnell on behalf

The *Fox* wintering in the pack ice.

of Lady Franklin and carried north by Captain Hartstene in his search for Kane three years earlier. When it was learned that the intrepid surgeon had made his own way southwards, Hartstene had left the memorial at Godhavn. Carved into the marble were the words:

To the memory of Franklin, Crozier, Fitzjames, and all their gallant brother officers and faithful companions who have suffered and perished in the cause of science and the service of their country. This tablet is erected near the spot where they passed their first arctic winter, and whence they issued forth to conquer difficulties or to die. It commemorates the grief of their admiring countrymen and friends, and the anguish, subdued by faith, of her who has lost, in the heroic leader of the expedition, the most devoted and affectionate of husbands.

And so "He bringeth them unto the haven where they would be.".

McClintock took the tablet away with him in order that he should be able to complete Lady Franklin's wishes.

More dogs were collected from the northern Greenland settlements before the time had come to head westwards across Melville Bay in the hope of passing north of the Baffin Bay ice. Unfortunately, contrary winds had prevented the ice from drifting to the south and, within days, the *Fox* found herself beset. To pass the time, rounders was played on the frozen surface as Petersen and Christian went hunting for seal, 'the liver fried with bacon is excellent'. Although desperately hoping for a northerly wind that might break up the ice, McClintock was eventually forced to come to terms with the fact that he was trapped by the ice and had the screw and rudder lifted clear. The ship's boats were put on the ice and the *Fox* housed over with its canvas roof. Instead of finding himself well beyond the entrance to Lancaster Sound, he was now at the mercy of the pack as it drifted at the whim of the wind.

The drift, which proved to be ever southwards, lasted 242 days and covered a distance of 1,194 miles. The dark, bleak, months were spent learning to handle the dogs, building igloos, and going out on hunting 'sorties'. Dr Walker set up a school to teach 'the three R's – reading, 'riting, and 'rithmetic' – and an organ (the same instrument that had been supplied by the Prince Consort to the *Prince Albert*) provided a cheering tune. The building of the 'snow huts' showed a remarkable improvement. At the beginning of the winter it took four men four hours to put up an igloo, by the end they could do it in thirty minutes. A tragedy clouded the dark season when Leading Stoker Robert Scott, the *Fox's* 'engine driver', fell down a hatch and died two days later. In accordance with naval custom, his belongings were auctioned and £12 6s 6d was raised for his widow and children.

On 24 April 1858, an 'ocean swell rolled in, breaking up the ice about us.' Two days later, after receiving a pounding from the loose ice, the *Fox* broke out into clear waters. Immediately heading northwards, Holsteinsborg was reached on the twenty-eighth and shore leave was granted to the crew. Led by Chief Petty Officer

The burial of Leading Stoker Robert Scott.

Harvey, they took with them a fiddle and several flutes, 'in order to get up a dance, soon all of the native population from the Governor downwards were squeezed together in a large shed.' McClintock wrote a letter to Collinson outlining his plan for the forthcoming search: 'Should I get down to the Magnetic Pole, I will pass on the east side of King William's Land, communicating with the natives, and into the Fish River.' A visit to Godhavn enabled the hospitable Danes to shower the yacht with parting gifts. Amongst other things, McClintock received an eider-down coverlet, a pair of fur boots, and a jar of pickled whaleskin. An additional Eskimo dog-driver – Samuel – was taken onboard complete with his gun, kayak and sledge.

Whilst passing Buchan Island on 8 June, the *Fox* ran aground on a submerged rock and was forced so far over to starboard that her upper deck was awash almost to the edge of the after-hatchway. It seemed as if the slightest movement would have capsized her and several large ice floes were drifting off her port side, any single one of which could easily have pushed her over. The vessel was saved by the turn of the tide and, after eleven hours of great concern the *Fox* was lifted clear and returned upright. Just under two weeks later, McClintock found himself once again in Melville Bay and heading for the waters around the northern edge of the ice. After some difficulty with ice and fog during the early days of July, the sea ahead suddenly lay open and he was able to press on to the west. Jones Sound was seen to be clear of ice but Lancaster Sound was choked with loose ice-floes. With time on his side, McClintock decided to call at Pond's Bay to see if the natives had any knowledge of Franklin, but none had.

Returning to the north, the *Fox* was gripped by a gale which pushed her into Lancaster Sound. By 11 August, she was anchored just to the west of Cape Riley and McClintock took a boat over to Beechey Island to organise the replenishment of his supplies from the storehouse left by Belcher. He found John Ross's *Mary* still in good condition with a number of smaller craft requiring little work to bring them up to a seaworthy state. He had brought with him the marble memorial tablet and erected it alongside the memorial to the dead of Belcher's Expedition and the tablet raised in memory of Bellot. With his storing completed, McClintock returned to his ship in time to see Able Seaman Robert Hampton, setting off in pursuit of a polar bear, fall into the ice-strewn water. Without hesitation McClintock leapt in after him and brought him safely back onboard, noting of Hampton merely that, 'the intense cold of the water had almost paralyzed his limbs'. Of his own condition he recorded nothing.

McClintock sailed from Beechey Island on the sixteenth to take advantage of an unusual lack of ice in Barrow's Strait. A visit to Cape Hotham, where he found the depot destroyed by bears, was followed by an unchecked voyage across the strait. Then, 'in a state of wild excitement', the open waters of Peel Sound were entered. Twenty-five miles further south McClintock's hopes were dashed as he saw ahead of him a solid mass of ice stretching across the sound from North Somerset in the east to Prince of Wales Island to the west. He did not dwell on his misfortune but returned to Barrow's Strait. The northern shore of North Somerset was rounded and Port Leopold visited before the *Fox* turned her bowsprit southwards for Prince Regent Inlet. Fury Beach was passed almost un-noticed in a snow shower and the entrance to Bellot Strait reached on the twenty-first. Much to McClintock's relief, ice could be seen streaming out of the strait indicating a strong current from the west. Beneath the remains of a cairn built by John Ross, McClintock landed and established a depot before entering the cliff-lined waterway. At about halfway along its twenty-mile length the *Fox* was brought to a halt by a mass of broken ice. From the crow's nest the barrier could be seen to reach six miles to the west, beyond lay open water and, true to McClintock's expectations, the turn of the tide began to move the pack eastwards. But it was to prove a slow process. Four attempts to find a passage through the ice were thwarted before McClintock took one of the yacht's boats into the strait to examine the passageway in detail. Climbing to the top of a hill halfway down the strait McClintock found he could see open water to the west although the bottom end of Peel Sound remained frozen. Unfortunately, however, the western exit of Bellot's Strait remained blocked with ice.

Despite what he had seen, McClintock took the *Fox* for a fifth attempt to break through to the west but was forced to turn back. Before he did so, he had another look at the open waters to the west and decided that, as the only man to have navigated his way through those waters was Franklin, he would name them 'Sir John Franklin Strait' (Franklin Strait). Reluctant to go into winter quarters whilst there remained the slightest chance of breaking through to the west, McClintock tried for a sixth time to breach the ice barrier at the western end of the strait, but no lane allowed his passage and he was forced to return to the eastern entrance to establish his winter quarters at a site he named Port Kennedy after the strait's discoverer. He had been prevented by a belt of ice no more than four miles wide from entering Franklin Strait and, with it, the strong likelihood of completing the Northwest Passage by sea.

On 28 September, preparations were put under way for securing the vessel for the winter as Hobson, with seven men and fourteen dogs, was sent across to the west coast of Boothia to establish depots as far down the coast as he could. He returned after being away for twelve days and was rewarded by a meal of caribou, plum pudding and rum. Two weeks later, Hobson returned to the west coast to extend the depots even further to the south. He arrived back at the ship after an absence of nineteen days. At one stage he and his party had been travelling over the ice when it broke away from the shore. In a violent wind and driving snow the floe on which they stood continued to break up until they were left standing on a piece of ice less than twenty yards in diameter. Fortunately, just as it seemed that they were to be plunged into the bitter waters the wind died down and the commotion ceased. This was followed by a night in which the temperatures dropped so low that, by morning, the sea had frozen hard enough for them to dash across its flexing surface to the safety of the shore. Hobson had done his work well and had achieved a chain of depots stretching between fifty to eighty miles from the ship.

Hobson had not long returned to the ship when tragedy struck. The yacht's engineer, George Brand, a married man with young children, was found dead on the floor of his cabin. He appeared to have suffered a stroke and had died some hours before he was found. A grave was dug ashore and a headboard erected to mark the spot. McClintock's engine-room department now consisted of two stokers who had little or no knowledge of the workings of the steam machinery, and his own experience with engines on the *Pioneer* and the *Intrepid*.

The programme of sledge journeys for the spring had been confirmed in McClintock's mind for some time. There would be three parties, one led by McClintock himself, the others by Hobson and Young. Each party would consist of four men hauling a sledge, in company with a dog-sledge driven by Christian for Hobson, Samuel for Young, and by Petersen for McClintock. Young was to cross Franklin Strait and search the coast of Prince of Wales Island from Lieutenant Browne's furthest point down Peel Sound to Sherard Osborn's furthest on the west coast. McClintock intended heading down the coast of Boothia to reach the mouth of Back's Great Fish River before returning via the south and west coasts of King William Island. Hobson would accompany McClintock until they reached Cape Victoria from where he would head westwards to Cape Felix – the most northerly tip of King William Island – and then make his way down the west coast to link up with McClintock as he made his way northwards.

Young had been unable to establish a depot on the shore of Prince of Wales Island in the autumn so he set off once again on 17 February to cover the seventy miles to his destination. He returned safely on 3 March and, a fortnight later, completed the 400-mile round trip to collect eight hundred-weight of sugar from Fury Beach (the sugar was needed to brew 'sugar beer' – believed to be a good remedy against scurvy). The stores at the beach – which had lain there for thirty-three years – showed no sign of being visited by any of Franklin's men.

On the same day that Young set out, McClintock began a journey to establish a depot at the site of the North Magnetic Pole, over 200 miles away on the south-west coast of the Boothia Peninsula. He also hoped to meet Eskimos in order to find if there was any evidence of Franklin. The temperature proved to be so low that the mercury in McClintock's artificial horizon froze solid and the rum took on the consistency of frozen treacle. Moccasins were worn over feet wrapped in pieces of blanket for travelling. At night fur boots were worn inside blanket sleeping bags. Igloos were erected but, even with Petersen's skills, took so long to build that a canvas tent was thrown over to act as a roof.

The magnetic pole was reached on 1 March without any sign of Eskimos. With his rations low and several of his dogs limping badly, McClintock felt he could only continue for one further day. Stopping for a rest, the party were surprised to look back and see four figures walking in their tracks. These turned out to be a party of Eskimos on a hunting trip. The strangers proved to be friendly, and as greetings were being made, McClintock noticed that one of the natives was wearing a naval officer's button on his clothing. The man told Petersen that it had come from 'some white people who were starved upon an island where there are salmon (that is, in a river); and that the iron of which their knives were made came from the same place.' Another of the natives told of seeing Rae and his party. After a gift of needles, the four Eskimos built an eight-foot igloo in an hour.

The following day Cape Victoria was reached and the natives went on ahead to their village. They returned the next morning with the entire village population – about forty-five Eskimos. Many carried items that could only have come from Franklin's party and McClintock traded knives, needles, files and scissors for six silver spoons and forks, a length of gold chain, buttons, and a silver medal awarded to Assistant Surgeon Macdonald of the *Terror*. He also noted that one of the villager's sledges had been made from wood that looked as if it had been part of a boat's keel. The older natives could remember James Ross and the abandoning of the *Victory*. Others talked of a ship that had been crushed by the ice to the west of King William Island. None, however, had seen the white men who, it was claimed, had landed safely from the disaster. There was no mention of cannibalism.

The *Fox* was rejoined twenty-five days after they had left her. In his journey McClintock had completed the uncharted stretch of coastline linking the site of the magnetic pole and Bellot's Strait, and had discovered the first practical sea-route through the Northwest Passage. He had confirmed that his plans led in the right direction, and had also, 'acquired the arctic accomplishment of eating frozen bear's blubber, in delicate little slices on biscuit, and vastly preferred it to frozen pork.'

McClintock trading with the Eskimos for Franklin relics.

Above: Exploring parties starting out from the *Fox.*

Opposite: Lieutenant Hobson's party search the cairn at Back Bay.

The two travelling parties under McClintock and Hobson mustered on the ice on the afternoon of 2 April. Doctor Walker was to be left in command of the *Fox* with just five men once Young had left for Prince of Wales Island. Flags were hoisted on the yacht to match the silk banners fluttering above the sledges. McClintock's sledge-flag was bright red, bordered with a white embroidered pattern, and bore the name 'Lady Franklin' in bold white letters.

Keeping company as far as Cape Victoria, McClintock and Hobson fell in with some of the Eskimos that had been encountered earlier. More articles from Franklin's expedition were found along with an account of a second ship that had been driven on to the shore of King William Island by the ice. They also heard tales of white men dragging their boats to a 'large river' where, later, their bones were found. The natives then told McClintock that at least one of his depots had been broken into, its contents stolen and, when items began to be pilfered from his sledge, he decided to move on refusing to answer the natives' demands to know where his ship was based.

Hobson separated from McClintock with orders to search the west coast of King William Island. If nothing was found he was to cross over to Victoria Land to complete the gap left between Captain Collinson's furthest and the point where McClure's unfortunate mate, Wynniatt, turned back. As they parted, McClintock noted that Hobson felt unwell, complaining of stiffness and pain in his legs but thought it was nothing more than the effects of the journey. The lieutenant's party reached Cape Felix on 2 May. There he found an empty cairn and traces of an encampment from which he removed a small white ensign and the heads of two boarding pikes. Over the next four days he travelled down the low rubble beaches of the north-west coast of the island with the heavily ridged ice of Victoria Strait pressing hard against the shore. On the morning of the sixth, he reached a wide curving bay (Back Bay) with, at its northern point, the small pillar of rocks with which James Ross had marked his Victory Point. In the distance, the coast could be seen stretching westwards to Cape Franklin. To the south the low-lying land was broken by a gently sloped hill ('Cape Jane Franklin').

Hobson continued around the edge of the bay for about a mile and a half when he saw a large cairn surmounting a low shingle ridge. As he approached the pile of rocks he became aware of a large amount of stores, clothing, and other abandoned equipment lying around the base of the cairn and the nearby beach. Part of the cairn had collapsed and, in the loose rubble at its base, Hobson picked up a metal cylinder. When opened, it revealed a message written on a standard 'bottle paper' used for placing in bottles and being thrown over a ship's side to test currents, or for attaching to balloons to research air currents. The message read:

H.M. Ships *Erebus* and *Terror*, Wintered in the ice in Lat. 70 05'N., Long. 98 23'W.

May 28, 1847. – Having wintered in 1846-7 at Beechey Island, in Lat. 74 43' 28"N., Long. 91 39' 15", and having ascended Wellington Channel to Lat. 77 and returned by the west side of Cornwallis Island, Sir John Franklin commanding the expedition. All Well. Party consisting of two officers and six men left the ships on Monday, May 24, 1847

Gm. Gore, Lieut.
Chas. F. Des Voeux, Mate.

That completed the original message but, eleven months later the paper had been taken from its original cairn and the following written around the margin:

April 25, 1848. – H.M. Ships *Terror* and *Erebus* were deserted on April 22 5 leagues N.N.W. of this, having been beset since September 12, 1846, the officers and crews consisting of 105 souls under the command of Captain F.R.M. Crozier, landed here in Lat. 69 37' 42" and Long. 98 41'W.

This paper was found by Lieutenant Irving under the cairn supposed to have been built by Sir James Ross in 1831 4 miles to the northward, where it had been deposited by the late Commander Gore in June 1847. Sir James Ross's pillar has not, however, been found and the paper has been transferred to this position, which is that in which Sir J. Ross's pillar was erected.

Sir John Franklin died on June 11, 1847, and the total loss by deaths in the expedition has been to this date nine officers and fifteen men.

James Fitzjames, Captain,
H.M.S. *Erebus*.

Along the top, with the paper inverted, had been written:

> F.R.M. Crozier, captain and senior officer, and start on to-morrow twenty-sixth for Back's Fish River.

Taking the note and a few other items, Hobson continued southwards crossing the ice of a two-mile wide inlet (Collinson's Inlet) and followed the coast as it swung first west then south. Whilst passing along the beach towards Point Franklin, another cairn was found containing a second bottle paper. It proved to be a duplicate of the early edition of the Back Bay message and added nothing to the fate of the survivors from the abandoned ships. It did show, however, that Gore and Des Voeux had passed that way on their exploration southwards.

The weather deteriorated into gales, and heavy snow showers made the sledge hauling difficult. Hobson was unable to help as his aching legs had worsened to severe pain in all his joints. It was quite obvious, both to him, and to his party, that he was suffering badly from scurvy.

As the coast curved first south then west in a huge arc (Erebus Bay), one of Hobson's men came across the upper part of a ship's whaler standing clear of the snow. Its upper strakes had been removed then replaced by thin fir planks and the stem post had been planed down – both modifications intended to reduce the weight of the vessel. When the snow was cleared away from the inside of the boat Hobson was shocked to see revealed part of a human skeleton at the bow with a more complete skeleton, still wrapped in furs, in the stern. The rest of the boat was filled with clothing and stores, but Hobson could carry out little more than a cursory search for records or journals (of which none were found). He had to get as far south as possible in the hope of meeting McClintock before making a dash back to the *Fox*. A gale confined them to their igloo for two days and, in order to rest his men, Hobson took Christian and just one man with him as they used the dog sledge to get as far south as he could. After two days Hobson's scurvy worsened and he was forced to call a halt. All he could do was to build a cairn and leave a message for McClintock. He was then left to lead a desperate race to get back to the yacht – any plans for crossing Victoria Strait would have to be abandoned. He arrived at the *Fox* twenty-three days later having been away from the vessel for seventy-four days. His personal journey had been an epic of survival, fending off the effects of scurvy until he could no longer walk and had to be carried on the sledge. To him, however, had fallen the honour of finding the vital clue revealing the fate of Franklin.

When Hobson left him for Cape Felix, McClintock made his way first to the Clarence Islands, where a small cache was deposited, and then onto the east coast of King William Island itself. Matty Island was visited in the hope of meeting natives but none were seen, and the first Eskimos they met were found on their return to King William Island. They proved to be an amiable group of about forty men, women and children, living in igloos. They claimed to have never previously seen white men, but McClintock managed to barter from them six

Lieutenant Hobson's party discover the boat at Erebus Bay.

forks and spoons bearing the crests or initials of Franklin, Crozier, Lieutenant Fairholme, and Assistant Surgeon MacDonald. More buttons were obtained and a considerable amount of wooden articles seen, including a stout sledge. Many claimed to have visited a wreck 'without masts'. A mention of fire led Petersen to assume that the masts had been burned down. A woman who said she had been to the wreck the previous year was closely questioned, and told Petersen that the white men, 'fell down and died as they walked along.' Some had been buried, others had not. Once again an outbreak of theft by the 'good-natured, noisy thieves' prompted McClintock to move on.

Further down the coast a feature named by Rae as 'Mathison Island' was corrected to 'Mathison Hill' and a solitary igloo found at Booth Point. The inhabitants of the snow house were, 'much alarmed by our sudden appearance' and very reluctant to emerge from their dwelling to discuss with McClintock the origin of the wooden poles found outside. The estuary to the Great Fish River was reached after crossing the ice of Simpson's Strait. After a delay of two days caused by a ferocious gale the party reached the grey rocky heights of Montreal Island on 15 May. No cairn was found, just a few items of iron and sheet copper. A heavy fall of snow delayed further progress for a day and gave McClintock a chance to rest one of his men who had become ill – others suffered from snow-blindness.

The return journey began on 19 May. On regaining King William Island McClintock headed westwards. A cairn was discovered as they marched towards Simpson's cairn at Cape Herschel, but no trace of a message was found. Just after

McClintock finding the skeleton on King William Island.

midnight the following day, McClintock was walking along a shingle ridge close
by the beach when he was stopped by the sight of a skeleton protruding through
the snow. The arm and leg bones were missing but enough clothing remained
to identify it as that of a steward or officer's servant. A pocket book was found
with the remains containing the service record of thirty-seven-year-old Petty
Officer, Henry Peglar, the *Terror's* Captain of the Foretop. Other papers – one
of which was a mildly pornographic parody of a well-known verse – were in
the hand-writing of Thomas Armitage, aged forty-one, the *Terror's* Gun Room
Steward who had served with Peglar on a previous vessel. The remains of the
clothing suggest that the bones belonged to Armitage, and he was trying to
reach home with the only thing he could carry that had belonged to an old
friend.

Simpson's cairn, crowning the high ground at Cape Herschel, was reached the
following day. McClintock had high hopes for the prominent rock pile. Now that
it seemed certain that Franklin's men had passed by the spot on the way to the
Great Fish River, it was reasonable to expect that they would have left a message
at such a well-known landmark. But nothing was found. There was evidence that
the natives had visited the site, and the fact that one side of the cairn had been
pulled down, suggested that there might have been something hidden inside
at one time. A close search of the area and digging with pickaxes failed to find
anything. McClintock was convinced that the natives had broken into the cairn
and found what they were looking for, otherwise, he felt, the rock would have
been levelled to the ground.

McClintock travelling over King William Island.

Twelve miles further to the west, beyond 'Washington Bay' (named after the Hydrographer to the Navy), another, more recent, cairn was found. Inside was a note from Hobson describing his journey down the west coast of the island and the discoveries he had made. Like McClintock he had seen no sign of any ship, but hoped one might be seen as he made his way back to the *Fox*.

From Hobson's cairn, the coast of King William Island falls away to low and undulating ground, crossed and re-crossed by shingle ridges. To the west, the shallow waters of Victoria Strait are frozen over with massed hummocks of ice that rear up in great, glittering, blocks. During warm summers this ice can become open water as far north as Erebus Bay but, beyond that, remains frozen the year round. A group of small islands kept the main pack at bay and allowed McClintock to take his sledges onto the ice close in shore and make good progress around the western-most point of the island ('Cape Crozier'). The coast then turned directly eastwards as it formed the southern edge of Erebus Bay. On 30 May, McClintock reached the boat earlier found by Hobson.

Although by now getting short of provisions, McClintock stayed long enough at the site to examine the boat's contents closely. Beneath the two skeletons and a pile of clothing he found five watches – one of which belonged to Edward Couch, a mate in the *Erebus*; twenty-six pieces of silver-plated cutlery (eight with Franklin's crest); a pair of decorated slippers; a pair of half-boots; and five books on the Christian religion – one of them a copy of 'Manual of Private Devotions' that had been given to Lieutenant Graham Gore by Captain Sir George Back. There was also an amazing amount of small items such as a tooth-brush, soap, towels, silk handkerchiefs, tools, munitions, knives, and two rolls of lead. A small amount of tea was found and forty pounds of chocolate. By clearing the snow away from the boat, two double-barrelled guns were revealed, propped muzzle-upwards against the boat's side. In each gun, one barrel was found to be loaded and cocked. Also discovered beneath the boat was a massive iron-shod oak sledge measuring over 23 feet long and 4 feet wide. Although the sledge had carried the boat in a cradle of supporting chocks, the boat had been lifted, possibly by an incoming tide, and returned to the side of its original position. Put together, McClintock estimated the weight of the sledge and boat (excluding the contents) to be at least 1,400lbs. An enormous weight that had been dragged for more than fifty miles using traces made of whale-line. A particularly surprising aspect of the boat and sledge was that they were pointing to the north-east rather than to the south. McClintock took this to mean that she was actually *returning* to the ships but, finding their load too heavy, two men had been left behind as guards as the remainder continued northwards – perhaps for more supplies from the abandoned stores at the Back Bay cairn, or in an attempt to reach supplies and safety at Fury Beach.

The snow-covered ground revealed no more skeletons, graves, or any other evidence from Crozier's party. McClintock continued following the coast until he reached Point Franklin – the most westerly point on the 'Gore Peninsula'. From there he explored the shores of Collinson's Inlet before reaching the site of the cairn at Back Bay (apart from Washington and Collinson, McClintock had decided that all the features along the route of the escaping parties should be named after the officers lost from Franklin's expedition). Scattered around the base of the cairn McClintock found a four-foot high pile of clothing, none of the articles were marked with an owner's name. Cooking stoves lay alongside part of a lightning conductor. Brass curtain rods rested next to a medicine chest, and a dip circle complete with its needles and magnets lay upon the honey-coloured shingle. A sextant belonging to Frederick Hornby, a mate in the *Terror*, was found with two cooking implements, one belonging to Corporal William Hedges, the other to Private William Heather, two of the *Terror*'s Royal Marines. A preserved meat can, adapted as a pannikin by one of the *Erebus*'s able seamen, had his name, 'W. Marks', scratched upon it. In his journal, McClintock wrote:

> These abandoned superfluities afford the saddest and most convincing proof that here – on this spot – our doomed and scurvy-stricken countrymen calmly prepared themselves to struggle manfully for life.

A copy of the message found by Hobson was placed in the cairn along with a record of both McClintock's and Hobson's visit. A further message was buried under a large stone 10 feet to the north before McClintock and his party set off to cover the 300 miles to the *Fox*. At Wall Bay (named by James Ross after one of the *Victory*'s seamen) the party crossed to the east coast of the island in order to reach a cache that had been deposited at Port Parry and to avoid the broken ice

Some of the artefacts collected by McClintock.

hummocks that lined the coast as far as Cape Felix. Before long, the increasing temperature reduced the surface ice and snow to a knee-deep slush that made the sledge-hauling exhausting work for both men and dogs. After sixteen days, and within sixteen miles of the ship, heavy rain forced the sledges to be abandoned. The party pressed on without stopping and reached the safety of the *Fox* the following day, 'in time for a late breakfast'. They had been away from the ship for seventy-eight days and had travelled almost 1,000 miles.

Hobson was found to still be lame from his journey, but recovering slowly from scurvy. Of Allen Young, however, there was no sign since he had returned to the ship two weeks earlier before setting off once again. Taking two sledges he had set off on 7 April and crossed the ice of Franklin's Strait to reach the southern tip ('Cape Swindburn') of Prince of Wales Island. From the cape, the low-lying shore turned north-west with the ice to the west piled up in a mass of jumbled ridges and hummocks. Young attempted to make his way across the ice ('McClintock Strait') to the coast of Victoria Island but progress was so painfully slow that his limited supplies forced him to return to Prince of Wales Island. In order to stretch his provisions to their maximum limit, he sent back three of the seamen and the Eskimo dog-driver with the man-hauled sledge, and continued on with the dog-sledge and Able Seaman George Hobday. Sleeping in igloos or on top of the sledge (the tent had gone with the returning men) they made their way along the coast against violent gales and storms. At one stage they were so exhausted that, having built their igloo, they slept solidly for twenty-four hours as the winds raged about them. The point reached by Lieutenant Sherard Osborn in 1851 was reached on 11 May and Young and Hobday turned around to complete their journey by searching up the east coast as far as Lieutenant Brown's furthest. Young's health, however, rapidly deteriorated and soon it was clear that he had no choice other than to return to the *Fox* as quickly as possible. They arrived on 7 June, both in very poor condition and with Young feeling markedly depressed. Under the care of Surgeon Walker, Young's condition improved to the extent that, after three days, he was determined to set off again. Walker protested vigorously and, when Young insisted on leaving with his sledge teams, the Doctor committed his doubts to paper, handing Young a copy. But there was no stopping the merchant navy officer and the whole party set off on the tenth.

Fifteen days after Young's departure, with his own recovery from his journey well under way, McClintock took four men to go out in search of the missing team. They were met on the western shores of Franklin Strait with Young so enfeebled that he had to be carried on the sledge. All were back onboard the *Fox* by the twenty-eighth. Young had travelled up the coast of south-east Prince of Wales Island as far as Browne's furthest and, after crossing the ice of Peel Sound, had returned by the western coast of Somerset Island. In all he had been away for eighty-two days, forty of which had been solely in company with Hobday. 380 miles of new coastline had been discovered which, when added to that explored by McClintock and Hobson, meant that almost 1,000 miles of new coasts had been searched and charted.

All that remained to be done was to get the *Fox* prepared for sea – and hope that the ice would allow them to escape. One immediate difficulty faced by McClintock was the fact that the yacht's engine had been stripped for maintenance by the engineer, Brand. Now he was buried beneath the shingle on the beach. As fortune would have it, the only man onboard with any engineering experience was McClintock himself who had earned a First-Class Steam Certificate as a mate in HMS *Gorgon* and had commanded the *Intrepid* under Belcher. Consequently, whilst Hobson supervised the upper-deck preparations, McClintock laboured in the engine-room fitting together the complex and oily arrangement of gear-wheels, pistons, and connecting-rods.

By mid-July, the *Fox* was ready for sea but the ice did not clear from Port Kennedy until the morning of 9 August. The boiler fires were lit and, at eleven o'clock, the yacht steamed out of Brentford Bay into Prince Regent's Inlet. A defect in the boiler caused scalding water to be ejected from the funnel with such force that it reached the top of the masts – much to the consternation of Young who was piloting the ship from the crow's nest and had to evacuate his position with great rapidity. McClintock was forced to spend many long hours operating the engines before the vessel was clear of the entrance to Lancaster Sound and a favourable wind helped them on their way to Discovery Bay.

Their arrival at the port of Godhavn was greeted by a desperately welcome supply of letters. There were messages from Lady Franklin and Sophia Cracroft and Hobson received a copy of the 'Navy List' through which he and McClintock pored in search of their friends' promotions. Whilst this was being done a large number of young Eskimo women scrubbed the yacht's decks and paintwork. Their reward for this effort was to be taken ashore by the seamen and treated to a dance in a wooden storehouse whilst being plied with rum punch. The two Eskimo dog-drivers were landed and, at their request, had their wages paid to the local inspector who was able to ensure that the two men would receive their income spread out over a lengthy period. McClintock took special pleasure in hearing that the two natives had left the vessel claiming that they had been treated 'all the same as brothers.'

Cape Farewell was rounded on 10 September and Portsmouth reached on the twenty-first. McClintock disembarked and took a coach for London, arriving at the Admiralty that night as Hobson took the *Fox* on to Blackwall. After making his report to the Lords of the Admiralty, McClintock rejoined the *Fox* with the news that those of her crew who had not previously been awarded the Arctic Medal would now be granted the honour. He was also able to inform Hobson that he was about to be promoted to commander. An award of £5,000 for the officers and men of the *Fox* was voted by Parliament (McClintock's share was £1,500) and, ten days after their return, all the officers were guests at a dinner hosted by Admiral Sir Horatio Austin and twenty-five other Arctic officers.

The Danish-Eskimo interpreter, Carl Petersen, returned to Denmark where he was awarded the Silver Cross of the Danebrog by the King to match his Arctic medal. This was followed by his appointment to the command of a lighthouse. He died, aged sixty-seven, in 1880.

Captain Allen Young entered the newly created Royal Naval Reserve, rising to the rank of Lieutenant RNR. He published an anonymous account of the voyage in which he reduced his own involvement to, 'discovered McClintock Channel, and proved Prince of Wales Land to be an island.' In 1860 he was appointed to command the *Fox* (purchased from Lady Franklin) and assisted McClintock in the survey of the North Atlantic Telegraph Route between Greenland and Labrador. Carried onboard for the Greenland land survey was John Rae whom Young had to rescue after Rae had reached no more than sixteen miles inland. Fifteen years later, Young was back in the Arctic. Lady Franklin – by now aged eighty-four – had sold her house to raise funds in order to charter the fourteen-year-old former naval steam-gunboat, *Pandora*. She had also resurrected the £2,000 reward for information regarding the fate of her husband and was particularly interested in finding any records left by his expedition. When Young heard of her project he volunteered to be its leader, offered to pay half the cost, and brought an Arctic yachtsman, Leigh Smith, as an additional volunteer. He would not, however, accept the reward, 'No gentleman could permit such a thing.' The *Pandora* sailed at the end of June 1875, with the additional object of attempting to sail through the Northwest Passage. Beechey Island was reached where Young noted that the storehouse built by Pullen of the *North Star* and used by Belcher for his accommodation had been wrecked by bears – a surviving barrel of rum proof that the site had been visited by 'neither Eskimo nor British sailor'. Peel Sound was then penetrated as far south as 'Pandora Bay' on Prince of Wales Island, and to within ten miles of Bellot Strait, but ice barred any further progress. Returning home, he found no-one to whom he could pass on news of his failure – Lady Franklin had died three weeks after he had sailed. Young was knighted in 1877 and introduced Lilly Langtry to the Prince of Wales. He was appointed as the Commanding Officer of the London Royal Naval Reserve in 1880. Two years later he set off with the whalers *Hope* and *Martha* in search of the private Franz Josef Land expedition mounted by Benjamin Leigh Smith and, delayed by a grounding, fell in with the missing expedition's boats just as he was about to sail northwards up the coast of Novaya Zemlya. Young joined McClintock at a dinner in 1907 held to mark the fiftieth anniversary of the voyage of the *Fox*. He died in November 1915.

After being promoted to commander, Hobson had to wait eighteen months before being employed. He was eventually appointed to the command of HMS *Pantaloon*, an eleven-gun wooden steam-sloop, based on the Cape of Good Hope Station. He had not been on the station for long when he was re-appointed to the East Indies Station to take command of the steam gun-vessel, HMS *Vigilant*. Hobson was promoted to captain in 1866 but received no further employment until being placed on the Retired List six years later. He died in October 1880, and was buried in the churchyard at Pitminster, Somerset. His widow paid for a new east window in his memory, a memorial which lasted for 100 years before being destroyed and replaced by a new one of garish abstract design.

On his return from Port Kennedy, McClintock busied himself in writing his narrative of the expedition. With the assistance of Captain Sherard Osborn, the book was written and ready for publication in just nine weeks. *The Voyage of the Fox*, first published in 1860, remained in print until 1939. With his work on the North Atlantic Telegraph Route completed in 1861, McClintock was appointed to HMS *Doris*, a frigate on the Mediterranean Station, with the son-in-law of Admiral Sir Horatio Austin as his first lieutenant. Nineteen months later he was appointed to another frigate – HMS *Aurora* – and witnessed a clash between the Austrian and Danish navies off Heligoland – the first battle in which both steam and shells were used. By stationing the *Aurora* on Heligoland's three-mile limit he prevented the Danes from pursuing the fleeing Austrians into neutral waters and, consequently, averted an international incident that could have widened the war. Sent out to the West Indies, McClintock found himself off the coast of Dominica when the black population grew restive about a new piece of legislation that was due to be passed by the Legislative Council. McClintock landed with sailors, marines, and the ship's band and occupied the Council House, leaving the band playing outside. The objectors grew threateningly violent and McClintock had to step in to prevent the marines from opening fire. He managed to delay the intended attack on the building for long enough to allow the attractions of the band to become apparent to the protestors who gradually clustered around the bandsmen and began dancing. At this, McClintock ordered the band to march away from the building and into the surrounding countryside, where they were followed by the happily dancing rioters: 'The members of the House were consequently able to pass their act in peace, while the negroes spent a most delightful day in the country.'

In 1865, McClintock was promoted to commodore and flew his broad pennant on board the *Aboukir* before his return to England the following year. After some persuasion he stood for election as a Conservative in the Irish town of Drogheda but found himself totally adrift in the religious conflict which surrounded the event. Following an outbreak of serious rioting in which the army had to be called out, McClintock withdrew his candidacy in order to save the lives and health of voters who were being attacked by mobs waiting at the polling stations. Whilst visiting an eighty-eight-year-old man who had been injured whilst trying to register a vote, he met the old man's grand-daughter, Annette Elizabeth. Six years later she became his wife.

Although still relatively low down on the 'Navy List', McClintock benefited from a number of 'deadwood clearances' in which senior captains were given the choice of remaining on half-pay or of being promoted to Rear-Admiral and immediately transferring to the 'Retired List' with a Rear-Admiral's pensions. Many captains chose to become 'Rear-Admirals of the Yellow' (as opposed to the active Red, White, and Blue squadrons) thus clearing the way for more junior officers to achieve flag-rank. McClintock's advancement to Rear-Admiral came in 1871 whilst he was serving on the councils of the Royal Geographical Society and the United Services Institute. He spent the next five years as Admiral Superintendent of Portsmouth Dockyard overseeing the launch of HMS *Inflexible*, the arrival of the Prince of Wales from a tour of India, and the return of troop ships from the Ashanti War. When he saw that the latter arrived with their wives and children wearing thin clothing more suited to a tropical climate McClintock organised shelter, hot coffee, food, and warm clothing to ease their emergence into an English winter.

Promoted to Vice-Admiral in 1877, McClintock was appointed as Commander-in-Chief of the North American and West Indies Stations two years later, flying his flag in the *Northampton*. His flag-captain was Captain John 'Jacky' Fisher (later First Sea Lord and moderniser of the Royal Navy with his introduction of the turbine-powered *Dreadnought*). He returned in 1883 to find himself just one place short on the Admiral's list with little chance of being promoted before his impending retirement. He had, however, good friends in high places who managed to persuade a senior Admiral to retire early and McClintock was able to take up the vacancy just one day before he was due to retire. Thus it was that Admiral Sir Francis Leopold McClintock left the Royal Navy after fifty years' service. He had proved to be a popular leader with a 'sunny temper' and practical outlook who became an example to all who served with him. His study and experience of sledging methods provided the pattern for all naval expeditions into the twentieth century, its dependence upon the reliability and endurance of British seamen at risk solely from the scourge of scurvy. McClintock had also come the nearest to taking a ship through the Northwest Passage, only a four-mile wide barrier of ice at the western outlet of Bellot's Strait had prevented him from achieving the goal of generations of mariners.

After almost a quarter of a century of active retirement (during which time he was elected as an Elder Brother of Trinity House), McClintock died, aged eighty-eight, in November 1907, and was buried at Kensington Cemetery. Among the many mourners at the ceremony were representatives of the King and the Prince of Wales, the First Sea Lord (Admiral Sir John Fisher), the President of the Royal Geographical Society, the Deputy Master of Trinity House, and numerous Arctic officers and seamen. A wreath was sent by the great Norwegian explorer, Frito Hansen. Later, a plaque was placed beneath Franklin's memorial in Westminster Abbey. On it – with greater accuracy than a similar comment on Rae's memorial – were the words, 'Discoverer of the Fate of Franklin'.

The *Fox* was chartered by the Atlantic Telegraph Company (and commanded by Captain Allen Young) before being sold to a Danish mining company operating out of Greenland. In 1905 she was sold on again, this time to the Royal Greenland Trading Company who, in addition to supplying settlements along the west coast of Greenland, also used her to transport scientific expeditions working on the island's glaciology. On 19 June 1912, the *Fox* ran aground on a small island before managing to limp back to the settlement at Qeqertarsuaq. There she was condemned as unseaworthy and abandoned. She remained heeled over on a sandbank for many years until a gale destroyed what was left of her hull in 1940. An Arctic work-horse, the *Fox* had achieved the height of her fame in her early years, survived to see the change of century, and found her final resting place just five years after the death of McClintock.

Although McClintock took the honour of discovering the fate of Franklin, it was to Franklin's widow that the laurels must go for sheer dedication, perseverance, endurance, and a willingness to spend all at her command in the search for her lost husband. Her fortune was not great and it was only by frequent appeals for help answered by naval friends, the British public, the people of Tasmania, and by American generosity, that she was able to achieve so much. Supported by her friend, niece, and companion, Sophia Cracroft, she used every contact she had to prosecute the search and, where she had no contacts, she went out and made them with directness rare in women of her time. On the return of the *Fox*, Lady Franklin was awarded the gold medal of the Royal Geographical Society and, five years later, was present at the unveiling of a Government-sponsored statue of her husband at Waterloo Place, London (other statues were erected at Hobart, Tasmania, and at Spilsby in Lincolnshire, Franklin's birthplace). The statue showed Franklin wearing a fur overcoat over a full naval uniform, worn in honour of the occasion when he informed his ships companies that the Northwest Passage had been found. The pedestal is decorated with two panels listing the names of the officers and men of the *Erebus* and *Terror*, a third shows a map of the Arctic, whilst

The memorial to Sir John Franklin in Westminster Abbey.

a fourth – designed by Walter May, who, as a mate in the *Resolute* and a lieutenant in the *Assistance* had taken part in the Franklin searches – shows a congregation of fur-wrapped men standing with heads bowed around a sledge-born coffin that is about to be lowered into a grave dug out of the ice. After years of travelling around the world with Sophia, Lady Franklin was afflicted by the infirmity of old age. Despite the onset of partial blindness she still found the commitment to pursue three final goals in connection with her late husband. She intended to buy the Spilsby house in which Sir John had been born and turn it into a museum to his memory, she raised money to send Captain Allen Young back to the Arctic to search for any records that might have survived, and – most important of all – to oversee the placing of a memorial to her husband in Westminster Abbey. The museum was never achieved, and Young was defeated by the ice of Peel Sound, but the marble monument – a bust of Franklin surmounting a carving of a ship trapped in ice – was unveiled by Rear-Admiral Sir George Back on 31 July 1875. There to read the verse carved into the monument (written by Franklin's nephew by marriage, Alfred Tennyson) were other widows, Sophia Cracroft, and Captain Hobson. The lines read:

> Not here! the white North hath thy bones, and thou,
>> Heroic sailor soul,
> Art passing on thy happier voyage now
>> Towards no earthly pole.

Only one person of note was missing at the sombre ceremony – Jane, Lady Franklin. She had died two weeks earlier. When news of her death was announced, further lines were added to the Westminster Abbey monument: 'This monument is erected by Jane, his widow, who, after long waiting and sending many in search of him, herself departed to find him in the realms of Light, July 18, 1875, aged 83 years.' Her coffin was placed in the catacombs of Kensal Green Cemetery as a poet wrote of her:

> Ye crystal mountains of the North!
> Ye guardians of the Pole!
> Lift up your gates! for at them waits
> A true and noble soul!
> Then open the everlasting door
> And raise the icy screen,
> Then let the hosts with solemn voice
> Say, 'Welcome! Polar Queen!'

CHAPTER THIRTEEN

'DEATH HAD BEEN STARING THEM IN THE FACE'

So what did happen to Sir John Franklin's expedition? The mystery was slightly muddled by two well-meaning American expeditions which set out for King William Island in search of more evidence. The first of these, consisting solely of the totally inexperienced Charles Francis Hall, left in 1860 with the hope of finding survivors. In order to achieve this, Hall intended to live with the natives, learn their ways, and then, with the help of hired whaling men and Eskimos, search King William Island. In the event, it took him five years to reach the island where he learned the penalty of 'going native' when the Eskimos refused to spend more than four days on the southern shore. With no other resources, he was forced to return with his guides as they turned on their heels and headed southwards.

Hall returned with a mishmash of tales, silver cutlery bearing the initials FRMC (Francis Rawdon Moira Crozier) and a complete skeleton. He had crossed over the ice of Simpson's Strait and landed on Todd Island, three miles south of Booth Point. On the islet he found part of a human bone and heard tales of five skeletons that had been seen there earlier. Landing on King William Island, he went a few miles to the west and came across a grave on the banks of a river. Upon opening it he found a complete skeleton and decided to take the bones home. He then returned to Booth Point before leaving the island. From the natives he heard lurid stories of knee-high boots stuffed with cooked human flesh, 'flesh cut off as if someone or other had cut it off to eat', and skulls with holes in them where the brains had 'been taken out to prolong the lives of the living'. Not surprisingly, the main source of these imaginative stories was none other than Innookpoozheejook – the same Eskimo that Rae claimed had given him the tales of cannibalism. Hall had none of the hostility towards the Royal Navy that affected Rae's opinions, but his gullibility was astonishing. Stories of bodies being found with hands sawn-off were accepted as evidence of cannibalism without examining the possibility that the hands might have been surgically removed as a result of frostbite-induced gangrene (it would be an exceptional cannibal that removed only the hands for a meal). A tale that one of Franklin's ships had drifted south after being abandoned and was looted by the natives was endorsed without any investigation that the natives might have actually been talking about a ship's boat and elaborating their story with memories of John Ross's *Victory* (one of the natives with Hall claimed to have met Ross). Even Hall's own simple faith in the stories he was told was shaken when he heard from a native woman that she had been the lover of both Parry and Lyon, especially when he later heard that she was spreading tales that she had been *his* lover.

It seemed clear, however, that the natives knew of the boat Hobson and McClintock had seen at Erebus Bay and had seen another boat in the near vicinity. They also talked of a tent at the head of Terror Bay on the south-west coast of the island, its floor covered with bones, and a site on the southern mainland where a boat and the remains of thirty to thirty-five men had been found. In factual terms, Hall's long effort had resulted in little more than a few relics, a skeleton, and confirmation of what was already known. He had seen little for himself and depended upon a wealth of second-hand information which he presented as evidence. As Lady Franklin noted in a letter to Henry Grinnell, 'his statement is full of omissions and so devoid of order and dates as to leave much confusion and perplexity in the mind. He makes no distinction between the places he visited himself and what he saw himself – and what he only heard of.' The skeleton disinterred by Hall was given to the British Embassy in Washington and was handed over to the naval attaché, Rear-Admiral Edward Inglefield, commander of the *Isabel* in her 1852 voyage into Smith Sound. He passed the bones on to Rear-Admiral Richards (formerly of the *Assistance*, 1852-54) who, with the help of a gold tooth in the skull, was able to identify the bones as belonging to Lieutenant Henry Le Vesconte of HMS *Erebus*. The bones were buried in the floor of the Painted Chapel at the Royal Naval College, Greenwich, and later removed to the college chapel.

In 1877, Thomas Barry, the captain of the American whaler *Eothen*, arrived at his home port with a startling tale. Apparently, some of Franklin's men had crossed the Boothia Peninsula to the Melville Peninsula where they had built a cairn. Inside it they had deposited items they had carried with them – possibly even journals and logs. When the Admiralty heard the story they consulted McClintock. He rejected the tale out of hand and advised that no action be taken. In America, however, the American Geographical Society decided that the story should be investigated and sponsored a small expedition to be led by Lieutenant Frederick Schwatka, an army officer serving with the US Cavalry.

On the expedition's arrival just north of Chesterfield Inlet on Hudson's Bay in August 1878, Schwatka soon discovered that the tale of a cairn on Melville Peninsula was groundless. Instead of returning, he resolved that his team should spend the winter living alongside the Eskimos before heading overland to King William Island the following spring. The summer of 1879 would be spent searching the south and west coasts of the island and the return journey made in the succeeding winter.

The party set out on the morning of 1 April with Schwatka, his three fellow Americans, thirteen Eskimos – including women and children – forty-two dogs, three sledges, supplies for one month, ten breech-loading rifles and 10,000 rounds of ammunition for hunting and 'personal security'. After crossing the Wager River the party kept to the banks of another stream ('Hayes River') which led them to Chantry Inlet and the mouth of Back's Great Fish River. A party of Eskimos was encountered and one of them was old enough to remember Back's journey down the river in 1834 and claimed to have visited one of Franklin's ships that had drifted south from where it had been abandoned in 1848. All that had been found inside the vessel was a number of cans of food – four of which remained unopened – various items of tableware, and a few books. The natives gained entry by cutting a hole in the side. This action had, according to the old man, caused the vessel to sink. Among the relics picked up by Schwatka was a wooden board with the letters 'LF' picked out in copper tacks (possibly 'Larboard Forward' – the designation of a seaman's mess).

Just to the west of Richardson Point, on the southern shore of Simpson's Strait, a large number of Netsilik Eskimos were encountered. On Schwatka's approach the natives ran out of their igloos and promptly formed up for battle. An old – and dispensable – woman was sent forward to test the reactions of the newcomers. On her shouting back that the strangers were white men, the natives lowered their weapons. Both sides had a narrow escape. It was the custom after the death of one of the tribe to kill the next stranger who entered the camp, and they had just suffered such a loss. Despite a truce, several of the Eskimo were still 'anxious to keep up the tradition' but were dissuaded from doing so. Nevertheless, one of Schwatka's Eskimos suggested firing a gun as the parties met just to ensure that the Netsilik were aware that the party was armed.

Lieutenant Schwatka at the site of Lieutenant Irving's grave, Back Bay, King William Island.

The following day, Schwatka heard of an inlet three or four miles to the west where the natives had discovered a boat, somewhere between six and ten skeletons, and one body with flesh still on it. Among a large collection of watches, books, papers and tableware taken from the boat was a tin box which contained books and another containing bones that had been sawn in half (to Swchatka, a sure sign of cannibalism). The body with flesh on it had a bizarre aspect that seemed unexplainable. Suspended from two gold earrings was a gold chain at the bottom of which was a gold watch. When the chain was pulled, the head of the corpse was pulled up by the ears. The site ('Starvation Cove') was visited by Schwatka, but a layer of snow hid any sign of the horror. Other tales told of brief contact between the natives and of men dragging a sledge along the southern shore of King William Island. A knife had been traded for some seal meat before the two parties separated. Just as in the story told to Hall, a tent had been seen at the head of Terror Bay with skeletons lying around both inside and out.

Simpson's Strait was crossed in the middle of June and a cairn erected by Hall found. At Washington Bay (where no sign remained of another supposed tent) the party headed inland with the intention of reaching Collinson's Inlet, instead they found themselves on Erebus Bay and spent the next fifteen hours wading through the slushy and broken ice at the bay's edge before camping to the south of Franklin Point. Two despoiled graves were found near the entrance to Collinson's Inlet before the remains of Crozier's cairn was reached – still surrounded by much of the wreckage seen by Hobson and McClintock. Close by, another open grave was discovered. Schwatka attributed this and other opened graves to the native's search for artefacts (but was much more likely to be the work of bears or foxes). A silver medal was picked up by the side of the grave. It had been awarded in 1830 as the second prize for mathematics at the Royal Naval College and bore the name 'John Irving'. Schwatka reasonably assumed that the bones belonged to Lieutenant John Irving of HMS *Terror*. They were collected up with the aim of returning them to Irving's family. After a search of the area, Schwatka pressed on to Cape Felix which was reached on 3 July suffering many of the 'disagreeabilities of travel in King William Land' yet finding ample game to provide for their sustenance. During the four days spent at the low cape little was found apart from a number of 'conspicuous cairns' which Schwatka believed to have 'been erected as points of observation from the ships' (although more likely to have been used to calculate the drift of the ships *from* the shore).

On his return south, Schwatka once again visited the tumbled-down cairn near Victory Point. This time, with less snow on the ground, he found McClintock's message describing the discovery of the Franklin bottle paper. At some stage during the twenty years since it was deposited, the paper had been removed from the tin canister in which it was placed. Of the container itself, there was no trace. Nor could the message buried by McClintock north of the cairn be found. Among a small number of items that were collected was a brush that had been the property of Henry Wilks, a Royal Marine Private in the *Terror*.

After re-crossing Collinson's Inlet and the Gore Peninsula, another opened grave was found at Point Le Vesconte with the bones scattered for up to a quarter

Lieutenant Schwatka's camp on King William Island.

of a mile. Gilt buttons attached to a remnant of blue cloth suggested that the deceased had been an officer, but no clue survived as to his identity.

The party continued on around the edge of Erebus Bay until the site of McClintock's boat was reached. Thirty years of exposure had caused many of the clinkered side planks to have fallen away, but the stem, keel, and stern remained intact. Four skeletons were found and buried and a small number of relics collected. Before leaving, Schwatka had the stem of the boat removed and brought it away with him.

Two more, incomplete skeletons, were found – one near Hornby Island on the south-west corner of King William Island, the other at Point Tulloch on the south coast. Schwatka then re-crossed Simpson Strait and once again visited Starvation Cove. With the snow cover now gone, four skeletons were discovered along with a pewter medal recording the launch of Brunel's *Great Britain* in 1843. The remainder of the bones had been 'gradually entombed' by the sea.

December was spent near to the entrance to Back's River before Schwatka took the brave decision to make a mid-winter dash back to his base on Hudson's Bay. He had expected to reach his destination within a month, but found that it took him until early March having lost twenty-four days through severe gales that prevented travel. On his arrival he found that Captain Thomas F. Barry, master of the *Eothen*, who had been entrusted with all their remaining provisions and a large quantity of other material, had stolen them on his departure from Hudson Bay. As a result he had to press on to Marble Island where he found a whaler in which he could take passage to New Bedford. He arrived in August 1880.

McClintock summed up Schwatka's achievements by noting:

We must all feel the greatest regret that the exhaustive and final search which Lieut. Schwatka has so very ably carried out has been unrewarded by the recovery of a single scrap of writing or by any new or important fact… His minute examination confirms my facts and strengthens my conjectures respecting the lost expedition.

As for Schwatka's contacts with the natives, McClintock found their evidence to be 'often conflicting, sometimes both contradictory and incredible in detail.'

The stem of the boat found at Erebus Bay was returned to England and proved to be the identical vessel seen by McClintock. It was placed alongside other Franklin relics in the Painted Hall of the Royal Naval College at Greenwich (and later transferred to the National Maritime Museum). The bones believed to belong to Lieutenant John Irving were returned to his native city, Edinburgh, and were buried in Dean Cemetery amidst great pomp and ceremony. He had passed his lieutenant's examination in 1834 but, as there were no immediate hopes of promotion, had gone out to Australia where he became a sheep-farmer before returning to England in 1843 on learning that his promotion was due. Two years later he had entered the *Terror* and sailed to discover the Northwest Passage.

Despite their hardships and endurance, neither of the American expeditions had added much to the mystery of what had happened to Franklin's men. A number of bones had been found and more second-hand rumours of cannibalism coupled with tales verging on the absurd. With the discovery of Irving's grave, Schwatka (supported by McClintock) believed that a party of men had returned from Erebus Bay to the site near Victory Point. Nothing had been seen of the missing ships, and the tales of a vessel found by the natives south of the island all pointed to a ship's boat rather than a large ship such as the *Erebus* or the *Terror*.

The *Erebus* and *Terror* trapped in the ice off Beechey Island.

In the summer of 1845, Franklin had passed through Lancaster Sound, gone north through Wellington Channel, returned to Barrow Strait by encircling Cornwallis Island, and had wintered on Beechey Island (not during the winter of 1846-47 as mistakenly noted on the bottle paper found by Hobson). When the ice broke up during the summer of 1846, Franklin left Beechey Island (no note was found recording his presence or his intentions, but this does not mean that one was not left) and, almost certainly, passed down Peel Sound – a waterway which, in some years, clears completely of ice. At some stage, probably well to the south of Franklin Strait, the *Erebus* and *Terror* encountered the massive stream of ice pouring down the McClintock Strait. Franklin would have been faced with the choice between returning to the north via Peel Sound (assuming that it remained open), of attempting a passage through the ice of Victoria Strait to the south-west (passing down the western coast of King William Island), or of steering to the south-east and entering James Ross Strait in the hope of passing to the east and south of King William Island. McClintock felt that the latter option was not available to Franklin as 'he was furnished with charts which indicated no opening to the eastward of King William Land'. Lady Franklin, however, repeatedly stated that her husband's charts *did* show King William Land as an *island*. But, even if Franklin did have charts showing – what later became – Rae Strait to the east of the island, he would have realised that the channel would have been very narrow. Furthermore, if he had assumed (and he would have been correct in doing so) that a south-eastern passage would also be shallow, it would have markedly reduced his chances of success in that direction. With less than 200 miles separating him from known waters, the option of a northerly retreat would have also offered no attraction.

Beechey Island with the three graves from the Franklin Expedition.

The *Erebus* and *Terror* being abandoned off the north-west coast of King William Island.

Franklin, unaware that on his starboard bow lay an unseen mass of ice slowly grinding its way south through McClintock Channel to be stopped only by the north-west shores of King William Island, chose to pass down the western coast. To him, the ice ahead of the ships was no different from the ice he had found further to the north. By accepting the risk of being trapped for one winter, there was always the strong possibility that, with the break up of the ice the following summer, he could reach the known, and open, waters along the northern coast of North America. From his standpoint, the risks were calculated and acceptable. Having pushed his way as far south as possible during the late summer of 1846, the ships would have been frozen into the ice and prepared to face the winter in the well-established manner.

In May the following year, with the ships firmly locked into the ice off the north-west tip of King William Island, Franklin needed to fully explore his circumstances. Two things were vitally important. He had to find his rate of drift with the ice and, secondly, find out at what stage he could expect to meet open waters during the approaching summer. Accordingly, he set up a camp in Cape Felix from which the rate of drift could be calculated by using readings taken from fixed positions (these were the 'conspicuous cairns' found by Schwatka). At the same time, Lieutenant Graham Gore and Mate Charles Des Vaux were sent with a party of six men to travel down the west coast of the island to ascertain where open waters could be expected. With the rate of drift, and the distance needed to be drifted before open waters could be reached, it would have been a simple matter to calculate how long they could expect to be trapped by the ice and, consequently, how their remaining supplies should be rationed. The information, when it was returned, would have been disappointing, but not insurmountable.

The rate of drift was very slow – probably not much more than a mile a month, and the break-up could not be expected to happen until, at least, eighty miles to the south. Franklin had been prepared to spend up to seven years in the Arctic on the assumption that he would have been able to supplement his provisions with local game. He had already spent two winters in the Arctic and, if his new information was correct, he could expect to spend another six years drifting slowly down Victoria Strait. There was little evidence that game was plentiful in the area and he had already lost a significant proportion of his supplies when his canned food turned out to be rotten. On the other hand, if the worst came to the worst, he could always send a party south to one of the Hudson's Bay Company forts. Such an enterprise would have required little more effort than he had used in covering the distance from the Great Slave Lake many years earlier, and there were now forts even closer than those on the lake. Once word reached civilisation of his position, the problem of supplying the expedition would not have been overly difficult and would have provided a stimulating challenge for both the Company and the Admiralty.

There were, however, other aspects that presented themselves during the course of the summer of 1847. When Gore returned with his party he could not have failed to have pointed out evidence to Franklin that suggested they were not trapped in a normal ice field. As he had passed up and down the coast, Gore would have seen the nature of the ice to the west. Reared up in great piles by pressure ridges and with massive fingers of ice reaching out across the shoreline it was clear that the ice was under an unimaginable pressure from the north-west as it collided with the north-west shore of King William Island. The *Erebus* and *Terror*, if their drift was to continue to the south-west, would not be able to avoid passing directly across the path of this immense stream of ice pouring down from over the horizon. Everyone onboard the two ships would have experienced, or have known of, other vessels succumbing to far less pressure than they were about to endure.

There was also the strong possibility of scurvy breaking out onboard the ships. There had been little, or no, access to fresh food for some time and its absence, despite the application of presumed anti-scorbutics, would have led to an inevitable outcome. When Gore had completed the bottle paper and buried it in a cairn near to Victory Point, he had written on it a cheery 'All well'. Less than a year later, Commander Fitzjames had noted on the same piece of paper 'the total loss by deaths in the expedition has been to this date nine officers and fifteen men.' What proportion of those losses was caused by scurvy cannot be known, but it is likely to have been high.

Finally, on 11 June, there would have been the great blow of the death of the expedition's leader. An extremely popular, and seemingly indestructible, captain, Franklin's death would have struck at the hearts of all his men. For almost half a century, his name had been at the forefront of all attempts to breach the Northwest Passage. Now, on the verge, and almost within sight of the goal being achieved, he was lost. He left in his wake many capable officers, not least his second-in-command – Crozier, but it must have been as if the expedition's own Pole Star had suddenly been extinguished, and its sure and steadfast guide lost for ever. He would have been buried on the nearby coast as ice-burials were generally only carried out when no shore was available (Walter May's plaque on the plinth of the Waterloo Place statue shows an idealised, albeit impractical, burial in the ice close to the ships).

Then, the very environment which they had frequently tempted in the past, extracted its own savage revenge. In late April 1848, the ships (or the last of the ships if one had gone earlier) gave in to the enormous pressure. With bulkheads collapsing and icy water pouring through the breaches, the ships were crushed beneath the unforgiving onslaught. Crozier had clearly expected this to happen. The ship's boats, already prepared for a river voyage, were clear of the vessels and massive oak sledges had been built for them to be transported over the ice. His orders would have been to save life first whilst rescuing whatever could be grabbed before the ships finally disappeared beneath the ice, thus accounting for the strange mixture of artefacts found at the landing site and in the boats. Watches were very important for future navigation and the officers ensured that their silver cutlery and personal mementos of Franklin were also saved. The ships may have gone down with frightening speed (the *Breadalbane* – although not as ice-strengthened as Crozier's ships – took less than fifteen minutes). If a large amount of wood had remained available, large fires would have been lighted ashore to keep the bitter cold at bay – but no evidence of any such fires have been found. Both ships, with their steam-engines in the holds, would have plummeted to the bottom of Victoria Strait. At the position where the ships went down, the bottom is far deeper than elsewhere in the strait, a basin probably carved out by the countless centuries of ice thundering down McClintock Strait. Within a few miles to the south the bottom rises to form the shallows around the islands clustering around the strait's southern exit. It would have been impossible for the ships to have worked their way up this rising sea-bed, and to pass unsteered through the shallow narrows to eventually end up on the west of the Adelaide Peninsula where the Eskimos claim to have seen and boarded one of them. It is equally highly improbable that one or more of the ships could have remained afloat and habitable. No-one would have abandoned such a haven in the sub-zero temperatures of an Arctic April unless they were forced to by desperate circumstances.

Once ashore, no time would have been wasted in getting the party of 105 men on the move to the south. At least three of the ships' boats (twenty-seven-foot whalers), topped to the gunwales with supplies (much had to be left at the landing site) and mounted on oak sledges, had to be hauled for more than 200 miles to the mouth of Back's Great Fish River if the ships companies of the two ships were to be saved. McClintock believed that they would have taken to the ice of Victoria Strait to reach their destination but, already knowing the outline of the coast from Gore's earlier expedition, and fully aware of the difficulties of dragging sledges over the heavily ridged ice, Crozier would have opted for the far shorter land route across Collinson's Inlet, then across the base of the Gore

'They forged the last link with their lives'. The Northwest Passage: HMS *Erebus* and *Terror*, 1849-50.

Peninsula to the head of Seal Bay. From Seal Bay his intention would have been to skirt the northern shore of Erebus Bay and to strike out overland to the south for the level, unridged, ice of Simpson's Strait. Such a route would have been over snow-covered, low-lying land, that undulated gently and provided no difficulty for the heavy sledges. The difficulty came, however, from the condition of the haulers. It is not known if, or how many of the men, were suffering from scurvy – but the experiences of other expeditions suggest that the chances are that a large proportion of them would have been affected by that scourge of seamen. Even in its early phases, scurvy induces a feeling of lethargy in its sufferers. This is followed by pain in the joints and a swelling and blackening of the gums to the extent that they can protrude from the mouth. Any form of exercise would have rapidly exacerbated the condition to the extent that the sufferer would be totally unable to take part in the sledge hauling. This, in turn, would have put an increased burden on the remaining haulers. It would not have taken long for deaths to have taken place, the graves of two possibly being found by Schwatka at Point Le Vesconte (not all of Schwatka's skeletal discoveries can be taken as being definitely from men of Franklin's expedition – some were later found to be of native origin).

At a point level with the southern curve of Erebus Bay, Crozier (or whoever remained in command) found that he had to modify his plans. Many of his men, possibly the majority, were totally unfit for any further progress and would have to be left behind if any of the remainder were to reach safety. It was not, however, a case of complete abandonment. Gore would have discovered that, in summer, the ice of Victoria Strait clears as far north as the bay. If the men could survive at the spot until then, they would be able to take their boats onto the water and head for the Coppermine River, or any other route that would take them to one of the Hudson's Bay forts. Even if that could not be achieved, there was always the chance that the fitter men would reach safety and send out a rescue party. Leaving two boats behind along with tents, provisions, guns and ammunition, the remainder pressed on (if native accounts are to be believed) to the head of Terror Bay. Once again, the desperately sick had to be left behind whilst the fittest of the survivors took to the ice of Simpson's Strait and headed westwards towards Chantry Inlet. This remaining group were capable of giving a formal burial to one of their number – Lieutenant Le Vesconte – but, having crossed over to the North American shore, were unable to survive beyond the barren shore of Starvation Cove.

It was probably then that the cruellest blow of all fell on the invalids waiting for the ice to clear at Erebus Bay (the same may have happened at Terror Bay, but there is no evidence that the site actually existed). When, in 1832, John Ross abandoned the *Victory* and the *Krusenstern* at Victoria Harbour they left a vast hoard of material wealth in the hands of the local Netsilik Eskimos. Prior to Ross's arrival, the Netsilik's only source of metal was by trading with other Eskimo tribes to the south. So rare was this commodity that, in almost all cases, blades for weapons, harpoons, and edged tools were made from slate. With the abandonment of Ross's two ships in their area, the Netsilik suddenly became the possessors of a huge amount of metal. Before long, weapons tipped and edged with iron, copper, tin, and brass, had replaced the stone-age slate. Even crudely made saws and scissors appeared for the first time in the hands of the Netsilik. The arrival of this giant leap forward in their fighting and hunting capabilities had an almost immediate effect on their neighbours. Before long, the tribes to the south had been sent reeling back and the Ookjulik Eskimos were driven westward, far from their tents on King William Island. In a very short time, the Netsilik had earned themselves a reputation as an aggressive people who were using their newly found and superior weaponry to clear other tribes off the land. Rae had been warned that the Netsilik had a 'very bad character' and his guide refused to hunt seal at night in case he fell in with them. Hall not only met a family fleeing from them, but was also warned about their violent nature. In May, 1848, the Netsilik suddenly found themselves faced with a new threat – and a new source of material wealth. Coming down the west coast of King William Island were 105 men, a grave threat to a people who depended for their very survival upon the game that could be found in their hunting grounds. Furthermore, the strangers had with them yet more treasures; metal, wood, canvas and glass.

When the attack – or attacks – were launched, the Eskimos found themselves up against muskets and shotguns, but only in the hands of desperately ill and weakened men who could barely lift the weapons, much less reload at speed. Falling upon the strangers with knives and axes, the Eskimos would soon have finished their bloody work. Only two men, guarding one of the boats, managed to fend them off, watching in horror as the natives carried out their traditional mutilation of the fallen enemy. Limbs, joints, and faces were hacked as the Eskimos ensured that the spirits of their enemies would not come back to haunt them.

Almost 150 years later, the bleached bones lying on the ground at Erebus Bay would reveal the extent of the attack. Long bones shattered as their owners lay defenceless on the ground, others bearing the deep cut of a hacking weapon. The majority of the marks on the bones were to be found on the hands, caused as the defenceless seamen raised their hands in a hopeless effort to protect themselves. So ended the lives of many men who, having set out on a noble mission intended to benefit the world, died a sordid death on the ice-bound, foggy, shores of an Arctic island. Just over two decades later, Lieutenant Hobson would gaze in horror at the skeletons of the two men who had guarded the boat. One young, the other older, they had propped their loaded guns against the side of the boat, then snuggled down beneath rugs and furs to fall asleep and die. The Netsilik, having completed their slaughter, and having looted the site of silver cutlery, Franklin's property, and anything else they could carry, had gone – unaware that further piles of treasure lay abandoned beyond a wide inlet to the north. They had not escaped unscathed. Among the bones found at Erebus Bay were those of a young native, sacrificed in the murderous struggle for existence in a hostile land.

It is possible that not everyone died in the Eskimo assault. The grave of Lieutenant John Irving (if, indeed that is who it was) suggests that a party – either before or after the supposed Eskimo attack and, perhaps made up of the fittest men – returned to the landing site. Irving died and was buried before the party set off in a ship's boat that had been left on the beach and headed north, either to Fury Beach (where it was well-known that supplies were still available), or to Lancaster Sound in the hope of meeting a whaler. The keel of a twenty-seven-foot whaler was found many years later at Back Bay on north-west Prince of Wales Island. Close by, lay a large 'tent ring' of non-native origin. If the boat was from the Franklin Expedition (and there is little chance of it being from another source) it is possible that the north-bound party passed up Peel Sound to Back Bay, camped in a tent made from the boat's sails, and waited for the sea to freeze. The boat was then broken up, its thwarts, frame, and strakes, used to make sledges which were then used in an attempt to reach Lancaster Sound. None survived.

There was no cannibalism, nor any reason to concoct improbable theories concerning lead poisoning arising from the construction of the food containers. A former Hydrographer of the Navy, Rear-Admiral George Richards (who as a commander had been in the *Assistance* with Belcher) was probably right when he wrote to the 'Times' in 1880 to protest about Hall and Schwatka's baseless propagation of the cannibalism myth. There was, he wrote, not 'one tittle of foundation' in the story. 'Death had been staring them in the face for months' and would have had 'no terror for men in their position'. As for cannibalism: 'The thing appears so monstrous to me that I am at a loss to conceive how it can have been suggested'. Wherever it had come from, 'The thing' was a shoddy, worthless, suggestion meant to denigrate brave men and sully a gallant enterprise.

Surrounded by death, the final survivor of the Franklin Expedition faces the cruelty of nature.

A medallion portrait of Sir John Franklin.

At great cost in lives, and after four centuries of struggle, the Northwest Passage had been discovered. But there was to be little gain from its discovery for those who had pushed its gates open. It would take another half-century before the Norwegian, Roald Amundsen, was able to take his tiny vessel *Gjoa* through whilst marvelling at the skills that had taken Captain Collinson from Icy Cape to Cambridge Bay. There was to be almost no commercial advantage and, in time, even the men whose names were marked on the charts of the Arctic would be forgotten. The greatest gain would be to the fledgling country, Canada, whose northernmost islands and waters were charted in a humanitarian search for missing countrymen.

But, tragedy or not, the Royal Navy had not yet finished with the north – there was still the chance of a last hurrah!

CHAPTER FOURTEEN

'OUT LIKE A ROCKET'

Following in the wake of Kane, two further American expeditions had pushed their way into the Kane Basin, Kennedy Channel and beyond. The first under Isaac Israel Hayes (a companion of Kane in the 1853-55 expedition) sailed from New London in the United States on 29 May 1860, with the intention of exploring the northern coasts and reaching an open polar sea before sailing to the North Pole. Smith Sound was penetrated with difficulty owing to heavy ice and Hayes was forced to winter at Foulke Fiord. Contact was made with the local Eskimos who replaced some of Hayes' dogs, all of whom had died during the winter. In early 1861, Hayes crossed the Kane Basin and explored the 'Grinnell Land' (Ellesmere Island) coast claiming to have reached beyond 81 degrees. On later examination, however, his navigational skills proved to be both defective and imaginative and it is unlikely that he reached beyond 80 degrees, 14'. With his return to his ship he decided to go home and make another attempt the following year. Unfortunately, his plans were thwarted by the outbreak of the American civil war.

In July 1871, ten years after Hayes' return, Charles Hall sailed in the *Polaris* on a Government-sponsored attempt to reach the North Pole. Favoured with a relatively smooth passage through the ice, Hall ascended Kennedy Channel and passed through open waters (Hall Basin) until he reached the north-west corner of 'Grant Land' (Ellesmere Island) where the ice brought him to a halt. Returning southwards along the Greenland shore, he hauled into a small bay he named 'Thank God Harbour' and prepared the ship for the winter. A short, exploratory, sledge journey was made northwards to Newman Fiord in late October and Hall returned convinced that he had found a sledge-route to the North Pole.

The voyage had not been a happy one and there had been much bickering between the officers. Two German scientists refused to obey Hall, the captain of the *Polaris* – Buddington – was caught stealing food, and the assistant navigator, George Tyson – who at one stage had been offered command of the ship, sulked at his reduced responsibility and considered the captain to be a 'coward'. Half of the crew were German and tended to stick together in opposition to the Americans. The first, and most terrible, sign of discontent came on 8 November when Hall was found teetering on the edge of his bunk trying to spell out the word 'murder'.

He died hours later and, although an official inquiry decided that he had died of a stroke, a later examination of his body revealed that he had died from arsenic poisoning.

The following spring saw a small number of sledge and boat expeditions, but the heart had gone out of the enterprise. On Hall's death, everybody had wanted to take over the command, Buddington took to drinking the preserving alcohol, and the Eskimo hunters left in disgust to live in an igloo ashore. All that could be agreed upon was that the ship should start her return voyage when the ice broke up in August. Three days after their release, Buddington – out of his mind with drink – ran the ship into the pack where it remained stuck for the next two months. When, at last, the ice began to break up around the ship, the sound of the floes grinding against the sides caused utter chaos and panic. Buddington ordered all the coal and provisions to be thrown onto the surrounding ice. Much was immediately lost as it disappeared through cracks in the crumbling floes. Tyson and several others then jumped onto the ice to save what they could – only to find that the floe on which they stood began to drift away from the *Polaris*. Before long the ship was out of sight and Tyson found himself alone with ten men – seven of whom were German, three Eskimo hunters, one Eskimo woman, and five native children. Over the next six months, as the floe drifted to the south, he had to rely both on the possession of fire-arms to fend off threats of cannibalism, and on the native's skill in hunting, whilst contending with the Germans setting up a camp of their own on a separate part of the floe. Their astonishing ordeal came to an end in April 1873, when they were rescued off the coast of Labrador by a Newfoundland sealer. Buddington, in the meantime, with fourteen men left, spent the winter at Foulke Fiord before abandoning the *Polaris* and heading south in the ship's boats. They were picked up by a Dundee whaler and taken back to Scotland before returning home.

When the expedition's journals and log books were finally collected from Foulke Fiord, it was discovered that all the pages covering the death of Hall, and the separation of the ship from the floe, had been torn out.

Although the voyages of Hayes and Hall had been separated by ten years they had served to start, and then to strengthen, British demands that the discovery of the North Pole should not be left to the Americans. Chief amongst those urging more British effort were Sherard Osborn and Clemence Markham. Osborn, a Rear-Admiral since 1873, had been agitating for more Arctic involvement since the return of Hayes. McClintock wrote to him in support; 'I am glad to know you are poking up the embers so as to keep the Arctic pot boiling. I wish I were now preparing for a trip to the North Pole, for I regard it as being within the reach of this generation.' Markham, who, as a midshipman had served under Ommanney in the *Assistance* and had taken part in two sledge journeys, was soon able to join Osborn's crusade from a considerably elevated position. In 1852 he had left the Service and spent a year rambling through the Inca ruins of Peru, an experience which led to his appointment as an honorary secretary of the Royal Geographical Society. He then joined the Civil Service and worked for the

A later portrait of Sir Clemence Markham with a model sledge and a picture of a cinchona flower.

Honourable East India Company before it was merged with the newly created India Office. Markham was then given the responsibility of collecting cinchona seeds and young trees from the forests of the eastern Andes and transferring them to India. The work was carried out successfully and the price of the quinine obtained from the trees fell to such an extent that the extract became widely and freely available. In 1867, Markham was appointed as Head of the Geographical Department at the India Office. The following year he was sent out as geographer on the Abyssinian Campaign, entered the city of Magdala with the troops, and was the first to discover the body of the Emperor Theodore. He was made a Companion of the Bath in 1871 and, two years later, elected as a Fellow of the Royal Society (the President was General Sir Edward Sabine, who had served on Arctic expeditions under both John Ross and Parry). Not unexpectedly, Markham had come to know many people of influence, and did not hesitate to use his contacts in pressing home the continuing case for the Royal Navy to take up Arctic exploration once again. Both his and Osborn's ambitions had been made easier by the appointment of the Imperial-minded Benjamin Disraeli as Prime Minister. In November 1874, encouraged by the Royal Society and the Royal Geographic Society, Disraeli gave his consent in support of 'that spirit of maritime enterprise that has ever distinguished the English People.' Parliament voted to commit £100,000 towards the expedition.

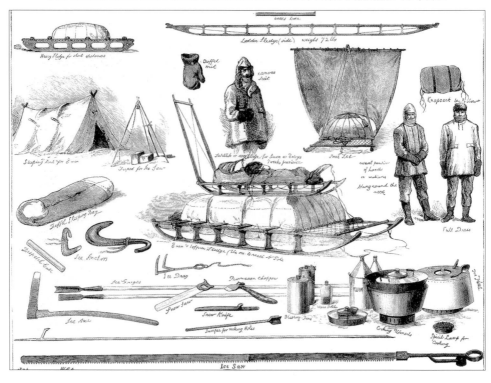

Above and below: Some of the Nares Expedition equipment.

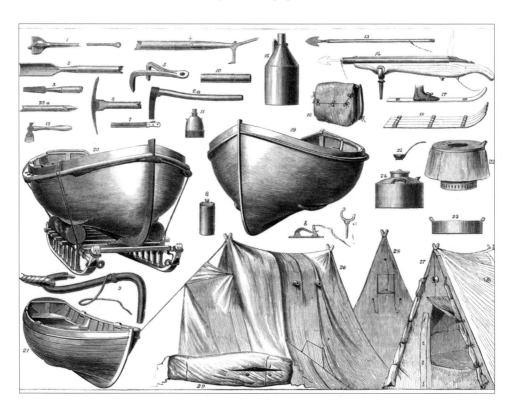

'Waiting to be Won' – a 1875 *Punch* cartoon.

WAITING TO BE WON.

Glad to be once more back in the hunt, the Admiralty lost little time in getting the proposed expedition launched. Two ships were commissioned and handed over to Portsmouth Dockyard where the Admiral Superintendent – Rear-Admiral Sir Leopold McClintock – personally involved himself in their preparation. HMS *Alert*, an eighteen-year-old steam sloop mounting seventeen 32lb guns, had already seen considerable service in foreign waters. She was given a seven-inch sheathing of teak, lined throughout with felt, and divided into watertight compartments. She was fitted to carry nine boats, three of which were fitted with swivel harpoon guns and three were light ice-boats with bows protected by copper sheeting. The Dundee whaler, *Bloodhound*, was purchased and commissioned as HMS *Discovery*. She was to carry a similar complement of ship's boats. Both ships had a figurehead of the Union Jack above the motto *Ubique*.

McClintock also supervised the preparation of the sledging equipment whilst Surgeon David Lyall – formerly of the *Terror* under Crozier and the *Assistance* under Belcher – and Paymaster James Lewis who had been in the *Resolute* under Austin and in the *Assistance* under Belcher, looked after the supplying of stores and provisions. Nearly 37,000lbs of canned meat were provided, along with 48,000lbs of biscuits, 100,000lbs of flour, 100 gallons each of gin, whisky, brandy, and champagne, 3,000 gallons of rum, 100lbs of curry paste, 8,000lbs of lime juice, and 500 tins of oysters. It had been intended to supply lemon juice as in previous expeditions, but it was found that commercial and political lobbying by West Indian lime growers had removed the markets normally giving access to the Mediterranean lemons – now only limes were available. A special brand of 'Arctic Ale' was provided by Allsopp the brewers, and Bryant and May provided tins of 'Arctic Matches'. A wide variety of games – including a football – were provided for the ships companies, and enough instruments for a drum and fife band. A piano and magic lantern were supplied for additional entertainment. Framed pictures were secured to the mess-deck bulkheads in the belief that, by staring at them, snow-blindness could be prevented. The Empress Eugenie contributed woollen caps for the seamen, and the ladies 'Christmas Box Committee' of Queenstown, Ireland, sent enough packages to ensure that both ship's companies received a gift at the appropriate season. The scientific work of the expedition was set out in a booklet *Scientific Instructions for the Arctic Expedition*. In it, senior

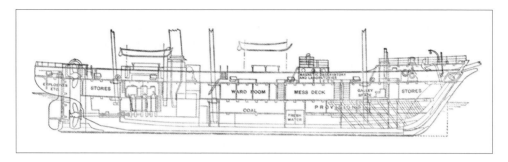

Sheer plan of the *Discovery*.

A 'nip' in Melville Bay, off the Devil's Thumb. (*Illustrated London News*, 22 May 1875.)

members of the Royal Society wrote suggestions for the study of astronomy, terrestrial magnetism, meteorology, atmospheric electricity, optics, zoology, botany, geology, and mineralogy.

To command the expedition, the Admiralty decided upon Captain George Strong Nares who, as a mate in HMS *Resolute* under Kellett, had gained considerable experience of sledging. Promoted to the post of lieutenant on his return, Nares took part in the Crimean War before serving as first lieutenant in the officer cadet training ship *Britannia*. On promotion to commander in 1862, he was appointed to the *Salamander* and sent to the Australian Station to survey the inside of the Barrier Reef and the Torres Straits. On the successful completion of the survey, Nares was ordered to the Mediterranean Station for further survey and oceanographical work.

In 1870, the Professor of Natural History at the University of Edinburgh suggested that the Admiralty should carry out a world-wide oceanographical survey. With Government approval gained, HMS *Challenger* was selected as the vessel for the work and Nares (promoted to captain in 1869) was appointed in command. His first lieutenant was Pelham Aldrich, a nephew of Captain Robert Aldrich who had been Austin's first lieutenant in the *Resolute*. After calling at Gibraltar, the Atlantic was crossed, Cape Town visited, and the ice of Antarctica encountered (the *Challenger* being the first steam-ship to cross the Antarctic Circle). At Hong Kong, Nares received news of his appointment to the *Alert* – the news also informed him that Aldrich was to be one of the officers on his new command. The *Challenger* continued on her hugely successful voyage under a new captain, her triumphal arrival home only marred by the loss of sixty-one seamen who succumbed to the lure of the diamond mines of South Africa and the gold mines of Australia.

The second in command of the *Alert* was Commander Albert Markham, a cousin and close friend of Clemence Markham. Having entered the Royal Navy in 1856, Albert Markham spent much of his early years on the China Station and earned a reputation as a brave and resourceful seaman. On one occasion, as a fifteen-year-old midshipman, he was given command of a boat with six seamen, the oldest of whom was aged nineteen. Following his orders, Markham boarded a Chinese pirate junk and, with his few young companions, captured it from forty men armed with cutlasses and pistols. He was later to see forty-eight such pirates line up to be beheaded one after the other. When he was aged twenty, Markham was given command of his own junk with a ship's company of twelve and twenty men borne for boarding the enemy. In his search for pirates he fell in with a large junk manned by eighty armed men which he captured after an engagement lasting four and a half hours with the loss of only five of his men. This action brought his promotion to lieutenant. During this period, Markham became a good friend of 'Chinese Gordon' – later General Charles George Gordon of Khartoum fame. In 1872, Markham was given command of the wooden steam-sloop, HMS *Rosario*, and ordered to carry out anti-slavery patrols off the Australian coast. Natives were being kidnapped from the South Sea islands and sold to Queensland planters for £3 each. Those unfortunates who were not purchased were decapitated and their heads sold to other natives as trophies. One slaver, operating out of Melbourne, was overhauled by Markham who boarded her in the knowledge that she was carrying slaves. On reaching the hold, however, all that could be discerned was the smell of fresh whitewash – all eighty slaves had been shot during the chase, thrown overboard, and their recent prison re-decorated. Realising that the real source of this human misery were the natives themselves in their eagerness to trade their fellow islanders to the slavers for trinkets, Markham embarked upon a campaign of action which led to the destruction of cannibal villages and the pursuit of rebel chiefs, whilst facing a hail of poisoned arrows. Markham's actions were criticised in some quarters, but they led to his promotion to commander on his return to England in 1872. Whilst on leave he took a voyage in the Dundee whaler *Arctic* and reported his experiences to Osborn. Two years later he was appointed to the *Alert*.

Captain George Strong Nares.

Above left: Commander Albert Markham.

Above right: Captain Henry Stephenson.

The newly promoted Captain Henry Stephenson was appointed to the *Discovery*. He had fought with distinction in the Crimean War, in the China War, and in the Indian Mutiny. He commanded a gun-boat on the Canadian Lakes during the Fenian disturbances before serving as flag-lieutenant to Admiral Sir Henry Keppel on the China Station. When the captain of the wooden steam-sloop, HMS *Rattler*, died, Stephenson was promoted to commander and appointed to take his place. The following year the *Rattler* was wrecked off the coast of Japan, but no blame was attached to Stephenson. Between 1871 and 1874 he was Commander of the Royal Yacht.

In addition to Aldrich, the *Alert*'s other officers were Lieutenant Alfred Parr, a gunnery expert who had served under Osborn; Lieutenant George Giffard, who had served under McClintock; Lieutenant William May who gave up a promising gunnery course to be with the expedition; and Sub-Lieutenant George Egerton. Staff-Surgeon Thomas Colan and Surgeon Edward Moss provided the medical staff. Appointed to the *Discovery* were Lieutenant Lewis Beaumont who, in addition to service in the Royal Yacht, was also a flagship gunnery officer; Lieutenant Robert Archer who had won his commission early through his examination results; Lieutenant Wyatt Rawson who had seen action, and was wounded during the Naval Brigade's march on Kumasi during the Ashanti War; Lieutenant Reginald Fulford, a member of a family who had provided the wife of John Davies of Davies Strait fame; and Sub-Lieutenant Crawford Conybeare. The *Discovery*'s medical staff comprised Surgeon Belgrave Ninnis and Surgeon Richard Coppinger. Lieutenant H.W. Fielden of the Royal Artillery was carried in the *Alert* as expedition naturalist whilst the Reverend C.E. Hodson looked after the expedition's spiritual requirements.

There was no difficulty in finding volunteers to complete the ships companies. One captain sent a message to Nares; 'An order has come to my ship for volunteers. What am I to do? The whole ship's company, nearly 800 men, have given in their names.' Where practicable, all applicants were interviewed, the most searching question being; 'Can you sing or dance? Or what can you do for the amusement of others?' (Markham had taken lessons in 'prestidigitation' in order to entertain his ship-mates.)

The expedition sailed from Portsmouth on 29 May 1875. Vast crowds thronged the harbour walls waving and cheering as the ships passed. A scarlet-coated guard of honour provided by the local garrison came to attention as their band crashed out 'Auld Lang Syne' to a background of ship's sirens and hooters. Small boats full of well-wishers bobbed alongside, and Sir Leopold and Lady McClintock waved from the deck of their yacht. It seemed as if the whole of England was keen to send Nares and his men off in style, and to celebrate the return to Arctic discovery. There was only one shadow that darkened the day – Rear-Admiral Sherard Osborn, who for a decade or more had pressed the Government and Admiralty to support such an expedition, had died three weeks before the sailing.

Lieutenant A. Parr.

Lieutenant G.A. Giffard.

Lieutenant W.H. May.

Sub-Lieutenant G.L. Egerton.

Lieutenant L.A. Beaumont.

Lieutenant R.E. Archer.

Lieutenant W. Rawson.

Above left: The Revd C.E. Hodson.

Above right: Lieutenant R.B. Fulford.

The *Alert* and *Discovery* were accompanied across the Atlantic by the old paddle-steamer, HMS *Valourous*, employed to carry the expedition's excess stores. She also carried Clemence Markham, desperately keen to oversee his and Osborn's brainchild for as long as he could. The *Valourous*, taking Markham with her, separated from the expedition ships at Godhavn once the stores had been transferred. At Upernavick the ships took on a Danish interpreter, Niels Christian Petersen, and sledge-dogs – with no real expectation of being able to use either. As they were leaving the settlement, fog fell and Nares accepted the services of two Eskimos in kayaks to lead him to a safe anchorage. Instead, they led him directly on to a beach just as the tide was falling. The hours of waiting for the return of the tide were spent sending the ships companies ashore to wash their clothes.

Nares met the 'middle ice' of Baffin's Bay in the early hours of the morning of 24 July. He decided to press straight into it in the hope that his steam engines would force a way through. The gamble paid off and, thirty-six hours later, the two ships emerged the other side to see clear waters stretching ahead into Smith

Left: A family wave farewell to Nares' ships.

Opposite above: The *Valorous* among icebergs.

Opposite below: Seamen dancing with Eskimo women at Godhavn.

Left: Far Away.

Below: Alert and *Discovery* in the harbour at Godhavn.

Sound and beyond. A message was left in a cairn erected on Littleton Island and a visit was made to Port Foulke in case the expedition might have to retreat there for the winter. Smith Sound was then crossed to the western shore and pack ice was met off Cape Albert and Victoria Head. The ships were trapped for a short time but Stephenson, positioning himself on the bowsprit of the *Discovery*, charged the ice with such force that each collision buried the bows of the ship up to the foremast. In the meantime, Nares busied himself correcting both Kane's and Haye's charts and bringing them back to the positions originally laid down by Inglefield. Free of the ice by 8 August, depots were established on the coast as they pushed on to the north. Kennedy Channel was found to be clear of ice and Hall Basin was entered on the twenty-fifth.

Once again ice forced the ships to stop and Nares took the two vessels into a sheltered harbour ('Discovery Harbour') that was protected from the ice by an island ('Bellot Island') guarding its entrance. To the south lay open water ('Lady Franklin Sound') with a broad opening to the south-west. To the east, directly across Hall Basin, lay Polaris Bay with its Thank God Harbour and Hall's grave. Nares decided that he would be lucky to find any site better than Discovery harbour and ordered Stephenson to secure his ship there for the winter whilst he probed even further north.

Taking Lieutenant Rawson and seven men with him from Stephenson's ship, Nares attempted to get the *Alert* out of Discovery Harbour on the twenty-sixth and made his way up a wide lane between the shore and the ice. However, he was forced back when the ice threatened to close in on him. Two days later he tried again and reached Lincoln Bay before being caught in the pack ice. It was his worst fear, to be trapped in the ice, and the ship drifted south, back along the route he had so successfully navigated. However, at high water, the ice was seen to slacken. Seizing the moment, and with his stokers desperately feeding coal into the boiler fires, 'a greater pressure of steam than had been exerted even during the official steam trial, the ship commenced to move.' Within hours Nares had reached the safety of Lincoln Bay.

A strong gale on 1 September drove the *Alert* up the western coast of the Robeson Channel beyond Hall's Cape Union and, at 82 degrees, 24' N, Nares ran up the White Ensign at the peak to celebrate the highest latitude ever reached by a ship. The wind was lost as the ship turned ever more to the north-west and Nares used steam to drive the *Alert* between the ice and the shore until, that evening, ice once again brought their progress to a halt. Nares was alongside a shallow bay ('Floeberg Beach'), already filling with ice, with solid pack to the north and no further open water to the west. Anchoring close enough to the shore to protect the ship from any large ice floes, Nares sent Markham and Aldrich to the west to see if there was a better harbour available should the ice allow passage in the next few days. They were soon back. A harbour had been found, but it was blocked off completely by heavy, grounded, ice. Rawson, sent to the east, came back after two days to report that the ice had closed in behind them. It was clear that Floeberg Beach was to be the wintering site for the *Alert*.

Left: Alert being cut into Floeberg Beach.

Opposite: Alert in her winter quarters.

Preparing to start a sledge journey.

Whilst depots were established along the coast to the west by Aldrich, Fielden and Moss, many eyes looked out across the solid jumble of ice to the north. Hall had claimed to see land in that direction, but nothing could be seen from the *Alert*, or by her sledging parties.

Three weeks after their arrival, Aldrich set off to pioneer a route around Cape Joseph Henry (seen and named by Hall, but 30 degrees out on his charts). Just inland from the cape both he and Petty Officer Adam Ayles (2nd Captain of the Foretop) climbed a 2,000ft mountain to celebrate the fact that they were north of Parry's highest latitude. Again no land was seen to the north. Markham, in company with Lieutenants Parr and May, had set out to establish depots at Cape Joseph Henry. He achieved his goal, but returned with eight of his party suffering from frostbite – several toes and fingers were lost to amputation. Rawson had been sent by Nares in an attempt to reach the *Discovery* in order to inform Stephenson of the *Alert*'s position. He returned after ten days, his route blocked just nine miles to the south by thirty-foot high floes pressing up against the cliffs. An attempt to continue over the land had failed when they came across valleys filled with soft snow. All the expeditions had suffered from broken sledges. It was discovered that they had been built too rigid for the deeply hummocked ice they had to face. The answer proved to require nothing more than the removal of the metal pins that connected the uprights to the upper part of the sledge, and their replacement by lengths of hide lashing. The sledges then worked well.

All those involved with the autumn sledging had been novices, and lessons had to be learned at the cost of lost fingers and toes, duckings in the icy waters, and broken sledges. But, when all were safely back, Nares could note that they had 'returned in wonderful spirits and full of pluck.' He then set about preparing the *Alert* for the rapidly approaching winter. The ship was housed over and the upper deck covered in trampled snow. Stores and provisions were placed ashore and

Chief Petty Officer Adam Ayles who, as a petty officer, served as a sledge captain to Lieutenant Aldrich. His name has been given to Ayles Fiord, Ayles Bay and Ayles Ice Shelf.

Rawson, with great difficulty as the snow seemed to be of a different consistency to that met at lower latitudes, built large igloos on the shore to house the scientific instruments. The officers set up schools that ran for five days every week. Thursday was reserved for lectures, 'songs in character', and readings. The ship's armourer occupied his time during the winter months by manufacturing wedding rings out of gold sovereigns given to him for that purpose by the officers. On 5 November – Guy Fawke's Day – a firework-stuffed 'Guy' was mounted on a barrel and paraded around the upper deck as the drum and fife band played the 'Rogue's March'. It was then placed on a large hummock of ice, set on fire, and danced around by the ship's company until frostbite threatened the fife players' lips and fingers. Surgeon Moss completed the night's entertainment by constructing a hot-air balloon out of coloured paper. Unfortunately, before the balloon ascended to any great height it caught fire and vanished in a cloud of spiralling ash. In the middle of the same month the 'Royal Arctic Theatre' was established. It was managed by Markham and was 'under the distinguished patronage of Captain Nares and all the nobility and gentry of the neighbourhood.' To a background of scenery painted by 'Professor' Moss and with actors wearing wigs of oakum (unpicked rope) and costumes of eider-down quilts and musk-ox skins, the favourite show was 'Aladdin, or the Wonderful Scamp'. Lieutenant Gifford played Aladdin ('more fortunate than he deserved to be'), and Fielden trod the boards as 'The Widow Twanky, Aladdin's ancient mother, who in her youth had never been beautiful, and who had not grown more lovely in her old age.' The music was arranged by 'Signore Aldrichi'. On 21 October – Trafalgar Day – the officers celebrated with the customary dinner. In honour of the occasion, an extra glass of wine was allowed, and the slightly amended version of Nelson's signal 'England expects every man *this day* to do his duty' was taken by the officers to mean that no scrap of food should be left on their plates. It was, however, not all fun and laughter. The mean temperature throughout the winter was -58.9 degrees Fahrenheit, the lowest reading – which lasted for five days – registered -66.29 degrees Fahrenheit. The mercury froze solid for a total of thirty days. Yet, everyday, the measurement of the scientific instruments were taken and recorded and, as soon as the first glimmer of light appeared in January, Sub-Lieutenant Egerton was out on the ice exercising the dogs.

On the first day of March 1876, Nares decided to open communications with the *Discovery*. He was especially keen that Stephenson should start to explore the coastline in the region of Discovery Harbour, and to send a party across to the north coast of Greenland. Rawson, accompanied by Egerton driving the dog-sledge and the interpreter Petersen, set off four days later to cover the seventy-six miles that separated the two ships. By the eighth they were back on board

Entertainment at the Royal Arctic Theatre.

carrying Petersen on the sledge. He had contracted severe frostbite. Moss had no option but to amputate both the Dane's feet. Petersen never recovered, and died three months later. On the twentieth, in temperatures of -30 degrees Fahrenheit, Rawson and Egerton set off again taking with them two seamen. Six days later they reached the *Discovery* to find that Stephenson and his ship's company had enjoyed a 'fair share of mirthful relaxation' during the winter.

Nares, in the meantime, began his preparations for the season's sledging journeys. He had decided that Markham and Parr would head out to Cape Joseph Henry before launching themselves out across the ice in the direction of the North Pole. They would haul two boats with them for use in ferrying across wide cracks in the ice and, if necessary, for navigation if open water was encountered. The two boat sledges (*Marco Polo* for Markham and *Victoria* for Parr) would be accompanied by three other sledges – *Bulldog, Alexandra,* and *Bloodhound* – 'as far as their provisions would allow.' Accompanying Markham's party as far as Cape Joseph Henry would be Aldrich and Giffard with the sledges *Challenger* and *Poppie*. They were then to continue on as far to the west as they could, charting the coastline of northern Grant Land (Ellesmere Island). Provisions for seventy days were to be taken. Some crews opted for extra tea rather than rum, but, apart from two bottles taken by Markham, no lime juice was carried as it had been discovered that it froze in the containers and required such a large amount of fuel to thaw it out that it became impractical to carry.

The *Alert* sledge party on their way to *Discovery*.

On the morning of 3 April, seven sledges and fifty-three officers and men stood ready for the journey ahead of them. Each sledge flew its commander's pennant and the boats flew a White Ensign and Union Jack. Additional colour was added by the seamen themselves. They had been ordered to decorate the backs of their canvas 'snow-jumpers' with any design that was to their taste so as to break up the monotony of the white surroundings in the vision of the man behind them on the sledge traces – 'the result being a display of comic blazonry.' Around everyone's heels raced Nellie – Markham's dog. She was to accompany her master to the north wearing flannel moccasins to protect her feet. Nares led prayers followed by the singing of 'God, from whom all blessings flow'. Then, with three cheers, the sledge parties set off.

The route to Cape Joseph Henry proved to be extremely difficult. The sledges had to be hauled over continuous ranks of ice hummocks and, where the ridges were too high or their sides too steep, a road had to be cut through with pickaxe and shovel. Parr set the pace and 'worked like a horse', wrenching aside the ice and clearing a path for the sledges. It took a week to reach the cape. There the auxiliary sledges returned to the *Alert* and the main sledging teams separated, Aldrich to continue westwards as Markham, Parr, and fifteen seamen struck out for the north.

There was no improvement for Markham's teams as they lined their sledges up with the 63rd meridian. The men soon became exhausted after a series of 'standing starts' were needed to move the sledges and, when the men had to haul one sledge forward and then come back for the other, the distance covered was tripled. Four days after they had said farewell to Aldrich, one of Markham's sledge crew complained of pains in his knees and ankles. On the sixteenth, another man began to exhibit the same symptoms. Just over a week from Cape Joseph Henry, Markham was forced to abandon the larger of his two boats as a third man fell ill.

A sledge party from the *Alert* making a push for the Pole.

Nights were spent huddled beneath blanket bags as Markham read extracts from Dickens's 'Old Curiosity Shop'.

The 83rd parallel, the highest point known to have been reached by man, was crossed on the twenty-fourth. Three days later, two more men became ill, but still the sledges were inched forward with every man who could hauling on the drag-ropes. Fog slowed things down for a day or two at the end of the month, yet any enforced rest seemed to do little to restore the invalids. On 2 May, Markham and Parr raised for the first time the possibility that scurvy might be the cause of their problems – the men, however, were not told. On the sixth, Markham noted in his journal that the sick men 'were perfectly helpless and require assistance in every little detail connected with their dressing, being totally incapacitated from doing anything themselves.' After a further three days, another three men began to complain of aches in their joints and found themselves incapable of eating.

On 10 May, Markham assessed his situation. Five men were totally disabled and, for much of the time had to be carried on the sledges. Five others showed clear signs of scurvy and some of the remaining men were affected by frostbite and snow-blindness. It had taken them forty days to reach their position and they had only thirty days' provisions to get them back. He decided that enough was enough – they had reached their furthest north. Writing in his diary, Markham noted:

> We felt that the absence of any greater success could not be attributed either to a lack of energy or of perseverance. It was, however, a bitter ending to all our aspirations, for which even the knowledge of our being homeward bound failed to compensate. In justice to my brave companions I must say that no men could have done more under the same circumstances.

Two days rest were taken as Markham and Parr repeatedly checked their position and carried out scientific measurements. The bottom was sounded through a crack in the ice and was found at 71 fathoms (426 feet). On the twelfth, leaving five invalids in the tents and two men to look after them, Markham and Parr took the remaining eight men to achieve the highest latitude possible. With flags and pennants flying they struggled for two hours to cover just one mile. There the artificial horizon was set up and their position fixed. It proved to be 83 degrees, 20' 26" North – 399 miles from the pole. Stamping their feet to keep out the cold, the seamen and officers raised their voices to sing 'The Union Jack of Old England', followed by a composition of their own, the 'Grand Palaeocrystic Sledging Chorus'. Finally, after Markham had planted a silk Union Jack that had been worked for him by Lady McClintock, the assembled group roared out 'God Save the Queen'. The motto on Markham's sledge pennant could have applied to them all – 'I dare do all that may become a man; who dares do more is none.'

On their return to the tents, Markham produced a bottle of whisky, the consumption of which led to many toasts and more singing. The following day, with heavy snow falling, the sledges began their return to the ship. The journey should have been easier as the road they had cut on their outward passage still remained, but the effects of the scurvy – particularly the sufferer's inability to eat and their constant thirst – bore down on everyone. Soon most were affected by the 'Marco Polo limp' and Markham observed that there were only 'four and a half sound pairs of legs in the whole party.' Eleven days after they had left their furthest north, and with 'Old Joe' (Cape Joseph Henry) looming on the horizon, Markham hoisted flags and issued all with a drink to toast the Queen's birthday. He also revealed that he had carried with him two bottles of lime juice which he now proposed to share out amongst the most sick. The contents of both bottles were frozen solid and, when he tried to thaw one out in front of a stove, the glass cracked and the contents were lost. Undaunted, Markham then took the other bottle into his sleeping bag with him and placed it between his legs. Despite an uncomfortable night, the next morning produced such a tiny amount of thawed lime juice that there was hardly enough for the smallest sip by the invalids.

On the twenty-seventh, five of the men were in a 'precarious condition' and had to be carried on the sledges. The five others could do no more than hobble painfully in the sledge tracks. With only two officers and two men 'effective', Markham decided to abandon the last boat. It was a difficult decision. Its weight helped reduce progress to a slow crawl, but icicles could be seen hanging from many of the hummocks. That could only mean that the temperature was rising and there was an increasing risk that the ice beneath their feet – especially as they approached the coast – would melt to a depth that would not bear their weight. They had to get off the ice as quickly as possible. On the last day of the month, just two days after they had raised their flags and drunk a toast to mark the first anniversary of their leaving England, one of the sledges went through the ice. It

Furthest North.

took a desperate struggle to hold on to the drag-lines whilst the invalids were pushed clear and the stragglers could add their enfeebled weight to the rescue. Before long, the surface of the ice had melted to such an extent that the few men able to haul had to wade through several inches of freezing water. Even worse, the road had been lost and a new one had to be hacked out across the crumbling hummocks. At last, on 5 June, the party found rock beneath their feet and could rest with the threat of the ice breaking up behind them. They had landed close by a depot which, when opened, revealed a note which told Markham that the site had been visited only two days earlier. It also told him that scurvy had broken out on the *Alert* and that Petersen had died.

They were now forty miles from the ship, but there was no strength left in the party. The few who had avoided scurvy, and on whom the burden of hauling had fallen, were exhausted, and the rest were capable of doing little more than attempting to survive. Markham knew that someone had to go for help. As the leader, he could not go, but Parr volunteered and set off alone on the seventh. The following day, George Porter, a Royal Marine gunner on Parr's sledge 'received that summons to which we all must at some time attend.' A grave was dug in the iron-hard ground and the body carried to it on a flag-draped sledge. Two sledge battens were used to form a cross marking the site. The internment was followed by a meal of preserved potatoes and bacon fat – the only food the invalids could eat whilst suffering from swollen gums.

The burial of Royal Marine Private George Porter.

Two days after Parr had left, on the afternoon of 9 June, a movement was seen among the hummocks to the south-east. Then the sound of loud yelling came across the ice. To the relief of all in the party, a dog-sledge driven by May, accompanied by Moss, hoved into view. Soon lime juice – well wrapped to keep it from freezing – was being issued, followed by a hot meal of mutton for those who could manage it. The following day, Nares himself arrived with a larger party. Out of the fifteen seamen and marines who had set out under Markham and Parr, one had died and eleven had to be carried on the rescue sledges. Only three, and Markham himself, were able to make the journey on foot. As they came alongside the *Alert*, three cheers of welcome rang out and prayers said in gratitude for their safe return.

On parting company with Markham on 11 April, Lieutenants Aldrich and Gifford and their sledge parties rounded Cape Joseph Henry and began to follow the shore closely – often finding difficulty in distinguishing land from ice. New names were soon appearing on the chart kept by Aldrich. 'James Ross Bay' and 'Crozier Island' were followed by 'Cape Hecla' and 'Clemence Markham Inlet'.

On the twenty-fifth, just short of 'Gifford Peninsula', George Gifford brought Aldrich's sledging rations up to forty-four days before setting out to return to the *Alert*.

Both sledges had experienced difficulty with deep, soft, snow and Aldrich urged his men on from standing pulls by shouting 'Main topsail, haul!' As well as being delayed by the soft snow, the succession of hummocks and floes piled up against the shore made exhausting work of the sledge-hauling. Just under three weeks after leaving the ship, Aldrich noted in his log that one of his men 'has just shown me a very ugly looking red patch or blotch just above the ankle; the limb is slightly swollen.' Ten days later he wrote: 'The men are nearly all suffering a great deal with their unfortunate legs, which appear to get worse every day … somehow the men do not appear up to the mark.'

Just to the west of 'Ward Hunt Island' (named after the First Lord of the Admiralty) which guarded the entrance to 'Disraeli Bay' (Disraeli Fiord) Aldrich noted that his men were 'less lively than usual'. The unremitting effort, combined with aching joints, was beginning to take its toll, but the seamen still heaved on the drag-ropes without complaint. The mouth of a wide bay ('Yelverton Bay') was reached on 15 May. It took them three days to cross its floe-barred entrance and, once the far shore had been reached, Aldrich decided that he had reached the limit of his men's endurance. Leaving two weakened men under the care of another seaman, he pressed on with the rest of his party to a stretch of low shore which he named 'Alert Point'. There he unfurled the Union Flag and drank the health of his sovereign at 82 degrees, 16', North and 85 degrees, 33' West. From Alert Point the land seemed to trend to the south, curving away into the far horizon.

A rest day was taken before HM Sledge *Challenger* was hauled round for the return journey. The health of most of the men continued to decline and, by the end of the month, Aldrich recorded that 'The men are regularly done.' A week later, on 7 June, four men began to complain of sore gums and Petty Officer James Doidge – the *Alert*'s Captain of the Foretop – asked Aldrich 'Is scurvy ever got while sledging, Sir?' Aldrich assured him that such a thing did not happen and blamed the sore gums on the biscuits they had been eating. Over the next few days conditions worsened dramatically. William Wood, a Royal Marine sergeant, collapsed and had to be carried on the sledge. Two other men, the *Alert*'s shipwright and blacksmith, were incapable of pulling and could only limp alongside. Two days later they were joined by two other seamen leaving just Aldrich and Petty Officer Ayles to pull the sledge on their hands and knees. On the seventeenth, so bad had matters become, that Aldrich's exhausted fingers wrote in his log 'I hope we shall come out all right'. That day, he and Ayles had started out hauling the sledge with four men riding on it. When this became too difficult, the invalids were taken off and told to make their way as best they could in the sledge tracks. After two and a half hours of gruelling effort, Aldrich and Ayles stopped and pitched camp. It took another four hours before the last of the seamen limped up to them. The following day, Aldrich decided to try something new.

Perhaps his men were depending upon Ayles and him too much and needed to be shaken out of their lethargy. With the ice melting, and several inches of water lapping around his ankles, he unloaded a collapsible boat from the sledge, filled it with 130lbs of provisions to reduce the sledge weight, and marched off towards Cape Joseph Henry after ordering his men to get the sledge moving. After staying out of sight for some time, he returned to find the men heaving under the command of Ayles. With their best effort they could only advance the sledge for five or six yards before stopping to get their breath. They had come only a short distance, but Aldrich was full of admiration for their full-hearted determination. 'Nothing', he wrote, 'could exceed the patience and endurance they showed.'

The morning of the twentieth found Aldrich dragging his boat and provisions. He had decided that if the sledge proved quite impossible to move, he would be able to haul the boat whilst the others walked in his wake with him providing the supplies. That way, they might just get back to the ship. The sledge itself was being dragged forward in a succession of slow heaves with one invalid riding on it. The painful monotony was broken when a pole was seen sticking up out of the ice. It had been placed there by Moss as a marker when searching for Markham's party. They had not long passed the pole, with Aldrich out in front dragging his boat, when the sharp crack of a gunshot rent the air. A shout followed and Aldrich replied with a shouted 'Challenger!' Turning round he ran back to the sledge and told his men to pitch camp immediately before returning to his boat. There he was met by May driving the dog-sledge accompanied by Able Seaman Malley. Nares had sent them out when the degree of scurvy had finally become apparent. He had realised that, if the disease had broken out amongst Markham's men, and onboard the *Alert*, Aldrich's team must be at risk. Before long the invalids were being carried back to the ship two at a time, but not before Aldrich, who had learned of the death of Gunner George Porter, had the cross over the man's grave temporarily removed – he did not want his men to be further depressed by the sight of their messmate's last resting place. It took five days before Aldrich saw the last of his men to safety. As he began to approach the ship he was met by Nares and Markham and, once again, Floeberg Beach echoed to the cheers of welcome. The next day, Nares wrote 'It is pleasant to hear Aldrich playing the piano in his usual cheerful manner.' It was, however, no time to relax – there was still one expedition out on the ice.

Three days after Markham and Aldrich had left the *Alert*, Lieutenant Lewis Beaumont, Surgeon Coppinger, and sixteen men set off from the *Discovery*. Their instructions from Stephenson were that they were to carry out the orders given by Nares that the north coast of Greenland should be explored. It had been decided that the best plan would be for the party to visit the *Alert* where they could be joined by a sledge-party under Rawson after topping up their supplies. Their first destination was reached on the sixteenth and, four days later, four sledges – the *Sir Edward Parry, Discovery, Stephenson,* and *Alert* – left Floeberg Beach along the route pioneered by Rawson the previous autumn. Upon reaching the coast of Greenland on the twenty-eighth, one of the support sledges was sent back, the party having reached Rawson's furthest. It had been planned that the route would remain on the shore as this would guarantee a return road if the ice melted during the journey back to the *Discovery*, but the cliffs were so high that the ice had to be resorted to in order to get around them. On 5 May, Cape Stanton was reached and Coppinger separated to begin his return journey. The following day, one of the seamen, Able Seaman James Hand, whilst crossing a bay that was to bear his name, informed Beaumont that his legs felt stiff and painful. The news caused grave concern to Beaumont who had read of Lieutenant Hobson's difficulties in McClintock's *Voyage of the Fox*. When Hand began to complain of sore gums, Beaumont talked the matter over with his sledge captain, Alexander Gray, the *Discovery*'s Ice-Master. Gray, with his whaling experience, confirmed Beaumont's fears – Hand appeared to be suffering from scurvy. Five days after Coppinger departed, Rawson and his team were sent back carrying Hand on their sledge. Knowing the urgency of his mission, Rawson pressed on hard only to find that all his men were becoming affected by scurvy. One by one they had to drop out of the traces to limp alongside the sledge. By the time the party reached the depot at Polaris Bay, only Rawson and one other man was capable of hauling. Rawson was blind-folded, his eyes closed with pain from snow-blindness. Hours after they arrived, Able Seaman Hand was dead.

Having buried their messmate, and with the pressing urgency now lessened, the party rested for four days. Just as they were about to continue their journey to the *Discovery*, they fell in with Lieutenant Fulford and Coppinger who were just returning from a survey of Petermann Fiord. Fulford took charge of the sick and, on the twenty-eighth, Rawson and Coppinger set off with the dog-sledge (driven by Hans, the *Discovery*'s Eskimo dog-driver) in pursuit of Beaumont who, they felt, must be in great danger.

After Rawson's departure on the eleventh, Beaumont and his six remaining men pushed on to cross 'St George's Fiord' to 'Dragon Point' where 'a wide reach of bays and fiords' presented them with a complex choice of routes. To the north lay nothing but heaped-up ice. To the north-east, a bold cape ('Cape May') could be seen, with, beyond it, a mountain Beaumont named 'Mount Hooker' after the distinguished botanist. South of Cape May, another tall hill received the name 'Mount Coppinger'. To his south-east, Beaumont was faced with a deep, wide, fiord ('Sherard Osborn Fiord'), its entrance guarded by 'Castle' and 'Reef' islands. He decided to cross the fiord entrance to reach its far shore and attempt to climb Mount Hooker.

The progress was made desperately slow by deep, powdery, soft snow. Before long, three of his men were complaining of aching joints and, at times, the sledge could only be moved by the whole party crawling on their hands and knees. A week after they had started out from Dragon Point the sledge could be dragged forward only ten or twelve yards at a time. On the nineteenth, barely a mile was covered during the whole day. It was Beaumont's birthday and he noted in his log that he did not 'want to be wished any happy returns of it.' The situation was worsened by the lack of any close visual reference. What had seemed a mere mile away was still in the distance after five hours of hauling. On the twentieth, Beaumont called a halt. It was quite clear that his men were not going to reach the fiord's eastern shore. The tent was pitched on the ice and, once Beaumont had seen to his men's comfort, he set off with Gray towards the land. After just two hours, the two men found themselves up to their waists in snow and with fog rolling down from the cliffs ahead of them. With no option but to turn back, they reached the tent after an absence of almost ten hours, only to find two men with clear signs of scurvy. There seemed to be no other choice but to head for the *Discovery* at their best speed. Fog and falling snow held them up for two days and it was not until late on the twenty-second that the sledge was able to get under way with two men limping alongside. Two days later the skies cleared and Beaumont found himself looking back at the beckoning sight of Mount Hooker. He decided on one last attempt and, leaving the two invalids in the tent, turned eastwards once more and, with the remaining seamen, made a dash towards his goal. This time they were successful and, standing on the 3,700-foot peak, Beaumont looked out across an immense view of fiords, islands, and mountains. Just to the east of north he could see an island ('Beaumont Island') with a hill he named 'Mount Albert' after the Queen's late consort. Further to the east, across the ice of 'Victoria Inlets', could be seen the craggy cliffs of 'Cape Britannia', the inlets themselves being separated by 'Stephenson Island'. To the south, a land of mountain ridges marched into the blue distance. Satisfied that he had done his best, Beaumont returned to the sledge and, despite being reduced to four men hauling, the tent was reached after just twelve hours.

A day after setting out for the ship, Beaumont, desperate to lighten the load, removed 200lbs of provisions from the sledge and made a depot at Dragon Point. He was now on the bare minimum of rations. Five days later, two men were crawling in the sledge tracks as the others – apart from Beaumont and Gray – were reduced to hobbling. Soon, two men were being carried on the sledge as the party trudged on with great, but wearied, resolution. Repulse Harbour was reached on 10 June and Beaumont considered the possibility of heading for the *Alert*, some thirty-five miles away across the ice, rather than attempting the forty miles to Polaris Bay. But the rotten state of the ice prevented any departure from the coast at that point. Continuing down the coast, the party began to turn inland rather than go around the high ground at Cape Brevoort. As they circled the eastern slopes of a tall hill they found themselves in a rocky defile ('Gap Valley'). With only Beaumont and Gray capable of hauling, the sledge could not be moved and it seemed as if the limit of their endurance had arrived. Beaumont, however, refusing to consider failure and urging his weakened team on, unloaded the sledge and had its load carried forward in a slow procession of limping men. He and Gray then returned for the sledge and dragged it painfully over the rocks whilst a gale roared in their faces. At the end of the day, everyone was so exhausted there was no energy left to erect the tent and the night was spent with the worst of the sick men lying on the sledge covered by the canvas sledge-sail. They lay together 'huddled up in a heap, wet through, and nobody could sleep.' For three days, by sheer leadership and example, Beaumont led his men down the valley until, on the nineteenth, they found themselves on the northern shore of Newman Bay (Newman Fiord). Two days later, off the shore of Hall Land, Beaumont's sledge crew could only walk a few paces before stopping to catch their breath. Less than a mile was covered, and Beaumont was beginning to feel the ache of scurvy in his own legs. On the twenty-fourth, he knew the game was up. His men had reached the end of their tether. They had done more than could have been imagined, and then gone further still. Only Gray and one other man were capable of the simple act of walking – and then in great pain. Beaumont decided that they should rest before one last effort be made to reach the shore of Hall Land south of the high ground. There a level plain connected Newman Bay across the peninsula to Hall Basin and Polaris Bay. He would then set out for the depot at Polaris Bay to see if there was anyone there to help him. If there was not, he intended to return to the sledge and upon 'sending Jones and Gray, who could still walk, to the depot, remain with the sick and get them on as the best I could.'

On the morning of the twenty-fifth, Beaumont began the gruelling last haul to the shore. Every step over the broken ice floes was racked with pain as he urged his exhausted body on. Grey and Jones lent a hand as best they could with two men riding on the sledge and the remainder plodding numbly behind. They had not gone far when they looked up to see the astonishing and exhilarating sight of three men and a dog-sledge racing across the ice towards them. Much to the relief of all, Beaumont 'soon had the pleasure of shaking hands with Rawson and Dr Coppinger.'

With the minimum of delay, the two worst invalid cases were put on the dog-sledge and driven by Hans – accompanied by Coppinger – to Polaris Bay. Rawson and Beaumont continued hauling the sledge with two men riding on top and another two walking slowly behind. The following day, Hans returned with the dog-sledge and a message from Coppinger – one of the invalids, Able Seaman Charles Paul, had died before the depot had been reached.

Beaumont, Rawson, and the last of the men limped up to the Polaris Bay depot on 31 June. A camp was set up where the six could recuperate whilst waiting for the ice of Hall Basin to break up and allow the party to cross to Discovery Harbour by boats previously brought across by Fulford. They finally arrived alongside the *Discovery* in the last week of August to find that their experience of scurvy had not been unique. They now brought the number of scurvy cases onboard up to twenty.

At Floeberg Beach, Nares found he had forty men down with the disease. It was, to him, 'most inexplicable.' Before sailing, the Navy's Medical Director General had assured him that there would be no scurvy during the first year. Some cases might be expected during the second year, and only if a third season was spent in the Arctic could he expect any serious problems. The difficulties he now faced were more serious than he had ever expected. Three men had already been lost to the scourge and a further sixty were in its grip. Between them, the *Alert* and the *Discovery* had fifty per cent of the expedition's members rendered incapable through scurvy. There was little sign, or even chance, of recovery for many of them unless they gained access to fresh food at the earliest opportunity. If he remained where he was for another year in order to try once more for the North Pole, there was every likelihood that large numbers of his men would succumb to the disease over the winter and, in all probability, there would not be enough fit men left to mount such an expedition.

Left: Nares in Polar dress.

Opposite: The *Pandora* in the ice.

Alongside his difficulties with scurvy, he could look at the achievements his expedition had secured. Markham's party had reached further north than anyone before. Aldrich had surveyed the northernmost coast of Grant Land, and Beaumont had reached out far across the top of Greenland. Also from the *Discovery*, Lieutenant Robert Archer had probed the opening at the head of Lady Franklin Sound and discovered a deep, cliff-lined, fiord ('Archer Fiord'). Fulford and Coppinger had crossed Hall Basin and surveyed Petermann Fiord. A full year of meteorological, magnetic, tidal, and ice movement measurements had been taken at a more northerly position than ever before. Natural history, geological, astronomical, and botanical studies had been carried out at the highest latitude reached by any expedition. Only the achievement of the North Pole itself remained, and – after Markham's experience – Nares was not convinced it was possible with the equipment he carried, nor was it worth the glory when compared with the lives of so many of his men. Accordingly, he decided to return home.

On 31 July the waters around Floeberg Beach were clear of ice and the *Alert* found no difficulty in leaving her home of the past year. Ice was met off Cape Union at the entrance to Robeson Channel but the pack was loose and the ship drifted with it south to Cape Beechey where they were stopped by a frozen barrier twenty miles short of Discovery Harbour. Nares sent Egerton and one seaman across to the coast with orders to make their way to the *Discovery* and inform Stephenson of the situation. The following day, Rawson turned up having been sent by the *Discovery*'s captain to confirm that all the sledging expeditions had returned safely from the Greenland side of Hall Basin.

Using a combination of ice-saws and pick-axes, the *Alert*'s ship's company forced a passage through the ice and arrived off Discovery Harbour on 9 August. They waited for eleven days for the ice to clear in Lady Franklin Sound and set off south on 30 August. Kennedy Channel and Kane Basin presented little difficulty until they reached Cape Victoria (Victoria Head) where a barrier of ice required the ships to charge the floes together 'line abreast' in order to make it give way. A party was landed at Cape Isabella and a cache of letters for them was found in a cairn. They had been deposited by Allen Young who had brought the *Pandora* into Smith's Sound at the request of the Admiralty. Young's original intention had been to try for a second time to sail through the Northwest Passage, but the Admiralty request had sent him in search of Nares. Stopped by ice, he had retreated to Upernavick before deciding to return home in mid-September.

Nares reached the *Discovery* on 25 September and crossed the Arctic Circle just over a week later. On 6 October the two ships fell in with Allen Young and the *Pandora*. Nares was concerned the faster yacht would arrive home with his news before he did, but Young merely shortened sail and removed his fears by offering to remain in company until he left to call in at Falmouth. HM Ships *Alert* and *Discovery* sailed into Portsmouth Harbour to a welcome of military bands, cheers, and salutes. The Queen sent a message of congratulations to the expedition and Nares was created a Knight Commander of the Bath. The Royal Geographical Society awarded him their Founder's Medal and the Geographical Society of Paris awarded him their gold medal. A special silver medal, suspended from a white ribbon, was designed and awarded to all who had been involved, including the crew of the *Pandora*. Markham was promoted to captain; Aldrich, Beaumont, and

Parr were made commanders; and Crawford Conybeare became a lieutenant. May, Egerton, Archer, Rawson, and Fulford had their services 'favourably noted'. Nares could not be promoted as he was already on the captain's roster for flag-officer – a promotion which would come in due course.

Not all, however, appreciated, or understood, the expedition's achievements. The public had been stirred by the newly created popular press into a frenzy of expectation. The main aim of the expedition had been the planting of the national flag at the North Pole. This had not been done and the public, again agitated by the press, felt let down. Even the Royal Navy's own supporters in the press joined in the chorus of disapproval. The magazine *The Navy* felt that the expedition had 'little of which to boast. It went out like a rocket, and has come back like the stick.' So great was the disappointment felt that the Admiralty set up an enquiry into the causes of the expedition's failings.

The 'Admiralty Committee on Scurvy' (or the 'Scurvy Committee' as it was more generally known with more than one naval officer enquiring whether the word 'scurvy' was being used as an adjective or a noun) was set up under the chairmanship of Admiral Sir James Hope. The other members were the experienced Arctic explorers Vice-Admiral Sir Richard Collinson (formerly of HMS *Enterprise*), Rear-Admiral Edward Inglefield (formerly of HMS *Isabella*), and James Donnet, the Inspector-General of Naval Hospitals and former surgeon in the *Assistance* under Ommanney. The fifth committee-member was Doctor Thomas Fraser. They had a difficult task. If there was failure on the expedition, there had to be blame – and blame had to be attributable. Twenty-one expedition members and twenty-nine expert witnesses were called by the committee, including officers who had been on previous expeditions, the Medical Director General of the Navy, and specialists from the Royal College of Physicians and Surgeons. Their final report, rendered to the Admiralty Secretary in March 1877, found that a pre-disposition towards scurvy was caused by:

> … the long winter, extending over 142 days, involving, during that period, absence of sunlight, confinement during the greater part of the twenty-four hours to a lower deck, accompanied by exposure to extreme changes of temperature and deprivation of fresh meat…

The sledging parties further suffered from the:

> … severe cold, and arduous labour…, their lack of food, and failure…to obtain sufficient sleep.

Over-riding all, however, was:

> … the absence of lime juice from the sledge dietaries.

The North Pole Expedition: a sledge party camping for the night.

The men of the Nares Expedition being welcomed home.

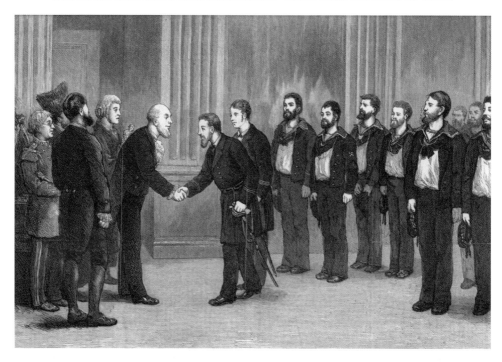

Nares and his men being welcomed at the Mansion House by the Lord Mayor of London.

Nares and his officers stand up at a banquet given by the Lord Mayor of London.

Nares, it seemed, was to blame for not following the advice of the Medical Director-General and ordering his sledging parties to carry lime-juice. How such advice could have been carried out was not examined – probably due to the fact that the committee members with Arctic experience knew it to be impractical. Unlike alcohol, lime juice froze easily and, in expanding, shattered the containers. Of course, less lime juice could have been put into the containers, but that would have meant more jars, and more risk of breakages. Furthermore, as Markham's experience had shown, it was very difficult, and required an inordinate amount of fuel, to melt frozen lime juice. But the committee had found its scapegoat and the public perception was satisfied.

Not everyone, however, was satisfied. Admirals McClintock and Richards wrote separately to the *Times* arguing that they had never supplied their sledge-crews with lime juice and that scurvy amongst their expeditions had been very rare. Clemence Markham weighed in with 'A Refutation of the Report of the Scurvy Committee' in which he repeated the fact that many sledge expeditions had been successful without the use of lime juice and that, even where lime juice had been supplied to the Nares Expedition invalids, it had failed to restore them to health. He also pointed out that, in many cases, where lime juice had been regularly issued on naval vessels, scurvy had still been found among the ships' companies. Furthermore, the Eskimos did not drink lime juice – and they did not suffer from the disease. The true answer probably lay in knowledge unavailable to the committee, to Markham, or to anyone else in 1876. The anti-scorbutic value of lime juice was only one-fifth of that of fresh lemon juice. The likelihood is that the demands of West Indian lime growers, in restricting the availability of Mediterranean lemons, had led to the outbreak of scurvy on Nares' expedition.

Unlike Collinson and Belcher, Nares continued with an active career in the Royal Navy. Returning to commission the *Alert* in 1878 he spent a year surveying the Magellan Straits before being appointed as Marine Adviser to the Board of Trade. He was promoted to Rear-Admiral in 1887 and to Vice-Admiral five years later. In 1896 he took over as Conservator of the River Mersey from Admiral Richards. George Strong Nares died in 1915 with, among his many achievements, the securing of the North American Arctic to, firstly British, then to Canadian sovereignty.

In addition to being promoted to captain, Albert Markham, was presented with a gold watch by the Royal Geographical Society and a silver-mounted sledge-staff bearing a naval crown beneath a pole star. He also had the *Alert*'s thermometer mounted on a sledge-batten with the inscription; 'This thermometer registered -77 degrees Fahrenheit., or -109 degrees Celsius, at HMS *Alert*'s winter quarters, on 4 March 1876. It was carried on 12 May 1876, to Lat. 83 deg. 20 min. 26 sec. N.'. With his return from the Arctic, Markham was appointed in command of the torpedo instruction ship HMS *Vernon*. On being relieved of the command in due course, he carried out a railway construction survey between Winnipeg and Hudson's Bay, and accompanied a private expedition to Novaya Zemlya.

He was recalled to active duty in 1886 and given command of the Training Squadron with the rank of commodore. Promoted to Rear-Admiral in 1891, Markham was appointed as second-in-command of the Mediterranean Squadron the following year. On 22 June 1893, the squadron, consisting of eight battleships and five cruisers, was off the Syrian coast steaming in two columns at six cables (1,200 yards) apart. The Commander-in-Chief, Vice-Admiral Sir George Tryon, onboard the *Victoria*, then ordered that the columns would 'come about' by turning inwards. Despite his staff officers pointing out that eight cables separating the two columns were needed for such a manoeuvre Tryon insisted that it be carried out. When Markham, with his flag in the *Camperdown,* received the signal he delayed its acknowledgement in the expectation that a more practical command would shortly be sent. Instead, a semaphore message from the flagship demanded 'What are you waiting for?' At this, Markham assumed that the Commander-in-Chief intended to circle around his ships thus giving him room to manoeuvre in the narrow waters between the two columns. The order was given and the lines of ships began to turn. To everyone's horror, the flagship also turned – directly into the path of the *Camperdown.* A collision was inevitable and the *Victoria* was struck abaft her starboard bow. Thirteen minutes later, after raising her stern into the air and with her screws still spinning, the *Victoria* was on her way to the bottom, taking with her the Commander-in-Chief, twenty-two other officers, and 336 men. The subsequent Court-Martial cleared Markham and the captain of the *Victoria,* although the press unfairly branded Markham as guilty of 'blind obedience'.

At the age of fifty-three Markham found a use for the gold ring he had made from a sovereign whilst in the Arctic when he married the sister of one of his midshipmen. He was appointed Commander-in-Chief at the Nore in 1901 and made a Knight Commander of the Bath in the new king's birthday honours. Placed on the 'Retired List' in 1906, Markham took a keen interest in the hazardous work of the mine-sweeping service during the First World War before his death in 1918.

Lieutenant Pelham Aldrich eventually received his flag and became the Admiral-Superintendent at Portsmouth Dockyard, among his many duties was the overseeing of Queen Victoria's coffin as it landed from the Isle of Wight on its way to London. Lieutenant Wyatt Rawson was killed in action in Egypt, and Sub-Lieutenant Conybeare was promoted to commander for his services ashore in the same country. He later became the Assistant to the Director of Naval Ordnance. Lieutenant George Gifford fought in the Egyptian campaign before being sent to the Newfoundland Station. Promoted to Rear-Admiral in 1903 and to Vice-Admiral four years later, he retired as an Admiral in 1911. Lieutenant Lewis Beaumont – of whose exploits in hauling his sledge through Gap Valley the explorer Knud Rasmussen was to write 'We others can only bow our heads to those who did it.' – became an Admiral in 1906 and was awarded the Grand Cross of the Red Eagle by the German Emperor when he acted as his host at the unveiling of the Victoria Memorial in 1911. He went on the 'Retired List' the following year. Lieutenant George Egerton served in the flagship under Vice-Admiral McClintock, fought in West Africa, and was present at the bombardment and capture of the Sultan of Zanzibar's palace in 1896. He was promoted to Vice-Admiral in 1909, knighted the following year and, in 1911, served as Second Sea Lord. In 1913 he was advanced to Admiral but, three years later, in company with two other Admirals, wrote that they 'expressed the wish to be retired in order to make room for the promotion of younger officers who are rendering important services to the Empire in this war.' His wish was respected. The greatest achiever, however, of all Nares' young officers was Lieutenant William May. Knighted in 1906, he served as a Lord Commissioner at the Admiralty, Controller of the Navy, Second Sea Lord, and Commander-in-Chief. He was promoted to Admiral of the Fleet in 1913.

So ended the Royal Navy's attempt on the North Pole. It was a bold effort, defeated only by an unknown, unseen, enemy that was to lurk unrevealed for the next three decades. Vitamin C can be obtained in the Arctic by the shooting of animals and birds, but there was almost none to be had at Floeberg Beach. Even the musk-oxen shot at Discovery Bay proved to be insufficient to fend off scurvy. The equipment was the best available and, although heavy, was successfully taken across some appalling ice conditions. Dogs had been used and had generally failed. Even the native dog-drivers found difficulty in crossing the jumbled, broken ice and, where the naval officers had acquired some skill in managing the dogs, they could not hope to achieve the same standard as the Eskimos. Disease had also affected the dogs. Yet again, the reliability of naval man-power – even under the threat of scurvy – had proved to be superior to the risk of employing dogs. To have 'gone native' as some critics suggested, would have been absurd – there are no natives on the northern coast of Ellesmere Island, no-one knew how humans could perform under such extreme circumstances. Even the much-vaunted (especially by John Rae) adoption of snow-shoes would have been of limited value. They may have been of slight assistance when in the vicinity of the ship, but would have been worse than useless in dragging a sledge (itself up to its battens in the soft snow) over huge ice ridges. In the end, the seamen of the Royal Navy were the first to face the fearsome ice of the polar sea, and had acquitted themselves with honour.

There remained still, however, one tiny spark of enterprise. Commander John Cheyne; who had served as a midshipman under James Ross in the *Enterprise*, in the *Resolute* under Austin as a mate, and as a lieutenant under Belcher in the *Assistance*; decided in 1879 that he would like to go to the North Pole – by balloon. Having announced his plans in the *Times*, Cheyne toured the country in an attempt to raise money for his idea. As this proved to be a slow process he tried to improve matters by writing and publishing a music-hall style song entitled 'Northward Ho! or Baffled not Beaten' (music by 'Commander Cheyne RN', words by 'Odoardi Barri'), and by setting up committees to organise fund-raising. When his final plan emerged, it merely had the effect of dampening down the enthusiasm of the few supporters that he had managed to get together. He intended to take a ship as far

Commander Cheyne's proposed balloon expedition to the North Pole.

north as he could through Smith's Sound. From there he would continue on with sledges whilst unreeling a telegraph line to keep him in communication with the ship. Once he had reached the limit of the sledges he would unpack three balloons – *Discovery, Enterprise,* and *Resolute,* and fill them with hydrogen. One balloon would have a crew of three men whilst the others had two each. Fifty-one days' supplies were to be taken, although Cheyne was confident that the actual flight to the pole would take only forty hours each way (whilst still continuing to unreel the telegraph cable). Unfortunately, by revealing his plan, Cheyne frightened off most of his support, the Royal Geographical Society refused to have anything to do with it, and a tour of the USA and Canada also failed to bring in any funds. He lived until 1902, enjoying probably a much longer life than if he had been successful in his attempt to fly to the North Pole.

With the Royal Navy retiring from the field, the banner of northern exploration was taken up by the United States of America. The arena was entered with that nation's ecstatic attitude of 'Win at all costs'. Sadly, as the 'costs' would demonstrate, it was not to be a happy experience.

As the inquest into the Nares Expedition was in full spate, Lieutenant George Washington De Long USN (having changed his original middle name from Francis) was looking over Allen Young's old ship, the *Pandora,* with a view to leading an expedition to what Charles Hall had called 'the crowning jewel of the Arctic dome'. He was being sponsored by James Gordon Bennett, an American publisher on a self-imposed exile in England caused by relieving himself in the fireplace of his fiancée's father's dining room – during dinner. The proposed expedition had received the support of Augustus Petermann, a German geographer with an intense dislike of the British, and a firm belief that there was open water around the Pole.

With the *Pandora* purchased and re-named as the *Jeannette*, De Long set off from San Francisco in July 1879, intending to reach the North Pole by way of the Bering Strait. The ship was trapped in the ice off Herald Island and spent the next eight months drifting in a generally north-west direction. With a civilian crew unused to attempts to impose naval discipline, the general morale broke down during the long winter months. Threats of Court-Martial were made in the wake of disobeyed orders and arrests were carried out. On 12 June 1880, the *Jeannette* was crushed and sank the following day. De Long, with three of the ship's boats, headed for the coast of Siberia. On the open waters off the Lena delta a storm caused the boats to separate. One was never seen again, and the others landed on different parts of the coast, their crews setting off to walk to the nearest native settlements for help. Of the thirty-three men who sailed with the *Jeannette*, only thirteen survived to reach their homes. De Long was not one of them.

Where the US Navy had failed, the US Army was keen to try its hand. Lieutenant Augustus Washington Greely took twenty-four soldiers and civilians north to Lady Franklin Bay – close to where the *Discovery* had wintered in June 1881. They built a base, 'Fort Conger', and spent a reasonably amicable winter preparing for the forthcoming sledging season. In mid-March 1882, Dr Octave Pavy set out to try and beat Markham's record using a dog-sledge. Cape Joseph Henry was reached, but an attempt to set off over the ice was thwarted by open water. Two weeks after Pavy's departure, Lieutenant James Lockwood left the base for the northern shores of Greenland. Gradually, his men broke down and had to be sent back. Lockwood, however, in company with Sergeant Brainard and Frederick, an Eskimo dog-driver, pushed on, not only to a point 100 miles further than had been reached by Beaumont, but also four miles north of Markham's furthest. After their brilliant achievement, Lockwood and his team returned safely to Fort Conger on the first day of June, having fended off scurvy by the use of lemon juice lozenges. Greely, in the meantime, had explored the interior of Ellesmere Island and had discovered a large lake he named after General Hazen, the Chief of the Army's Signal Service.

A relief ship, that had been expected during the summer, failed to arrive and dissention began to break out among the men who had expected to be leaving for home before the winter set in. Their second winter (the first ever second wintering at such high latitude) was spent in an atmosphere of surly gloom, drunkenness, and squabbling. In the spring, Lockwood tried to better his northern latitude but was defeated by the break up of the ice. Not to be outdone, he then crossed Ellesmere Island to the south-west and discovered 'Greely Fiord' – a journey that took him further to the west than the Yelverton Bay reached by Aldrich. And so, with the furthest north, east, and west, to his credit, Greely waited for the relief ship to arrive, unaware that she had been crushed by the ice of Smith Sound.

On 9 August, Greely and his men departed from Fort Conger. The dogs were left behind, but Greely took with him his dress uniform – including sword and epaulettes – in an effort to remind his men that he was in charge. The party, towed south in three boats by a steam launch, soon began to fall apart, one group even attempting to take command by declaring Greely to be insane. After six weeks they landed on the coast of Ellesmere Island and trekked north to Cape Sabine where they hoped to find provisions. Caches were found, including some from the Nares Expedition, but the contents were very meagre and unlikely to see them through the approaching winter. The next nine months were a time of unmitigated horror. Scurvy and frostbite began to take their toll. The theft of food led to one of the soldiers being shot. Insubordination and fighting broke out, starvation and scurvy led to deaths. But there were moments of great courage and compassion as men tried desperately to keep their friends alive. Lockwood died on 9 April. Soon, all that remained to eat was the occasional green plant and any lichen that could be scraped off the rocks. No-one was strong enough to bury the increasing number of corpses.

On 22 June, just before midnight, Greely heard a sound outside. It was men from a rescue expedition consisting of three ships – one of which was the former HMS *Alert*, now transferred to the American Navy. Having met two of the gaunt survivors on the shore, the sight that was yet to be revealed to the rescuers was horrific. In the gloom of the partly collapsed tent, five men lay still or moved with painful slowness. One appeared to be on the point of death; another, with his hands and feet missing, had a table-fork tied to one of his stumps. Two were struggling to pour brandy into a tin cup whilst another, with just enough strength to stay on his hands and knees, carefully put on his spectacles, and announced in a croaking voice that he was Greely. Eighteen men had died, only seven men had survived the ordeal, and one of those would not live to see the shores of his homeland. There was, however, an even greater shock for the rescuers. When they removed the dead, they found, to their horror, that six of them had been cannibalised.

Twenty-five years later, Robert Peary set off with dog-sledges from the northern shore of Ellesmere Island in an effort to reach the North Pole. Peary, a civil engineer with the United States Navy who had a penchant for awarding himself naval rank, had considerable experience in the Arctic. He had twice previously tried to reach the Pole and held the record for highest latitude at 87 degrees 06'N. On 1 April 1909, leaving behind the last of his supporting parties at 87 degrees 47'N, Peary pressed on with four Eskimos and his man-servant, Matthew Henson. Twenty-four days later – just five days after the last of his supporting parties – he was back at his ship claiming to have reached the North Pole. If his claim was true, Peary had achieved an extraordinary feat. The distance to the Pole from the point where he separated from his last supporting party was 133 miles. He had spent thirty hours at the Pole and had returned to the separation point eight days after leaving it, having spent much of the time on the sledge whilst suffering from pain in his feet. To do this, it meant he had been travelling over piled-up, broken ice, at the rate of around thirty-nine miles a day, compared to the twelve miles a day he had been achieving before the separation. He achieved this feat in the company of five men, not one of whom could take a navigational fix to accurately determine their position, and thus confirm his calculations. Furthermore, his return route showed none of the westward ice-drift he would have been subjected to. The ice had been moving, driven by easterly winds, but Peary somehow, according to his calculations, managed to come back on a straight, southerly, course. He could, however, have completed the journey back to the ship, within the time he claimed to have reached the Pole and back, if he had begun his return trip just north of the point of separation. But, within a very short time, it seemed as if his claim, and the doubts surrounding it, would be little more than of academic interest – someone else was claiming to have beaten Peary to the Pole by a year.

Doctor Frederick Cook, an American of German descent, started out in July 1907, on an Arctic hunting expedition. He had already accompanied Peary on an expedition to Greenland and had served alongside the great Norwegian explorer, Amundsen, during Adrien de Gerlache's 1897 *Belgica* Expedition in search of the South Magnetic Pole. In 1906 he had climbed Mount McKinley, North America's highest peak and had published a bestselling book about his achievement. Now, almost on a whim, he left the hunting base at Annoatok, Greenland, and crossed Smith Sound. Travelling over Ellesmere Island he reached Svartevoeg (Cape Stallworthy) on the tip of Axel Heiberg Island and struck out for the North Pole with two Eskimos. Eleven months later, Cook and his two companions returned to Annoatok after a winter spent in a cave on Jones Sound – and with a claim that they had reached the North Pole on 21 April the previous year. Leaving his navigational notes and instruments at Annoatok (never to be seen again) Cook took a passage to Copenhagen where he was being feted by his Danish hosts when news arrived that Peary was claiming to be the first to the Pole. Almost at the same time, Cook's claim to have climbed Mount McKinley was being challenged and, before long, proven to have been a fraud. Then his Eskimo companions claimed that they and Cook had travelled only a short distance northwards on the ice and had never even lost sight of the land.

With glory dulled by claim and counter-claim, by allegations of fraud, and by questionable records, America fell into two camps, one for Peary, the other for Cook. Debate led to argument and argument led to squabbles that were to last for decades and would never be satisfactorily resolved. A sad, sour ending to what should have been a triumph of man over the elements – a triumph almost certainly not achieved without mechanical aid until the Englishman, Wally Herbert, arrived at the Pole on 6 April 1969 (the sixtieth anniversary of the date Peary claimed he reached the same desolate spot). Wally Herbert's team of three companions and forty dogs had, however, not just made it to the Pole – they had made the first surface crossing of the Arctic Ocean by its longest axis. A journey which no one has ever attempted to repeat. They set out from Point Barrow on the north coast of Alaska and their epic trek took them via the Pole of Inaccessibility (the point furthest from land on the Arctic Ocean) and the North Pole to the Arctic Island

The way it was meant to be. An imaginary sketch by Sir John Ross showing the Union Jack flying at the North Pole.

of Spitsbergen – a journey of 3,800 miles which had taken them sixteen months (including the first ever wintering on the drifting pack ice by a travelling party).

The Royal Navy, the instigator of the push to the North, stayed clear of the Cook/Peary conflict. It had failed to send a ship through the Northwest Passage and had to watch as Roald Amundsen stole the laurels in his little vessel, *Gjoa*. It had hauled its flag and sledges to its furthest North only to be overtaken by the grimly competitive Americans. But where it had failed, it had done so with honour. Its wake and its footprints had served as routes for others to follow. Now, thwarted in the North, it turned its back on those regions and looked towards the South.

Opposite above: No more hauling sledges over the Arctic. (Sledges from Sir Edward Belcher's expedition.)

Opposite below: The last farewell. The Royal Navy leaves the field of Arctic exploration.

CHAPTER FIFTEEN

'MY COMPANIONS ARE UNDEFEATABLE'

Whilst the Arctic had become the scene of great activity during the latter half of the nineteenth century, the Antarctic had lain quiet and undisturbed after James Ross's visit in 1841. That was to change when the whales of Baffin Bay and other places in the Arctic began to be 'fished out'. Whales were well-known to flourish in the cold southern waters and, in January 1895, the Norwegian whaler *Antarctic* landed a party of men at Cape Adair – the first men to set foot, and place their flag, on the main Antarctic continent.

A second thrust at the Antarctic was set under way by the 1895 Sixth International Geographical Congress. Held in London, the Congress resolved that 'the exploration of the Antarctic regions is the greatest piece of geographical exploration still to be undertaken' and urged that scientific expeditions should be sent out to explore its mysteries.

The first to take up the challenge was Lieutenant Adrien de Gerlache of the Belgian Royal Navy. Against official indifference, De Gerlache obtained a ship – the *Belgica* – and assembled a crew of mixed nationalities. Among the officers was a young Norwegian named Roald Amundsen, and an American doctor, Frederick Cook, who was later to challenge Peary's claim to be the first at the North Pole.

The *Belgica* sailed to the south on 23 August 1897, and arrived off the South Shetland Islands in January the following year. De Gerlache's entry into Antarctic waters was darkened by the death of one of his Norwegian seamen. This incident looked set to become a gloomy omen for the expedition when, after passing through an unknown channel ('De Gerlache Strait'), and landing parties ashore, the *Belgica* found herself trapped in the pack-ice. For the next twelve months the ship drifted with the pack as three of her crew went mad, De Gerlache fell out with Amundsen, and scurvy broke out. The expedition's saviour turned out to be Cook who, using the experience he had gained with Peary in Greenland, fed the crew raw seal-meat, thus holding the scurvy back.

The ship was freed from the ice in March 1899, and arrived at the Chilean port of Punta Arenas two weeks later – her crew being the first men to winter in Antarctica.

De Gerlache was followed by the 'British Antarctic Expedition', sponsored by the wealthy publisher, Sir George Newnes, and under the command of Carsten

Borchgrevink, a Norwegian who had been in the *Antarctic* during her 1895 visit to Cape Adair. Sailing in the *Southern Cross*, a Norwegian-built wooden bark, the expedition left London in August 1898, and arrived off Cape Adair six months later after losing forty-three days frozen in the pack. After a winter ashore at the cape – the first ever wintering on the Antarctic mainland – during which one man died, Borchgrevink set off to explore the nearby Robertson Bay with sledge parties. Considerable natural history work was done, but the notebooks recording the results were handed over to Borchgrevink, who promptly lost them.

With the return of the *Southern Cross* in January 1900, Borchgrevink sailed along Ross's 'Great Ice Barrier'. At one stage he landed on the ice and, in company with Lieutenant William Colbeck RNR and Savio, one of two Laplanders carried on the expedition, sledged to 78 degrees, 50'S – the most southerly point ever reached by man.

Above: The *Southern Cross* in the Antarctic ice, 1898.

Opposite above: Lieutenant William Colbeck repairing a sledge.

Lieutenant Wiliam Colbeck taking magnetic observations.

Sir Clemence Markham.

Leaving the *Southern Cross* in Australia, Borchgrevink and his party returned to England in a Royal Mail steamer to a somewhat muted reception. The delay in the pack had prevented any serious attempt to reach the Pole and, thanks to the loss of some of the scientific journals, there was little to show on that front. Among those who congratulated Borchgrevink on his safe return (but not on his achievements) was the President of the Royal Geographical Society – Sir Clemence Markham. Markham had been watching developments in the Antarctic with a keen – if agitated – interest. To him, the great southern continent was the proper destination of solely Great Britain, the Empire, and, more specifically, the Royal Navy. Quite apart from his own connection with the Service, stretching back to the Franklin searches, Markham's belief that the Royal Navy should lead the exploration of the Antarctic was based on entirely reasonable assumptions. With over a thousand years of history, with a tradition of victory, and with experience of frozen wastes embedded in the background of many of its senior officers, the Royal Navy was unique in its record of polar enterprise. The only problem was that the Royal Navy was not keen to become involved.

Markham had been appointed President of the RGS in 1893 and had immediately set about pointing the Society in the direction of the Antarctic. An Antarctic Committee was created and included in its ranks Admirals Sir Vesey Hamilton (*Assistance* 1850-51, *Resolute* 1852-54), Sir Erasmus Ommanney (*Assistance* 1851-52), and Sir George Nares (*Resolute* 1852-54, *Challenger* 1872-74, *Alert* 1875-76). Science was represented by Sir Joseph Hooker (*Erebus* 1840-43). Not surprisingly, the committee came to the conclusion that, 'apart from the valuable scientific result of an Antarctic expedition, great importance must be attached to the excellent effect that all such undertakings, in which our country has been prominent, have invariably had on the navy, by maintaining the spirit of enterprise.' Markham then invited the Royal Society to become involved, only to find to his disgust that they promptly made a bid with the Admiralty to mount their own expedition. Their attempt 'to steal a march', however, was refused out of hand. Undeterred by the Royal Society's chicanery, Markham continued pressing the case for Antarctic exploration and put forward a resolution on the subject at the 1895 International Geographical Congress. But an attempt to send a delegation to the First Lord of the Admiralty to explain the need for an expedition was rebuffed. Three years later, the Royal Society held a debate on 'The Scientific Advantages of an Antarctic Expedition'. Markham spoke at the meeting and was supported by Fridtjof Nansen, the Norwegian explorer who had earned well-deserved world acclaim by drifting across the Arctic Ocean in his tiny vessel, *Fram*. The Admiralty remained unimpressed and replied to a letter from Markham saying that he should not 'hold out any hope of Her Majesty's Government embarking upon an undertaking of this magnitude.' Vesey Hamilton then wrote in the *Times* that, 'The refusal of the Government to despatch a naval Antarctic expedition has caused considerable surprise, especially since the Admiralty has fully admitted the great scientific importance of such an enterprise.' He then continued:

> The maritime supremacy of Great Britain must be founded on quicksand if it cannot spare eight or nine lieutenants to enable it to maintain its supremacy in maritime discovery... At the present moment an expedition is being fitted out for Antarctic exploration by an influential publisher who, I cannot but think, unfortunately has given the command to a foreigner (Borchgrevink) instead of one of his own countrymen.

But even this combined threat of commerce and foreigners failed to move the Admiralty.

With a succession of Government refusals, Markham decided that the only answer was to mount a private expedition, and he set about persuading the Royal Geographical Society to embark upon such an enterprise. It was difficult work but, in April 1897, he was given permission to start raising funds. Letters were sent to anyone Markham thought might have enough influence or wealth to lend substantial support. Much to his later regret he, once again, invited the Royal Society to become involved in the belief that their eminent support would lead to greater contributions. By the end of the year he had raised just £14,000, but the big breakthrough came in March the following year when a wealthy paint manufacturer, Llewellyn Longstaff, offered to donate £25,000. As a result, the Prince of Wales became patron of the fund, and the Duke of York vice-patron. At that point the Government began to take notice and Markham was allowed to put his case to the First Lord of the Treasury. He came away with the promise of £45,000 if it could be matched from private sources. The RGS made up the difference, the Government's contribution was secured, and the expedition became a reality.

Markham immediately turned his mind to the expedition ship. A visit to Norway and an interview with Nansen led to the possibility of her being built in Norway, but patriotic sentiment held that the ship should be British-built. No suitable whalers were available and Stephenson's *Discovery* – although still on the Navy List – was only fit for 'comparatively easy service'. The only answer was to have the ship purpose-built. Accordingly, a Ship Committee was set up under the chairmanship of Admiral Sir Leopold McClintock and included Nares, Albert Markham, Aldrich, and May from the 1875-76 Arctic Expedition and Vesey Hamilton who, like McClintock, first gained experience in the search for Franklin. It was decided that Stephenson's vessel had shown all the requirements of a good polar vessel and it was decided that she would be the pattern for the new ship.

Tenders were invited, but only two were forthcoming. One – from Vickers – proved far beyond the purse of the committee. The other, from the Dundee Shipbuilder's Company, was also too expensive but, after a few modifications was reduced by £17,000 to £33,700. She was to be 172 feet long, 33 feet at the beam, and capable of displacing 1,570 tons. Bark-rigged (i.e. square-rigged on the fore and main masts, with fore and aft on the mizzen), she was to be fitted with a 450 horse-power engine giving her a range of 5,100 miles at 8 knots on a full load of 240 tons of coal. She was to have a rounded, overhanging, stern and a rudder and screw that could be lifted clear of the ice. Her bows, also overhanging, were to be sharp, massively supported on the inside, and with iron-plate protection outside. The sides of the vessel were to be built up on 26 inches of oak frame from layered pine, mahogany, and elm. In addition, she was to be given extra support from three tiers of massive beams running athwartships. Her keel was laid down in March 1900 and she was launched by Sir Clemence' wife, Minna, a year later. Following a succession of ships that had added lustre to the name, Lady Markham named her, *Discovery*.

With the vessel safely in the hands of the Ship Committee, Markham could turn his attention to the personnel of the expedition. Through his connections with the two senior Naval Lords, Markham was able to put enough pressure on the First Lord who 'screwed himself up' and allowed the services of two serving naval officers – one for the appointment of captain of the *Discovery*, the other as first lieutenant. Markham knew exactly the type of man he needed to lead the expedition:

> He must be a naval officer, he must be in the regular line and not in the surveying branch, and he must be young. These are essentials. Such a Commander should be a good sailor with some experience of a ship under a sail, a navigator with a knowledge of surveying, and he should be of a scientific turn of mind. He must have imagination and be capable of enthusiasm. His temperament must be cool, he must be calm yet quick and decisive in action, a man of resource, tactful, and sympathetic.

And Markham knew the man he wanted.

Lieutenant Robert Falcon Scott.

Thirteen years earlier, Markham had paid a visit to his cousin, Albert, who was then the commodore of the Training Squadron, cruising in the West Indies at the time. Whilst there he saw a cutter race between a number of midshipmen. The winner, an eighteen-year-old named Robert Falcon ('Con') Scott, seemed to Markham to have just the sort of qualities he would be looking for in a leader of an Antarctic expedition. On 5 June 1899, Scott (by then a lieutenant and serving in the *Majestic*) met Markham in London and volunteered for the command of the expedition. His captain, George Egerton – formerly of the *Alert* under Nares – had no hesitation in approving Scott's application. Scott was, he wrote:

> an officer of great capabilities and possesses a large amount of tact and common sense, he is of strong physique and robust health – a scientist and an expert in electricity, very keen, zealous, of a cheerful disposition, full of resource, and a first-rate comrade.

Just five days after meeting Markham, Scott was appointed to the command of the expedition. He did not wait long to stamp his personality on the position. Before the month was out he had listed the conditions under which he would lead. He had to have complete command of both the ship, and the shore parties, 'There cannot be two heads'. He was to be consulted on the landing party equipment. There must be four other executive officers apart from himself, and he must be consulted on all other appointments – the doctors, in particular, must be 'medical men' first, scientists second, 'not vice versa'. Such demands gave Markham confidence in Scott's 'firmness and clear insight'. On the last day of June 1900, Scott was promoted to commander.

Lieutenant A.B. Armitage RNR.

Five years after watching Scott win his cutter race, Markham was on his way to another boat race. This time he met a young cadet – Charles ('Charlie') Royds – who turned out to be a nephew of Wyatt Rawson, one of Nares' lieutenants. Once again, Markham had mentally noted the name of a possible future explorer. On 3 April – less than a month after Longstaff had offered his support – Royds volunteered for the expedition, but had to wait almost exactly a year before receiving his official appointment.

In addition to the serving Royal Naval officers, Markham had also gained permission to appoint Royal Naval Reserve officers to the expedition. Such permission gave him the opportunity to appoint the first of only two expedition members with polar experience. Lieutenant Albert Armitage RNR was a thirty-seven-year-old Yorkshireman who had spent much of his life at sea with the P&O Line. In 1894 he had taken part as second-in-command in the Jackson-Harmsworth Polar Expedition to Franz-Joseph Land. The original intention had been to reach the North Pole with the aid of ponies but, when this proved to be impossible, the next three years were spent exploring the archipelago. In June 1896, Armitage was astonished to see a lone figure approaching him over the sea-ice. It was Fridtjof Nansen who, with Hjalmar Johansen, had left his ship, the *Fram*, as it drifted locked in the ice of the Arctic Ocean, and had attempted to reach the North Pole by sledge. Defeated by the southward drift of the ice, Nansen had headed for Franz-Joseph land and then spent the winter in a crude hut living on polar bear and walrus meat. Armitage was greatly impressed by

The expedition officers on the quarterdeck of the *Discovery*. Dr Wilson (Assistant Surgeon), Shackleton, Armitage, Skelton, Dr Koettlitz (Surgeon), Barne, Scott, Royds, Bernacchi (Physicist), Ferrar (Geologist) and Hodgson (Biologist).

everything about Nansen and called him, 'A prince of men and explorers, and a born leader.'

With three winters in the Arctic to his credit, Armitage had doubts about serving under the untried Scott. When first invited to join the expedition as navigator he refused, but offered to help with the equipment. Markham then offered him the appointment of second-in-command and navigator and suggested that Armitage meet Scott before making up his mind. He met Scott and was 'charmed by him from the first.' He agreed to go, even though he privately felt he would have to act as a 'dry-nurse' to his new leader. Armitage also put in place a number of demands of his own. He wanted to lead his own expedition by being placed ashore with a hut and supplies for two years. He needed eight men, a doctor, and a dog-team; and his pay was not to be more than £50 a year less than Scott's. Both Markham and Scott agreed to these conditions. There was one further problem. Armitage was a Royal Naval Reserve lieutenant, and he would find it difficult to command any officers, such as Royds, who wore the two straight stripes of the regular service on their cuffs. To meet this difficulty, Markham used his influence and, before long, Armitage was ordered by the Captain of Reserves to place the 'half-stripe' of a senior lieutenant between the two inter-woven stripes of his RNR lieutenant's rank.

In order to complete Scott's demand to have four executive officers on the expedition he was given permission to appoint a former shipmate, Lieutenant Michael ('Mick') Barne, a twenty-four-year-old Suffolk-born great-grandson of an Admiral.

The expedition's fourth officer came as a result of his connection with Llewelyn Longstaff. Ernest ('Shackles') Shackleton was a Merchant Navy officer who had been serving in a Union-Castle ship which took Longstaff's son, Cedric, to the Boer War. They had become good friends and, when Shackleton heard about the expedition, used his friendship to gain a nomination after having been turned down on his first attempt. Markham obtained a commission as a Sub-Lieutenant RNR for Shackleton and the twenty-seven-year-old Irishman of Yorkshire stock soon impressed his fellow officers with his unbounded energy and rapid wit.

One further naval officer was appointed as ship's engineer. Twenty-nine-year-old Reginald ('Skelly') Skelton was a Lincolnshire-born engineer-lieutenant and, therefore, could not be considered as an executive officer. In addition to his engineering duties, Skelton, was also given the job of expedition photographer.

Four warrant officers were appointed, an engineering artificer, a boatswain, a ship's steward, and a carpenter. Six petty officers were drafted along with nine seamen, five stokers, and two royal marines. Four merchant navy seamen, one donkeyman, and three civilians – a laboratory assistant, an assistant steward, and a cook – were recruited. The most senior petty officer was Edgar ('Taff') Evans. A Welshman who had served with Scott in his previous ship – the *Majestic* – Evans was noted for his great physical strength and his ability to spin yarns.

Reginald ('Cutlets') Koettlitz, who had served with Armitage on the Franz-Joseph expedition, was appointed as expedition surgeon. Of German extraction, Koettlitz believed that scurvy came about as a result of eating food with scorbutic qualities. He did not believe that anti-scorbutics existed, nor that fresh vegetables were any use at all in combating scurvy. Koettlitz had, however, designed the pyramid-shaped tent that was to prove invaluable on the gale-swept southern ice.

The assistant surgeon was Edward ('Billy') Wilson, a Cambridge graduate who had contracted tuberculosis whilst working among the London poor. He had a great delight in nature which he used in support of his deep, but undemonstrative, Christian beliefs. An artist of considerable merit, Wilson was also one of nature's optimists for whom tolerance was a pre-eminent virtue. Often preferring his own company, he was equally capable of being the life and soul of a party. When he joined the expedition, Wilson had been engaged for several months to the splendidly named Oriana Souper. They were married just before sailing.

The director of the marine biological laboratories at Plymouth, thirty-six-year-old Thomas ('Muggins') Hodgson, was appointed as the expedition biologist. Hartley Ferrar, recently graduated from Cambridge, became the expedition geologist, and Louis Bernacchi accepted the position of physicist. Bernacchi was the only member of the expedition to have Antarctic experience, having been with Borchgrevink during the 1899 wintering at Cape Adair.

The entire expedition almost foundered, however, on an appointment that had been proposed by Markham himself. He had been looking for an eminent scientist to take the post of Director of Civilian Staff, i.e. the head of the

The expedition ratings on the quarterdeck of the *Discovery*. Petty Officer 2nd Class Edgar Evans is sat on the boom with one foot on the support rope.

expedition's scientific work. His eyes fell upon Dr. John Gregory, the head of the geological department at the British Museum. Gregory was, in many ways, admirably suited to the post. He had been an explorer in Africa and Spitsbergen and had demonstrated both organisational ability and leadership skill. When his appointment was approved by the joint committee of the two Societies, Gregory, supported by the Royal Society, began to demand that he have absolute control of the scientific side of the expedition, including the landing parties. This cut directly across Scott's perceived role and threatened to reduce him to little more than the captain of a ferry taking a group of scientists to Antarctica. Both sides retreated to their entrenched positions and a bitter war broke out between the two Societies. After a long period of sterile accusations and personal abuse it was decided to appoint a select committee to look further into the matter. The key was eventually found by McClintock, representing the RGS. He pointed out that the *Discovery* might be required to spend a winter in the Antarctic. Such a decision could only be made by Scott. Would Gregory agree that Scott had such authority, regardless of its effect on the scientific programme? Gregory – by now looking at another job in Australia – telegrammed his reply: 'No'. The answer was taken as a resignation, and Scott was confirmed as commander of the entire expedition.

At last Markham could now concentrate on those aspects of the expedition he enjoyed the most. Scott left for Norway to discuss the expedition with Nansen followed by a visit to Berlin to meet Professor Erich von Drygalski who was to lead a German Antarctic Expedition in 1901. Royds and Skelton were sent to supervise the fitting out and the engines of the *Discovery* while Barne found himself on the top of Ben Nevis studying magnetism. Shackleton went to Aldershot with Leading Stoker William Lashly to learn the art of handling an observation balloon. He also became responsible for gathering props for amateur theatricals, for the testing of explosive detonators, and the stowage of stores in the *Discovery*. For Markham himself, one of the supreme pleasures was the designing of the expedition's sledge-flags – just as he had done for Nares a quarter of a century earlier. With the exception of Shackleton's, all bore the cross of St George at the hoist with the fly bearing an appropriate device and motto. On Scott's swallow-tailed pennant, Markham placed the motto 'Ready, Aye, Ready'. Markham and Scott had one other difficulty to resolve. Although commanded by a naval officer, and manned for the most part by naval officers and men, the expedition and its ship remained a private enterprise. It meant that all the ship's company had to sign 'Articles' under the Merchant Shipping Act which, 'however adequate these may be for commercial purposes, they fail to provide that guarantee for strict obedience which I believe to be a necessity for such exceptional conditions as exist in Polar service'. Scott's answer to the problem was simple and straightforward. The ship would be run as if under the Naval Discipline Act with a separate wardroom, gunroom, and messdeck. Just as in a warship, 'Captain's Rounds' would ensure the ship's cleanliness and 'defaulters' would take care of any disciplinary problems. This solution was accepted by all despite everyone knowing 'that this pleasing state of affairs was a fiction.' Markham had gained the King's approval for the ship to fly a White Ensign, but the Admiralty Secretary had opposed the idea. Scott could not fly a Blue Ensign as he was not an RNR officer. The answer came with Scott's election to membership of the Harwich Yacht Club, and with it permission to fly the Blue Ensign along with the club's burgee.

The *Discovery* sailed from Dundee on 3 June 1901, and was berthed on the Thames at the East India Dock where her loading began. In addition to sledges, tents, and warm clothing, there had to be enough provisions for three years. Much of the food was supplied at a special price by the leading names of the day. Colman's provided nine tons of flour and the expedition's mustard. Cadbury's gave 3,500lbs of chocolate and cocoa, and Bird's supplied nearly half a ton of custard and baking powders. There were also:

> Ice implements of various kinds, explosives for destroying the ice, guns and ammunition, and fireworks for signaling … tobacco, soap, glass, crockery, furniture, mattresses, and all such requisites for personal comfort; oil lamps and candles for lighting, and stoves for heating; medicines and medical comforts; a photographic outfit, a library of many hundreds of volumes; also a balloon equipment; canvas boats of various kinds, huts for our shore station, instruments of many descriptions; and so on almost ad infinitum.

Shackleton's service on merchant ships soon proved invaluable in stowing the vast amount of cargo away in the very limited space available in the *Discovery*.

After a farewell dinner for the officers at the Ship Inn, Greenwich, *Discovery* left London on 31 July to three cheers from an assembled crowd of well-wishers. There were five additions to the ship's company; Scamp – Scott's Aberdeen terrier, Armitage's Samoyed dog, Vinker, plus three kittens.

Markham had taken passage from London and, after the ship arrived at Spithead, gave Scott his official instructions. He was to sail along Ross's Great Ice Barrier and to explore beyond its end. The coast of Victoria Land was to be used as a wintering base and sledge parties were to explore as far inland as possible. A magnetic survey was to be carried out below the 40th parallel and research was to be undertaken in the fields of meteorology, oceanography, geology, astronomy, and biology. Charting and surveying of the areas discovered was to be carried out, and soundings taken. Scott, however, was given considerable discretion in the order and manner in which his instructions were observed.

The ship was 'swung' for the calibration of the compasses off Cowes during Cowes Week and, shortly before noon on 5 August, the King and Queen came onboard to tour the ship and meet Scott and the ship's company (Wilson, falling in with the spirit of the occasion, made sure his most colourful medicines were on display). Also there to meet their sovereign were Sir Clemence Markham, Admiral Albert Markham, Admiral Sir Leopold McClintock, Sir Allen Young, Llewelyn Longstaff, and Scott's mother. The King, dressed in Admiral's uniform, was escorted by his senior aid-de-camp, Admiral Sir Henry Stephenson – formerly of HMS *Discovery* in the Nares Expedition.

After inspecting the men, the King addressed them, saying:

> I have often visited ships in order to say farewell when departing on warlike service; but you are starting on a mission of peace, and for the advance of knowledge. The result of your labours will be valuable not only to your country, but to the whole civilised world. I trust you will be able to achieve the great work that is before you, and that you will all return safe and well.

He then reached around to a pocket at the rear of his tail-coat and, with some difficulty, plucked from its depths a case containing the insignia of a Member of the Victorian Order. This he handed to Scott's mother with the instruction to pin it on her son's uniform.

Discovery finally slipped from her buoy at noon on 6 August and, twenty four hours later, the last sight of England disappeared below the horizon. An ecstatic Markham, with the core of his ambitions breasting the channel waves, wrote, 'May all success attend the gallant explorers. They are engaged on a glorious enterprise; fighting no mortal foe, but the more terrible powers of nature arrayed against them. Truly they form the vanguard of England's chivalry.'

The 'vanguard' was rapidly finding that the *Discovery* – taken in hand without the extensive sea-trials normally associated with a new ship – had some serious

The departure of the *Discovery* from Cowes, 6 August 1901.

flaws. The engine did not produce the power expected and the sail-area was much too small for a vessel of her size. Consequently, the maximum speed that could be maintained was around seven knots – a speed that could be markedly reduced by even a moderate head-wind. The ship's iron-work was of very poor quality and numerous flaws appeared in parrells, goose-necks and spurs, much to the detriment of the vessel's yards. Worse still was the amount of water the ship took in. Some leakage was always to be expected in a wooden ship, especially a new wooden ship, but the *Discovery*'s leaks were so bad that much of the stores were damaged and the hold had to be constantly pumped to keep the water level down. The combination of poor speed and constant leakage threatened the time-table Scott had set for himself. He had to reach the Antarctic whilst enough of the summer remained to test their polar equipment.

The Cape was reached on 3 October. The ship was coaled, the engines overhauled, and an attempt to find the leaks failed. A planned visit to Melbourne was abandoned because of the lost time and the ship headed for New Zealand. The sixtieth parallel was crossed in mid-November and, the following day, the ship had her first experience of ice as a succession of small pieces gave way to heavy pack:

> The novelty of our surrounding impressed us greatly. The wind had died away; what light remained was reflected in a ghostly glimmer from the white surface of the pack; now and again a white snow petrel flitted through the gloom, the grinding of the floes against the ship's side was mingled with the more subdued hush of their rise and fall on the long swell, and for the first time we felt something of the solemnity of these great Southern solitudes.

A gale which, on one occasion, caused the *Discovery* to heel over to an angle of 55 degrees, welcomed them to New Zealand and the hospitality of its people. Harbour dues at the port of Lyttelton were waived, stores were transported free of charge and the ship's company were given unlimited travel on the railways (of considerable assistance, no doubt, to one of the merchant seamen who deserted at the port). The ship was put into a dry-dock and the full extent of the poor Dundee workmanship revealed. Nevertheless, not all the leaks could be located and the constant in-flow of water remained a wearying toll upon the ship's company for the duration of the expedition. Because of the damage the water had caused to the stores, the ship had to be emptied and re-stored – a gift of coal from a New Zealand well-wisher being packed into every remaining space. With the stowage completed, forty-five sheep were put in pens on the after part of the upper deck whilst twenty-three yelping sledge-dogs were kennelled forward.

To help with the extra work of stowing, men from HMS *Ringarooma* were sent across to the *Discovery*. One of these was Able Seaman Thomas Crean, a twenty-five-year-old Irishman who had recently been disrated from Petty Officer – probably as a result of his hard drinking habit. Crean, nevertheless, had other qualities. His capability for hard work, his strength and his evidently likeable character, was brought to Scott's attention and, in the absence of the absconding merchant seaman, Crean was taken on board the *Discovery*.

On the afternoon of 21 December, *Discovery* made her way out of Lyttelton as thousands of cheering onlookers crowded the wharves and quays. In response, several seamen climbed into the ship's rigging and clambered up masts to return the waves. Able Seamen Charles Bonner, aged twenty-three and engaged to be married to Miss Minnie Greyburne, hauled himself to the truck of the mainmast. Using the wind vane to steady himself, Bonner stood up. Seconds later he was dead, lying on the deck of the ship with the wind vane still clutched in his hand. The body was transferred to the *Ringarooma* – a sad exchange for Crean.

Two and a half weeks after leaving New Zealand, and after 'splicing the mainbrace' in celebration of passing safely through the pack, Scott and his men gazed for the first time on the glittering peaks of Antarctic mountains – the Admiralty Range named by Ross more than half a century earlier. Only one, Bernacchi, had seen the sight before and, the following day, he was able to show the others around the hut he had shared with Borchgrevink, Colbeck and the others.

On leaving Cape Adair, the *Discovery* was caught in a tidal stream which drove the pack against a line of grounded icebergs. For a short time it looked as if the ship was to be thrown against the mass of ice but, with the engine at full power, she managed to claw herself away from the danger. Heavy snow-storms and ninety-mile-an-hour head-winds delayed the progress further south for some days. A message was left in a tin cylinder on Coulman Island before the glacier-ringed and ice-blocked Lady Newnes Bay was crossed. The west coast of the Ross Sea proved to have few places that offered themselves as possible wintering sites and Scott pushed on until he came to McMurdo Bay. Mount Erebus (named after Ross's ship), with its plume of smoke drifting from its top, had been in sight from at least 120 miles to the north. Now on the port bow, and with mountains to starboard it seemed clear to all that they were blocked by land from any further progress to the south. The southern end of the bay, however, seemed to show a 'plain stretching directly south'. Clearly, McMurdo Bay offered both a good site at which to winter, and from where sledging operations could be based.

Before any thoughts of setting up a shore base could be contemplated, there was the need to range along the Great Ice Barrier in both Ross's and Borchgrevink's wake. The vast wall of ice – reaching up to 280 feet – could be seen stretching away to the east from Cape Crozier, its face scarred blue and white and darkened by sea-gouged caverns. As it unfolded to the gaze of the ship's company, the barrier led them to a position further south than any ship had been before. All along its front, soundings were taken and the water dredged revealing many species new to science. After nine days they reached the spot where Ross had claimed to have seen land, and lookouts strained to be among the first to report, but nothing could be seen. Early that evening, the ice wall could be seen to veer sharply to the north, directly across their bows. Beyond its ice-rimmed shore, what seemed to be land could be seen, only to be lost in a descending fog. By dinner time, the mist had lifted and, just as the meal was about to be served, it was reported that black patches could be seen on the ice. This was the first indisputable proof that they were off land. Soon other areas of bare ground could be made out, rising up to 2,000 feet. Scott named the newly discovered territory 'King Edward VII Land' and a range of mountains after Alexandra, the Queen.

The officers, ratings and scientists of the *Discovery*.

Intending to press on further east, Scott passed through a narrow opening between icebergs before going to his cabin to catch up on his sleep. The officer of the watch – Royds – handed over to Barne who found that he was sailing along a wall of icebergs, each connected to the other by solid pack. Following his orders, Barne kept the *Discovery* clear of the ice mass only to find the icebergs curving across his bows without a break. He was relieved on watch by Shackleton who continued to search for a way through whilst, at the same time, coming to the conclusion that they were completing a full circle. Instead of alerting Scott to the obvious hazards, Shackleton completed his watch, and was about to hand over to Royds, when Scott returned to the bridge. The situation that faced the *Discovery* was one of great danger. Surrounded by linked icebergs, and with the sea freezing rapidly, there was every possibility that the ship would be trapped. Even the way they had come in – eight hours earlier – could have been closed. With Scott now on the bridge the ship crunched through the young ice as all eyes looked out for an exit. Suddenly, Royds, looking astern, recognised the shape of one of the icebergs that had allowed passage into the trap. At first, Scott was doubtful, but agreed to turn the ship around. Royds was right, and the gap – although narrow – still existed and the *Discovery* escaped into open waters.

The rapidly freezing sea convinced Scott that the time had come to look for a place at which to winter. Nothing had been found to be more suitable than the land around McMurdo Bay and so he turned the ship's bow to the west. There was, however, just time to carry out one important task. An inlet in the ice wall was found (possibly the same one reached by Borchgrevink) where the height fell to a level at which the *Discovery* could be secured alongside. With that achieved, Scott ordered the balloon to be unpacked and readied. At the same time, Armitage, Bernacchi and three seamen set off south with a sledge to carry out magnetic observations.

Due to the temperature being 16 degrees Fahrenheit the balloon (named *Eva*) required more cylinders of hydrogen than had been thought to fill it. But, eventually, held to the ground by mooring ropes, the balloon was ready. The whole thing being a very risky business, Scott 'selfishly' (his own word) decided he should be the first to go up and take 'the honour of being the first aeronaut in the Antarctic Regions' (and, of course, the first risk). At about 500 feet the balloon was halted by the weight of its cable and Scott heard someone shout 'sand!' from below. Picking up bags of sand from the basket floor, Scott threw them over the side instead of emptying them gradually. The result was that *Eva* shot up 200 feet and left Scott clutching the sides of a violently rocking basket. When the motion had ceased, Scott found he could see nothing but the ice disappearing in a series of waves to the far horizon. A group of tiny black dots about eight miles away showed him how far Armitage's party had reached.

Shackleton was the next to go up and took a number of photographs. Wilson refused the opportunity, believing that those who did go up, and survived, did so only 'because God has pity on the foolish'. As it was, a rising wind put paid to any more flights and, when the balloon was finally brought down by winding in its

The *Discovery* in the ice.

Inflating *Eva* at Balloon Inlet.

cable, it was found that had its valve been opened to lower the balloon when aloft, it would not have been possible to close it again – 'nothing would have prevented the whole show from dropping to earth like a stone!'

Armitage and his party returned safely from their magnetic survey. They had reached 79 degrees, 3'S. The furthest south reached by man.

A strong easterly wind allowed the *Discovery* to make its way west from 'Balloon Bight' by sail alone, skirting the ice barrier as snow fell heavily. Cape Crozier was reached and McMurdo Bay entered on 8 February. An attempt to penetrate further south was stopped by unbroken ice and Scott turned the ship eastwards and entered a small bay. Protected both from drifting ice and from pressure once the sea had frozen, it was decided that this would be their wintering site. A low shore was ideal for the construction of huts and a range of hills provided shelter from the prevailing winds. To the south, the flat ice of the barrier could be seen fringed to the west by a previously unknown range of mountains. Over all, the top of Mount Erebus glowed deep red. Leading Stoker Lashly was not particularly impressed:

> This looks a dreary place to spend twelve months in, but we are going to set about it and make it as comfortable as possible. There are three huts to build, and the windmill to put up. Played football today on the ice. Very good game.

The original purpose of the main hut had been to provide accommodation for a small party to spend the winter with the *Discovery* returning to New Zealand. However, with the ship safely tucked inside the harbour at 'Hut Point' it was clearly more sensible to use her as the living quarters. Nevertheless, the hut could be used for the stowage of equipment and supplies, as a refuge, and as a place of relaxation. The building had been based on the design of an Australian outback bungalow and come complete with a surrounding covered veranda. The chief problem in its erection lay in its need to have supports sunk 3 or 4 feet below ground level – an extremely difficult task when iron-hard permafrost was encountered little more than an inch below the surface. The two smaller huts, brought to hold scientific instruments, were merely asbestos sheets over a wooden frame. A further problem was found after the 'windmill', used to drive an electric generator, failed to stand up to the high winds. Eventually it collapsed altogether and was abandoned.

Whilst all this labour was taking place, Scott insisted on providing relaxation, usually in the form of football matches played on the ice. The officers beat the seamen two goals to one before the ice broke away, 'completely spoiling our football ground'. Skiing practice took place resulting in Warrant Officer Charles Ford shooting over a precipice and breaking his leg in two places. Others tackled the question of sledge-dogs. A race was arranged in which Armitage would drive his dogs with strictness and force and Bernacchi would use more gentle measures. Whilst Armitage shouted and cracked his whip, Bernacchi coaxed and cajoled his dogs and, to everyone's delight, won easily. Thus was set the style of work with dogs for the remainder of the expedition. All, however, were glad when the dog's kennels were put ashore and the upper deck could be cleaned and made useable. Scott was also given an opportunity to demonstrate his intention to run the expedition on naval lines. When the civilian cook, an Australian who had been taken on at New Zealand, refused Shackleton's orders to cook seal-meat, Scott (who did not even like seal-meat) had the cook brought before him on charges of insubordination. The cook continued to display a misunderstanding of naval discipline so Scott taught him some manners by chaining him to the ship's windlass for eight hours.

There was still time to send out sledging parties before the winter finally set in. The first to go were Shackleton (who won after tossing a coin with Barne), Wilson, and Ferrar. Their target was 'White Island', a peak that pushed through the ice twenty miles south of McMurdo Bay. They were away for three days and came back in a state of high excitement. Having climbed to almost 3,000 feet they had looked south and seen that the level ice continued on beyond the far horizon. They had seen beyond a cape ('Minna Bluff') that obscured a clear view southwards from the ship, and confirmed that the western mountains continued to the south. They also confirmed that Ross Island, containing Mounts Erebus and Terror, was a true island and that McMurdo 'Bay' was, in fact, McMurdo 'Sound'. One disconcerting discovery was brought back. The surface of the ice, although appearing to be firm and level, actually hid deep crevasses which were extremely difficult to see. Sometimes the snow covering acted as a passable bridge which could be crossed with care. At other times the thin snow gave way, threatening to send the unwary to almost certain death.

Before the sun dipped too low towards the horizon, it was necessary to send a party to Cape Crozier to amend a message that had been left there at the start of the cruise along the barrier. Leaving the message unchanged could mean that a search ship would not be aware that the *Discovery* was at anchor at the south-west corner of Ross Island. Scott had hoped to lead the party himself, but had damaged his knee whilst out skiing. He appointed Royds to go in his stead. The party, consisting of Royds, Skelton, Barne, Koettlitz, and eight ratings, left Hut Point with two sledges and eight dogs on 4 March to cover the forty miles to the Cape.

Koettlitz was the only man to have any experience of sledging, and the lack of experience of the others soon began to show. The dogs proved to be absolutely useless. Unwilling to pull the sledges, they were joined by the men and soon gave up any pretence at hauling. Only three of the party, Royds, Koettlitz, and Skelton, were wearing skis, the remainder sank up to their knees in soft snow. It quickly became clear that those on foot could not keep up with the skiers and Royds decided that he would take the other two skiers with him to Cape Crozier. Barne was ordered to take the rest back to the ship.

On the summit of a 1,000-foot hill, and about three miles from the ship, the return party were hit by a blizzard. Barne ordered the tents to be put up and they sheltered until – later in the afternoon – the visibility had increased to about fifteen yards. He then ordered his men to make a dash for the ship. As they were making their way across the face of a snow-covered slope it was noticed that Clarence Hare (the twenty-one-year-old ship's clerk) was missing. Barne, assuming that Hare had lost his footing and had gone down the slope, set off in that direction only to slip and disappear out of sight. Petty Officer Evans set off in pursuit, hit a patch of clear ice, and he, too, shot out of sight. Then Petty Officer Arthur Quartley (a Baltimore-born American) made his way down the slope, and suffered the same fate as Barne and Evans.

After waiting for twenty minutes, Able Seaman Frank Wild, the only man who had the foresight to put nails through the soles of his fur boots, began to make his way down in search of the lieutenant and the two petty officers. But, 'after descending far past where the others had disappeared and finding nothing but a continuation of the slope' Wild returned to the others. Under his leadership, the men decided to try and make for the ship. They had not gone far when they found themselves on another slope whilst supporting Able Seaman George Vince who was suffering from frostbite. Suddenly, Vince collapsed, pulling Wild over and sending the whole party down the slope. For over 1,000 feet the five men plummeted down with Vince hanging on to Wild until Wild managed to stop himself in a patch of soft snow. Vince continued sliding, but Wild was able to grab the others as they reached him. When they had caught their breath, they inched their way gingerly down the slope until they reached an edge. On looking over, they were horrified to see below them a straight drop of 300 feet to the icy sea. Vince had gone over, and there was no sign of him. The climb back up the slope was a nightmare. A snow-storm raged about them as they slowly made their way across the bare ice with every slip threatening to begin a slide to death. But, by remaining calm, and with the support of Wild's nailed boots, they made it back to the top. There was still no sign of any of the others so they made their way back to the ship as quickly as they could. On their arrival, Scott found himself facing four agitated men all trying to tell him what had happened. Pulling Wild to one side, he got the story and promptly organised rescue parties. Armitage, with Bernacchi and Ferrar, set off overland, and Shackleton took one of the ship's boats to look at the sea beneath the slope. Warrant Officer James Dellbridge hurried to the ship's boiler room to raise steam so that the ship's siren could be sounded as a guide. Three hours later, Ferrar was seen bringing in Barne, Evans and Quartley. They had managed to stop their slide down the slope, but had become completely disorientated. When they heard the ship's siren they had set off in its direction and had met Armitage's party. Armitage and Bernacchi had continued to search for Vince and Hare but, eventually, like Shackleton, had to return empty handed.

More search parties were sent out the following day, but no sign of the missing men was found and Scott found himself having to face the loss of at least two of his men. Then, at about 10 o'clock the next morning, a lone figure was seen staggering down a hillside. At first it was assumed that it was someone returning from a morning walk, but when the men working on the hut began to race towards the approaching man, those watching from the ship knew that it had to be one of the missing men. It proved to be Hare. When he had separated from Barne's party he had become exhausted and had lain down, curled up, and gone to sleep. The falling snow rapidly covered him, thus protecting him from the worst of the storm. After an estimated thirty-six hours, he had woken up and made his own way back to the ship without even the slightest suggestion of frostbite.

The loss of Vince was to seem even more futile when Royds, Skelton, and Koettlitz returned from their journey. They had got almost to within sight of the bright red cylinder containing the message, but were faced by a long stretch of bare mountainside. The sledges could not be dragged across such a surface and, even worse, the volcanic rock made walking almost impossible in soft fur boots. These conditions were made considerably worse by the arrival of the same blizzard that had caused the death of Vince. Three attempts were made to cross the treacherous terrain but, without any of the proper equipment, the party were forced to turn back. They returned to the ship badly frostbitten and, after a fortnight in low temperatures, Royds was often seen on the upper deck in his pyjamas in the early hours of the morning trying to cool down after finding the heat of his cabin unbearable.

There still remained one sledge journey left to do. Scott was determined to get a depot south on the ice in readiness for the spring sledging. It would also give an opportunity for those who had not yet been on a sledging expedition. He intended to start after the Easter weekend – a holiday, as Lashly noted, marked by 'hot cross buns or bricks, could hardly tell which.'

The depot party set off on the Monday with Scott, Armitage, Wilson, nine men, eighteen dogs and eight sledges. They soon learned that the dogs had no interest in pulling the sledges and combining men and dogs merely led to tangled traces. Progress was dreadfully slow and, at what should have been the end of the first day found them still on the sea ice. They had to press on in order to reach the permanent ice with its covering of snow in order to get water and use the snow to hold down their tents. The nights were spent in three-man reindeer fur sleeping bags that had frozen rigid on the sledges and had to be forced apart to enter. The perspiration that had frozen beneath their clothing during the day then melted and turned everything damp. The fur got into mouths and noses, and their breath melted the rime around their hoods causing water to run down their necks. Once tucked into the sleeping bags, nobody dare move for fear of disturbing their neighbours who might just have managed to drift into sleep. Nobody liked the pemmican. It was too rich as it was, and too greasy when made into soup. After three nights, and only nine miles covered, the depot stores were cached and the party headed for Hut Point. To their amazement, the dogs, who had been totally lethargic on their way out, raced to get back. Scott put their poor performance down to the fact that they had started losing their fur, their bodies having been used to a northern climate where April saw the start of the warm season.

The autumn sledging parties had been, for the most part, a disaster, and Scott recognised it as such. He noted: 'our ignorance was deplorable… Not a single article of the outfit had been tested, and amid the general ignorance that prevailed the lack of system was painfully apparent in everything.' There were many lessons to be learned, and a long dark winter in which to learn them.

An expedition depot.

Once a useful supply of penguin and seal-meat had been obtained, the expedition settled down to a winter routine. A large number of meteorological instruments had to be checked every two hours. This meant a 100-yard tramp from the ship regardless of the weather and was done solely by the officers. The least favourite instrument was the Ashmann's aspirator which required a small clockwork motor to be wound up to drive a fan which blew air across two thermometers before their measurements could be recorded. As gloves had to be removed to wind the motor up, and then there was a long wait for the fan to do its work, the aspirator was a deeply unpopular instrument.

The wardroom was run on naval lines with a 'formal' dinner every night. Instead, however, of the usual practice of the first lieutenant automatically being the mess president, it was decided that each officer should take his turn. This meant that when a fine of a round of port was handed out for misbehaviour, it was not just one officer risking a measure of unpopularity. When he was president, Bernacchi fined Shackleton five times when the rumbustious 'Shackles' repeatedly tried at the table to bet that someone was wrong.

Scott was determined that the messdeck should be a place for the ratings to relax and even allowed smoking – a most unusual freedom in a wooden ship. The seamen's day started with 'lash up and stow' at 8.00 followed by breakfast at 8.30. Prayers were held at 9.15, after which the day's work was got under way. The officers envied the men their warm, dry, hammocks as the cabin bunks, situated

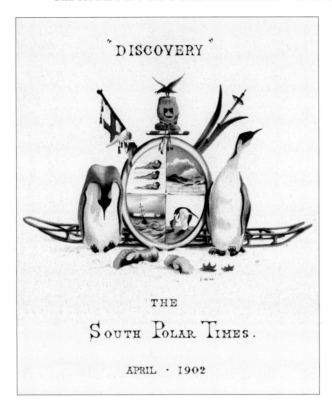

Left: The title page of a copy of the *South Polar Times*.

Opposite: Midwinter's Day celebrations on the mess-deck.

alongside the outboard bulkhead, suffered from damp. Scott insisted that the food be exactly the same for both wardroom and messdeck. Consequently, he was not amused when, during an inspection, one of the merchant seamen pulled an indescribable lump of matter out of his pocket and demanded 'Do you call this cake?'

The 'Royal Terror Theatre' was set up in the hut. Photographic slide or 'minstrel' shows were held followed by the singing of comic, patriotic, or sentimental songs. Shackleton and Wilson published the *South Polar Times*, a single-copy magazine, illustrated by Wilson, and packed with poems, articles, and 'sports reports'. Whilst the seamen played 'shove-halfpenny', the officers debated issues such as 'Women's Rights' and the rival merits of Browning and Tennyson. On one occasion the highlight of the entertainment was the removal of a cyst from Royds' face by Koettlitz, the patient lying on the wardroom table, surrounded by the other officers. No-one wanted to miss the first surgical operation in the Antarctic. Sundays were marked by 'Captain's Rounds' followed by an inspection of the seamen and a church service.

On 23 June, a mid-winter festival was held. Both the wardroom and the messdeck were decorated with coloured streamers, paper chains, bunting, and rosettes. The messdeck tables were decorated with ice carvings illuminated from the inside with candles, the officers put out their best silver-plate. Mince pies, plum puddings, and 'Christmas cakes' were washed down by an extra ration of

rum (the officers having to settle for dry champagne). The day ended with a walk on the ice to watch the *aurora australis*, an exercise which caused several cases of frostbite.

The sun returned on 21 August and Scott began his preparation for the coming season's sledging parties. He had decided to launch a number of reconnaissance expeditions to provide further experience and to test the dogs. Scott, in company with Wilson, Shackleton, Skelton, Ferrar, and the boatswain – Alfred Feather – spent three days travelling northwards along the coast of Ross Island with four sledges before meeting open water. He was able to examine the five mile 'Glacier Tongue' which jutted out from the coast, but was unable to come to any conclusion as to what had formed such an unusual feature. Armitage took a party and brought back the stores from the depot Scott had established before the winter – it was too close to the ship to be of any practical use. The unusual errand had meant that the sledgers had returned with greater weights than when they set out and, as a result, were 'positively cooked'.

Royds and Koettlitz, along with Evans, Quartley, Lashly, and Wild, headed off to the south-west to see if there was a way through the western mountains. Armitage, Ferrar, Petty Officer Cross, Able Seamen Heald and Walker, and the Royal Marine Private, Gilbert Scott, went directly west to see if a more northerly route existed through the same mountain range. Both parties were entirely man-hauled.

Scott left for the south with Barne and Shackleton, two sledges and thirteen dogs. They had been going for about six hours when they met Royds' party making their way back to the ship. No passage through the mountains to the south-west had been discovered and the journey had proved to be very difficult over broken, boulder-strewn ice. Two days out, Scott and his companions turned in for the night in single sleeping bags to test their warmth when compared to the three-man bags. A blizzard was blowing but Scott managed to get off to sleep without too much difficulty only to be awoken by snow forcing its way into his bag. Looking out, he discovered to his shock, that the tent, Barne, and Shackleton, had vanished. Wriggling around to look in the other direction he saw the tent, side flapping in the wind, and realised that he must have rolled out during the night. The snow used to weigh the sides down had been inadequate. Rolling himself back inside, he found his tent-mates just waking up to their situation. All they could do was to spend most of the next twenty-four hours sitting on the bottom of the tent wall holding it down as the blizzard attempted to tear the tent away. For Scott it was the 'most miserable day I have ever spent… More miserable conditions could scarce be imagined.' At one stage Barne and Shackleton made a dash for the sledge to get food. Both came back after two minutes, frostbitten but each clutching a bag of pemmican and chocolate. With the tent and sleeping bags full of ice, and with the clothes they were wearing frozen into 'sheet iron', once the storm had abated Scott decided to return to the ship 'having accomplished nothing except the acquisition of wisdom.'

After a rest, Scott determined to set off once again. Barne's fingers had suffered badly from frostbite so he was replaced by Feather. Four days out they came across a succession of frozen waves 20 to 30 feet high. The tops were bare, blue ice, whilst the valleys were lined with sastrugi – frozen wind-drifted snow. Beyond this, the ice levelled out to present a new threat. Scott, leading at the front, heard a shout from behind. Turning round he saw dogs and a sledge but no leader. Feather had disappeared down a crevasse and was discovered suspended over a void by his sledge-trace. The warrant officer was hauled out without too much difficulty and the march resumed. Half an hour later, Scott again heard a shout. This time he turned to see that one of the sledges had fallen down a crevasse. Fortunately, the sledge had been properly packed and secured, and was now hanging vertically without anything having dropped off. The weight was too much for the three men to haul up, so Feather volunteered to go down on a rope. Suspended with nothing beneath his feet but a yawning chasm, Feather slowly unpacked the hanging sledge, sending each item up to Scott and Shackleton. When the task was completed, Feather was hauled up followed by the sledge, the only damage being a broken ski.

Two weeks after setting out, Scott had reached the easternmost edge of Minna Bluff, a long, narrow, peninsula of rock jutting out from the western mountains. They could see that the mountains continued in a gentle curve beyond the southern horizon but, from where they disappeared, the horizon to the south, east, and north to Mount Terror on Ross Island, was an unbroken arc of flat, white, snow-covered ice. They were 'gazing with curious eyes on the road to the south.'

The return journey over eighty-five miles was completed in an extraordinary three days. The dogs, shaken out of their normally truculent behaviour by facing north, had dashed home as fast as they could. Scott was pleased with his results having seen what lay ahead, but on his return, Armitage brought him some bad news. The second-in-command's journey to the west had reached the mainland safely, but had been held up for several days by high winds. Eventually, they were able to reach the face of a glacier leading to the west ('Ferrar Glacier') but found the masses of broken ice at its base a formidable obstacle. By the time they had returned to their base, Ferrar was in a state of collapse. As soon as they could, the party dragged its sledges up towards the glacier but it soon became obvious to Armitage that there was to be no way through the mountains from where they stood. With no other options immediately available, he decided to return to the *Discovery*, noting as he did that his men seemed unusually tired. On arrival at the ship most were in a state of complete exhaustion. All were examined by Wilson and scurvy was detected in Ferrar, Cross, Heald and Walker. Others also showed early symptoms of the disease. Armitage had immediately banned the provision of tinned meat, issued bottled fruit, and taken the cook 'in hand' to such a degree that palatable seal-meat was served to everyone.

In early October, Royds, Skelton, Lashly, Quartley, Wild, and Evans, tried once again to reach the message canister at Cape Crozier. A week later they were within five miles of their target. Skelton and Evans set off and managed to place the new message with little difficulty, but returned to find a blizzard just about to descend upon the camp. A snow wall was hurriedly thrown up around the tents before the men retreated inside to wait for the storm to blow itself out. Unfortunately, two days later they were still inside with the walls pressing in as a result of the snow drifting inside the snow walls. During a brief lull a dash was made to the sledges to get the cookers so that a warm meal could be provided. It was to be another three days before they could start their return journey. Whilst in the vicinity of the cape, Skelton had discovered a rookery of Emperor penguins – a cause of much excitement amongst the scientists on arriving back at the ship as the life of the Emperors was a mystery to science.

Whilst the Cape Crozier party had been out, there had been a great deal of activity in the *Discovery*. Scott was to make his way to the south and the preparations of the sledges, stores, and provisions were nearing completion by the end of October. He had decided to take as his companions, Wilson – now well recovered from his tuberculosis – and the young, energetic, Shackleton. His team, therefore, represented the Royal Navy, the merchant navy, and the civilian scientists. Wilson and Shackleton had become good friends, and both could be expected to support their leader, Scott. The only difference between them on the eve of leaving was the question of sledge flags. Scott, ever keen to keep the weight of the sledges down, had decided that only a Union Jack would be taken, but Wilson, backed up by Shackleton, protested. Consequently, at mid-morning on 2 November, and to the cheers of the men remaining, Scott left the ship with nineteen dogs, a train of five sledges, and three sledge flags fluttering with a burst of colour against the white ice. Ahead of them, Barne, with twelve men and a flag declaring 'No dogs need apply', was hauling more sledges carrying depot and forward supplies. Scott soon caught his advance party up. The dogs had behaved extremely well and Scott and the others had found themselves running alongside as the dogs forged ahead with a rare enthusiasm for an outward journey. The only irritant was a constant coughing that affected Shackleton, and was causing Wilson some concern.

There were some small delays due to bad weather and the initial spirit of the dogs had dampened down as they left Ross Island to their rear. Their manner changed, however, when, to the south-east of the tip of Minna Bluff, they saw the waving black flags of Depot 'A'. Three days later the two parties joined together, all flags were flown, and fifteen unwashed men cheered and toasted each other when Scott's daily sighting revealed that they were just north of the 79th Parallel – Borchgrevink's record had been broken. Half the supporting party were sent back under the command of the Warrant Officer carpenter, Frederick Dailey, followed, two days later by Barne and the remaining men.

Now with no-one to follow, the dogs rapidly began to lose heart and Scott was forced to start relaying. This meant that every journey was trebled as the sledge loads were halved, brought forward, and the empty sledges returned to collect the remaining half. The dogs were also badly affected by the surface over which they travelled. A thin crust of snow would give way 'over some acres' with the sound of

Lieutenant Barne's Southern Support Party set out ahead of Scott.

a pistol shot and the resultant collapse and rush of air caused the dogs to cower in terror. Crevasses remained a problem but the men had almost come to terms with them. Legs would frequently disappear down narrow cracks whilst larger crevasses tended to be plugged by a large wedge of snow that acted as a bridge. Only at the very edges were the wider crevasses a risk. A covering of ice crystals clogging up the sledge runners made the going more difficult when compared to the bare ice. Three weeks after leaving the ship, all the party were suffering from cracked lips and peeling faces. Sun-blindness, with its excruciating pain of hot sand in the eyes, began to appear. To advance five miles they had to cover fifteen in relays. The beating of the dogs to get them to work had become 'soul sickening'.

On 25 November, Scott took a sighting and found that they were south of the 80th Parallel. He noted in his diary that 'this compensates for a lot of trouble'. But the dogs continued to fail and staggered along with heads down as Shackleton, hauling on the lead trace, tried to encourage them on. On some days, their situation was cheered by amazing displays of dazzling effects when the sky was full of intersecting rainbow coloured halos, mock suns, and brilliant white arcs. To their right, on clear days, a range of mountains could be seen marching alongside, forming the western coastline of the ice-sheet over which they were crossing.

Taking it in turns to be cook, their meals consisted of a breakfast of tea, fried bacon and ship's biscuit, lunch was a biscuit with hot Bovril chocolate, and supper was a 'hoosh' made of pemmican, pea meal and bacon powder ('red ration'), crumbled biscuit, a soup cube, and powdered cheese. Before turning in, they had a cup of cocoa and a biscuit. Later, dried seal meat was added to the daily ration. Unlike the Arctic, there was no animal life of any description that could be used to supplement their provisions – all edible materials were carried on the sledges. The food was cooked on a 'Nansen cooker', designed by the great Norwegian explorer himself, or on a Primus stove. Once, when Scott was 'cook of the day', he pumped the Primus to such an extent that a flame shot out of the top and set fire to the tent. Luckily, Wilson was on hand to put the flame out, and Shackleton found himself with the job of sewing a patch to cover the large hole. The time spent in the tent during periods of bad weather was used to read aloud chapters of Darwin's *Origin of Species* – a favourite of Scott's, but something of a puzzle to Wilson whose religious faith found difficulties with Darwin's catalogue of assumptions.

A calamity struck on 6 December when they awoke to find that one of the dogs had gnawed through his trace and had broken into a bag containing the seal meat. Altogether, a week's ration had been eaten by the animal. Four days, later the first dog died. After being examined by Wilson, the remains were fed to the other dogs and devoured with 'no hesitation'.

A giant chasm, full of huge broken blocks of ice, was found crossing their path in mid-December. Scott decided that it would be a good place to make Depot 'B'. In it was placed enough food for four weeks, just enough to get them back to Depot 'A'. This left them enough provisions for a further four weeks and five days. Enough for two weeks further advance with a few days in reserve in case of bad weather. He also abandoned most of the dog food. He had brought with him Norwegian dried fish on the advice of, 'one who had had great experience in dog-driving' – Armitage. Probably through poor quality, it seemed as if the fish had deteriorated to the extent that it had badly affected the dogs. By the time Depot 'B' was established, they were almost useless. From then on, the dogs would have to be killed to feed the others. This task fell, in the main, to Wilson. Scott was quite unable to carry out the butchery, freely admitting, 'a moral cowardice of which I am heartily ashamed'.

With lightened sledges there would be no more relaying. They had done it for thirty-one days without a break, but now the grind of repeated hauling over the same ground had finished. In that time they had gone 112 miles to the south – and been forced to haul their sledges for 336 miles to do it. Their chief concern now was hunger. Wilson saved one of his biscuits and took it into his sleeping bag with him. He had found that when he woke with his stomach crying out, he could not go back to sleep unless the ache was assuaged. Christmas day, therefore, was a special day indeed. Beneath glorious clear skies, a breakfast of pemmican and seal-liver hoosh, and a spoonful of blackberry jam, were followed by the flying of flags and the taking of a photograph. A ten-mile haul was interrupted by a lunch of Bovril chocolate, biscuit and more jam. That evening, in a warm tent, supper consisted of a 'double whack' of thick hoosh, the whole being crowned by a tiny Christmas pudding that Shackleton produced from the toe of a spare sock. As an extra flourish, Shackleton also furnished a sprig of artificial holly to decorate the pudding.

Scott needed a break in the sledging routine to boost morale. Just a few days earlier he had been told by Wilson that Shackleton was beginning to show the 'angry-looking gums' associated with scurvy. Even Scott himself had not escaped – he also had the first signs of the disease. Wilson admitted to no indications of scurvy, but, by Boxing Day, had to be blindfolded in an attempt to lessen the agonising effects of snow-blindness. Scott knew that he was close to the point where he must turn and head northwards. Quite apart from any considerations for the party's medical problems, he was near the end of his outward supplies. Ahead of them they could see mountains where the coastline to the west curved around to their front. A mountain directly south of them was given the name 'Mount Christchurch' and a cape to its east, 'Cape Lyttelton', in grateful recognition of the help given by the people of New Zealand. Further away, to the south-west, a twin-peaked mountain was named 'Mount Markham' and another, to the south-east, was honoured by the name, 'Mount Longstaff'. Despite the urgency the threat of scurvy was placing upon them (Shackleton had not been told about the scurvy but could not be unaware of his symptoms), they all agreed there remained one geographical feature that had to be examined before they turned for the ship. Mount Christchurch formed the southern entrance to an inlet that might just provide the route for a future expedition. If they could take a peep into the inlet, they might have been able to see to its head.

The camp at Furthest South.

The Southern Party at their furthest – Shackleton, Scott, Wilson.

Unfortunately, the camp they made on 30 December was surrounded by thick fog. Scott and Wilson used their skis to push on for a mile or so to the south-west but soon lost sight of the camp and had to return. The nature of the inlet would have to remain a mystery. Scott named it 'Shackleton Inlet' and its northern cape, 'Cape Wilson'. As for their furthest point south, it would have been churlish to have excluded Shackleton who had not been on the short ski journey. Instead, Scott decided that their final camp would be their 'southerly limit', and fixed it at 'between 82 degrees 16S and 82 degrees 17S' (his eventual chart showed 82 degrees 16' 33"S).

The following morning the party turned to the north, but had not gone far when Scott attempted to carry out his obligations to science. Using skis, the three men headed westwards to try and reach land in order to obtain rock samples for the geologists. As they approached the base of the foothills, they found their way barred by a huge ice chasm. Still not to be outdone, they left their skis and, roped together, tried to get across only to find that they were about to be up against a series of deep crevasses followed by a forty-foot ice cliff. Defeated by the sheer magnitude of the task, they returned to camp. Their failed attempt to reach land was underlined that evening when Shackleton knocked over the pot of hoosh. Because of the shortage of food they were reduced to scraping the mixture off the waterproof ground cloth.

The dogs were so weak by now that, incredibly, one of them had to be carried on the sledge for the last few hours before he died. Scott, seeing that all the dogs had very little time left, unloaded the last of the dog food and let the animals help themselves, 'at any rate, poor things, they will not die of starvation'. Help came in the form of a southerly wind allowing a sail to be raised to get the sledge along. By 7 January, all the dogs were let out of the traces and the three men took to pulling the sledges. They all felt great relief at being able to chat easily amongst themselves as they hauled instead of having to scream and yell at the gravely weakened dogs.

Having got into damp sleeping bags after a meal of short rations, Scott was lying in the tent when, through the canvas, he saw the sun appear at midnight on the thirteenth. Grabbing the chance to fix their position he went outside and set up the theodolite. He had only been looking through the telescope for a moment when a black speck caught his eye. Seconds later he was shouting 'Boys, there's the depot'. Almost immediately, everything was thrown on the sledges and the party strode out for the depot. It took them two hours, but they were soon tucking into a hot 'fat hoosh'. Scott now felt that he had left the worst behind him. The next depot was 130 miles away, he had three weeks' rations, the sledges were much lighter, and he would be crossing known ground. He had, however, forgotten human frailty.

Shackleton had seemed to be getting weaker over the previous days, but it was assumed that a good meal from the depot supplies would give hope for improvement. Before they set off on the fourteenth, Wilson gave the other two a medical examination. Scott's gums had gone from pink to red and a swelling at the joints had been detected. Wilson himself had a purple lump on his gums. Shackleton, however, had gums that were purple and swollen, he had difficulty breathing, and was coughing up blood. By the end of the day, Wilson felt sure that Shackleton was close to collapse. Scott now knew that they had to reach the ship as quickly as possible. Shackleton had to be kept on his feet, for if he had to be carried, it could only be done by relaying and Scott did not believe that he and Wilson would be able to manage it, and make it back to the *Discovery*.

Over the next few days, Shackleton's condition worsened and Scott was forced to order him not to haul, but to walk alongside the sledge. It was a difficult situation for all of them. Scott needed all the man-power he could get, but could not afford the risk of having to carry Shackleton. Shackleton's feeling of uselessness was a direct assault upon his characteristic energy and activity, making him feel even worse. At night he was not allowed to do any duties in camp as Scott impressed upon him 'the folly of pretending to be any stronger than he is.'

For the next week, the party pushed on as the weather closed around them. Scott and Wilson noted an improvement in their condition and, for a while, it seemed as if Shackleton was also getting better, but, on the eighteenth, 'Shackleton gave out' and they were forced to camp. Three days later, with the sail up, it was found to be difficult to control the sledges. Scott ordered Shackleton onto the rear sledge and to use a ski pole as a break. The effort involved, however, proved too much for Shackleton and, after an hour or so, he was taken off, put onto skis, and told to walk alongside. When the weather closed in again, Shackleton was sent on ahead, either with a compass, or directed by Scott, to act as a forward marker. It was in that position on the twenty-eighth that Shackleton was the first to see the black flag marking Depot 'A'. That night was spent luxuriating in their sleeping bags with full stomachs and reading the messages left for them by their friends. Within hours, Shackleton and Wilson were having much fun at Scott's expense as the effect of eating too much made him go out of the tent and run around in an effort to ease his bloated stomach. Not long afterwards he was joined by Wilson.

The following morning, Shackleton took a turn for the worse. The others dressed him and managed to get him onto his skis, but he was incapable of making any progress so Scott had him put onto the rear sledge for the remainder of the forenoon. On the completion of lunch, he had recovered enough to go back onto his skis and, by sheer will-power, urged himself forward. Curving around the tip of Minna Bluff, Scott and Wilson, with the sledge under sail, frequently found themselves falling down crevasses that Shackleton's skis allowed him to pass over safely. For the next few days, Mounts Erebus and Terror, the former with a plume of smoke trailing from its top, could be seen getting closer and closer. White Island was passed by 2 February. The following day, having been under way for about two hours, two dark spots were seen ahead. At first they were taken to be penguins, but soon materialised into the shapes of the 'clean and tidy looking' Skelton and Bernacchi. The welcomers were greeted by three men with faces burnt brown, with cracked and swollen lips, blood-shot eyes, and long hair and beards. All bore the marks of scurvy and one, Shackleton, was clearly desperately ill. They had been away for ninety-three days and, including relays, had covered 960 miles. They had discovered 300 miles of new coastline and had penetrated further to the south than any human had before.

The ordeal was over. With Cape Armitage rounded, they saw before them the *Discovery*, dressed overall with brightly coloured signal flags, and with the ship's company in the rigging cheering wildly. That night, Scott and Wilson were entertained in the wardroom to 'drink, noise, and songs', but Shackleton, after having a bath had retired, ill and exhausted, to his cabin. He was awoken in the early hours of the morning by Scott saying 'I say Shackles, how would you fancy some sardines on toast?'

Discovery dressed overall for the return of the Southern Party.

Along with his return, Scott was given some excellent news. Not long after the *Discovery* had sailed, Clemence Markham had set about raising funds for a relief ship. The King and the Prince of Wales had given donations as had Llewelyn Longstaff and the Government of New Zealand. A Ghurkha regiment had sent in contributions and support had come from the Sub-Lieutenant's Course at the Royal Naval College, Greenwich. Markham was soon able to purchase a Norwegian whaler named *Morgenen* which he anglicized to *Morning*. To be her captain, he appointed Lieutenant William Colbeck RNR – formerly of the Borchgrevink Expedition. Colbeck selected Lieutenant Rupert England RNR to be his first lieutenant. The Admiralty allowed two sub-lieutenants to join the relief ship, Edward Evans, and George Mulock. After calling at New Zealand, and just south of the Antarctic Circle, the *Morning* had run aground just off a small, uncharted, island. With his vessel successfully refloated, Colbeck named his new discovery 'Scott Island'. The message at Cape Crozier had been found and, by the time, Scott had rejoined his ship, Colbeck had brought the *Morning* to within ten miles of Hut Point – the closest the ice would allow.

The *Morning* had brought out a set of orders for Scott. He was to transfer stores to the *Discovery* and then sail in company with the relief ship to New Zealand. Unfortunately, however, the *Discovery* was still locked in the ice and there was little chance that she would get free in time. Some gun-cotton charges were buried in the ice in an attempt to break it up, and the *Morning* was able to get closer and closer to Hut Point, but the ice around Scott's ship remained immoveable. With time running out, Scott was forced to make a decision. He could abandon the

The *Morning* – Lieutenant W. Colbeck RNR.

Discovery, but that seemed unthinkable. He could keep his ship's company together through another winter, or he could reduce the number of his men. Scott chose the latter option. Sending a list around the messdeck he found it returned with eight names on it, not only exactly the number by which he wanted to reduce his ship's company, but the list was also made up of the very men he would have chosen to go. In the main, they were merchant navy men (the recalcitrant cook also went), men whose career ambitions would have gained little from remaining for a further winter. No officers volunteered to go, but Scott was very concerned about Shackleton.

On the journey south, Scott had seen Shackleton at close quarters. His courage and determination were never in doubt. Nor was the fact that he had contracted scurvy brought into the balance, the disease had affected them all. But Shackleton's coughing up blood had been symptomatic of something different, something that had forced his collapse and, for a while, had rendered him quite incapable. Two of Scott's men had died on the expedition, he did not want a third, especially when there was an opportunity to remove the man to a place of safety and medical assistance. He asked Koettlitz, the senior surgeon, for his opinion on Shackleton's health. Could he, 'at any moment be called upon to undergo hardships and exposure?' The doctor replied, 'I cannot say that he would be fit to undergo hardships and exposure in this climate.' When told of his fate, Shackleton was distraught, pleading to stay, but Scott was not prepared to take the risk. On 2 March, to the echo of three cheers from his friends, Shackleton slowly made his way over to the *Morning*. He was still suffering from the effects of the southern journey and had only been out of the *Discovery* twice since his return. Some hours later, he was followed by most of the ship's company of his old ship, invited by Colbeck for a farewell party. The drinking went on throughout the night and, after breakfast the next day, it was discovered that young ice had formed around the ship threatening to lock them into the adjoining floe. To avert this threat, the two ship's companies 'sallied' the ship by running from side to side in unison until she began to roll and the ice around her cracked. Shortly afterwards, the *Morning* slipped and proceeded to the north with Shackleton, tears cascading down his face, answering the waves of his former mess-mates standing on the floe, among them Sub-Lieutenant George Mulock, transferred to the *Discovery* in his place.

Shackleton had not been the only one of Scott's officers whom he suggested might like to consider returning home. Armitage's wife had given birth whilst the *Discovery* was away and Scott felt that his second-in-command might like the opportunity to see his new-born child. Regrettably, this news was scarred by the information (brought out by the *Morning*) that Mrs Armitage had become involved in an unsavoury scandal. Armitage, however, refused the chance to go home. He was able to do so by referring to the original arrangement he had with Markham and Scott. This had given him the right to command his own expedition from his own base ashore. That this had not happened, still gave a degree of independence that Scott would have had difficulty getting around. Despite his refusal to go, Armitage was becoming embittered by his situation. He was aware that his suggested dog food had proved to be a hazard to the expedition, he had not been given the independent command he had been promised, his good news about his child had been soured by allegations of his wife's behaviour, and he had become fixated with the idea that Scott wanted the expedition to be a solely Royal Naval affair. He was soon to receive another blow to his injured pride.

Before heading south Scott had ordered Armitage to have another look at the western mountains to see if a way through could be found. Instead of returning to the face of the Ferrar Glacier, Armitage decided to see if there was a route just to the south. In company with Skelton and ten men, and with Koettlitz, Ferrar, the Warrant Engine Room Artificer – James Dellbridge, and six men in support, Armitage set off on 29 November. Their first obstacle was a steep snow-slope over which, by relaying, they dragged their sledges up to 5,000 feet where they found a surface of level ice. A northern outlet of the ice-field overlooked the Ferrar Glacier almost 2,000 feet below them. The glacier surface revealed a great amount of blue ice and Armitage came to the conclusion that it would be extremely dangerous to put his sledges on such a hazardous slope. Instead, he would continue up the snow-covered slopes that led westward from the ice-field on which he was currently camped, as the support party returned to the ship.

Faced with a steep expanse of snow, itself with an increasing gradient, Armitage was forced to use a crowbar and ice-axe to make a secure point from which he ran a block and tackle. By this means the sledges were hauled up, secured, and the crowbar moved higher up ready for the next heave. It was gruelling work that lasted for two days, only for Armitage to find his further progress barred by a rocky outcrop guarding a succession of deep crevasses. The party was forced to return to their previous position and Armitage now knew he had no other option than to descend to the Ferrar Glacier.

'Descent Pass' – the only way down – was filled with snow and obscured by cloud. Armitage had the sledges tied together in pairs and lowered over the edge with the sledge-teams hauling back on the traces. Before long the weight of the sledges had taken charge and the party were sent plunging over 600 feet before being brought up by a more gentle slope. This, in turn, was followed by another slide of 400 feet. Eventually, the surface of the glacier was reached and, much to his relief, Armitage found its angle of descent to be so shallow that it represented little danger to his party and could be ascended with relative ease.

At the top of the glacier, its walls of rock fell away leaving just the tops of mountains – 'nunataks' – sticking through a wide, white, plain. A depot was established by one of the rocky outcrops and the party continued on in a direction just south of west. On New Year's Day 1902, they were 7,500 feet above sea-level when Petty Officer William MacFarlane suddenly collapsed with pains under his heart. The tents were pitched immediately and MacFarlane given time to recover, but Armitage decided that he would leave the invalid with half of his party at the new camp and push on with the rest. A gentle climb followed which took them to 9,000 feet where, on 5 January, Armitage found himself facing a smooth snow-covered surface that stretched to the horizon in all direction but the north and north-east. He had led a party that had been the first to see the Antarctic plateau – the great inland ice-sheet covering millions of square miles with an average depth of over 6,000 feet; ice that was constantly on the move feeding the un-numbered glaciers that emerged from the continent's rim.

The party set off to return the following day and reached the *Discovery* two weeks later, they had been away for fifty-four days and covered 377 miles. The ailing MacFarlane volunteered to return home with the *Morning*. Scott not only considered Armitage's journey to be 'excellent pioneer work' but decided that his route would be the main thrust of the following summer expeditions. To Armitage's deep disappointment, Scott decided that he would lead the next western journey. At the same time, he refused to give Armitage permission to lead an expedition to the south on the grounds that there was nothing further to be learned in that direction.

The preparations for winter went ahead in the usual manner whilst recreation was found in playing hockey on the adjoining floe. Sometimes the officers played the seamen, at other times it was 'married' against 'single'. The game was played without rules and no-one could be found to act as umpire – 'Occasionally there is a cry of "Off side!" but no one pays very much attention.' Royds would have paid attention, however, when, after giving the ball a mighty blow, Scott was forced to leave the field with a resulting black eye. Mid-winter days were spent, for the most part, as in the previous year, with the exception that the officers invited the warrant officers for dinner. Devilled wing of skua was washed down with champagne before the table was cleared away and Royds played the piano as the remainder danced the 'Lancers'. The evening ended with a tug-of-war – 'altogether we had as festive an evening as we have ever spent.' To extend the fun, Barne dressed up one night as a bear and waited for Koettlitz as he went out to take temperatures at Cape Armitage. The effect of meeting a strange hairy beast on the doctor was immediate and Mulock reported seeing the light of Koettlitz's lamp fleeing across the floe at great speed. On the messdeck, the seamen spent the winter reading, helping the officers with their instrument readings, making model sledges, or playing card-games for a giant medal with the King's head, made out of the lid of a chocolate box.

The spring sledging journeys began on 7 September with Royds and Wilson visiting Cape Crozier in the hope of finding an Emperor penguin egg just before it was about to hatch. Barne went out to lay a depot on the ice to the south, whilst Scott led a party to the foot of the Ferrar Glacier to see if a path existed to reach the glacier surface directly rather than follow Armitage's route across the snow-slopes to the south. Once the initial mass of broken ice at the base of the glacier was negotiated, Scott and Skelton found they were able to climb with little difficulty. Before long, they had travelled up the glacier to a point where they could leave a depot for the main expedition. On their return they found an even easier route to the north of the glacier. Scott came to the opinion that Armitage had been hasty in abandoning the base of the glacier as a route. Having, 'seen the disturbance on the south side, (Armitage) had concluded that it must extend right across.' The news would have been hardly welcome to Armitage when Scott and his party returned.

Barne had been successful in establishing his depot off White Island, his chief difficulty being a frozen foot belonging to Able Seaman Ernest Joyce. To bring the foot back to life the other team members took turns to place it under their upper garments so that it rested against their bare chest. They took turns because, after ten minutes, the icy foot against their skin 'was not a pleasing sensation'. Royds and Wilson returned from Cape Crozier not just with Emperor penguin eggs, but also with two chicks armed with increasing appetites that rapidly changed them from being 'small tanks' to 'bottomless pits'.

The end of September and the first few days of October presented a scene of feverish activity as the summer expeditions prepared themselves for the coming journeys. Barne and Mulock left on 6 October. They were to go south-west towards a large gap in the western mountains ('Barne Inlet') and survey as much of the coastline as they could. Royds and Bernacchi had the least attractive of the marches ahead of them. They were to go south-east to see if the barrier continued in an unbroken plain in that direction. Bernacchi was to use the opportunity to carry out magnetic measurements in an area assumed to be totally free of any external influences on the dip circle he was using.

Scott and his party left the ship on 12 October. The lower part of the Ferrar Glacier was ascended without difficulty and he soon found himself at a point that had taken Armitage twenty-seven days to reach. He had done it in six. But the party was then hit with a serious problem. The metal sledge-runners had been damaged by the hard ice of the glacier and would have to be replaced. Scott faced up to the problem ('It was no use even discussing the matter') and began the return journey to the ship. It was done 'as near flying as possible' and the eighty-seven miles between them and the *Discovery* were covered in under three days.

Scott and his team were back on the glacier by the twenty-seventh only to have their run of bad luck continue. On reaching the depot, they found that the wind had blown the lid off an instrument box, and the copy of 'Hints to Travellers', with its tables that Scott intended to use to fix their position on the plateau, had blown away. They had not got much further before Skelton and Lashly were at work with files and hammers repairing the sledge-runners once again. Crampons had to be used to haul the sledges over the long stretches of bare ice 5,000 feet above sea-level and, at the base of the upper reach of the glacier, a blizzard kept them in their sleeping bags for twenty-two hours a day for the best part of a 'most miserable week'.

The plateau was reached on 14 November. Ferrar and his party were detached in pursuit of geological specimens as Scott, Feather, and Evans hauled one sledge and Skelton, Lashly, and Able Seaman Jesse Handsley, pulled another out onto a glistening white ice-sheet 9,300 feet above sea-level and bound only by the horizon. The two sledges found great difficulty in passing over soft snow. Relaying had to be resorted to, and Scott became aware that some of his team were beginning to fade. For a week he kept an eye on those who were 'relaxing their strain on the traces' before deciding that he would be able to press on better with just two men and one sledge. Scott chose Evans and Lashly to form his new team and sent the others back. Handsley, in particular, had found the going hard, and, at one stage had broken down. He begged Scott not to send him back, but Scott had no alternative; 'What children these men are! and yet what splendid children! They won't give in till they break down, and then they consider their collapse disgraceful.'

With the new team in harness, Scott was able to press on regardless of the sledging conditions. Soft snow continued, followed by long stretches of hard ice, followed, in turn, by the solid, frozen, waves of *sastrugi* that collapsed their sledge and brought them tumbling down onto its sharp edges. A continual, keen wind slashed at their faces, cracking their cheeks, noses and lips, and producing a rawness that made even a gentle smile painful ('jokes are not to be encouraged'). On 30 November, Scott made his way up a gentle slope and looked out upon yet more of the same. He had reached his limit – 'we have reached the end of our tether, and all we have done is to show the immensity of this vast plain.' The party had reached 146 degrees 33'E – 200 miles almost due west from the top of the glacier. It had taken them seventeen days to reach that point and they had fifteen days' full rations left, with enough oil for the stove for twelve days. Scott could console himself that those seventeen days had been the result of a slow start with the men he had sent back, but he also knew that he could not be complacent – delays could cost their lives.

Problems and difficulties were not long in appearing. Starting the return journey on 1 December, it was not long before the sun disappeared and a gloom descended preventing them from seeing their route. The *sastrugi* sent them sprawling and forced them to camp just at a time when 'we could not afford an hour's delay'. Whenever the opportunity presented itself, they broke camp and pushed on until forced once again by the elements to stop.

Despite the conditions, Scott was probably happier than he had ever been. In the company of two other long-serving naval men, the sheer effort required combined with the awful surroundings, produced a bond between them that would have been unthinkable under other circumstances. Scott, a commander, could laugh freely at the jokes of Evans, a petty officer with a gunnery and physical training background, and attempt to join in the songs sung by Leading Stoker Lashly. Everything was shared equally whether hauling on the sledge traces, or cleaning out the mess traps after a pemmican hoosh. In their discussions, as the wind rattled the canvas over their heads, they concluded that they could run the navy 'a great deal better than any Board of Admiralty' and Scott learned more than he could ever have hoped about life on the lower-deck. 'My companions', he wrote in his diary, 'are undefeatable.'

The *nunataks* announcing the top of the glacier appeared over the horizon after ten days. Their oil was desperately low and, in an effort to make it last for as long as possible, lunch consisted of cold pemmican as the weather closed in around them obliterating the far-off land. Five days later, Scott was having to come to terms with the fact that he was lost. The weather had lifted and he could see mountain tops ahead and to each side, but none were recognizable. There were also signs that the improvement in the weather was to be short-lived. Snow crystals were being lifted in a stiffening breeze and it was clear that the tent would soon have to be pitched. That, however, could mean they might have to spend days waiting for a blizzard to blow itself out, but the rations would certainly not last that long. The situation ahead was as bad or, if anything, even worse. Before them lay a downward slope of wildly uneven ice, as if a river torrent, or cascade, had been instantly frozen. Hazardous under normal circumstances, to attempt to go down with a storm about to break over their heads seemed an absurd risk. Scott discussed the matter with Evans and Lashly. The outcome was unanimous – they all agreed to press on.

It was not long before the sledge, uncontrolled at the rear, began to try and overtake them as they began the descent of the slope. Scott put Evans and Lashly behind to act as brakes whilst he guided them gently over the slippery hummocks and across the succession of crevasses. Then, despite wearing crampons, Lashly slipped and lost his footing. The sledge, swinging uncontrollably, pulled Evans off his feet and both men began to slide down the slope. Scott tried to hold the sledge as it shot past but was jerked into the air and fell on to his back. All three of them, accompanied by the sledge, began to bounce over the broken ice with an increasing velocity. Scott's first thought was that it would be inevitable that limbs would be broken and tried to shout out that they should not attempt to stop themselves, but his words were lost against the crashing sound of the somersaulting sledge and the gasps of his companions as their bodies were repeatedly slammed against the ice. After what seemed an age, there was suddenly only the sound of rushing wind as a last frozen ridge hurled them through the air to land on a patch of compacted snow. Scott, badly shaken, painfully raised himself up and, much to his delight and relief, saw Evans and Lashly doing the same. Apart from having the wind knocked out of them, and having collected a mass of bruises, they had come through the ordeal without serious injury. There was also more good news. The rapid descent of about 300 feet had not only brought them below the wind which was gathering strength at the top, but revealed to them that they had fallen to the top of the very glacier for which they were searching. After a month without a single landmark, they found themselves surrounded by familiar terrain. Even the smoking summit of Mount Erebus could be seen far to the east.

Much of the sledge's cargo had been scattered in the fall and the next hour was spent in recovering what they could and repacking. They rewarded themselves with a cup of cocoa before setting off to the depot which, they now knew, was well within marching distance. Another frozen cascade was carefully negotiated before a level plateau was reached that would lead them to the depot. Scott was hauling on the centre trace with Evans to his left and Lashly on the right when a strong wind began to take charge of the sledge. To counteract this, Scott ordered Lashly to move further out to the right. Just as he said this, he and Evans disappeared down a yawning crevasse and the sledge rushed towards the edge. Lashly threw himself back in an attempt to stop the slide but could only watch as he was dragged over the surface of the ice. To his utter relief, the sledge, instead of following Scott and Evans down the crevasse, jumped the gap and wedged itself precariously across the top.

Suspended by their traces above a seemingly bottomless chasm, Scott and Evans swung between the blue ice of the crevasse walls. Regaining his breath, Scott looked up and saw Evans hanging just above him. Twelve feet above Evans, the sledge could be seen clearly and Scott could not avoid noticing that one side of the frame had cracked. If the other side gave out, the sledge would fall apart and they would plunge to certain death. Having ascertained that Evans was uninjured, Scott began to swing on his trace, using his legs to kick off the sides of the crevasse. In doing this he discovered a large piece of ice was wedged between the walls and acted as a fragile bridge. Grabbing hold of the ice Scott hauled himself onto it, secured his position, and then helped Evans to join him.

Above them, Lashly had been grimly hanging on to his trace for fear that the sledge might give way. He had also noticed the damaged frame and inched his way towards the edge of the crevasse until, holding on with just one hand, he pulled a pair of skis off the sledge and worked them underneath it to act as a support. He could not, however, assist Scott for, as soon as he relaxed his attempts to haul back on his trace, the sledge began to slide. There was little else that Scott could do other than try to make his way up his own trace. Taking his mitts off, he reached up the rope with his frostbitten hands and began to climb. How long it took him, he never knew, but with a mighty gasp he eventually hauled himself over the edge where he lay gasping for breath. The first thing he had to do was to plunge his hands beneath his shirt to try and get some feeling back into them.

After five minutes he was able to reach down and pull Evans up from the abyss (Scott records that Evans' comment on reaching safety was; 'Well, I'm blowed'). That night, safe at the depot, and in absolute calm, Scott and Evans sat chatting and laughing as Lashly cooked the evening meal. Only then did the petty officer seem to fully realise how close he had been to death and injury earlier that day. 'My word,' he said to Scott, 'but it was a close call!'

Far from making a dash for the ship and safety, Scott decided to investigate a northern arm of the glacier. Camping in the lee of a giant rock, they could not help but notice that the ice was melting around them, making the obtaining of water the easiest they had known during their time in the Antarctic. The next day, the three men set off roped together to see what lay at the foot of the ice slope as melt-water streams raced past them. Much to their surprise, the ice came to an end in a muddy moraine which Lashly declared to be, 'a splendid place for growing spuds!' An even greater surprise awaited them. After passing two frozen lakes and moraines, they found themselves in a sandy-bottomed valley laced by small streams feeding shallow ice-free lakes. The sand even felt relatively warm, and, as he ran it through his ungloved hands, Scott thought the valley was, 'a very wonderful place' but, 'certainly a valley of the dead.' He and his companions had been the first humans to see the Antarctic 'dry valleys' or ice-free Antarctic oases which, in time, were to become of great interest to both geologists and naturalists.

Returning to the main slope of the Ferrar Glacier, Scott was deeply disappointed to look out across McMurdo Sound and see that the ice extended twenty miles beyond the ship and showed no sign of breaking up. He knew that if a relief ship was to arrive with the *Discovery* still trapped he would have to abandon her, something he would find very difficult to do.

The ship was reached on Christmas Eve, and Scott was made welcome by the four men remaining onboard. Koettlitz, Ford, Handsley, and Quartley were the only ones not at work at a camp halfway to the ice edge, trying to saw a passage through to the ship. Scott was keen to join them, but had to spend a few days recovering from his journey (whilst being fed by Ford who was learning cookery by reading Mrs Beeton's cookery book). He, Evans and Lashly had been away from the ship for fifty-nine days and had travelled over 700 miles. Nine days had been lost due to blizzards and other forms of inclement weather leaving an average daily distance covered of fourteen and a half miles – considerably more than had been achieved by using dogs on the southern journey.

Whilst resting, Scott was informed of the other expeditions that had taken place during his absence. Barne had reached the western mountains beyond the eightieth parallel. From there, Mulock had been able find the height and fix the position of over 200 mountains. Whilst returning, Barne had visited Scott's old Depot 'A' off Minna Bluff. To his surprise, the site had drifted northwards by 608 yards in the intervening thirteen and a half months, thus giving the first ever measurement of the rate of drift of the barrier itself.

Using sheerlegs to saw through the ice.

The thrust to the south-east undertaken by Royds had confirmed that the barrier continued without interruption in that direction. Bernacchi had completed a successful series of magnetic observations well clear of any land mass and almost directly along a line from the magnetic South Pole. Wilson had returned to study the Emperor penguins at Cape Crozier and had learned that the Emperor chicks, too young to take to the water, left the area by floating with the parents on floes breaking away from the ice-edge. As the Emperors left the region, their place was taken by Adelie penguins coming in for the summer. Wilson had been able to extend his and his party's time at the cape by the time-honoured Arctic practice of using seal-blubber to cook seal meat. On his return, Wilson, with Armitage and Heald, crossed McMurdo Sound and carried out a survey of the Koettlitz Glacier.

Scott joined the ice-sawing party as soon as he could and found them in good spirits despite the hard work. In twelve days they had only managed to cut 150 yards through the 7-foot thick ice and there appeared to be no possibility of cutting a channel ten miles to the ship. He decided that instead of wasting time in continuing sawing, the time could be better used in preparing the ship for another winter, just in case no relief ship arrived. Taking Wilson with him, Scott headed off to the ice-edge to see if he could gain some idea of the rate of break-up. Off Cape Royds, just as they were about to come to open water, Wilson spotted a rookery of Adelie penguins and both men went to investigate. They set up their tent on a stretch of sand and settled down to study the habits of the friendly birds. The following day, 5 January 1904, after having breakfasted, Scott and Wilson sat in the tent planning the day's work when Scott saw a ship sail into the view framed by the open tent flap. In an instant, he and Wilson had tumbled out of the tent and were putting on their boots when Wilson said, 'Why, there's another.' Sure enough, to the bafflement of both men, a second ship had appeared.

A nearby penguin-hunting party were alerted and sent to the *Discovery* with the news as Scott and Wilson headed across the ice to meet the new arrivals. Colbeck, out once again with the *Morning*, had his ice-anchors secured at the ice edge by the time Scott reached him. When the two men met, what Colbeck had to tell Scott came as a great disappointment. In sending a message out with the *Morning* the previous year, Scott had explained that the *Discovery* was iced-in, but that their situation presented no difficulty or danger. He also mentioned that scurvy had been experienced – not to cause alarm, but to prevent the possibility of exaggerated rumours. But alarm had been caused. Sir Clemence Markham had immediately set about raising funds for another relief expedition, and, when he applied to the Government for help he found they would only help if the Admiralty took over the entire relief effort. When this was eventually agreed, the Admiralty commandeered the *Morning* and purchased a Dundee whaler, the *Terra Nova*. The command of the new ship was given to an experienced whaling captain, Harry MacKay and her crew made up of whaling men. Shackleton had been offered the appointment of chief officer, but refused. To get the *Terra Nova* out to New Zealand and put her in company with the *Morning*, a relay of cruisers towed her through the Mediterranean and the Suez Canal ('at a speed which must have surprised the barnacles on her stout wooden sides'). Now, with both ships secured to the ice, Scott received orders from the Admiralty telling him, that if the *Discovery* could not be freed in time to join the relief ships as they sailed northwards, he and his men were to go with them and abandon her. It was the wrong order at the wrong time. Neither Scott, nor his men, felt they were in any danger and the *Discovery* was safe at harbour. They had intended to leave the area once the ice cleared, but if events turned against them, another winter held no fears and there was still much work to be done in the region. Scott's freedom of action was suddenly curtailed, and it was with a heavy heart that he began the work of transferring stores, equipment, and specimens to the *Morning* and the *Terra Nova*.

From the date of arrival of the relief ships it was reckoned that there were just six weeks before they would have to leave. Between them and the *Discovery* lay a twenty mile unbroken sheet of thick ice. Sawing had proved to be ineffectual and attempts to blast it apart with explosives had little effect. Attempts to ram the ice were made by the *Terra Nova* using her powerful engine, but the ice fended her off with little difficulty. A line of signals was set up between the ice-edge and Hut Point in case the ice should start to break up. Up to 23 January, the only signal to come through was 'No change in the ice conditions'. On the following day, hopes soared as large floes parted company with the main ice-sheet and the relief ships were able to advance seven miles closer. A week later they had come within eight miles and Scott felt that there were 'even chances' of escaping – 'It's a toss-up'. Calm weather slowed things down again and Scott found himself in the extraordinary position of hoping for a gale to break the ice up.

The use of explosives was tried again with Scott marking out the holes needed for the 35lb charges. After each explosion the resulting craters were checked for linking cracks. Usually they were successful, but they still needed a rolling sea to part the newly created floes. By 10 February, the ships were still six miles apart – 'Everyone now is making an effort to be cheerful, but it is an obvious effort.' Berths in the relief ships were allocated to the *Discovery*'s ship's company and Scott wrote the instructions needed for the abandonment of his ship. On the twelfth, the ships had closed to four miles. Two days later a south-easterly blocked the view with blown snow. It was known that more ice had drifted out, but the escape of the *Discovery* still seemed an unlikely event. Scott and his officers were at dinner that evening when they heard shouting on deck. This was followed immediately by someone shouting down the hatchway, 'The ships are coming, sir!' From the deck, Scott looked out on an extraordinary sight. The ice-sheet was being torn apart by the unseen hands of nature. Black cracks could be seen and heard racing across the surface and huge floes were drifting silently out of McMurdo Sound. From the opposite direction the relief ships could be seen getting closer and closer. The *Morning* slowly edged her way along widening cracks and surged into areas of open water as the *Terra Nova* rammed the ice, her crew 'sallying' from side to side, the rocking ship forcing floes apart. Before long the *Terra Nova* had a line across to the *Discovery* and the combined cheers of the ships echoed from the bleak rocks of Ross Island. That night 'wild revelry' took place into the early hours as men went from ship to ship, shaking hands and celebrating their good fortune. Even Scott was moved to note; 'Much can be excused on such a night.'

The sixteenth saw the final preparations being made for leaving. The hut was secured and the final grip of the ice was severed by a 67lb charge of gun-cotton.

As a light snow fell on bared heads, Scott held a service at the foot of a large cross. The sombre memorial had just been erected on the summit of a nearby hill to the memory of Able Seaman Vince, the expedition's only fatality in the Antarctic.

The following forenoon, having raised steam, the *Discovery* weighed anchor and began to move slowly out of the small harbour against a gale-force wind. As the bows of the ship rounded Hut Point, the wind seized her, spun her round, and forced her onto a submerged bank. Soon she was beam on to the wind, to the current, and to a raging sea that crashed over her decks. The engine failed and the vessel began to rise and fall on the bank, each fall producing a mighty crashing sound followed by the groans of tortured timber. It was clear to all that the ship could not take such punishment for long. Wilson took to the upper deck, risking a drenching as an increasing wind threw icy waves high into the rigging, and saw the ship buckling along its length. Ten-foot sections of timber floated up to the surface as they were torn from the vessel's false keel, and the glass dead-lights

The *Terra Nova* and the *Morning* get within hailing distance of the *Discovery* (left).

After the final explosion, *Discovery* breaks free. The *Morning* waits on the far side of an ice floe.

– used to provide daylight to the deck below – cracked in their brass frames as the ship twisted in her agony. Scott wandered about the ship gaining strength from the way his men were reacting to this dreadful turn of events. Skelton and Feather were calmly working on ways to lighten the ship or prepare anchors to hold her. Marine Private Gilbert Scott got on with polishing the wardroom silver.

The officers, helpless against the elements, decided to go to dinner only to have a, somewhat gloomy, meal interrupted by the officer of the watch – Mulock – who reported to Scott, 'The ship's working astern, sir.' Sure enough, the wind had fallen slightly, just enough to allow the *Discovery* to swivel on the bank and begin to slide off it stern first. Slowly, seemingly an inch at a time, the ship scraped backwards until, at last, she broke free of the hazard. To Wilson it had been, 'almost the worst eight hours I have ever experienced.' Scott wrote in his diary, 'We have had a day and no mistake.' Skelton, Dellbridge, and Lashly soon had the engine going and Scott took the ship over to the ice-edge to join the *Terra Nova*. Coal was taken onboard in the usual Royal Naval tradition of officers working alongside the seamen and stokers, all forming 'an indistinguishable party on the coaling whips.' But such work alongside the men was nothing new to Scott's officers – they had regularly pulled sledges, erected tents, and served as 'cooks-of-the-day' all in their turn, in addition to their scientific and seamanship tasks.

It was Scott's intention to carry out further exploratory work to the west around Cape North. Consequently, the much slower *Morning* was sent on her way with orders to rendezvous at Port Ross in the Auckland Island as the remaining ships headed north-west. McMurdo Sound was left as the sun set at midnight beyond the western mountains, its dying rays catching the bright snow around the upper slopes of Mount Erebus. Wood Bay was entered with the hope of watering and to carry out a magnetic survey. The bay, however, was full of pack ice and all that could be done was to take ice from a floe.

In the early hours of the next morning Scott was awoken by Skelton. The ship was taking water badly and the pumps had ceased to work. It was the start of a long night that only came to an end when it was discovered that the bottom end of the pump was clogged with ash. Two days later it was found that the ship's rudder was badly damaged and would have to be replaced. The *Discovery* hauled into Robertson Bay on Cape Adair to carry out the work, only to find the pack closing in from seaward. She escaped without being trapped, but, accompanied by snow-storms, the pack followed her, forcing her away from the shore. Eventually, Scott realised that he was not going to get to the west through the menacing pack and headed to the north.

Reaching north of 68 degrees, and having lost sight of the *Terra Nova*, Scott decided to head west and search for the Balleny Islands. John Balleny had discovered the islands in 1839. They had been seen again by James Ross, but their position had never been definitely fixed. The islands were met within a few days and Mulock was able to obtain enough bearings to get an accurate fix on their position. Much to Scott's surprise, having expected to encounter more pack, he found the waters to the west open and took the opportunity to search for Wilke's

Land, reported by the American explorer in 1840. But, like Ross before him, no land was to be found. Now, with his coal stocks low, Scott decided that his time in the Antarctic was at an end, and, with whales blowing around him, he turned the bows of the *Discovery* to the north.

Scott arrived at the appointed rendezvous on Auckland Island on 15 March and promptly set about making the ship presentable for her arrival in New Zealand. Decks were scrubbed, paintwork washed down, brightwork polished, and 'travel stains' painted out. The *Terra Nova* and the *Morning* joined within a week and the little flotilla sailed on the twenty-ninth. A month later they arrived at Lyttelton to find the jetty packed with people waving a welcome and the harbour ablaze with bunting. Also waiting for him were congratulatory telegrams from the King and the Admiralty.

The *Discovery*'s voyage home took her via Cape Horn, the Falkland Islands, and the Azores. She arrived at Spithead on 10 September to a welcome from relatives, dignitaries, and fleets of small boats that swarmed around the ship with a buzz of wide-eyed fascination. Scott and his men had been away for three years and one month. They had seen lands on which no other eye had settled, and had experienced adventures almost beyond description. Death had been stared in the face and made to back down, the combined forces of cold, isolation, and danger, had been overcome. Leadership, teamwork, courage and determination had all triumphed. And now it was over. Scott wrote – '...there was not one of us, I think, who did not feel the sadness of the day which brought the end of our close companionship and the scattering of those ties which had held us together for so long.'

Scott, who had been a commander for almost four years, was 'in zone' for promotion. He received the fourth gold lace stripe of a captain the day after his return – a cleverly calculated dating that demonstrated his promotion was as a naval officer, not as an Antarctic explorer. The King improved his class of the Victorian Order to that of 'Commander'. In a more relaxed time than the Edwardian Age, Scott would have been knighted, but the tradition had grown in the Royal Navy that only flag-officers normally received knighthoods. The Royal Geographical Society created a special award in the shape of a three-inch gold medal bearing a portrait of him in naval uniform. The reverse was decorated with a scene showing the *Discovery*, sledges, and penguins. The ship's company and scientists of the expedition received a copy of the medal in silver. A grateful Government authorised the issue of a medal to be known as the 'Polar Medal'. Returning to the Arctic Medal for its octagonal shape, the Polar Medal bore the King's head on one side whilst the reverse showed the *Discovery* in winter quarters with a sledging party. With the exception of a few men, the award went to all those who served in the *Discovery*. A bronze version of the Polar Medal was awarded to the men of the *Morning* and the *Terra Nova*.

Scott obtained six months' leave from the Admiralty (later extended by a further three months) to write his account of the expedition. *The Voyage of the Discovery* was published in October 1905 and proved to be a best seller – 'a masterly work' was how it was described by the *Time's Literary Supplement*. Much against his

The newly promoted Captain Scott
wearing the Polar Medal.

modest nature, Scott was required to give a succession of talks and lectures, always
travelling third class in order to keep costs down. In August 1906, no doubt greatly
to his relief, he was appointed to HMS *Victorious* to serve as Flag-Captain to the
Arctic explorer, Rear-Admiral George Egerton. The lure of the great southern
continent, however, became too great to be ignored and, in January 1907, he
wrote to the Secretary of the Royal Geographical Society outlining a plan to
reach the South Pole from his former base at Ross Island.

Lieutenant Albert Armitage RNR, returned home an embittered man. His
expectation of leading his own expedition had come to naught, and a request to
take a sledge party to the south had been refused by Scott. Much of the blame
for the failure of the dogs on Scott's journey south had fallen on his shoulders,
and his discovery of the Antarctic Plateau had been overshadowed by Scott's
western journey. Both his return home and his finances were ruined by his wife's
scandalous behaviour during his absence, and he spent nine months without pay
before being appointed to a ship. His experiences in the south were described in
Two Years in the Antarctic which, without regard to the normal courtesies, he had
published before Scott's account. Promoted to captain in 1907, he commanded
mail, supply, and troop ships during the First World War. He was torpedoed
off Weymouth in 1917. Armitage was promoted to P&O Line commodore in

1923, retiring from the company just over a year later. He died in 1943 at the age of 79. His most enduring attack on Scott's reputation came when he wrote that he had learned from Wilson that, on the journey south, Scott had behaved boorishly towards Shackleton and that Shackleton had retaliated, thus opening a breach in their relationship. He also wrote that, when asking Koettlitz's advice on Shackleton's health, Scott had told the surgeon, 'If he does not go back sick he will go back in disgrace.' Neither comment was ever substantiated. Both were made long after Scott, Wilson, Koettlitz, and Shackleton were all dead. Nevertheless, they have been frequently used to try and belittle Scott's achievements.

Lieutenant Charles Royds was promoted to commander in 1909, and to captain five years later. After the First World War he was appointed to command the Royal Naval College at Osborn before being selected to become the Director of Physical Training (taking over from his brother). In 1923 he was appointed commodore of Devonport Royal Naval Barracks and became an Aide-de-Camp to the King – with whom he shared an interest in stamp-collecting. Royds was advanced to Rear-Admiral in 1926 and was made Deputy Commissioner of the Metropolitan Police. He was knighted in 1929 and made Vice-Admiral the following year. He died in January 1931, at the age of fifty-four.

Lieutenant Michael Barne came close on two occasions to raising his own Antarctic expeditions after his time on the *Discovery*, but neither achieved fruition. After commanding a destroyer he left the Service in 1910, rejoining at the outbreak of war. He was commander of the *Majestic* when she was sunk off Gallipoli in 1915 before taking command on the Dover and North Sea Patrols where he earned a Distinguished Service Order. Barne was promoted to captain on the retired list in 1922 and served in the Second World War. He died, aged eighty-three, in 1961.

The *Discovery's* engineer, Lieutenant Reginald Skelton, went on to achieve a spectacular career. By the outbreak of the First World War he was an Engineer-Captain. He served at the Battle of Jutland and was awarded the DSO before being appointed to the Admiral's staff at Archangel where his services earned him the awards of Commander of the Bath, and Commander of the British Empire. After service as Fleet-Engineer officer on the Mediterranean Station he was promoted to Engineer Rear-Admiral before being appointed to the Admiralty in the rank of Engineer Vice-Admiral. In 1928, Skelton was promoted to the highest rank in his branch – Engineer-in-Chief of the Fleet and was knighted in 1931. He retired the following year and died in 1952.

Sub-Lieutenant George Mulock earned an award from the Royal Geographical Society for his work on the expedition's charts and later commanded destroyers and a Yangtze gunboat. Following the outbreak of war he saw considerable action at Gallipoli as a Beach Master, was awarded a DSO and promoted to commander. After the war he retired from active service to become Marine Superintendent at Shanghai. Promoted to captain in 1927 he served in the Second World War and spent time as a prisoner of the Japanese. He died in 1963.

Reginald Koettlitz left to live in South Africa and died of typhoid in 1916. Edward Wilson went to study grouse diseases. The expedition biologist, Thomas

Hodgson became curator of the Plymouth Museum and died in 1926. Hartley Ferrar was appointed to the Geological Survey in Egypt and would disappear into the desert for months at a time. After service in Palestine during the war he joined the New Zealand Geological Survey and remained with that department until his death in 1932. Louis Bernacchi served with the Royal Naval Volunteer Reserve in both the First and Second World Wars before dying in 1942.

Leading Stoker William Lashly was rated Chief Stoker on his return and sent to the officer cadet training establishment at Osborn House on the Isle of Wight. Edgar Evans was rated Petty Officer 1st Class and returned to the Gunnery School at HMS *Excellent*, Whale Island. Tom Crean and Frank Wild both jumped from Able Seaman to Petty Officer 1st Class. Crean became Scott's coxswain, and Wild went to train young seamen.

The *Discovery* was purchased by the Hudson's Bay Company and used by them until she was laid up in London in 1920. Bought by the Crown Agents a few years later, the *Royal Research Ship (RRS) Discovery* returned to the south on an oceanographic expedition between 1925 and 1927. The 1929-1931 'British, Australian and New Zealand Antarctic Research Expedition' (BANZARE) saw her in service before she was laid up, once again, in London and, subsequently, transferred to the Sea Scouts. During the Second World War, the *Discovery* became a parachute mine-watching station and lost her masts and engine. In 1954 she was transferred to the Royal Naval Volunteer Reserve as a drill ship and, in a ceremony that would have gladdened the hearts of Scott and Sir Clemence Markham, the ship was commissioned as HMS *Discovery*. This happy state of affairs lasted until 1979 when she was handed over to the Maritime Trust and reverted to being the *RRS Discovery*. The Trust took her in hand and restored, what had become just a hulk, to the condition she was during the 1925 oceanographic expedition. A stately passage north in the embrace of a floating dock took her to Dundee in April 1986. There the *Discovery* rests in her original dry-dock, proud in her achievements and history, a worthy emblem of a gallant enterprise.

CHAPTER SIXTEEN

'DEATH LAY AHEAD AND FOOD BEHIND'

Among the men who had been with Scott in the *Discovery*, only one returned to England under a cloud. Ernest Shackleton, far from being feted as a polar hero, found he had to earn a living. A few lectures were given on his return, but as they led to no exciting offer of employment, he accepted a job as a sub-editor with a magazine. Journalism, however, was not to prove his forte, and he soon accepted the post of Secretary to the Royal Scottish Geographical. He resigned after eighteen months to stand for Parliament only to come third in a three-cornered fight. Shackleton then found employment with the industrialist, William Beardmore, at an engineering works at Parkhead, Glasgow. It was the stroke of luck that Shackleton had been looking for – before long he had persuaded Beardmore to be the main sponsor of an expedition that he had been quietly planning for some time.

Between 1901 and 1905 the Antarctic had been the focus of a number of expeditions. Apart from Scott, the continent had been visited by the German, Erich von Drygalski; Otto Nordenskjold of Sweden; the Scotsman, William Bruce; and the French explorer, Jean Charcot. All had been successful to a degree (Bruce, for example, had charted the coast of 'Coats Land' and carried out an oceanographic survey of the Weddell Sea). There were clearly challengers in the offing (Charcot was known to be considering a return to the Antarctic) – and only one South Pole. Shackleton had no intention of failing to be first through want of enterprise. Unfortunately, his decision looked as if it would cut across the plans of Scott, already in the hands of the Royal Geographical Society.

Scott, at that time, was commanding HMS *Albemarle*, and learned of Shackleton's intentions at Gibraltar, correspondence followed, and eventually a meeting. Scott was keen that he should be granted priority for a base at Ross Island and that Shackleton should find a new base from which to strike out for the Pole. Being merely a matter of honour and precedence such an idea could have no legal substance, but the principle was widely accepted that, where one explorer had forged a path, and intended to return along the same route to extend his personal limit, other explorers should keep clear. Shackleton agreed to Scott's demands and decided to make a base on King Edward VII Land.

To go with him, Shackleton looked first at Scott's men. He asked Wilson to join him as second-in-command, but was turned down. Both Barne and Mulock also refused. He had better luck with Petty Officer Frank Wild who was given permission to go by the Admiralty, and with Petty Officer Ernest Joyce who bought himself out of the Navy in order to go. Lieutenant Jameson Adams RNR was appointed second-in-command. With the exception of the expedition cook, motor mechanic, and two doctors, the remaining men were all academics, from student to professor, aged from nineteen to fifty. In an effort to keep such a disparate group together, Shackleton did away with any idea of naval discipline such as had been used by Scott. Instead, with no distinction between 'wardroom' and 'lower deck' he practically regarded everyone as an officer – or as a rating, depending on the current need. Consequently, academics could find themselves scrubbing decks, or a petty officer could be given complete responsibility for an expedition department, such as stores. It was not, however, a democracy. Shackleton soon established his position as 'Commander of the Expedition' and would brook no opposition to his ideas. Any challenge to his authority was seen as disloyalty, and would be rewarded as such.

An elderly Arctic sealer – the *Nimrod* – was purchased as the expedition vessel and Lieutenant Rupert England RNR (first officer in the *Morning* during the Scott relief expeditions) put in command – Shackleton had no experience of captaining a ship. A novel form of transport (first thought of by Skelton at Balloon Bight) was provided in the shape of a motor-car. Shackleton, who intended to do long daily distances on his way south, was convinced that the 15 horse-power vehicle would drag his sledges over the ice with little difficulty. A few dogs were

The *Nimrod*.

taken, but Shackleton, who had first-hand experience of the failure of the dogs on the southward journey in the summer of 1902, relied on Manchurian ponies for hauling where the motor-car could not operate.

The 'British Antarctic Expedition' assembled at Lyttelton, New Zealand, and sailed on New Year's Day 1908, under tow by the steamship *Koonya*, captained by Lieutenant Frederick Evans RNR. The 1,500 mile voyage to the pack-ice was difficult in the extreme with violent storms threatening to swamp the tiny *Nimrod* with each successive wave. One of the ponies was so badly injured that it had to be put down. The ships parted company on the fifteenth and Shackleton headed for Scott's Balloon Inlet where he intended to set up a base rather than go to King Edward VII Land. The inlet, however, had disappeared, probably having broken free of the ice-barrier, leaving a wider, less protected indentation that Shackleton named 'Bay of Whales' after the large number of spouting whales to be seen in the area. To land and make a base on the barrier at that point would have placed the expedition sixty miles closer to the Pole than Scott had been at Hut Point. But Scott had been on dry land, and to establish a base on the barrier meant the risk of the base breaking away and drifting northwards into oblivion. After a weak probe further to the east, Shackleton decided that, regardless of his agreement with Scott, he was going to make his way to Ross Island. Eric Marshall, the expedition's cartographer and one of its doctors, was furious. In his diary, he accused Shackleton of 'funk' and of not even having 'the guts of a louse' (Marshall, a tough former boxer, was to become his leader's most vociferous critic).

Ross Island was reached in late January and Shackleton found that the ice of McMurdo Sound prevented him from reaching Scott's Hut Point. Instead he had to land at Cape Royds and accept that he was twenty-three miles north of Scott's base. When added to the sixty miles he could have gained at the Bay of Whales, it meant an extra total of approximately 166 miles that would have to be travelled in any journey south from Cape Royds. The frustration caused by his erroneous decisions began to affect Shackleton and, when England refused to hazard his ship by closing with the shore until the weather conditions improved, Shackleton grabbed the engine-room telegraph handle from the captain. An undignified scuffle ensued, and when the *Nimrod* sailed for New Zealand on 22 February, her captain was unaware that the ship's engineer carried a letter, signed by Shackleton, containing his dismissal.

With his hut erected, Shackleton decided that a party of his men should climb Mount Erebus. He would not be going, and so Adams was put in overall charge of the ascent with the unusual order that he was to command a three-man support party whilst a separate three-man party, under Professor Edgeworth David – one of the expedition's geologists – would strike out for the summit. In the event, the inevitable happened and Adams decided that he and his support party would also aim for the top. The party returned a week later, their attempt having been successful at the cost of one toe amputated due to frostbite.

If Shackleton's first attempt at campaign leadership had been somewhat muddled, the following winter cruelly exposed his lack of disciplined structure.

When told to exercise the ponies, Raymond Priestley – a second year student and the expedition's second geologist – refused, reminding Adams that he was a scientist. Adams, in direct nautical language brought to Priestley's attention the fact that, regardless of his imagined status, he was just another expedition member and should get on with whatever he was told to do. One of the expedition doctors, Alistair Mackay, had to be pulled away from trying to throttle the cook, and Joyce and Marshall shouted or glowered at each other over petty accusations. Shackleton twice publicly threatened to shoot Mackay, and – according to Marshall – was either boasting that he was a better man than any of the others, or was 'in a regular panic'. Not unnaturally, without a formal structure, cliques soon developed with Wild and Joyce making a naval front against the, occasionally united, university men. The three Australians combined in a colonial cabal.

An attempt to calm things down was made by introducing weekend smoking concerts, and by holding special dinners to mark birthdays. A number of articles were combined to form a book, *Aurora Australis*. It was a lacklustre affair when compared to the *South Polar Times* and was only produced with an eye to future sales – which did not happen.

With the return of the sun in late August, Shackleton set into motion his plans for the main sledging expeditions. The motor-car was tested and found to be hopeless on soft snow, but useable on ice. Only four of the ponies had survived the winter. The losses amongst the animals were to have a great effect upon

Some of Shackleton's shore party. Petty Officer Ernest Joyce is standing far left, Petty Officer Frank Wild is standing third from left with Lieutenant Jameson Adams to his right. Shackleton is standing fifth from right with Eric Marshal looking over his left shoulder.

Shackleton's subsequent achievements. He had decided that there would be three sledge expeditions. One, with David, Mackay, and the expedition physicist, Douglas Mawson, would head northwards along the coast of Victoria Land to reach and fix the position of the South Magnetic Pole. The pony handler, Bertram Armytage, Priestley, and Sir Philip Brocklehurst – a young Etonian in his second year at Cambridge – would cross McMurdo Sound to carry out geological research in the Victoria Land mountains. Both parties had a vague expectation of being picked up from the Victoria Land coast by the *Nimrod* on her return from New Zealand.

For Shackleton, the prize was to be the South Pole itself. Scott's hut was to be used as a depot and a further depot was established 120 miles from Cape Royds. The party was expected to be out for ninety-one days and carried supplies for just that length of time. A support party, led by Armytage, was to accompany Shackleton for part of the way. The expedition biologist, Joseph Murray, who would be remaining at the base camp, was ordered to keep a look-out for Shackleton's party until 25 February 1909. If nothing was seen by that date, fuel, stores, and clothing to last seven men for one year was to be left at the base. Three volunteers were to be found to stay and wait for the southern party as the *Nimrod* left for New Zealand. Should, however, conditions allow, the ship could remain off Cape Royds until early March, but had to leave by the tenth at the latest.

The southern party set off on 29 October. The supporting party left first with the motor-car hauling their sledges. Half an hour later Shackleton set off with his team of Adams, Marshall, and Wild, each leading a pony. In his baggage Shackleton carried a Union Jack, given to him by Queen Alexandra to fly at the South Pole. Within an hour the first pony went lame and they had to slow down to allow the animal to recover. As they rested for lunch, Adams was kicked just below the knee by another of the ponies. It was an unfortunate start to the great enterprise and a week later Wild was noting that Shackleton had become, 'rather irritable and excited.'

Four days after leaving Hut Point they had only covered twenty miles. The following day the support party was sent back. Poor light soon put Shackleton's party at risk of crevasses and bad weather forced them to stay in their tents for a whole day. Such delays, so early on, threatened to markedly reduce their chances of reaching the Pole. All they could hope for was an improvement that would allow a good passage, at least to Scott's furthest point. Fortune seemed to be on their side for a time when the weather cleared, but Shackleton was affected by mild snow-blindness. The depot was reached safely and Shackleton used the time at the site to reduce his load. A week later, one of the ponies was shot and much of its meat deposited with a tin of biscuits and a can of oil beneath a black flag flying from a bamboo pole. On 26 November, twenty-four days out from Cape Royds, a noon observation revealed that they were at 82 degrees 18'S – one mile further south than Scott's best. Even the critical Marshall considered it to be 'a great day'. They celebrated by shooting another of the ponies, depoting its meat for their return journey. Ahead of them mountains were beginning to rear up, and it was clear that, unless they could find a way through to the south, they would have to start marching eastwards along the mountains' front.

Mount Hope on the left. The first inlet to its right is the route to the Beardmore Glacier.

The third pony was shot on the first day of December, just before Shackleton decided that he had better approach the southern mountains head-on. The mighty range barring their way continued on to the east and offered little but a pointless march in the wrong direction. He headed for a small hill ('Mount Hope') which, on being climbed, revealed how right he had been to press on to the south. Before their astonished gaze, a giant glacier, at least thirty miles wide, flowed silently towards them between rugged walls of snow-laced rock. On its western flank a huge mountain stood with its head in the clouds. Shackleton named the glacier after his chief benefactor, William Beardmore, and the mountain 'Cloudmaker'. This then, was to be the route to the Pole.

Three days up the glacier slope, Wild was leading the sole remaining pony when the ice opened up under his feet. His fall was halted by a sharp jerk a split second before the pony dealt him a glancing blow as it fell past him. By sheer good fortune the sledge had become jammed at the crevasses' mouth and Wild was left hanging by his left arm. Taking prompt action he hauled himself out just as the others raced over to help. The loss of the pony was a disaster. Shackleton had depended upon it to assist in dragging the sledges up the glacier, and to provide its meat for their way down. Now they had to haul the sledges on reduced rations, and Shackleton was nearly blind from refusing to wear tinted snow-goggles. The only high point in the day for Wild was the realisation that he would not have to shoot his pony.

The gruelling climb up the broken glacier surface continued day after day to a background of hunger and breakdown of team-spirit. Shackleton was failing

Shackleton's 'Furthest South' – flying the flag given by Queen Alexandra to be flown at the South Pole.

to keep his men motivated and belief in the expedition itself was beginning to falter. The tough little man, Wild, raged in his diary about Marshall and Adams. They were, he wrote, 'two grub-scoffing useless beggars'. Adams, he admitted, sometimes did his best, but it was a 'poor best'. As for Marshall, 'I sincerely wish he would fall down a crevasse about 1,000 feet deep.' Nor did he always keep his comments to himself, complaining openly to Adams about Marshall's 'slack trace'. Marshall, on the other hand, approved of Wild and saved his bile for Shackleton whom he considered, 'an old woman. Always panicking', and 'hopeless'. The shared experience of hauling sledges for a full month up a broken glacier surface to reach over 10,000 feet should have welded them together into a life-long bond of companionship; on reaching the plateau, their combined will-power as a team should have forced them to plant their Queen's flag at the Pole, regardless of the consequences. Instead, worn down by suspicion and petty enmity, they all began to look for reasons to turn back. They did not have long to wait. On 9 January, leaving their camp and sledges in the early hours of the morning, the four men pushed on to the south. After seven hours, they stopped, planted the Queen's flag and Shackleton took possession of the plateau in the King's name. They had to guess their position as they had left their theodolite at their camp. It was decided that they had reached 88 degrees 23'S – just ninety-seven miles from the Pole after travelling 730 miles from their base. There were no handshakes, no mutual congratulations, no cheers. Just a desire to get home.

With their food in desperately short supply, the party were keen to get under way towards the north. They were helped by a strong blizzard at their backs which drove the sail-rigged sledge on at a good pace. The top of the Beardmore Glacier was reached after eleven days. Shackleton was in a bad way with split heels and had been badly shaken up by a number of hard falls; consequently, he had to walk by the sledge for part of the way. Wild began to be affected by dysentery, and both he and Adams collapsed from exhaustion as they made their way down the glacier. One by one the depots were picked up. Each was reached with little or no food remaining on the approaching sledge. Hunger became the predominant feature in all their minds. Even the frozen blood of one of the ponies was found and used to make a 'beautiful soup'. Shackleton felt a 'distinct grievance' if, when hoosh was available, anyone managed to make it last longer than the others.

Minna Bluff was reached six weeks after they had left their furthest point south. Much to their relief they found a depot that, following Shackleton's instructions, had been established by Joyce. It was stuffed with provisions ranging from crystallised fruit to freshly boiled mutton. There was, however, little time to rest and enjoy the delicacies that Joyce had brought out. With the food was a letter telling Shackleton that the *Nimrod* had arrived. The depot had been reached on 24 February, and Shackleton had given orders that stores and party of three volunteers should be landed on the twenty-fifth. If he had not appeared by that date, the landing party should set off south to look for him. The ship, ice permitting, was expected to remain until 10 March – giving Shackleton ample time to reach it before it was due to depart.

The day after leaving the depot, Marshall went down with dysentery. He proved capable of hauling on the twenty-sixth, but collapsed in the evening. It was clear to Shackleton that someone would have to push on to the base, or to the ship, to seek help. Adams was fit and Wild, although suffering with his feet, was in a better condition than Shackleton who not only had split heels, but was also suffering from severe headaches. This, alone, would have given Shackleton the reason he needed as leader to remain with the exhausted Marshall. Almost every previous example of polar leadership had found the commander of the expedition remaining at the point of greatest danger as a comfort and example to the rest of his men (an exception being Franklin, ninety years earlier, but he had to leave Doctor Richardson to nurse Midshipman Hood whilst his authority was needed to deal with the Indians). Surprisingly, Shackleton decided that he would leave Adams at the place of greatest risk as he and Wild made a dash to Hut Point. Such a decision also ensured that his diaries – and, consequently, the story of his achievements – would reach civilisation whatever the outcome.

The two men set off on the late afternoon of the twenty-seventh and arrived at Hut Point the following evening to find neither ship nor relief party. After a night huddled in the hut they were attempting to set light to one of the outbuildings when the *Nimrod* sailed into view. The meeting was not how Shackleton had imagined and hoped it would be. In answer to the question 'Did you reach the Pole?' he was forced to answer that he had not. Not only that, but he had left

The Southern Party on their return to the *Nimrod* – Wild, Shackleton, Marshall, Adams.

two men out on the ice. He also found himself in the middle of a storm caused by his lack of a disciplinary structure. Shackleton had left a letter with Murray putting him in charge and giving him instructions regarding the relief party. The captain of the *Nimrod* – Lieutenant Frederick Evans, formerly of the towing ship *Koonya* – decided that he would take command. There were plenty of volunteers for the relief party, but they promptly fell into factions. David announced that a party consisting of Australians and New Zealanders would make up the relief. Mackay fumed that such a choice represented a slight against the British, and Joyce declared that he was staying, whatever anybody else might say.

Shackleton handled the problem by leaving it. He went back over the ice with three men to collect Marshall and Adams. The invalid had recovered well, and was able to make his way back unaided.

Despite his failure to reach the pole, Shackleton's expedition had been a magnificent achievement. He had pioneered a route to the Pole and had beaten the previous furthest southern record by 366 miles. Mount Erebus had been climbed and the party led by Edgeworth David had reached the South Magnetic Pole. Not a man had been lost. Shackleton was determined that his reception in England would differ from the muddle and mayhem he found at Hut Point. At the first opportunity he telegraphed the *Daily Mail* to ensure that the high points of his expedition would receive wide-spread attention, and on his voyage home he took with him a journalist to polish up his account of his travels. At Port Said, he transferred to a mail packet under the command of none other than Captain Albert Armitage – a good friend from his *Discovery* days. Armitage noted that Shackleton struggled to find a phrase or 'catchword' to provide a gloss for his turning back when so close to the Pole – 'I've got it at last', he cried. 'Death lay ahead and food behind, so I had to return.' (He, nor anyone else, knew that within a few years, hundreds of thousands of men would have death 'ahead', but still gallantly advanced into the horrors of no-man's land regardless.) Now ready to meet the public, Shackleton made sure the press knew that he would be arriving at Charing Cross station at 5pm.

Shackleton received the adulation he sought. Crowds turned out to cheer his arrival, he was awarded the CVO by the King, a gold medal came from the Royal Geographical Society, and his Lieutenant RNR uniform soon had a chestful of foreign decorations. The high point came with a knighthood awarded with the Birthday Honours. Among the first to offer their congratulations on his achievement was Captain Scott.

The only shadow to fall across this blaze of glory was the question of the latitude gained. When geographers examined Shackleton's claim to have reached 88 degrees 23'S they found that it depended upon the final dash south on 9 January. Despite being weak with hunger, and exhausted from the climb up the Beardmore Glacier, Shackleton recorded that he and the others covered sixteen miles of soft snow in five hours, ran up the flag, took some photographs, and then returned to their tent in the same time. Thirty-two miles of hard going had been covered in ten hours by men who could not raise the energy to press on to the Pole. Some people found this claim difficult to believe.

PUNCH, OR THE LONDON CHARIVARI.—MARCH 31, 1909.

THE EXCLUSIVES.

NORTH POLE (*to* SOUTH POLE). "HALLO! ARE YOU THERE? I SAY, OLD MAN, THEY NEARLY HAD YOU THAT TIME."

VOICE FROM SOUTH POLE. "YES, I KNOW. THERE'LL SOON BE NO SUCH THING AS PRIVACY."

[With *Mr. Punch*'s best compliments to Lieutenant Shackleton.]

Above: Punch's 'best compliments to Lieutenant Shackleton'.

Opposite: The menu from a dinner given at the Savage Club by Captain Scott to welcome Shackleton's return.

As recommended by Shackleton.

Two of Shackleton's best men, Mawson and Wild, returned to the Antarctic on Mawson's 'Australasian Antarctic Expedition.' It was to prove Mawson's finest hour as he; an English army officer, Belgrave Ninnis (the same name as one of the surgeons on Nare's 1875-76 Arctic expedition); and Doctor Xavier Mertz, a Swiss mountaineer, set off with their dog-sledges. The expedition intended to explore the land west from Cape Adair and Mawson chose for himself a route that would take him to the south before swinging to the east. 300 miles from their base, Ninnis fell down a crevasse along with his dogs and sledge. Quite apart from the loss of Ninnis, the crevasse had also swallowed most of the expedition's food – including all of the dog food. There were six dogs remaining and a tent cover. Mawson decided that their only hope was to return as quickly as possible using the dogs as food. Before long Mertz became very ill as a result of eating the dogs' livers. With the base still 100 miles away, Mertz died. Dreadfully weakened, Mawson cut the sledge in half to reduce its weight and plodded doggedly on. Nine days after Mertz's death, Mawson fell down a crevasse but was saved from instant death by the sledge jamming across the mouth of the crack. He found himself hanging by one hand with nothing but a black void beneath his feet. With almost superhuman effort, and with hands blistered by frostbite, he managed to pull himself out and to safety. Two weeks later, much of which he had spent hauling the half-sledge on his hands and knees, he reached an ice cave five miles from the base. A blizzard was to prevent him from leaving the sanctuary for another week and, when he managed to escape, he ran into five men who were setting out to search for him. They had desperately bad news – the ship had just sailed to pick up a party led by Wild – and Mawson and his men were condemned to another winter in the Antarctic.

CHAPTER SEVENTEEN

'WITH AN EYE TO MEDALS OR SOMETHING'

When Wild returned to England in 1913, he found Shackleton in a frenzy of activity. A new expedition was to be launched. The South Pole had already been reached leaving just one chance for glory – the crossing of Antarctica. The idea was not new. The Scottish explorer, Dr William Bruce, had come up with the idea of putting a ship into the Weddell Sea, landing a sledging party on the coast, and then meeting them using the same ship from the Ross Sea. The idea had foundered through lack of funding. The German, Wilhelm Filchner, had actually taken a ship into the Weddell Sea with the same aim, but had been frozen in and spent nine months drifting with the ice before being freed. He had not been able to put anyone ashore.

Shackleton's life had not been easy since his return from his *Nimrod* expedition. A succession of failed ventures, and the shadow of a brother's criminal activities, had done little to burnish the fame he had found on his return. His book, *Heart of the Antarctic*, however, had been a success, and his name counted highly in the world of polar exploration. As always, raising funds was the greatest difficulty he had to face and, once he had worked out the basis of his plan – to cross the continent from the Weddell Sea to the Ross Sea – he was not above a little deception to start his fund-raising. Pretending to already have a rich benefactor, Shackleton applied to the Government for money. The Admiralty, under Winston Churchill, would have nothing to do with him, especially as the Hydrographer (a grandson of the great Arctic explorer – William Parry) was still aggrieved by Shackleton's 'meagre' production of hydrographic and magnetic survey information from his *Nimrod* expedition. The Chancellor of the Exchequer, David Lloyd George, on the other hand, could see clear political advantages in having his name linked with such an enterprise and offered Shackleton £10,000 providing he could match the same figure from private sources. The Royal Geographical Society was then approached. To Shackleton's good fortune, Sir Clemence Markham had retired as President. He still tried, nonetheless, to put a spoke in Shackleton's plans by writing to the Society's secretary and saying that, 'I have been astounded at the absurdity of Shackleton's plan, alike useless and expensive, and designed solely for self advertisement.' A contribution of £1,000 was the best that the Society was prepared to donate.

Sheer plans for the *Endurance*.

The plans for 'The Imperial Trans-Antarctic Expedition' were published after an announcement in *The Times* of 29 December 1913. In them, Shackleton, declared that he would secure 'for the British flag the honour of being the first carried across the South Polar Continent.' To achieve this he intended to land a party of six men with dogs and sledges on the shores of Prince Leopold Land on the shores of the Weddell Sea. From there, over the next five months, they would march 1,800 miles to the Ross Sea via the South Pole.

The Weddell Sea party would be landed from a newly built vessel. Originally named *Polaris*, Shackleton had her name changed to *Endurance* to reflect his family motto *'By endurance we conquer'*. Once the crossing party had been landed, the *Endurance* would spend the winter at South Georgia. On the other side of the continent, the Ross Sea party would land from the *Aurora*, recently purchased from Mawson. These men would construct a line of depots and wait for the crossing party to join them, 'probably' at the top of the Beardmore Glacier.

There was, of course, a great flaw in the plan. With no means of communication, the Ross Sea party would not know if Shackleton and his team of sledgers had left Prince Leopold Land during the first season. If there was a delay, it would be another year before they could get underway, leaving the Ross Sea party stranded at the top of the glacier. Such detail, however, seemed to go unnoticed as the funds began to come in. Chief among the backers was a Dundee industrialist, James Caird. Two others were Dudley Docker and Miss Janet Stancomb Wills. Each of them had one of the *Endurance* ship's boats named after them.

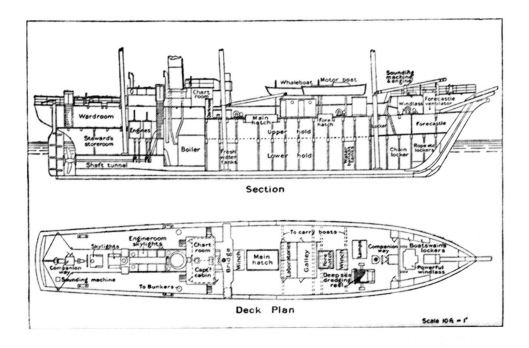

Above: Sheer plan of the *Aurora.*

Right: Lieutenant Frank Worsley RNR – the captain of the *Endurance.*

The expedition office mail was soon full of applicants wishing to gain a place – among them fourteen women. Apart from Wild, Shackleton chose only four others with Antarctic experience for the *Endurance*. George ('Putty') Marston, formerly of the *Nimrod*, was taken as Expedition Artist and given charge of the clothing; Petty Officer First Class Tom Crean was appointed as Second Officer, while Alf Cheetham, the Third Officer, had been to the Antarctic on three occasions. The fourth was an Australian, Frank Hurley. His experiences under Mawson earned him the job of expedition photographer. A New Zealander, Frank Worsley, a lieutenant in the Royal Naval Reserve, was appointed as captain of the *Endurance* (Shackleton had hoped for John Davies – the *Aurora's* captain under Mawson – but was turned down).

Shackleton was keen to have the *Aurora* manned by men of the Royal Navy but was refused. Instead the Admiralty agreed to send just one officer, Captain Thomas Orde Lees of the Royal Marines – the head of the Corp's physical training school, and a noted trick-cyclist with a penchant for throwing himself off bridges to test parachutes. Shackleton appointed him to the *Endurance* as 'Motor Expert'. Among the other men chosen was a dog-driver recommended by the Royal North West Mounted Police. On his arrival in England the man learned to his horror that there were no trees, plants, or animals in the Antarctic. His prompt reaction was to catch the next ship home leaving Wild to take charge of the dogs.

Captain Thomas Orde Lees RM.

Above: The *Aurora* party. Sub-Lieutenant Aeneas
Mackintosh RNR is third from left in the centre row
with the tall figure of the Revd Spencer-Smith to
his rear.

Right: Sub-Lieutenant Aeneas Mackintosh
RNR, captain of the *Aurora*.

Sub-Lieutenant Aeneas Mackintosh RNR, a merchant navy officer, was placed
in command of the *Aurora* and the Ross Sea party. He had intended to join
Shackleton ashore on the *Nimrod* expedition, but had lost an eye in an accident
whilst the ship was being unloaded. Ernest Joyce, who had been with Scott in
the *Discovery* and Shackleton in the *Nimrod*, was appointed to the *Aurora* with
responsibility for the sledging equipment. He was joined by Frank Wild's brother,
Ernest, who was put in charge of general stores. The *Aurora* herself was in Australia,
and much of her crew would have to be raised from volunteers in that country.

The *Endurance* left England on 8 August 1914, just as the country was about to slide into war. Shackleton did not sail with the ship but left to join her at Buenos Aires after attempting to sort out the expedition's growing financial problems. At the Argentinean port he picked up, not only the photographer Hurley, but also a stowaway – a nineteen-year-old ship's steward, Percy Blackborrow, who was assured that, if the expedition had to resort to cannibalism, he would be eaten first.

A month was spent in final preparation among the stench of decaying whale carcasses at Grytviken, South Georgia's main whaling station. Informed by the whalers that the ice in the Weddell Sea was particularly thick, Shackleton changed his plans and decided that he would allow the *Endurance* to be frozen in for the winter off the coast where the crossing party were to be landed. He also decided that the party would not leave for the Ross Sea until November the following year. Although he told the British press of his new plans, the news never reached Mackintosh and the *Aurora*.

The stay at Grytviken was enlivened by Hussey, who, on paying a social call on one of the whaling captains on a dark and snowy night, found his way across the open 'flensing plan' (where the whales were cut up) barred by a huge whale. Finding no way around the head of the creature he tried the tail end only to find that blocked off by a pile of offal. Determined not to be defeated, Hussey climbed up the side of the animal. Just as he reached the top, the flesh gave way beneath his boots and he fell into its bowels and had to lay trapped in his evil-smelling prison, 'anxious to avoid publicity', until his eventual shouts brought help. For this achievement he was awarded a special 'Jonah' medal made of leather. On 5 December, the *Endurance* sailed for the Weddell Sea to the sound of whaling factory sirens and the salutes of harpoon guns. She had onboard twenty-eight men. Shackleton, Wild, Crean, Marston, Macklin, and Hurley would make up the crossing party leaving four scientists, one surgeon, and one motor expert with the ship's crew.

A long, slow, battle with thick ice was followed by a sighting of the coast of Coats Land ('Caird Coast') on 10 January 1915. 'Glacier Bay' looked an ideal place to land, but Shackleton had his eye on Filchner's Vahsel Bay, almost 200 miles further south. And it seemed as if he was to be right. Open water for 120 miles to the south allowed a swift passage towards his goal. But, just over a week after seeing land, the *Endurance* was firmly trapped with a glittering white plain extending in all directions. 281 days later, to the sound of the ship's ribs cracking as she writhed beneath the pressure of the ice, eight Emperor penguins approached the ship's side and began to sing what sounded like a mournful dirge. The eerie sight and sound of the penguins shook Shackleton. The next day, the *Endurance* was abandoned, and everyone assembled at a pile of recovered stores 200 yards from the ship's starboard bow nicknamed 'Dump Camp'.

They were in a desperate situation. The ship had drifted for almost 1,500 miles, first to the south and then northwards. To their north-west, the Graham Land peninsula curved gently eastwards, but was hundreds of miles away. Even if they managed to make land, no-one would know where they were, and many months would pass before anyone started looking for them. Their feet rested on nothing more than a sheet of ice above a deep ocean. As the ice drifted north it would begin to break up beneath them. Shackleton knew that he had to install some sense of hope into his men and came up with the idea of dragging the boats across the ice to Paulet Island, 346 miles away. In 1902, Nordenskjold had built a hut on the island and it was known that a cache of food had been left at the site. From there it would be possible to cross the peninsula to Wilhelmina Bay, an area where whalers might be encountered.

The *Endurance* almost on her beam ends as the ice begins to lift and crush her.

Shackleton's men dragging a boat from the *Endurance*.

The boat hauling began on 30 October. As the dogs dragged sledges of stores and provisions, fifteen men began to haul on the largest of the boat sledges, its weight of almost a ton soon causing exhaustion. After two hours they had done less than a mile and had reached their limit. Two days later Shackleton gave up and decided to simply camp on the flow and wait as it continued its northward drift. According to Hurley, 'Ocean Camp' looked like 'a deserted Alaskan mining village that had been ransacked by bandits.' Over the next six weeks the camp drifted 120 miles, and morale fell – especially amongst the seamen who were convinced that their pay had stopped when the ship sank. To counteract this encroaching mood of discontent, Shackleton decided that he would attempt, once again, to haul the boats towards the land. They set off on 22 December only to find that what had been difficult before, was now nigh on impossible. The snow covering the ice had turned to a knee-deep mush, wide leads and open cracks frequently lay across their path, and pressure ridges and hummocks reared up in all directions. After three days of sheer grinding effort, just six miles had been achieved. Shackleton, who had been ahead of the boats, returned to find Worsley in direct confrontation with Harry McNeish, the ship's carpenter. McNeish had come to the conclusion that if he was not being paid, it followed that he had no superiors, therefore, he did not have to accept anyone's orders – and the most ridiculous order he had been given demanded that he drag a boat over impossible conditions. It was a threatening moment that called for great leadership in its resolution. Instead, Shackleton resorted to subterfuge, claiming that he was the captain of the *Endurance* (thus reducing Worsley to the position of first mate) and had authority on both sea and land. The question of pay was easily dealt with – he told the seamen that it had always been intended that their pay would continue until they reached a recognised port. It was a lie – Shackleton's funding of the expedition had failed to cover even the basic costs – but it diffused the situation and McNeish returned to the traces.

Shackleton had been badly rattled by the display of disloyalty and he never found the magnanimity to forgive McNeish, despite the fact that the carpenter proved to be right. After two more days, and at a point no more than ten miles from Ocean Camp, even Shackleton realised that his men could haul no more and called a halt.

'Patience Camp' remained their home for the next four and a half months. By March the floe on which they were camped had gradually reduced in size as large pieces broke off – only the three boats could save them. The dogs were shot by Wild and added to their store of food as the boats were prepared for the forthcoming voyage. Shackleton had decided that he would head for Elephant Island, a small island north of the Graham Land peninsula, about 100 miles from 'Patience Camp'. The boats entered the water on 9 April with Shackleton in the largest – the *James Caird* – followed by the smaller *Dudley Docker* and *Stancomb Wills*.

It took five days to reach Elephant Island. A rough sea constantly threatened to swamp the boats, many of the men suffered from sea-sickness, and thirst became an ever-present problem – Shackleton had not taken the simple precaution of collecting ice to provide drinking water. When the cliff-lined shore approached, it became clear that the smaller *Stancomb Wills* stood the best chance of reaching safety first, and Shackleton transferred into her, 'to ascertain the possibilities of landing.' It was sixteen months since they had last stood on solid ground. Two days later the party moved westwards along the coast to a better beach discovered by Wild.

A hot drink on the beach at Elephant Island – the first for seven days. Petty Officer Frank Wild is standing to the far right looking at the camera.

The *James Caird* being launched.

The next few days were utter misery. A blizzard raged as the men, wet through and exhausted, huddled in their sleeping bags beneath tents that were ripped to shreds. In some ways, however, they had improved their situation. There was plenty of food and fuel in the shape of penguins and elephant seals (their name being given to the island). Their boats had survived and, in six months' time, could be used for an attempt to reach Deception Island and the whaling grounds, 140 miles away to the south-west.

Shackleton, however, had no intention of spending months on the island. He decided that an attempt should be made to get help by sailing 800 miles to South Georgia (although both Cape Horn and the Falkland Islands were closer, the strong westerlies would have prevented any boat under sail from reaching them). Such a boat journey was certainly one of the options available to him but, surprisingly, yet again, Shackleton used the single option that took him away from the point of greatest danger. To help ensure his own survival he decided to take Worsley with him. He had little time for the *Endurance*'s captain, either as a leader or as a seaman. He did, however, recognise that Worsley was a superb navigator, and good navigation was vital if South Georgia was to be located in the vast waters of the South Atlantic. Worsley's later comments typically verged on the sycophantic (or, possibly, sarcastic), 'It was certain that a man of such heroic mind and self-sacrificing nature as Shackleton would undertake this most difficult task himself.' There was no need for Shackleton to have gone at all. If the boat journey had to be made, there were plenty of volunteers who had the skills needed to make the voyage whereas Shackleton could have remained with his men to lead and encourage them through the approaching winter (he admitted to Worsley that he knew nothing about small boat sailing). As it was he took Crean, McCarthy, and Vincent – three seamen all used to small boat work. He also took McNeish, the ship's carpenter, as added insurance.

The price those remaining would have to pay was significant. The chances of reaching Deception Island were dramatically reduced. The *Dudley Docker* was dismantled by McNeish to 'deck in' the *James Caird,* the *Stancomb Wills* lost her mast to provide her with fore and aft strengthening. Penguins were in the process of being killed and stored up for the winter but, as soon as Shackleton left, Wild (put in command of the Elephant Island party by Shackleton) played down the need to lay in an adequate store of penguin meat. Not only was he convinced that the penguins would be available throughout the winter, he also believed that Shackleton would be back with a relief ship 'in less than a fortnight' and to obtain meat for a whole winter would only cause despondency among the party. As a result, the threat of starvation later became a reality.

The *James Caird* sailed from Elephant Island on 24 April and, thanks to Worsley's navigation, reached King Haakon Bay fourteen days later. It had been a difficult voyage under dreadful conditions made worse by Shackleton's insistence that the boat be over-ballasted. The result, according to Worsley, was 'unnecessary misery'. The landing had been made on the southern coast of the island and it was necessary to get to the whaling stations strung out along the northern shore. But, not only was the *James Caird* in no shape for a further voyage in the inhospitable waters around the island, Vincent was suffering from exposure. Consequently, Shackleton realised that his only practical chance of reaching assistance was to cross the island – something that had not been done before.

After resting for a few days in a small cove and living on albatross chicks, Shackleton and his party sailed across the bay to a low stretch of sand where he left McNeish in charge of Vincent and McCarthy. The boat was upturned to provide accommodation for the three men and McNeish was told that, if no help came, they should see the winter out living on the many elephant seals that lay on the surrounding beaches before sailing the *James Caird* around the coast to the whaling stations.

With neither proper clothing nor mountaineering equipment, Shackleton, Worsley, and Crean set off to cross the island. It proved an epic journey that lasted for thirty-six hours and tested the three men to their limit. The afternoon of 20 May however, saw them arrive exhausted and dishevelled at the door of the manager's house at Stromness whaling station – almost seventeen months after they had left South Georgia for the Weddell Sea. They had not washed for three months nor changed their clothing for seven months. After a bath, clean clothes and a meal, Worsley joined a steam whaler and sailed round to King Haakon Bay to collect the three men left beneath the upturned *James Caird*. Following a good night's sleep, Shackleton and Crean visited the nearby Husvic whaling station where they found a British-owned whaler. Shackleton used this vessel to try and reach the twenty-two men he had left behind on Elephant Island. He got within sixty miles of the beach, but was forced to retreat when the pack-ice prevented further progress. The whaler then took him to Port Stanley in the Falkland Islands where he sent a telegram to the King, informing him of the expedition's predicament. A reply came the following day wishing him well, but when the captain of HMS *Glasgow*, anchored in Port Stanley, requested permission from the Admiralty to make an attempt to reach Elephant Island he was refused – clearly, at a time when there were men dying in their thousands on the Western Front, it was no time to waste the services of a cruiser on a self-inflicted side-show. The Falkland Islanders also showed a remarkable lack of sympathy merely observing that Shackleton should have been fighting in the war 'instead of messing about on icebergs.'

The Admiralty, however, had already been organising a relief expedition. They decided that the best ship for the job would be the *Discovery* and appointed Temporary Lieutenant Commander James Fairweather RNR to command her. She left England on 10 August under tow and reached Montevideo a month later carrying a letter informing Shackleton that Fairweather would remain in command regardless of Shackleton's wishes. In the meantime, Shackleton had accepted a Uruguayan offer of the trawler *Instituto de Pesca No.1*. He was picked up at Port Stanley by the trawler and managed to reach within twenty miles of Elephant Island before the ice forced his return. Shackleton then sailed for the Chilean port of Punta Arenas where he hired the schooner *Emma*. Under tow by the small Chilean steamer *Yelcho*, the *Emma* got to within eighty miles of the stranded men before having to turn back in the face of the pack. Calling at Port Stanley before returning to Punta Arenas, Shackleton learned for the first time of the *Discovery* relief effort and Fairweather's orders to take over command of the search. Ignoring the Governor of the Colony's advice to wait for the *Discovery* (and the consequent removal of his authority), Shackleton returned to Punta Arenas and asked the Chilean Government for permission to use the *Yelcho* in a fourth attempt to rescue his men. Permission was granted and the steamer left on 24 August. This time the ice cleared a passage and the island was reached on the thirtieth. In less than an hour the twenty-two men were onboard and heading for the Chilean port. They bathed, dined and were given new clothing, but Shackleton refused to allow them to cut their hair and beards as he wanted publicity photographs to be taken on arrival at Punta Arenas.

The return of the *Yelcho* with Shackleton and his rescued men was greeted with all the hectic warmth of a Chilean homecoming. Crowds packed the jetty and bands led the returning heroes through the streets to the Royal Hotel. Receptions, dinners, and parties were laid on, Shackleton made speeches, and his men were taken into the homes of the townsfolk. Not everyone, however, was quite so impressed.

The Admiralty was beginning to look upon Shackleton's activities as little more than a publicity stunt. One of his *Nimrod* expedition members, Douglas Mawson (now Sir Douglas and a member of the Admiralty's expedition relief committee), had heard the reports given by McNeish, Vincent, and McCarthy on their return to England. He wrote to the Hydrographer:

> Their story shows that Shackleton's cable rather exaggerated matters particularly the plight of the Elephant Islanders. There was a rookery on Elephant Island where the party landed and before they left 500 penguins had been cached. They state also that there were plenty of seals and sea elephants. They state there is NO anxiety as regards food for the party and they expect to be relieved in November. In my opinion it is a pity that the Government has been troubled in the matter and put to expense.

Shortly afterwards, Mawson revealed his view of Shackleton when he again wrote to the Hydrographer that Shackleton, 'is up in Chile now – presumably with an eye to medals or something.' The hydrographer – Captain Parry – replied, 'The rescue of the Elephant Island party by Shackleton having taken place immediately after his having ascertained that he was not to have charge of the *Discovery* was to my thinking more than a coincidence.' They were not alone in their doubts about Shackleton. His ship, the *Aurora*, had ended up in New Zealand and he wanted to take her back into the Antarctic to pick up his Ross Sea party, but the Australian Government (helping with funds and with a number of Australian citizens involved) did 'not want Shackleton to have anything to do with it'.

There was good reason for the Australians to view any involvement of Shackleton's with a jaundiced eye. When Aeneas Mackintosh arrived in Sydney in November 1914 he found his part of the expedition in chaos. The money Shackleton claimed to have sent had not arrived, the stores were woefully short, and the *Aurora* was still registered in Mawson's name. The Australians, who were sending men to fight in the war, could not summon up a great deal of interest in an Antarctic side-show. They were outraged at the costs of refitting the ship and the assumption that they would supply her with free coal.

The ship had left Australia on Christmas Eve and arrived off Ross Island on 16 January 1915, with orders from Shackleton that she was not to anchor in McMurdo Sound as he did not want to risk her being frozen in. Both Mackintosh and Ernest Joyce were keen to set off southwards to establish depots as they expected Shackleton to start his crossing during the summer of 1914-15. The only problem was that, thanks to Shackleton's confusing orders, both men thought they were in charge of the sledging operations and early conflict between the two men was not helpful. Mackintosh, Joyce, and Ernest Wild established a depot at 80 degrees South only to return through appalling conditions which saw them reduced to eating biscuit crumbs, being badly frostbitten, and having all their dogs die in harness. On arrival at Scott's *Discovery* hut they joined three other men to wait for the ice in McMurdo Sound to freeze over and allow them to reach their base at Cape Evans. They had expected the *Aurora* – temporarily under the command of Sub-Lieutenant Joseph Stenhouse RNR, the ship's chief officer – to have delivered stores to the hut, but nothing had arrived.

Consequently, they were forced to burn one of Scott's scientific outbuildings for fuel and live on seals. Nine weeks later they were able to cross the ice and reach the Cape Evans base where they found that the *Aurora* had drifted out with the ice a month earlier and not been seen since. Even worse, the ship had not had time to complete her unloading. Most of the food, all of the sledging clothing, much of the sledging equipment, tents, sleeping bags, fuel, and cookers, had vanished with the ship. Ten tons of coal that had been landed on the ice had also drifted out and were lost. The ten men that had been marooned on the island faced an Antarctic winter without sufficient clothing or fuel.

The season was spent with little of the relaxed bonhomie of previous expeditions. The area was searched for remnants left from earlier visits and clothing stitched from the remains of a canvas tent. Seals were killed and cached for food and fuel. Morale was not helped by the jostling for position between Mackintosh, Joyce, and Stevens – the head of the scientific staff. As usual, Shackleton had not established a clear chain of command and each man felt that he should be leader whilst disregarding the other's claims.

Early the following spring, and despite the poor equipment with which they had been left, sledging parties determined to complete the task Shackleton had set out for them. They were to establish a depot on each line of latitude with a final depot on Mount Hope at the base of the Beardmore Glacier. Any plans for leaving a party at the final depot had to be abandoned. Mackintosh and Joyce had disagreed over the weights to be carried on the sledges and Mackintosh was keen that man-hauling should be used to set up the depots, but Joyce demanded that the five remaining dogs be taken. Before the depot at the 80th degree of latitude had been established, Mackintosh, complaining of a sprained knee, handed over the leadership of the sledging parties to Joyce.

Just beyond the 83rd degree depot, one of the party, the Reverend Arnold Spencer-Smith collapsed with scurvy and was left in a tent with a fortnight's food as the rest pressed on to Mount Hope. Mackintosh who by now was very weak, was beginning to show clear signs of the same disease.

With the final depot established, the return journey began with Mackintosh limping with swollen legs, Joyce suffering from snow-blindness, and, when he was picked up, Spencer-Smith riding helpless on the sledge. A month later, just short of the depot they had laid at Minna Bluff, Joyce decided that Mackintosh and Spencer-Smith would have to stay in a tent looked after by Wild as he pushed on to the depot. Living on nothing more than scraps of dog food, it took three days to reach the site. As the spot was reached, one of the other men – Hayward – collapsed with scurvy. Two days were taken to recover before they returned to the tent where Mackintosh, expecting to die, had written in his diary that he intended to do so 'in the British manner as our tradition holds us in honour bound to do.'

With Mounts Erebus and Terror clear on the skyline, three men – now all affected by scurvy – and five dogs, pulled three sick men on the sledges. After a week, the effort of hauling could no longer be sustained and Mackintosh

The Revd Arnold Spencer-Smith being carried on the sledge.

volunteered to stay alone in a tent as the others tried to gain Hut Point. He was given three weeks' food. Shortly after, Spencer-Smith died just before his thirty-second birthday and was buried beneath a cairn of snow surmounted by a cross made of bamboo poles. Two days later, on 11 March, Joyce and the remainder of his party reached Hut Point and safety. Within a week, after nine days of being alone, Mackintosh had been collected and brought in. They had covered 1,561 miles in appalling conditions, dressed in inadequate clothing, and dragging defective sledges. All so that Shackleton's orders should be carried out. Now that they had completed their mission and returned to Ross Island, there was no sign of the *Aurora* and they knew that, once again, they would have to wait for the ice to cover McMurdo Sound before they could attempt to reach the base at Cape Evans.

The next nine weeks were spent living almost solely on seal meat cooked over a blubber fire as they waited for the ice to freeze over in the sound. Mackintosh, in particular, was keen to find out how the four men left at Cape Evans had fared since the sledging parties departed eight months earlier. On 8 May, he decided that the ice had frozen to a thickness where it was safe enough for him and Hayward to strike out for their main base. Joyce disagreed, arguing that the young ice was not yet ready to bear the weight of a sledging party and that Mackintosh should wait just a few more days. But Mackintosh would not hear of it and set off with Hayward. Two days later, Joyce and the others decided to follow. Ahead of them they could clearly see the footprints left by Mackintosh and Hayward and followed them until they stopped at the edge of the ice. On arriving at Cape Evans their fears were confirmed, Mackintosh and Hayward had not arrived. All the evidence pointed to them having been taken out to sea on a floe that had detached itself from the ice of McMurdo Sound. Neither man was ever seen again.

Left: Lieutenant Shackleton RNR wearing his Polar Medal.

Opposite: Lieutenant-Commander Frank Worsley ('Depth-charge Bill') receiving a letter of thanks for saving lives from the captain of a U-boat he had rammed.

On 10 January 1917, the seven men left on Ross Island were overjoyed to see the *Aurora* off Cape Royds. Shouts of 'Ship ho!' were followed by handshakes and broad smiles. It had been twenty months since she had disappeared and all had feared the worst. In fact, when her ice-anchors were torn away in early May 1915, she had drifted northwards until she was locked into the pack. She remained trapped for the next eight months, only breaking out on 13 February 1916. Stenhouse took the battered and leaking *Aurora* to New Zealand where she arrived on 3 April. The remainder of the year was spent in refitting the ship, getting her ready for a return to the Ross Sea. Much to the annoyance of the British, Australian, and New Zealand governments, Shackleton turned up in December expecting to take charge of the relief expedition. Captain John Davies (ex-*Nimrod* and ex-*Aurora* under Mawson) had been appointed to the command of the vessel, and he promptly threatened to resign if Shackleton was allowed to take charge. His resignation was not accepted and the Australian Government, in particular, was adamant that Shackleton should not be given command. Consequently, in order to gain his share of the glory from the rescue, Shackleton was forced to 'sign on' what was still (legally speaking) his own ship at the rate of one shilling a month.

With the return of the *Aurora*, Shackleton went to Australia and gave speeches on the importance of the men of the country taking part in the war. He followed this by spending a month in America exhibiting none of the desire to get into the conflict he had been urging others to show.

He arrived home in late May 1917, but had to wait for some months before he was given any chance to play a role in the war. During this time he pursued the award of the Polar Medal for his expedition. In this he was successful, and the medal (or clasps for those already in possession of it) was awarded to all his men with the exception of four men including the carpenter, McNeish. This petty-minded action lay in direct contrast to Scott who had ensured that Shackleton was awarded the medal despite his frequent outbursts of indiscipline. In September, Shackleton was sent to South America on behalf of the Department of Information to put the British case among the neutral countries. The job lasted for seven months and he was back in England at the end of April 1918. Again, he was forced to wait until, at last, in August he was given the rank of major in the British Army and put in charge of the winter stores destined for the North Russian Expedition. Before leaving, Shackleton became involved with a mining expedition to Spitsbergen along with Temporary Lieutenant Frank Wild RNVR who had spent much of the previous year in Russia. He had actually sailed with the expedition when he was recalled by the War Office when the ship reached Tromso.

At Murmansk he was joined by Worsley (who had already distinguished himself in the war as 'Depth-Charge Bill') and by the surgeon Maclin, sporting a Military Cross he had won on the Italian Front. Two months later, Shackleton resigned his commission to pursue a scheme in which he would develop Murmansk and surrounding resources on behalf of the Tsarist Government. Inevitably, the proposal collapsed with the Soviet victory in the November Revolution of 1917. His New Zealand journalist ghost-writer had completed the draft of his account of the Imperial Trans-Antarctic Expedition and the book was published in late 1919 to great acclaim. Unfortunately, Shackleton had been forced to sign away his profits from the book in an attempt to reduce his personal debts.

In 1920 Shackleton was able to raise funds for the rather vague idea of circum-navigating the Antarctic continent. He had originally intended to sail into the Beaufort Sea with a possible chance of reaching the North Pole, but a change of Government in Canada put paid to any Arctic ambitions. Now, with funding available he decided to return to the south. As captain of his newly purchased ship *Quest* he appointed the exceptional navigator Frank Worsley. Frank Wild was appointed ship's first-officer and second-in-command of the expedition. Wild promptly gave himself the rank and address of 'Commander' (it was Wild who, some years earlier, had first called Shackleton 'the Boss' – the usual title awarded to captains of merchant ships). Frank Hurley, whose superb photographs of the *Endurance* were to become almost a monument to Shackleton's memory, was taken on as expedition biologist. The two surgeons from the *Endurance*, Maclin and McIlroy, joined the *Quest* in the same role.

The *Quest* sailed from Plymouth on 24 September 1921 and reached Rio de Janeiro two months later. There Shackleton suffered a heart attack, but managed to convince Macklin that he could continue with the expedition. South Georgia was reached on 4 January. At three o'clock the following morning, as the *Quest* lay at anchor off Grytviken, Macklin was by Shackleton's side as a massive heart attack brought his life to an end. He was forty-seven years old.

The body was embalmed and taken by a Norwegian vessel to Montevideo where it was accorded the highest honours, including a memorial service attended by the President. It had been expected that the body would be returned to England, but a telegram from Lady Shackleton requested that it be buried on South Georgia. As a result, Shackleton was buried in the Grytviken whaling station cemetery. Following a decision that Shackleton would no doubt have approved of, the grave was dug along a north-south line, and the coffin lowered with Shackleton's head to the north. The *Quest* had been at sea during the ceremony, but on their return, Wild, Worsley, and the others built a small cairn surmounted by a cross on a promontory on the opposite side of the bay. At the base of the cross a plaque was attached which read – 'Sir Ernest Shackleton. Explorer. Died here January 5 1922. Erected by his comrades.' In 1928, a granite headstone was taken down to South Georgia and erected over the grave. At its head was engraved a nine-pointed star – the number 'nine' being considered by Shackleton to be lucky. As on the cross, Shackleton is described on the headstone simply as 'Explorer'.

Apsley Cherry-Garrard, who had served with Scott and Wilson, wrote; 'For a joint scientific and geographical piece of organisation, give me Scott; for a Winter Journey, Wilson; for a dash to the Pole and nothing else, Amundsen: and if I am in the devil of a hole and want to get out of it, give me Shackleton every time.' The comment was well thought out, for it was constantly Shackleton who had put, both himself and his men, into 'the devil of a hole'. On examination, his greatest achievements came about when he was getting *himself* out of trouble. He was frequently described as a 'leader' by his contemporaries. Raymond Priestley, the young second-year student with the *Nimrod* Expedition, described Shackleton as; 'The greatest leader that ever came on God's earth, bar none.' And yet he had

Shackleton's *Quest*.

failed repeatedly to show leadership. He had failed to keep his men's morale up in his attempt on the Pole, and retreated from the prize when it lay less than 100 miles away. He had handled the McNeish incident badly, and retaliated with spite. Worst of all, on, at least three occasions, he had, in effect, been the first to jump into the lifeboat, leaving others to cope at the scene of the greatest danger. In the profession of the sea, and the call of exploration, Shackleton stands alone and apart from a galaxy of leadership examples. Why then is he considered to be a great leader?

A clue may lie in the late 1990s elevation of Shackleton as a leading example of 'man-management' amongst the business culture of the United States. In 'management' terms it might be entirely appropriate for the 'Boss' to look after his own interests first for, without doing so, the company or business might founder. Then, having saved himself, the 'Boss' can expect the noisy plaudits of his staff for having, in turn, saved them. It might be good 'management' to show ruthlessness in the face of a differing opinion, even if that opinion is later proved to be correct and the individual concerned plays a vital part in the company's subsequent recovery. It is, however, not a form of leadership that would be recognised by Nelson, Franklin, or Scott.

Shackleton failed at every strategic enterprise he undertook. He failed to reach the Pole, he failed to cross Antarctica, he failed in journalism, politics, finance, and business. He was, nonetheless, a master tactician, and a splendid companion who could be depended upon for courage, determination, and humour.

CHAPTER EIGHTEEN

'GO FORWARD AND DO THE BEST FOR OUR COUNTRY'

Just under thirteen years before the death of Shackleton, Captain Robert Falcon Scott's mind had been a whirl of contradictory thoughts and emotions. Happily married for six months, and with his wife pregnant, he had been appointed as Naval Assistant to the Second Sea Lord. It was the equivalent of a seat close to the high table. Surrounded in his daily work by useful contacts, and working directly for the head of the Royal Navy's personnel, he could sit comfortably, be seen to work hard, and set his ambition at promotion. As a captain approaching six years seniority, he would soon be 'in zone' for his flag, or at least in line for a significant command that could end with his advancement to Rear-Admiral. On the other hand, news had come through that Shackleton had failed to reach the South Pole. The prize still remained, a chance to place the British flag at the southernmost point on the earth. On September 13, the day before the birth of his son, Peter Markham, Scott announced that he was to return to the Antarctic. Telling the public that the achievement of the Pole was to be his main aim, he was really disguising the fact that he was actually more interested in the scientific exploration of the Ross Sea area. The Pole, however, was more likely to catch the public's interest – and more likely to raise funds.

Scott was keen to get the *Discovery* for his forthcoming expedition, but the Hudson Bay Company refused to make her available. Instead, he turned to the *Terra Nova,* the ship that had caused him so much consternation when she appeared, unbidden, in McMurdo Sound in early 1904. Thanks to Scott being elected a member of the Royal Yacht Squadron, the *Terra Nova* could be classed as a yacht rather than a merchant ship and, therefore, not subject to Board of Trade regulations. To command her and oversee her refit, he appointed the first of his team, Lieutenant Edward ('Teddy') Evans RN, whom he had first met when he turned up in the *Morning* relief ship. Evans had seriously considered setting up his own expedition, but had been persuaded by Sir Clemence Markham to throw in his lot with Scott when offered the chance of being second-in-command. He was a tough, energetic, naval officer who was overjoyed at being given his first command. He still 'blushed', however, when, after the ship had been moved to London, she was visited by Admirals who had to endure the strong stench of her whaling past. Lieutenant Victor ('The Wicked Mate') Campbell RN was appointed as the ship's chief officer. He was an old-Etonian who had volunteered

Lieutenant Henry Rennick wearing a seaman's blue-edged 'flannel'.

Henry Bowers as a sub-lieutenant in the Royal
Indian Marine.

to go on the Retired List in 1902 to follow an interest in skiing. Scott decided
that Campbell should lead a party southwards down the King Edward VII Land
mountain range that skirted the eastern shore of the ice barrier. Lieutenants Harry
('Penelope') Pennell and Henry ('Parnie') Rennick were appointed as, respectively,
navigation officer and hydrographer. Two naval surgeons were loaned by the navy,
Edward ('Atch') Atkinson, and George Murray ('Toffarino') Levick.

In September 1905, Sir Clemence Markham had been visiting the training
ship *Worcester* when a young officer cadet, Henry Bowers, was introduced to him.
Bowers, expressing a keen interest in polar matters impressed Markham and, when
Scott was getting his team together, he suggested that he consider Bowers – now
a lieutenant serving with the Royal Indian Marine (the precursor to the Royal
Indian Navy). Never doubting Markham's judgement, Scott wrote to Bowers,
inviting him to join the expedition. The deeply patriotic Bowers was overjoyed
and accepted eagerly. He was a man of short stature, stockily built, with red hair
and a huge beak-like nose that earned him the nickname 'Birdy'.

Scott's own judgement was never in doubt when he appointed his chief of
scientific staff. After seeing Dr Edward Wilson's abilities at close hand during the
Discovery expedition, he was extremely keen to obtain his services for the new
venture. 'Uncle Bill' needed little persuasion, especially when Scott asked him
to find his own team of scientists. Before long, he had gathered around him the

best available men for the job. Two Australian geologists, Griffith ('Griff') Taylor (who tended to refer to those he worked with as 'my mates'), and Frank ('Deb') Debenham were joined by a third geologist, Raymond Priestley – formerly of the *Nimrod* under Shackleton. Two biologists were appointed, Edward ('Bronte') Nelson and Dennis ('Hercules') Lillie. The expedition's physicist was a Canadian, Charles ('Silas') Wright, and George ('Sunny Jim') Simpson was appointed as meteorologist. Wilson also recommended to Scott that he find room for a young friend of his as assistant zoologist. Apsley Cherry-Garrard, without the slightest qualification in zoology and with extremely poor eyesight, wrote to Scott offering to pay £1,000 if he could go. Scott turned him down, but when Cherry-Garrard wrote again offering the money as a donation without strings, Scott recognised a noble spirit and 'Cherry' was found a place.

Another £1,000 was offered by a wealthy cavalry officer serving in India. Captain Lawrence Oates had earned himself a reputation for bravery during the Boer War where 'No surrender Oates' had held his position despite having a thigh shattered by a bullet. A life centred on horses, hunting, and yachting had begun to pall, and with little interest in pursuing promotion along an endless line of social events, Oates cast around for something different. Scott took 'Titus' to look after the ponies he had decided to take south after the example of Shackleton. Despite Oates' obvious qualifications for the job, Scott sent a widely travelled adventurer, Cecil Meares, to Siberia to purchase the expedition ponies. They had to be white or dappled grey as Shackleton had discovered that the darker-coated animals died first.

Motor sledge tractor trials. The rearmost passengers on the sledge are Captain and Mrs Scott.

Motor sledge tractor.

It was intended to take three newly designed motor sledges. Originally, the vehicles were to be under the charge of Engineer-Commander Reginald Skelton who had been with Scott in the *Discovery*. Evans, however, felt uncomfortable with the idea of having an officer of such seniority in the *Terra Nova* despite the fact that, being an executive branch lieutenant, his status as captain of the ship would not be affected. Consequently, much to Skelton's disappointment, Scott selected Bernard Day, another *Nimrod* veteran.

To record the experiences yet to come, Scott selected the 'camera artist' Herbert ('Ponko') Ponting. A much-travelled man, Ponting had tried ranching in California before settling down to become a photographer. His work had appeared in many leading periodicals and journals, and he had become proficient in the, still new, art of cinematography. Finally, at the recommendation of Nansen, Scott took the ski expert, and former Norwegian naval officer Tryggve ('Trigger') Gran. When Nansen had expressed concern about the expedition's lack of skiing skills, Scott was astute enough to take note and accepted the offer of Gran.

Three lower deck members of the *Discovery* expedition were made available to join Scott. Chief Stoker William Lashly, and Petty Officers Edgar Evans and Thomas Crean. They would be joined later by Petty Officer Thomas Williamson – an able seaman on the *Discovery*.

As usual, funding proved to be a problem. At least £40,000 was needed and six months after the expedition was announced only £10,000 had been raised. However, that figure convinced the Government that they should become involved and they offered £20,000 providing Scott could raise an equal amount from other sources. One way of cutting down the costs of the expedition was to allow schools, colleges, other groups or even individuals to sponsor a dog, pony, tent, sleeping bag or sledge. Master H. Gethin of Lewis paid three guineas to sponsor a dog he named 'Hughie' – its Russian name was 'Gerachi', but it was known to all on the expedition as 'Ginger'. The ships company of HMS *Invincible* collected enough money for two ponies, two sledges, and one sleeping bag (used

Petty Officer Evans (to the right of the front rank) training the 1907 Portsmouth Command Field Gun crew for that year's Royal Tournament.

by Surgeon Levick). In a link to another era, Sir John Franklin's old school, King Edward VI Grammar at Louth, sent £2 for a sleeping bag that was eventually used by Surgeon Atkinson.

Other savings were made by gifts, or special arrangements with manufacturers. Fry supplied chocolate; Huntley and Palmer, biscuits and cakes; Colman, mustard; and Frank Cooper, marmalade. The sugar came from Tate, and the golden syrup from Lyle. Shipphams provided potted meat; and Heinz, baked beans. Price's Patent Candle Co. supplied edible candles; Reckitt, starch; and Wolsey, underwear. Broadwood and Co. provided a player piano, Shell gave the fuel for the motorised sledges, and the Gramophone Co. – two gramophones.

Six weeks before sailing, the ship's company and expedition members began to arrive at the West India Docks to join the *Terra Nova*. Campbell, Pennell, and Rennick, soon had their duties in hand. Oates turned up looking like a farmer, with a buttoned up raincoat and a bowler hat on the back of his head – Crean took some persuading that the cavalry captain was actually an officer. Bowers, who had been appointed as the expedition's stores officer, began his duties by falling 19 feet from the main hatch onto the pig-iron ballast. The onlookers, who included Campbell, were convinced that he had either killed, or seriously injured, himself, and were amazed to see Bowers jump to his feet, shake himself, and return directly to the job in hand.

The *Terra Nova* was ready to sail on her appointed date, 1 June 1910. She was allowed to wear a white ensign as a result of Scott's membership of the Royal Yacht Squadron and would be the first steam vessel to fly the flag within sight of

THE GREAT BARRIER.

Ice Maiden (*to Captain Scott*). "COURAGE YOU HAVE, BUT YOU MUST HAVE GOLD TOO BEFORE I LET YOU PASS."

[There is grave fear lest the South Pole Expedition should fail for lack of funds. Contributions may be sent to Sir Edgar Speyer, 7, Lothbury, E.C.]

Punch on the problem of funding. Under the heading 'The Great Barrier', the Ice Maiden tells Scott, 'Courage you have, but you must have gold too before I let you pass.' An address for the collection of contributors follows.

Left: Advertisement from biscuit suppliers to the expedition.

Left: Suppliers of exposure meters to the expedition.

Opposite above: Pocket watch, speed indicators and mileage recorder suppliers to the expedition.

Opposite below: Using notepaper headed with the expedition's badge, Scott approves of the jam supplied by a manufacturer.

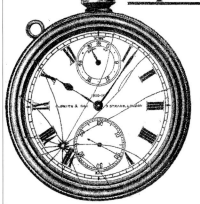
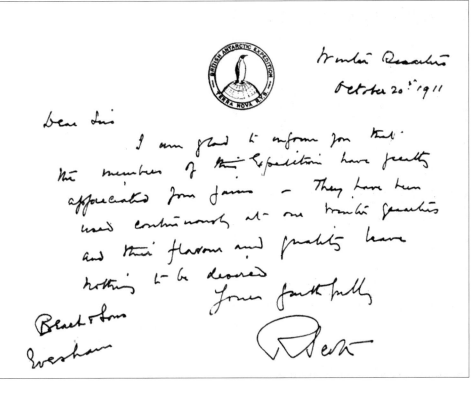

A supply of free petrol for the motor sledges arrives at the *Terra Nova*.

the Antarctic Continent. To give the ensign a more naval aspect, it was broken out at the hoist by the wife of the First Sea Lord. Lady Markham hoisted the burgee of the Royal Yacht Squadron. At 4.45 p.m. the ship slipped her moorings and headed down the Thames. Portsmouth was visited four days later. Scott (who, in common with other naval captains of the time, was known to all as 'The Owner') joined the ship at Spithead, the compasses were 'swung', and the nearby battle-cruiser, HMS *Invincible*, had her boatswain's stores raided whilst everyone looked the other way.

The Welsh mine-owners had offered Scott unlimited free coal so he intended Cardiff to be his last port of call. On his way west, the *Terra Nova* called in at Portland and was towed through the cheering lines of the Home Fleet by the cadet training ship HMS *Cumberland*. At the Welsh seaport a 'rattling good time' was had by all as the coal was loaded and the Lord Mayor presented Scott with a cheque for £1,000. There was still more fund-raising to be done, and Scott left the ship to make his own way to Cape Town as the *Terra Nova* sailed to the sound of ship's sirens, cheering crowds, and detonators exploding beneath the wheels of railway wagons.

It was not long before the ship's company had shaken themselves down into the warm conviviality of close comradeship. In the wardroom, spirits were high and the geologist, Frank Debenham, described the typical after-dinner entertainment:

It was a grand scrap, a free-for-all, though no one quite knew what it was all about and no one cared. The general principle was that no one must be left standing so; if, when under a pile of struggling humanity, you caught sight of a leg in an upright position you grabbed it and tugged, regardless of whether it belonged to friend or foe. It raged up and down between the solid wardroom table and the cabins for a long time and great was the damage to shins and elbows. Everyone achieved great glory; it was a noble battle.

From Madeira, Wilson wrote to Scott saying, 'You have got a crew of pirates that would be exceedingly difficult to beat – or equal. I have never been with such a persistently cheery lot before.' Evans, Campbell, Rennick, and Pennell were, 'simply splendid', the scientists were 'workers', Cherry-Garrard had been first up the rigging, and, 'there is far more to Oates than meets the eye – or ear, for that matter – in his rather amused taciturnity.' It was turning out as Scott would have hoped. Without his presence, and of their own accord, his men were turning into a team.

At Cape Town, Scott rejoined the ship and sent Wilson on ahead by steamer in order that he might meet the Australians who were joining the expedition. This gave Scott the opportunity, as the *Terra Nova* continued on her way to Melbourne, to have a close look at the officers and seamen who were to form his landing parties. For the most part he found he agreed with Wilson's assessment, noting, however, that Rennick was 'blank', Levick was amiable with a 'vacant smile', and Lillie had his 'head in the clouds.' He was also less than impressed by Gran's reluctance to wash, ignoring with distaste the Norwegian's claim that it was 'not the custom of his country.'

Melbourne was reached on 12 October. As the ship was berthed alongside that evening, Scott was handed a telegram. To his stunned surprise the message read 'Madeira: Am going south, Amundsen'. Suddenly, an unlooked for, and unwelcome, complication had cast its shadow across his plans. Amundsen, the first man to take a ship through the Northwest Passage, a man who had already experienced an Antarctic winter, would not spend much of his time in pursuit of scientific aims. He would go for the Pole. Scott's public reply was to tell the press that his plans would go on unchanged.

At Lyttelton, Scott found Meares waiting with nineteen ponies and thirty-three sledge dogs. He had also brought along a Russian groom, Anton Omelchenko, for the ponies, and a dog driver, Dimitri Gerof. Oates thought the ponies to be of very poor quality, they were, after all, to be his responsibility, but it was too late to make any changes. As the ship was dry-docked for a final caulking, stables were built under the forecastle and on the upper deck. The stores were disembarked and restowed by Bowers, and the expedition hut was erected ashore to ensure that it was complete and sound. Yet again the New Zealanders excelled in hospitality and gifts to the extent that the ship became dangerously overloaded (Evans had painted out her Plimsoll line so that her deep lading was not obvious to the eyes of officialdom). In addition to the ponies, the upper deck was also used to store thirty tons of coal, three crated motor sledges, and two and a half tons of petrol.

On the night before sailing, Petty Officer Evans, in true Gunner's Mate manner, accepted too freely of the hospitality and fell into the water alongside the ship.

The *Terra Nova* sailed from Lyttelton on 26 November to the cheering of a vast crowd who had come down to see her off. Scott was picked up at Port Chalmers and the ship finally left for Antarctica on 29 November taking with her a ship's cat and Crean's pet rabbit.

The voyage south was to prove extremely stormy. On 2 December, mountainous seas rolled across the decks, threatening to swamp the ship. The coal broke free and ten tons of it had to be dumped overboard to prevent damage to the other deck cargo. Worse still, coal dust in the bilge blocked the steam pump. With the water level increasing to the boiler ash-pan, the fires had to be put out to protect the boiler. This left just the hand-pumps, but they were also blocked. As the ship bucked and rolled violently, a hole had to be cut in a bulkhead so that Lieutenant Evans, Bowers, and Lashly could reach the blocked inlets. Crawling into the narrow space, the two men plunged themselves into the freezing oily bilge water to bring out handfuls of clogging coal dust. The pumps were restored to working order and the water-level reduced. Scott had been shown what his men were made of. But there had been a cost. Despite the careful handling of Oates and Atkinson two of the ponies had died and one of the dogs had drowned.

The ice was met five days later, much further north than had been anticipated and Christmas day was spent locked in the pack. As usual banners, flags, and all manner of bunting were hung out in the wardroom and mess. The same fare of penguin breast, roast beef, plum pudding and mince pies were issued to both officers and men, the latter at midday, the former in the evening. On the mess deck, beneath the forecastle, the seamen accompanied their singing with a 'squeegee band' whilst far aft, beyond the boiler room, and a deck lower, the officers sang non-stop carols and shanties for five hours. Scott would rather have been pushing hard to the south, but it took twenty days and 370 miles of charging the pack before open waters were reached – a delay that caused him great concern.

Wilson was very keen that a base should be made at Cape Crozier in order that he could study closely the Emperor penguins in their local rookery. Scott was amenable towards the idea, but when the cape was reached on 3 January 1911, no safe landing place could be found. Evans took the ship into McMurdo Sound, passing Shackleton's *Nimrod* hut near Cape Royds, until he saw a beach beside a small cape. On inspection, Scott decided that the site was admirably suited for his base and named it 'Cape Evans'.

Campbell was given charge of the unloading of the ship whilst Evans supervised the building of the hut. With the weather on their side, the unloading went well and was completed within a week. Only two incidents of note happened. When one of the motorised sledges was being unloaded, it was swung out clear of the ship and placed on the floe in exactly the same manner as two previous sledges. On this occasion, however, the ice gave way, and the sledge made its way 100 fathoms to the sea bottom. Scott took the loss 'awfully well'. He did not take quite so well the result of his pointing out a pod of killer whales to the photographer,

Terra Nova in the ice.

Landing hay for the ponies from the *Terra Nova*.

Ponting, who was in the process of filming the unloading. The cameraman, eager to film the whales at close quarters, set off to the floe edge. Just as he was about to start filming, the floe beneath his feet reared up and began to break as the whales – seeing Ponting as their next meal – charged the ice on which he stood, breaking it up with their backs. Clutching his camera, Ponting raced away, jumping from one small floe to another as eight whales cruised alongside waiting for him to fall in. To Scott's immense relief, the camera artist survived with nothing more than a fright.

The hut was finished by 18 January. Divided into 'Wardroom' and 'messdeck' it was a solid structure that would give good protection during the winter months. It was soon echoing to the sound of 'Home, Sweet Home' on the player piano, with Dame Nellie Melba's operatic best on the Wardroom gramophone countered by the messdeck gramophone thumping out the latest song by Harry Lauder. Only Scott had a private corner, but Ponting was given the privilege of sleeping alone in his tiny darkroom. Stables for the ponies were built on the north side.

A visit to the *Discovery* hut deeply depressed Scott. When he arrived he found that Shackleton had left a window open. Consequently, the hut was full of snow. Even worse, on attempting to dig the snow out, he found the hut to be in an appalling condition and chose to camp outside: 'I went to bed thoroughly depressed. It seems a fundamental expression of civilised human sentiment that men who come to such places as this should leave what comfort they can to welcome those who follow, and by finding that such a simple duty had been neglected by our immediate predecessors oppressed me horribly.'

On 24 January, Scott left Cape Evans to establish depots in readiness for the following season's attempt on the Pole. At the same time, Campbell, Priestley, and Levick, with Petty Officers Abbott and Browning, and Able Seaman Dickason, were taken in the *Terra Nova* 400 miles eastwards towards King Edward VII Land where they were to survey the eastern edge of the barrier. Before transporting them to the far edge of the barrier, Pennell, now temporary captain of the ship, was to drop off the geologist, Taylor, along with Wright, Debenham, and Petty Officer Evans, on the western side of the sound to undertake a geological survey in the western mountains.

Using dogs and ponies, Scott brought his stores to 'Safety Camp' – a point some two miles from the barrier edge – before striking out just south of east to 'Corner Camp'. From there he intended to turn south to run slightly to the west of the 170th meridian. Corner Camp was reached on 5 February, but a blizzard held them in their tents for the next three days. Bluff depot was made fifty-four miles south of Corner Camp on 12 February. Scott was keen that his next depot should be at 80 degrees South, but a sharp drop in temperatures began to produce frostbites. The ponies were having great difficulty in soft snow and Oates had begun to resort to his 'gloomy view' about their condition. He suggested to Scott that the ponies be taken on to their limit, killed, and cached as dog food. But Scott would not hear of it. On 17 February, 150 miles north of Hut Point, thirty miles short of where he had intended, and with a bitter wind driving snow

Hut Point with a grounded iceberg
and the Western Mountains in the
background.

from the south, Scott decided to make his last depot of the season. Because of the
amount of supplies it contained, the 6-feet-high cairn, with its black flag fluttering
overhead, was named 'One Ton Depot'.

The journey out had been a trying time for the ponies. Their hooves sank in the
snow and the effort they needed to haul themselves clear soon exhausted them.
Three of the weakest had been taken back at Corner Camp. Scott, leaving Oates,
Bowers, and Gran to bring in the five remaining ponies, returned northwards with
the dog-sledges. Eager to get back to his base to hear if Campbell and his party
had reached King Edward VII Land safely, Scott swung to the west earlier than he
should and, on 21 February, saw the horrifying sight of his dogs disappearing into
the snow – only the lead dog remained on the surface, its claws taking the strain on
the far side of a crevasse. The sledge was unpacked and the tent poles laid across the
gap. Meares crossed and took the weight off the heroic lead dog, then the sledge
was driven over the crevasse and used as a bridge to haul out the eleven dogs that
had remained in their harness. Two dogs had fallen free and were howling pitiably
as they clung for dear life on an ice bridge that had saved them from disappearing
into the darkness of the icy canyon. Scott had himself lowered on a rope and sent
the dogs up one after the other. The rescue took almost two hours.

Safety Camp was reached the following day. Evans was waiting with the
depressing news that two of the three ponies sent back had died. Taking the
surviving pony in tow, the party set off for Hut Point. On reaching the hut they
found a message pencilled on the wall telling them that there was a bag containing

Bower's party escaping from the ice floe.

mail waiting inside for them. But no bag could be found. After a few moments thought they decided that Atkinson and Crean had picked up the bag and taken it to Safety Camp, the two parties having missed each other. Their guess turned out to be right and, on returning to Safety Camp, Scott opened the single letter the bag contained. What he read put all his other difficulties in the shade.

As the *Terra Nova,* carrying Campbell's party, approached the Bay of Whales, towards the eastern end of the barrier, her ship's company were taken aback to see mast-tops standing above the ice. Inside the bay they found the *Fram*, the same ship Nansen had locked into the Arctic ice, and now under the command of Amundsen. The Norwegian had decided to make his base at exactly the spot that Shackleton had refused before retreating to McMurdo Sound in the *Nimrod*. Amundsen had 130 dogs with him, and had just one ambition – to get to the Pole. His base, 'Framheim', was already sixty miles closer to the Pole than Scott's at Cape Evans.

Some of Scott's men were deeply angry about the Norwegian's appearance on the scene, and more than one of them wanted to go over to the Bay of Whales to 'have it out with Amundsen and his men.' But Scott had no time for such antics. Realising that Amundsen was 'a serious menace', he still intended to 'Go forward and do the best for our country without fear or panic.' Gran was placed in a very awkward position. He was a Norwegian, and Oates had already told him that he simply did not like him on the grounds that he 'was a foreigner.'

Campbell, on discovering Amundsen, had returned with the *Terra Nova* to Cape Evans, there being no point in continuing with the eastern expedition. Instead, he had chosen to be landed at Cape Adair where they became the 'Northern Party', living in their hut in the middle of an Adelie penguin rookery.

When Oates, Bowers, and Gran arrived at Safety Camp with the ponies. Scott sent the dogs ahead to be followed by Bowers, Cherry-Garrard, and Crean who were to lead the four fittest ponies. Bowers was told to go over the sea ice to Hut Point as it was the quickest route for the tired animals. All went well until Bowers found that the ice around him was beginning to break up. With cracks opening up in all directions, he hurriedly led his party towards an area of old sound ice. Now well clear of the danger, camp was set up and the men rested in their tent to recover from their narrow escape. Two and a half hours later, Bowers woke up with a jolt and looked out of the tent. To his horror he found that the ice on which his party had been sleeping had also broken away, and was now drifting into the sound. Raising the alarm, Bowers went to look at the ponies only to find that the crack along which the floe had broken free had also claimed one of the animals. A desperate scrabble ensued in which the sledges were packed and the ponies harnessed. They then began to cross from floe to floe whenever the opportunity arose to get them closer to the barrier edge. At times the ponies could just jump across; at others it was necessary to use the sledges as bridges. At last they arrived at a floe which had clearly just broken away from the barrier and climbed its slope in the hope that they could find safety on its southern edge. Instead they found a gap, 30 to 40 feet wide, full of loose ice and with killer whales churning the waters as they sought for prey. Bowers knew that he could get his party no further unaided and would have to get help. As leader, he could not desert his men: 'To go myself was out of the question.' Both Cherry-Garrard and Crean volunteered. With Cherry-Garrard being the least experienced and seeing little without his spectacles, Bowers decided to send Crean. The petty officer worked his way to windward along the ice front, leaping across the gaps with killer whales closely following his movements until he was lost to Bowers' sight. For the remainder of that day, with the killer whales rising perpendicularly out of the water to gaze at the marooned party with menacing, unblinking eyes, Bowers waited calmly as every passing minute threatened to take the floe out to sea. At 7 o'clock that evening, figures were seen on the top of the barrier edge. It was Scott, with Oates and Crean. Soon, with the help of a rope, and using the sledges as ladders, the two men and all the stores were safe. An attempt to get the ponies across saw one of them saved, but the remaining two had to be shot in the water as the whales closed in for the kill.

The depot-laying had not been as successful as Scott had hoped. One Ton depot was over thirty miles north of where he had intended and, of the eight ponies he had started out with, six had died. He could assume, however, that Campbell's Northern Party were battening down for the winter and that the *Terra Nova* was

Left: Captain Scott about to play football.

Opposite: Scott's birthday party, 6 June 1911.

safely on its way to New Zealand. The Western Party arrived at Hut Point on 15 March. They had carried out geological work in the area from the Koettlitz Glacier to the dry valleys and, for the most part, had enjoyed good weather. Petty Officer Evans had mixed well with the two Australians and the Canadian and, free from immediate naval authority, had entertained the university men with raucous anecdotes. They were especially delighted with his pronunciation of the name of his favourite author, Alexandre Dumas – which he pronounced 'Dum-Ass'.

The depot-layers and the Western Party – a total of sixteen men – settled down in the *Discovery* Hut to wait for the sea to freeze over. Now restored from the shambles Shackleton had left behind, the hut provided warm and dry accommodation. The day started with a breakfast of bread, butter, and tea followed by a stroll down to the ice to see how it was freezing. Lunch was more or less the same, followed by more exercise. Dinner usually consisted of fried seal liver spiced up with curry powder and cooked over a blubber stove, its smoke, and that from the blubber lamps, giving the entire company blackened faces. Most then retreated to their sleeping bags to read before enjoying a long sleep.

It took until 13 May before all the men, ponies, and dogs were back at Cape Evans. The following day, as Oates and Debenham scattered the furniture in a mock fight, Scott wrote, 'It is a triumph to have collected such men.'

During the winter months they lectured each other, Ponting put on slide shows, and the scientists carried on with their experiments and recordings. Football was played whilst the light was good enough, Cherry-Garrard produced a new edition of the *South Polar Times*, Oates pampered the ten surviving ponies, and Wilson produced exquisite watercolours. On 6 June, a surprise birthday party was sprung on Scott. The cook, Clissold, produced a magnificently decorated cake for lunch, whilst dinner was a lavish affair held beneath a ceiling bedecked with sledge pennants. The evening ended with robust debates on politics, the origin of matter, and military tactics. Scott fell asleep as the biologist, Nelson, offered Taylor a pair of socks in exchange for lessons on geology. The event proved to be a genteel rehearsal for the mid-winter festival at which the flags were brought out once again and champagne flowed freely. After-dinner speeches were made and Scott was forced to put a ban on the repeated compliments being made about him,

particularly by the scientists. On completion of the meal, the table was removed and, as the gramophone played, Ponting gave a slide show of his latest photographs – each appearing to a great cheer. The room was then cleared again and riotous dancing introduced. Petty Officer Evans went around spreading rumours in a stage whisper, Petty Officer 'Pat' Keohane grew, 'intensely Irish' and was desperate to find someone to draw into a political argument whilst – to the deep shock of the naval men present – the cook forgot himself to the extent that he proposed a toast to Scott as 'Good old truegg' ('truegg' being a popular type of dried egg). Bowers then appeared with a Christmas tree made of sticks and coloured paper. In its branches candles flickered their light onto small packages that had been made up many months earlier by Wilson's sister-in-law – Miss Souper. There was a gift for everyone. The winter also provided Wilson with an opportunity to undertake some research that was impossible at any other time of the year. He was keen to obtain some Emperor penguin eggs to see if they could explain questions about the evolution of birds. To get the eggs would mean a journey of sixty-seven miles over desperately difficult ground in the darkness of winter, and in temperatures of -60 degrees Fahrenheit and below. Taking with him Bowers and Cherry-Garrard, and hauling two nine-foot sledges, Wilson set off on 27 June with the support of a 'small hurrah party'. Very soon they were forced to resort to relaying the sledges. Consequently, the journey to the cape took eighteen days. The conditions were appalling with their clothing and sleeping bags becoming so frozen that they assumed the rigidity of sheet metal. Sleep became practically impossible, and the slightest movement brought down a shower of the white rime which thickly coated the inside of the tent. The temperature during one of these nights fell to -77 degrees Celsius (-109 degrees Fahrenheit). At 800 feet above the rookery they built a circular enclosure of rocks, put one of the sledges across the top of the wall, and covered the whole thing with their tent.

A dangerous climb in the darkness down and back to the rookery produced six eggs, two of which broke as they approached their shelter. That night the wind tore the tent away and the three men spent the next forty-eight hours shivering in their sleeping bags as the gale roared around the inside of the stone walls and buried them in snow. Wilson prayed fervently that they would be saved, and Bowers sang hymns to pass the time. Occasionally, they would thump each other to check that they were still alive. When, at last, the storm died down, they ventured out and were astonished to find their tent wedged against a rock. Following this stroke of good fortune, Bowers devised a 'tent downhaul' by attaching a rope to the apex of the tent with the other end secured to his sleeping bag. Thus, if the tent blew away, it would take him with it.

On the return journey, Bowers' balaclava helmet was so frozen that it encased his head in ice. This meant that he could only look down by leaning forward and, as a result, he fell down a crevasse. As he hung suspended by his harness, he heard Wilson shout to him, 'What do you want?' Bowers requested a rope with a bowline (i.e. a non-slip loop) at the end for his foot. Then, by a combination of hauling on the rope and then on the harness, he was pulled to safety. This method was later adopted as the usual means of getting someone out of a crevasse – a method invented, as Cherry-Garrard noted, 'on the spur of the moment by a frozen man hanging in one himself.'

The party staggered into the hut at Cape Evans with their precious cargo on 1 August – five weeks after they had started out. With the exception of the two days trapped beneath the open, hostile sky when their tent blew away in 84-mile-an-hour winds, Bowers had faithfully recorded the meteorological conditions three times a day, each time by candlelight. So precise was the record that Simpson, the meteorologist, regarded Bowers' log as a 'masterpiece'.

The arrival of spring saw the final preparations for the attempt on the Pole. Petty Officer Evans took charge of the sledging equipment. The twelve-foot sledges, made of elm with hickory runners, carried a waterproof canvas 'tank' for the food. Methylated spirit bottles and instruments were secured at the rear in wicker or 'venesta' boxes beneath the 'Nansen' cookers and primus stoves. At the front, tins of paraffin were secured above a venesta board. Sleeping bags and the tent were fastened on top and, to the rear, a wheel sledgemeter counted the miles and yards.

Lieutenant Evans was sent out with two men to check the stores at Safety and Corner Camps. The latter was found to be buried to the tip of its flagstaff and had to be dug out and re-stowed in temperatures sometimes even colder than -70 degrees Fahrenheit. In the meantime, Scott led a party out to the Western Mountains to lay a depot for Taylor who was to lead another geology expedition whilst the southern party was away.

Wilson, Bowers and Cherry-Garrard on their return from their egg-hunting expedition to Cape Crozier.

Much work was done by Scott and Bowers on the weights and packing of the sledges before the final plan of the assault on the Pole was announced. It was an extremely complicated affair that needed to include clothing, food, fuel, motor sledges, ponies, dogs, food for the animals, weights to be hauled by men and animals, and daily distances expected and hoped to be covered. Men had to be matched to animals and to each other to make effective teams. Included in the weight to be dragged out were supplies and provisions for the depots needed for the return journey. On top of everything was the unpredictability of the weather, long delays could throw out even the most carefully prepared calculations. There was one further great unknown – Amundsen. Scott took the pragmatic view:

> If he gets to the Pole, it must be before we do, as he is bound to travel fast with dogs and pretty certain to start out early. On this account I decided at a very early date to act exactly as I should have done had he not existed. Any attempt to race must have wrecked my plan, besides which it doesn't appear the sort of thing one is out for. After all, it is the work that counts, not the applause that follows.

Scott's plan was to send out the motor sledges first under Lieutenant Evans taking fuel and forage for the ponies. They would be followed by the pony sledging party. Finally, the dog teams would set out to join Scott at One Ton depot. From there

Left: Lieutenant Henry 'Birdy' Bowers RIM.

Below: Scott working in his corner of the hut.

the main objective would be to get three sledge teams of four men each to the foot of the Beardmore Glacier. They would then press on until a single team of four men would strike out for the Pole as the supporting parties returned to Cape Evans. The route to the Pole had been pioneered by Shackleton, and there were unlikely to be any surprises in the 100 miles he had left unexplored. Organisation, determination and leadership were all in place – all that was needed was luck.

The two motor sledges left Cape Evans on 24 October under the command of Lieutenant Evans. He took with him the motor mechanic, Bernard Day, Lashly, and Hooper – a former naval steward. Great difficulties were experienced on the hard blue ice where the tracks failed to get a grip. Connecting rods snapped and bearings broke apart under the pressure. When the barrier surface itself was achieved, the main problem was, surprisingly, overheating. Safety camp was reached after four days, and from there the motors could only crawl forward, stopping every few minutes to cool down. The next day another connecting rod smashed through a piston and Evans abandoned the vehicle. Two days later Corner Camp was found but, within twenty-four hours, a bearing had gone and Evans, taking six weeks' food for four men, continued southwards on foot. The motors had taken their loads for fifty-one miles before finally expiring. One Ton depot was passed on 9 November and Evans continued for a week before making camp to wait for Scott and the ponies. The time was passed with the help of Day reading aloud from the *Pickwick Papers*. In the early hours of the morning of 21 November the ponies began to catch up and, by the following day, sixteen men, thirteen sledges, five green canvas tents, ten ponies, and twenty-three dogs were mustered on the vast, white, plain.

Scott had done well with the ponies. There had been some slight delays due to the weather, but most of the animals had proved willing and held out reasonable promise that the base of the Beardmore Glacier would be reached in accordance with Scott's plans. The dogs had also done well under Meares and Dimitri

Day and Hooper were sent back on 24 November having done excellent service. Their place on the man-hauled sledge was taken over by Atkinson. His pony was shot to provide food for the dogs. Four days later, Wright's pony suffered the same fate and the physicist joined Lieutenant Evans at the traces. Land was sighted on the thirtieth, the day before the third pony fell to Oates' pistol. This time, much to their delight, the man-haulers were treated to a joint of pony meat. So far all was going well. On 4 December the ponies were reduced to five and the base of the glacier lay just fifteen miles to their left front. Then a ferocious blizzard descended which kept them in their tents for three days. The temperature increased, melting the snow as soon as it fell. Soon, all the equipment, including clothes and sleeping bags, was sodden. The tent groundsheets lay in pools of water as the walls bowed in under the weight of wet snow. Oates, who had carefully managed the ponies' fodder so that it would last until the glacier, now found he had to feed the animals the last of their food without the return of progress. Respite did not come until the ninth. 'Shambles Camp' was left behind with the man-haulers helping the ponies over the deep, wet snow. By the end of the day, the last pony had been shot.

Meares, Dimitri, and the dogs were sent back on the eleventh leaving three teams of four men to haul their sledges up the fearsome, 120-mile, slope of the Beardmore Glacier. All had been marching for 400 miles. Lieutenant Evans, and Lashly had also been man-hauling for the previous six weeks over the same distance. Now everyone was man-hauling on skis. Bowers in particular, was delighted. He had written to Scott's wife before leaving Cape Evans telling her that, 'it will be a fine thing to do that plateau with man-haulage in these days of the supposed decadence of the British Race.' But the lower slopes of the glacier proved to be extremely difficult as the sledges ploughed into the soft snow. Day after day they climbed upwards over crevasses, bare ice, pressure ridges, and frozen waves that threatened to break their sledge runners. On the twenty-first, at 'Upper Glacier depot' – 8,000 feet above sea-level, Scott decided that Atkinson, Wright, Cherry-Garrard, and Keohane should begin their 584-mile return journey. All, especially Wright, were bitterly disappointed and Scott found it 'heartrending' to have to choose who would not go to the Pole. Just two teams remained. Scott led Wilson, Oates, and Petty Officer Evans. Lieutenant Evans led Bowers, Crean, and Lashly.

Christmas Day started well but, after an hour's good hauling, they found themselves in an area crossed by hidden crevasses. Time and again legs would disappear and their owners throw themselves back to save disappearing completely. Such reactions did not always work and Lashly fell through a snow bridge pulling the sledge after him. Bowers and Crean were swept off their feet and careered towards the edge in pursuit. Luckily the twelve-foot sledge jumped the ten-foot gap and Lashly was suspended at the full length of his harness with another 80 feet below his boots to the floor of the frozen cavern. It was his forty-fourth birthday. Pulled to safety, the chief stoker continued on as if nothing worth commenting upon had happened. That night, Bowers produced a 'great feed' of provisions he had kept hidden since leaving Cape Evans. Their meal consisted of:

> A good fat hoosh with pony meat and ground biscuit. A chocolate hoosh made with water, cocoa, sugar, biscuits, raisins, and thickened with a spoonful of arrowroot. Then came two-and-a-half square inches of plum duff each, and a good mug of cocoa washed down the whole. In addition to this we had four caramels each and four squares of crystallised ginger.

Feeling full to bursting, and snug in his sleeping bag, Bowers turned to Lieutenant Evans and said, 'Teddy, if all is well next Christmas we will get hold of all the poor children we can and just stuff them with nice things, won't we?'

Three days after the Christmas excesses, Lieutenant Evans found that his sledge was becoming increasingly difficult to pull. Scott went across and pointed out that – as a result of seeing Oates' sleeping bag fall of his sledge – the retaining straps had been pulled too tight and the sledge was being distorted.

The effort in hauling the warped sledge had tired the team out, a situation not improved by the conditions of the following two days. Consequently, on New Year's Eve, approaching 10,000 feet, and on the lip of the plateau, Evans gained Scott's approval to depot his skis, ski boots, and climbing rope in order to save

Petty Officer Evans, Bowers, Wilson and Scott having a meal in their tent.

weight. Scott had no difficulty with this decision, for, in three days' time, he was to announce the final team that would strike out for the Pole. Before that happened, however, a camp was made at '3 Degree depot'. More weight could be saved by reducing the sledges from 12 to 10 feet. The work was carried out by petty officers Evans and Crean as Scott cooked the evening meal. During the work on the sledges, Petty Officer Evans, his fingers numbed by the -40 degrees Fahrenheit temperatures, cut his hand badly. True to his stoic nature, and anxious to avoid a fuss, Evans replaced his mittens and carried on with his work.

The hour Lieutenant Evans feared came on the morning of 3 January 1912. And it arrived double-edged. Not only was he to return, but Scott asked him if he could do it without Bowers. Both Lashly and Lieutenant Evans had man-hauled, without relief, for almost 750 miles. Although they were fit and keen to go on, to add another 300 miles to the Pole and back on top of the 800 miles to Cape Evans was to test them beyond a reasonable limit. Crean was in fine shape and might be needed if the exertions of the other two began to tell on them. Furthermore, Evans was the only one who could navigate and would be needed to pilot the sledge back to Ross Island. On being told of his decision, Scott noted that, 'Teddy Evans is terribly disappointed but has taken it very well and behaved like a man. Poor old Crean wept and even Lashly was affected.'

Like the others, Bowers was desperately keen to have a go at the Pole. He had, nevertheless, prepared himself for disappointment and, in a letter written to his

Petty Officer Edgar Evans.

mother before leaving Cape Evans, he had said; 'you may be sure I shall consider no sacrifice too great for the main object, and whether I am in one of the returning parties or not – I am Captain Scott's man and shall stick by him right through.' To Scott, for whom loyalty was always a two-way emotion, the sheer courage, single-mindedness, and 'indefatigable zeal' of Bowers was an inspiration. He had formed a splendid team to take his sledge and his country's flag to the Pole, but to do so without the brave little Bowers was beyond him. He could even rationalise his decision. Whilst he represented the Royal Navy as a whole, and Petty Officer Evans the lower deck in particular, Oates stood for the army, and Wilson for both civilians and scientist. With Bowers of the Royal Indian Marine onboard, he now had someone to represent the British Empire with its Dominions and Colonies spread around the world. What better team could possibly exist?

Once the sledges had been re-arranged, there remained just one problem. Bowers had left his skis three days' march to the rear. For Bowers himself, the lack of skis was no problem at all and he was quite happy to plod along in the middle of the skiers, but Scott asked Lieutenant Evans to accompany them for a short distance in case the new arrangement did not work. When it became clear that the ski-less Bowers provided no impediment to their progress, Scott stopped and shook the hands of those about to start their return journey. That done, Lieutenant Evans and his men gave three cheers before standing, watching, and waving, until

Lieutenant E.R.G.R. Evans.

Scott and his party were 'a tiny black speck on the horizon.' The Pole was only 146 miles away but, on 4 January, fate forced Evans to turn to the north, and to the dash for the bleak cape Scott had named in his honour.

As he made his way back to the top of the great glacier, Evans calculated that he and his men would have to cover at least seventeen miles a day if they were to travel on full provisions. Anything less would mean reduced rations, hunger, and a decreasing mileage. So desperate was he to keep up his daily distances that, when a blizzard came on them three days after separating from Scott, they simply hunched their shoulders, lowered their hoods, and walked through it.

On the thirteenth, they found themselves looking down on the Beardmore Glacier from the top of a great ice falls that Scott, at Evans' request, had named after Shackleton – the first man to climb up them. Evans, however, was now faced with the choice of spending up to three days making his way down to the glacier by a roundabout route, or by attempting to go *down* the falls. After a 'short-lived' discussion with Lashly and Crean it was decided that they would risk the rapid descent. The skis were secured on the sledge and crampons attached to their fur boots before they began the slow, careful business of controlling a 400lb sledge on steeply sloping, badly crevassed, ice. Before long, they were overtaken by the forces of nature. The sledge began to slide faster than they could hold it so, throwing caution to the wind, the three men jumped onboard as it began tobogganing down the broken ice. The exhilarating, uncontrollable slide ended when it leapt over a yawning crevasse and crashed on the far side to roll over and over until brought to a halt by a ridge of ice. Miraculously, no-one was injured apart from a severe bruising. They had come down many hundreds of feet and saved three days hauling and food. Evans rewarded his men by winding his watch forward before getting up in the morning and winding it back later in the day. Thus, when they thought they were doing ten hours of hauling, they were actually doing twelve.

Despite his efforts to keep the daily distances as high as possible, Evans found the journey down the glacier to be both difficult and slow. Food had been picked up at the Upper Glacier depot but, by late afternoon on the seventeenth, after having been delayed by fog, they found themselves lost, short of food, and in a maze of wide crevasses. The great chasms could only be crossed by either finding an ice bridge, or by walking along the edges until they found the end. This worked without too much difficulty until they came across a crevasse which seemed to go on for ever. All they could find was an ice bridge that was so narrow the sledge runners would inevitably fall on either side of it. Eventually, Lashly, sitting astride the fragile bridge worked his way across taking a rope. Then, hauling carefully, with Evans and Crean hanging onto the sides of the sledge and with their crampons biting into the sides of the bridge, he inched the load across until the two men could clamber up the slope on his side. All three then prepared to pull the sledge across and up to safety. Just as they began, the sledge toppled and rolled into the abyss. With crampons digging into the ice on which they stood they held onto the rope for dear life, gradually pulling the sledge up. It took a huge amount of effort but, at last, they hauled it clear. They tried to continue, but their exhaustion soon told and Evans had to call a halt. The situation was indeed desperate. Weak from hunger and effort, surrounded by seemingly limitless broken ice, and without a clear patch on which to put up the tent, they sat in silence on the sledge. At last, Evans decided that he had to do something and wandered off by himself. In fact, he had gone to pray. Finding an area of clear ice, he fell to his knees and 'prayed to God that a way out should be shown to me'. Regaining his feet, he pressed on up an ice slope to see a sight that made his heart leap. Ahead lay an un-crevassed slope of the glacier and, in the near distance, was a red rock marking the next depot. By that evening, they were eating hot pemmican hoosh and preparing for a night of sound sleep.

During the day's events, Evans had been forced to remove his snow-goggles. As a result, the following morning, he woke up to the searing pain of snow-blindness. For the next twelve days, attached to the sledge trace by the lanyard of his pocket sundial, he was led down the glacier and onto the barrier surface by the other two men. By 30 January, fourteen weeks after setting out from their base, Evans began to detect a stiffening of the joints. Soon he could not straighten his legs and the knees were swollen and green. Then his gums began to swell and bleed as his teeth became loose. There could be no doubting that he was in the grip of scurvy. He tried to keep up with the sledge by pushing himself along on a pair of skis but eventually fainted from the pain. Crean and Lashly put him on the

Chief Stoker William Lashly.

sledge tucked inside his sleeping bag and continued the long haul to Hut Point. One Ton depot was passed, then Corner Camp until, thirty-five miles short of the hut, the sledge ground to a halt as Lashly and Crean collapsed in the traces. They could go no further with the weight of the sledge. The tent was put up and Evans made comfortable inside from where he could hear voices. It was Lashly and Crean discussing what to do next. By now Lashly had been hauling for close on 1,500 miles. Crean had walked that distance, but had been hauling for about 400 miles less. The two men agreed that Crean was probably in a better shape and that he should attempt to reach Hut Point to see if help was available. If none could be found he would have to go on to Cape Evans – a further fifteen miles. Taking a few paraffin-soaked biscuits and a bar of chocolate, Crean set off, striding out into the distance as Lashly made porridge for Evans from the tiny amount of oatmeal they had left. The lieutenant was sinking fast and was soon 'past caring' as Lashly did what he could for him. Two days after Crean had left, both men were lying in the green gloom of the tent, when Lashly suddenly sprang to his feet and pushed open the tent entrance. Sure enough, coming across the surface of the snow and ice, he could hear the sound of dogs. Moments later, a sledge reached the tent and the lead dog burst in to lick Evan's face. Atkinson and Dimitri had been delayed at Hut Point by a blizzard when Crean burst in after covering the distance from the tent in eighteen hours – much of it through the same blizzard.

They had harnessed their dogs immediately when a lull in the weather allowed them and set out in the hope of getting to Evans in time. After a hot meal and a rest for the dogs, Evans and Lashly were safe at the *Discovery* Hut within three hours of leaving their camp.

Atkinson had been left in command at Cape Evans whilst the sledging parties were out. Wright and the others of the first support party had returned safely albeit with a touch of scurvy, and the *Terra Nova* had returned after transporting Campbell's northern party south from Cape Adair to Terra Nova Bay. They had intended to stay at that site for just a few weeks, but sea ice off the bay had, so far, prevented the *Terra Nova* from collecting them. The ship had also brought out seven mules which Scott intended to use in exploring the Victoria Land Coast where it met the barrier ice – and Petty Officer Thomas Williamson, who had been with Scott as an able seaman on the *Discovery* expedition.

Apart from the team he had with him, Atkinson's first thoughts were for Scott and the returning southern party. He had no reason to worry about their safety, but was keen that they should be brought in as quickly as possible once they were within range of his dogs. To that end he sent Cherry-Garrard and Dimitri out with supplies to increase the stores at One Ton depot. It was a very risky decision as Cherry-Garrard, 'had never driven one dog, let alone a team of them'. Also, One Ton depot was 130 miles away and the assistant biologist knew nothing about navigation. But Atkinson was needed to look after Evans, and Wright had taken over as expedition physicist as Simpson was returning to New Zealand in the *Terra Nova*. The two men set off with their dog teams on 26 February with Dimitri leading (Cherry-Garrard's spectacles frequently fogged up, preventing him from seeing much further than his lead dog). Their progress was surprisingly successful with Cherry-Garrard only losing control of his sledge once before they reached One Ton depot. Blizzards greeted their arrival and stayed with them as they waited for Scott and the southern party to arrive. Six days in total were spent at the site with only two in which the high winds eased back. Cherry-Garrard was desperately keen to press on even further south despite the conditions, but his youth and inexperience held him back. Atkinson had told him that, on arrival at One Ton depot, he was to, 'judge what to do'. He had also told Cherry-Garrard that the dogs 'were not to be risked'. The blizzard had used up much of their stock of dog food and there was no dog food at the depot. Consequently, Cherry-Garrard's options were severely limited. He could risk both their lives and those of the dogs by a dash to the south in search of someone who might not be there, or he could start his return journey. Seeing 'no reason for disobeying' his orders he started his return on 10 March and arrived back at Hut Point six days later after a hair-raising journey over deep crevasses and with Dimitri on the point of collapse. Both men needed Atkinson's medical attentions.

As for Scott and his men, although hope was piled upon hope, Atkinson could find no realistic expectation of their survival.

Lieutenant Pennell, still in command of the *Terra Nova*, brought her south towards Hut Point, and Evans was sledged across to her in his sleeping bag.

Right: Petty Officer Tom Crean.

Below: Surgeon E.L. Atkinson.

A further attempt to reach Campbell's party at Terra Nova Bay failed, and the ship sailed for New Zealand, taking with her – in addition to Evans – Simpson, Ponting, and the groom, Anton. Those remaining to see a second winter though were, Atkinson, Wright, Debenham, Nelson, Cherry-Garrard, Gran, Archer (a former Chief Steward who came out with the *Terra Nova*), Lashly, Williamson, Crean, Keohane, Hooper, and Dimitri. Somewhere to the south was Scott and his team, whilst, to the north, there was Campbell and five men, known to be almost without supplies or equipment.

Atkinson was determined to get help to both parties if the possibility of doing so remained. On 26 March he set off south with Keohane, man-hauling a sledge of supplies, but got no further than Corner Camp before atrocious conditions drove them back. The surgeon then led a party first west then north to lay out depots in case Campbell was making his way along the Victoria coastline in an effort to reach Ross Island before the winter finally set in. On his return, Atkinson knew that nothing further could be done apart from seeing the winter through at the Cape Evans hut. Under trying circumstances Atkinson succeeded in keeping his party's morale high during the dark season. The gramophone and pianola played their part alongside lectures, reading, celebrations of birthdays, and the mid-winter festival. It was during the latter event that Atkinson revealed his plans for the forthcoming spring. He, like everyone else, had to assume that Scott and his party were long dead. His own belief was that they had fallen down a crevasse on the Beardmore Glacier. Cherry-Garrard agreed with him, but Lashly though scurvy more likely. Campbell, and the northern party were also probably dead, but there was just the slightest chance that they could have survived – they, at least, would have had access to penguins and, possibly, seals. The chief objective of the expedition, however, had been the Pole and Atkinson felt they were duty bound to try and find evidence that it had been achieved. Therefore, a search party would go south to search for Scott, at the same time praying that the northern party would get through the winter alive.

Most of late October 1912 was spent in supplying the depot at Corner Camp in readiness for the search expedition. The expedition itself got under way on the thirtieth with a mule party consisting of Wright, Gran, Nelson, Lashly, Crean, Hooper, Williamson, and Keohane. Two days later, the dogs followed with Atkinson, Cherry-Garrard and Dimitri.

Seven days after the mules had set out, Debenham and Archer, the two men remaining at Cape Evans were out taking readings. On their return to the hut they were baffled to see signs of activity. On getting closer, they found to their delight, that it was Campbell and the northern party. When the *Terra Nova* had failed to reach them for the final time, Campbell found himself facing an appalling situation. The party of six men could muster six 45lb tins of biscuits of which two would have to be saved for any attempt to go south along the coast, a small amount of cocoa and tea, some bars of chocolate, a few dozen sugar lumps and a bottle of Wincarnis wine. Enough raisins were available to give twenty-five to each man on their birthday – unless each man found he had 'a birthday once a month'. In addition they had killed 120 penguins and eleven seals, but their meat would not get the party through the winter – even on half rations. And seals were getting very scarce. Their tents were already in bad condition and would certainly not see them through a winter, so Campbell decided that they should dig a large hole into some compacted snow in the lee of a small hill.

After a few days of effort the 'hut' had a three-foot thick roof of snow with walls of ice. Snow and seaweed was used to insulate the walls and a layer of pebbles provided a floor. A blubber stove was concocted along with blubber lamps made from 'Oxo' tins. The number of seals killed was eventually brought up to sixteen and seal hooshes were served once a day, cooked in sea-water with old seaweed pretending to be cabbage. To preserve naval discipline, Campbell scored a line down the centre of the ice cave and declared that one side was the wardroom, the other, the messdeck. Anything said about the ratings by an officer whilst in the 'wardroom' could not be heard on the other side of the line. Equally, anything said about an officer by a rating whilst on the 'messdeck', could not be heard by any of the officers. A stick of chocolate was served out on Saturday evenings followed by a concert and the following day was marked by an issue of sugar lumps and a church service. At mid-winter's day they celebrated by having a hoosh of seal liver and biscuits, four sticks of chocolate, twenty-five raisins, and a sip of Wincarnis wine. The return of the sun on 10 August was greeted with an eagerly anticipated seal brain hoosh washed down with cocoa.

By the middle of September, Campbell was leading his men in doing 'Swedish exercises' to get them ready for the long walk back to Cape Evans. They set off on 30 September, towing sledges loaded with precious geological specimens. A month later, they came across a depot that had been left by the western party the previous year. Campbell granted a day's holiday to enjoy the extra pemmican, biscuits and cocoa. Three days later they stumbled across one of the depots established by Atkinson the previous April. This find gave them ample food to get around McMurdo Sound. On their arrival at Cape Evans, they found letters waiting for them that had been brought down by the *Terra Nova,* clean clothes, and a meal which they attacked, 'in a way that made Debenham hold his breath.'

Meanwhile, out on the barrier, Atkinson had found the going easy. The surface had remained good and the slight wind came from the north-east. One Ton depot was reached on the morning of 11 November and Atkinson ordered a day's rest as the depot was checked. It was found that one of the one-gallon tins of paraffin had leaked and spoiled some of the stores beneath. No hole could be found, but the evidence made it quite clear that something was wrong with the tin.

Wright led-off with the mule party that evening and was still ahead at six o'clock the following morning. Suddenly he noticed a dark speck to his right, about a quarter of a mile away. Putting on his skis, he went over to have a closer look at what had caught his eye. It turned out to be the top of a green tent sticking out of the snow for about 6 inches. In his heart, Wright knew what he had found, and turned to wave vigorously at the column of sledges – to shout, he felt, would have been, 'like desecration'. A camp was made some distance from

The Southern Search Party. Front row: Gran, Williamson, Keohane, Wright, Dimitri. Rear row: Archer, Hooper, Nelson, Atkinson, Cherry-Garrard, Lashly, Crean.

the site and Wright and the rest waited for about two hours for Atkinson to catch up with them. On his arrival, the surgeon ordered the tent to be cleared of snow. Like all the tents used on the expedition, entrance was gained via a funnel tube which was then closed and secured on the inside. Atkinson pulled the tube out and released the lashing. Then, under the eyes of the entire party, he crawled into the tent. There was a pause for a minute or so until his head and shoulders re-appeared and he motioned Lashly to join him. Shortly afterwards, the tough chief stoker re-emerged with tears in his eyes and passed on Atkinson's order that all the men should enter the tent to see what had been revealed.

The sight they saw was, according to Williamson, 'ghastly'. Gran thought, 'a terrible nightmare could not have shown more horror.' Inside, softly illuminated by the light filtering through the green tent-cloth, Scott lay on his back with his sleeping bag half open. His left arm lay across the body of Wilson who was lying with his arms folded across over his chest like a medieval knight. Bowers rested as if he had simply slipped into a quiet, well-earned, sleep. There were no obvious signs of scurvy, but clear evidence of 'exposure and want'. Around them the tent presented a neat and well-ordered appearance. Scott's diary was found beneath the head of his sleeping-bag. In it were instructions to the finder that they were to read of the death of Captain Oates before ensuring that the book was taken to England.

Atkinson read the account and then told the others of its contents. Oates had died some miles to the south, and the manner of his death was such that Scott wanted

The cairn of snow covering Scott's tent.

the world to know. Having carried out Scott's last request, and having retrieved all the records, personal belongings, and a small white ensign, Atkinson had the tent collapsed over the bodies. The party stood bare-headed beneath a sky of evening crimson, as he read from St Paul's First Epistle to the Corinthians in remembrance of their fallen comrades. Then a cairn of snow was erected over the collapsed tent and Lashly used Gran's skis to make a cross to place at its summit. Scott's sledge had been dug out and found to contain 35lbs of rocks – geological specimens that Wilson, especially, had wished to bring back. The sledge, and one from Atkinson's party, was upended and planted upright in the snow, one on each side of the cairn. According to Cherry-Garrard, 'The whole', was 'very simple and most impressive. Of all the fine monuments in the world none seems to me to be more fitting.' A record, signed by all the party, was buried between the eastern sledge and the cairn. It gave the cause of the deaths as 'Inclement weather and lack of fuel.'

The next two days were spent in searching for Oates. His sleeping bag was found, but the snow had claimed his body. Atkinson had another cairn and cross erected. Lashed to the cross was a record stating that, 'Hereabouts died a very gallant gentleman, Captain L.E.G. Oates of the Inniskilling Dragoons.'

With their sad duties completed, Atkinson led his party back to Cape Evans. There they found some cheer in the form of Campbell and the northern party, safe from their winter ordeal at Terra Nova Bay.

There was little for them to do at the base apart from waiting for the *Terra Nova* to return. Priestley took Debenham, Gran, Hooper, Abbott, and Dickason on an ascent of Mount Erebus. The rim of the crater was reached by Priestley and Gran, and a record was left in a small cairn. However, on the way down, Priestley discovered that instead of leaving a record he had left a tin of exposed photographic film. Gran volunteered to return and effect an exchange. Just as he had completed his task, the Norwegian heard 'a gurgling sound' coming from the crater. Before he could take any action, a small eruption covered him in sulphurous fumes and threatened him with a shower of lava. The experience was, Gran noted 'disagreeable in the extreme' and 'no joke'. Whilst this had been going on, Debenham had carried out a creditable topographical survey of the volcano, the key to the resultant map unashamedly illustrating his inexperience in such matters – 'Contour lines 250ft very approximate. Scale 2.7 miles to the inch (about).'

On 13 January 1913, the party were beginning to prepare for a third winter in the Antarctic when the black hull and lofty masts of the *Terra Nova* hove into view. The ship, back under the command of a recovered Evans, closed the cape with flags flying from the mastheads. Onboard, cabins had been prepared and bunks made up for Scott and the southern party. Three cheers from Campbell and the group assembled ashore were answered by three from the ship. Evans, taking up a megaphone shouted out 'Are you well, Campbell?' The reply silenced the excited hub-bub on the ship; 'The Southern Party reached the Pole on January 18 last year, but were all lost on the return journey – we have their records.' The flags were immediately sent down; only the ensign was allowed to remain – fluttering at half-mast.

No time was lost in getting the shore party, their equipment, and the scientific collections onboard. The hut was secured with enough stores inside to, 'see a dozen resourceful men through one summer and winter at least.' Cape Evans was left the following day and the *Terra Nova* made her way to the ice edge of McMurdo Sound. Atkinson landed with a sledge and a party of seven men. They took with them a stout cross made of Australian jarrah wood to erect on the top of Observation Hill. From its heights, the barrier, the *Discovery* hut, and Cape Evans could all be seen. After listing the names of the men lost with the southern party, the cross carried the following words from Tennyson's *Ulysses* – 'To Strive, To Seek, To Find, And not to Yield.'

When the news of the expedition's fate reached England, the nation, still reeling in shock from the loss of the *Titanic*, went into mourning. Shackleton said, 'I cannot believe it is true. I am distressed beyond belief.' Nansen had, 'the greatest admiration for Captain Scott and his gallant band' whilst, for Amundsen, it was 'Horrible! Horrible! I admire Captain Scott as a fine and brave man.' Flags were lowered across the country, newspapers devoted whole editions to the tragedy, and churches throughout the land held special services to remember the dead. The King, after issuing a special message of mourning, led a memorial service held in St Paul's cathedral, the congregation overflowing into the surrounding streets. Wearing the uniform of an Admiral of the Fleet, the sovereign was accompanied by the First Lord of the Admiralty (Winston Churchill) and the Lord Mayor and

A Lord Mayor's Fund contribution card.

Sheriffs of London. A 'Scott Memorial Fund' was established to provide gratuities and pensions for the dependants of those who had died. At the Prime Minister's request, the King authorised Scott's widow's elevation to the rank of 'Lady Scott' exactly as if her husband had survived to be knighted on his return.

Lieutenant Edward R.G.R. Evans was promoted to commander on his return and presented the King with the small white ensign that Atkinson had found among Scott's belongings. It was framed and placed in the Royal Yacht. He served at the Battle of Jutland, and as the captain of HMS *Broke,* he achieved a brilliant victory against German destroyers that earned him wide popularity as 'Evans of the *Broke*'. He was given his flag in 1929 and made commander-in-chief of the Royal Australian Navy. After service on the Africa Station as commander-in-chief and deputy high commissioner of the British Protectorates, he was appointed during the Second World War as London Regional Commissioner. He was elevated to the House of Lords as a Labour Peer with the title Baron Mount Evans. His death came in 1957.

Lieutenant Victor Campbell was specially promoted to commander on the Emergency List and later earned the Distinguished Service Order as commander of the Drake Battalion of the Royal Naval Division during operation on Gallipoli. He was consulted by the Admiralty during the Second World War on the subject of incarceration for long periods. His experience of wintering in the ice-cave at Terra Nova Bay was put to use in preparing secret caves for occupation by a few men for up to seven years on Gibraltar should the Rock ever be captured. Perhaps fortunately, the expected invasion never took place. Surgeon Edward Atkinson was promoted to Staff Surgeon and had already earned the Distinguished Service

Victor Campbell as commander.

Order when he was near to the coastal defence ship, HMS *Glatton*, as she blew up in Dover Harbour in September 1918. Although badly injured and with one eye destroyed he took part in the rescue of men from the ship, earning the Albert Medal as a result. He died, aged forty-six, in 1929. Surgeon George Murray Levick served as a Staff Surgeon during the First World War and was present at the landings on Gallipoli. His popularity was ensured when he adopted the practice of sending whisky ashore to friends – the bottles being labelled 'Medicines, very urgent'. He died in 1956, aged eighty.

Chief Stoker William Lashly and Petty Officer Thomas Crean were both awarded the Albert Medal for their rescue of Lieutenant Evans. Lashly left the Navy on his return and settled down with his pension only to be recalled on the outbreak of war. He was serving in the battleship *Irresistible* when she was sunk in the Dardanelles by a shore-launched torpedo. He was then drafted to the light cruiser, *Amythest*. In 1932, Lashly built a house at Hambledon which he named 'Minna Bluff'. Shortly before he died there, eight years later, he was described by Evans as a, 'steel-true Englishman whose example sets us all a-thinking. He is one of those Yeomen of England whose type gave us Drake's men and Nelson's men and Scott's and Shackleton's men, and will do so again.' After serving with Shackleton in the *Endurance* followed by service in the war (during which time he was promoted to Warrant Officer), Crean returned to

Ireland and bought a public house which he named 'The Pole Star'. He died in 1938.

The only survivor from the Cape Crozier winter journey, Apsley Cherry-Garrard, took Wilson's precious Emperor penguin eggs to the Natural History Museum where they were accepted with neither thanks, nor appreciation. Left waiting for a receipt, the normally mild-mannered assistant zoologist passed the time by imagining what he would like to do with his boots to the Chief Custodian, 'by way of teaching him manners.' With the outbreak of the war, 'Cherry' entered the Royal Navy and served with the Royal Naval Armoured Car Service. For much of his life he was troubled by the possibility that, by ignoring his orders and pressing on beyond One Ton depot, he might have saved Scott. At that time the southern party were less than seventy miles away and Cherry-Garrard had enough dog food to get him to their camp. But that was all. Had he struck out in search of them, he might have added his name to the list of the dead. None of his polar companions ever suggested that he had failed in his duty. With the help of the playwright, George Bernard Shaw, he was later to write, *The Worst Journey in the World*, one of the best accounts of the expedition to be written. Apsley Cherry-Garrard died in 1959.

Both Cecil Meares and Tryggve Gran served in the Royal Flying Corps, and Herbert Ponting continued to earn a living from his photography, eventually producing a film, *90 Degrees South*, from the results of his expedition cinematography. Griffith Taylor became a professor of geography, Frank Debenham founded the Scott Polar Research Institute in 1926, and Charles Wright and Raymond Priestley were both knighted for their academic and scientific achievements.

CHAPTER NINETEEN

'ENGLISHMEN CAN STILL DIE WITH A BOLD SPIRIT'

Just over two years before the memorial service in St Paul's Cathedral, Scott, Wilson, Bowers, Oates and Petty Officer Evans had hauled their sledge south to the cheers of the last support party. The day after the separation, all seemed to be going well, but Scott was cautious; 'At present everything seems to be going with extraordinary smoothness, and one can scarcely believe that obstacles will not present themselves to make our task more difficult. Perhaps the surface will be the element to trouble us.' He was right. A covering of ice crystals made the hauling extremely difficult. Instead of the friction of the sledge runners melting the surface beneath – thus producing a smooth 'glide' – the crystals refused to melt. It was as if the sledge was being dragged through sand and made the pulling heavy and exhausting work. To make the situation worse, waves of 'sastrugi' swept across their front; their sharp, crystal-edged rise and fall forcing the party to remove their skis and practically lift the sledge over the repeated obstacles.

After four days the white plain levelled out, but the ice crystals remained. A blizzard halted progress on 8 January. Evans' hand was dressed by Wilson, and Scott used the time they were forced to remain in their tent to look closely at his companions. Wilson was 'tough as steel' and 'never wavering'. Evans and Oates were 'invaluable', and Bowers 'a marvel' who was 'thoroughly enjoying himself.' The tough little man with his trademark hooked nose had kept up gamely on foot, 'It is a long slog with a loaded sledge, and more tiring for me than the others, as I have no skis. However, as long as I can do my share all day and keep fit it does not matter one way or the other.'

The wind eased the following day and, on the tenth a depot was laid at 88 degrees 29'. Taking eighteen days' food forward on a lightened sledge, they still found the surface against them; 'None of us ever had such hard work before.' In places, the ice crystals were replaced by soft snow which had to be ploughed through and Scott found it hard to keep up the distances he needed to stay within his rations. Another depot – their last before the Pole – was left on the fifteenth. They had been walking for sixty-six days and their goal was just twenty-seven miles ahead.

On Tuesday, the sixteenth, the morning went successfully with a march of seven and a half miles. A lunch rest was taken and the march resumed with 'high spirits'. About two hours after they had started, Bowers spotted something that could

Above: Four of the five members of the final Polar Party. Scott and Wilson lead followed by Evans and Oates. The photograph was taken by Bowers.

Opposite: The Polar Party at their destination. Oates takes his weight on one foot in an attempt to relieve the pain from his feet and from an old war wound. A gaunt Bowers pulls a string to operate the camera. Scott appears to be feeling the anguish of being beaten by Amundsen. Wilson looks almost calm and untroubled whilst Evans glowers with weary defiance.

have been a cairn, but tried to persuade himself it was probably more sastrugi. Within half an hour the mysterious feature had resolved itself into a black speck. On approach, it turned out to be a black flag flying from a sledge bearer. Such an item could only mean one thing. Someone – and it could only have been the Norwegians – had been there ahead of them. The game was up, and the laurels lost. In his diary, Scott wrote, 'It is a terrible disappointment, and I am very sorry for my loyal companions. All the day-dreams must go.' The find cannot have been a total surprise. Despite ignoring Amundsen's presence, and despite pushing the threat to the back of his mind, Scott – and the others – knew that there was every chance that they would be beaten. That did not stop them trying, nor did it make them turn back in the face of a lost cause; 'Tomorrow we must march on to the Pole.'

At the site of their thwarted ambition they found a brown tent beneath a Norwegian flag. The scarlet cross of St Olaf waved above the spot at which Amundsen and his men had achieved a signal triumph for his country. Inside, Scott found a note informing him that the Norwegians had been there almost exactly a month before his own arrival. 'Great God!', he wrote, 'this is an awful place and terrible enough for us to have laboured to it without reward of priority.' If Bowers was equally disappointed, he failed to show it in a letter to his mother – 'I don't suppose you ever thought that your son would be at the Apex of the Earth. Well, here I really am and very glad to be here too. It is a bleak spot – what a place to strive so hard to reach.'

Bowers took a number of photographs of the site. Group photographs were taken by operating the camera by a length of string as they stood or sat in company with the Union Jack and their sledge pennants. In one of the photographs, Scott is caught with his eyes closed giving his face a pained expression, a thin-looking Bowers is operating the release string, and Oates is leaning on his left leg as if avoiding putting weight on a frostbitten foot or his old Boer War wound. Wilson looks as if he is trying to smile and Evans seems as rock-hard as ever, if a little gaunt, 'We built a cairn, put up our poor slighted Union Jack and photographed ourselves.' In the meantime, Wilson made a sketch of the tent – noting its colours for a later painting.

Leaving the Union Jack flying, the party began their 900-mile journey back with a sail rigged on the sledge. The surface had not improved and the sand-like drag made a 'dreary' haul. On the twenty-first, a blizzard delayed their start and Scott began to calculate, 'forty-five miles to the next depot and six days' food in hand – then pick up seven days' food and ninety miles to go to the "Three Degree Depot". Once there we ought to be safe.' Two days later they were forced to stop when Evans was attacked by frostbite, 'There is no doubt that Evans is a good deal run down – his fingers are badly blistered and his nose is rather seriously congested with frequent frostbites.' They were all beginning to feel the cold.

On the twenty-fourth, Scott noted in his diary, 'Things beginning to look a little serious'. With only seven miles achieved, a blizzard forced them into their tent seven miles short of the next depot. The red-flagged cairn was reached the next day and nine and a half days rations were recovered. Oates had 'a very cold foot', Evans continued to suffer from frostbite, and Wilson was affected by snow-blindness. An increase in temperature on the twenty-seventh meant damp sleeping bags to go with a shortage of food. Three days later, Wilson damaged a tendon in his leg and Evans' hand took a turn for the worse when two finger nails broke away – 'to my surprise he shows signs of losing heart over it. He has not been cheerful since the accident.'

The 'Three Degree Depot' was reached on the morning of the thirty-first, and Bowers' skis were picked up shortly afterwards. He had pulled on foot for 360 miles without respite and without complaint. Scott added himself to the list of injured when he, 'came an awful purler', slipping and crashing down hard on his shoulder. Then, with the end of the plateau journey almost in sight, they found themselves in an area of crevasses. Evans fell through into one and was hauled out with little damage but, shortly afterwards, he fell down another one, this time with Scott. Both men were pulled out. Scott had suffered bruising, but Evans was concussed. He continued on without complaint, but Scott noted that the large petty officer had become 'rather dull and incapable'.

The Upper Glacier depot was reached seven weeks after they had left the same spot for the Pole. Now faced with a 120-mile descent of the Beardmore Glacier, Scott remained hopeful as 'the outlook is much more promising.' Evans, however, was starting to look 'played out'. Mount Darwin was visited to get specimens of its pink limestone rock, and a visit to a moraine beneath Mount Buckley proved to be so interesting that Scott decided to spend the rest of the day 'geologising'. Among exposed coal seams, much to Wilson's delight, several rocks were found with plant impressions. Thanks to the supplies from the last depot, the food situation had eased, but it was necessary to keep up the daily marches to keep within their closely calculated rations.

Unable on the slope of the glacier to see what lay immediately ahead of them they found their way into a jumble of broken ice, crevasses, and dangerous ice falls. It was a time of great hazard and took them twelve hours to find a way through. But they had come out some way off their track and rations had to be reduced in order to reach the next depot. The next day they found one of their old camps and so were cheered to know they were back on track. Yet again, however, they stumbled into another region of crevasses. By pushing on they found their situation worsening and Scott decided to camp. After a much-reduced supper, they found that there was just one meal remaining. Scott wrote in his diary, 'In a very critical situation.' He did not even know if he was close to the next depot.

Snow fell that night and continued on into the next day, forcing them to remain in their sleeping bags until they were able to get away at mid-morning. Fog hindered their progress for some time but, at last, they came out onto another moraine. Making their way down the slope they were all delighted to hear Wilson shout out that he had spotted the depot. Food for three and a half days was collected along with notes from Wright and Lieutenant Evans informing him that their respective parties had managed to reach the site safely on their return journeys. The close encounter with possible starvation had alarmed Scott and, as Wilson went to collect more rocks, he decided that he must be more frugal with his supplies and make allowances for bad weather – 'We mustn't get into a hole like this again.' He was not helped by having lost the sledgemeter as they came down the moraines, and could no longer be sure of his distances.

The next three days saw a sharp decline in the condition of Evans. On the lower slopes of the glacier he had proved to be of no assistance in hauling and caused their progress to be stopped for a series of minor equipment adjustments. Scott felt that the petty officer had, 'broken down in brain' and had 'absolutely changed from his normal self-reliant self.' On the seventeenth he had to leave the traces to replace his ski boots which had worked free. The rest pressed on for about an hour and then waited for Evans to catch up. Again, he fell out with boot trouble and lagged far behind the others. Scott decided to camp and cook a meal as they waited for him to catch up. When he failed to appear, all four went back on skis to look for him. Scott was in the lead when they found him. Evans was on his knees with his clothing undone and his mitts off. Slowly, he tried to explain that he must have fainted. They managed to get him to his feet but, after just a few steps, he pitched forward once again. He was clearly incapable of moving under his own effort and Oates was left to look after him as the rest returned to the tent to collect the sledge. By the time he was brought to the camp, Evans was unconscious. He died shortly afterwards.

Shambles Camp was reached the following day with its wealth of pony meat and Scott ensured that they all had a good meal after their recent shortages. Any hope, however, of a better surface on the barrier vanished in the face of yet more soft, loose snow that left deep ruts in their rear. It was 'like pulling over desert sand, not the least glide in the world.' The next depot was reached on the twenty-fourth. Much to their consternation, it was discovered that the oil supplies were less than had been expected. The leather washers used as a seal for the stoppers had perished, allowing the oil to evaporate. This loss seriously affected their ability to cook food and melt snow for water – especially with the low temperatures they were experiencing.

For the next few days the surface conditions improved markedly accompanied by a steady fall in temperatures. They all began to feel cold, a situation not helped by the impossibility of drying their ski-boots overnight. Consequently, they had to put their feet into frozen footwear to start out. Before long, the ice around the boots had melted and their feet became both cold, and wet. The shortage of fuel was also causing concern with the next depot being almost eighty miles from their last supply.

They arrived at the Middle Barrier depot on 2 March to find, yet again, that the fuel was short. Even with the greatest economy it seemed unlikely that they would be able to reach the next depot – seventy-one miles to the north. Oates also revealed the appalling state of his feet. His toes were badly frostbitten and an agony to walk with. The following morning the temperature fell to -40 degrees Fahrenheit and it took them one and a half hours to get their ski-boots on. Once again the bad surface returned to taunt them as, with backs bowed, they struggled against its grip. Pemmican just warmed through was all that could be provided from the fifth. They all pretended that they preferred it that way – 'Amongst ourselves we are unendingly cheerful, but what each man feels in his heart I can only guess. We mean to see the game through with a proper spirit.' The same day Scott noted that, 'the poor Soldier is nearly done.' Oates was in dreadful pain with his feet, yet still hauled at the trace in a defiant effort not to let the side down.

Over the next days, Oates' condition worsened. On the tenth he asked Wilson what his chances were and, on the following day, he openly discussed his condition with the others. Scott responded by obtaining from Wilson, 'the means of ending our troubles…so that any one of us may know how to do so.' Each man was given thirty opium tablets each, Wilson retaining a tube of morphine. With little chance of exceeding six miles as a daily march, and with seven days' food remaining, Scott calculated that they would be thirteen miles from their next depot – One Ton – when their food ran out – and that figure took no account of bad weather. Two days later a northerly wind blew directly into their faces and they were unable to leave their camp.

On the fifteenth, worn down at last by pain, Oates declared that he could go no further and asked to be left in his sleeping bag. The others persuaded him to keep on going and he struggled forward with them for the rest of the day. That night he lay in his sleeping bag in the hope that he would not wake in the morning. But wake he did, as a blizzard raged around the tent. Hauling himself from his bag, he made his way on hands and knees to the tent entrance, pulled at its securing cord and announced, 'I am just going outside and may be some time' before disappearing into the wind-driven snow. He knew that by remaining, he would be a fatal burden upon his companions, and chose to relieve them of that responsibility in the only way he knew. For Scott, it was, 'the act of a brave man and an English gentleman. We all hope to meet the end with a similar spirit, and assuredly the end is not far.'

For the next two days they trudged on in the face of a northerly wind and with temperatures around -40 degrees Fahrenheit. Scott's right foot became seriously frostbitten. In one unkind stroke he had gone from having the best feet in the party to having the worst. On the night of the nineteenth, the tent was erected eleven miles from One Ton depot as a blizzard grew in strength around them. Scott knew he could go no further but, if the weather improved in time, there was just the chance that the other two might make it to the depot. There they should find ample fuel and supplies to either take them forward, or to bring them back for him. Such a forlorn hope, however, was dashed by the continuing blizzard.

For the next nine days, as their lives ebbed away, Scott tidied up the end of his life. To his friend, Sir J.M. Barrie, the author of 'Peter Pan', he wrote:

> We are pegging out in a very comfortless spot. We are showing that Englishmen can still die with a bold spirit, fighting it out to the end. I may not have proved a great explorer, but we have done the greatest march ever made and come very near to success.

In a letter to his wife, he gave her instructions regarding the upbringing of his son, Peter:

> Make the boy interested in natural history if you can; it is better than games; they encourage it at some schools. I know you will keep him in the open air. Above all, he must guard and you must guard him against indolence. Make him a strenuous man. I had to force myself into being strenuous as you know – had always an inclination to be idle.

As for her future, he encouraged her to not disregard the possibility of finding a new husband:

> You know I cherish no sentimental rubbish about remarriage. When the right man comes to help you in life you ought to be your happy self again – I wasn't a very good husband, but I hope I shall be a good memory.

He did not forget to honour the memory of the two companions who lay at his side. He left a letter for Bowers' mother:

> I write when we are very near the end of our journey, and I am finishing it in company with two gallant, noble gentlemen. One of these is your son. He had come to be one of my closest and soundest friends, and I appreciate his wonderful upright nature, his ability and energy. As the troubles have thickened his dauntless spirit ever shone brighter and he has remained cheerful, hopeful, and indomitable to the end.

To Wilson's wife he wrote:

> His eyes have a comfortable blue look of hope and his mind is peaceful with the satisfaction of his faith in regarding himself as part of the great scheme of the Almighty. I can do no more to comfort you than to tell you that he died as he lived, a brave, true man – the best of comrades and staunchest of friends.

With his personal duties taken care of, he then turned his thoughts to giving an explanation for the events that had brought him to meet his fate on the windswept Antarctic ice barrier. In a 'Message to the Public' he gave the reasons for the tragedy as the loss of the ponies during the depot-laying journeys in March 1911; the weather on the outward journey; and the soft snow on the lower reaches of the Beardmore Glacier. There was no self-pity, and no recriminations:

> We took risks, we knew we took them; things have come out against us, and therefore we have no cause for complaint, but bow to the will of Providence, determined still to do our best to the last. Had we lived, I should have had a tale to tell of the hardihood, endurance, and courage of my companions which would have stirred the heart of every Englishman. These rough notes and our dead bodies must tell the tale.

Punch in mourning.

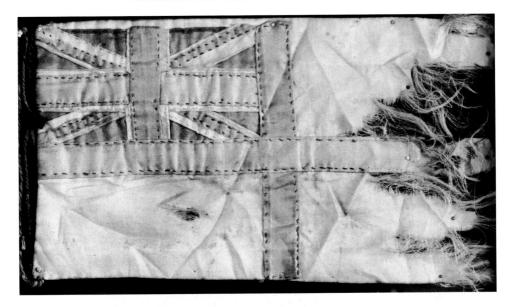

The miniature white ensign carried to the South Pole by Captain Scott. It was recovered from the tent where Scott and his companions died. The ensign was presented to King George V by Commander Edward Evans in May 1913.

He ended his message with an appeal for the provision of care for the dependents of those who had lost their lives, 'for the honour of our country'.

On Thursday 29 March, he pencilled-in the last entry into his diary:

> I do not think we can hope for any better things now. We shall stick it out to the end, but we are getting weaker, of course, and the end cannot be far. It seems a pity, but I do not think I can write any more. R. Scott.

The death of Scott and his companions, far away on the Great Ice Barrier, meant more than the loss of husbands, sons, and friends. It brought home to a nation about to face the horrors of a protracted and bloody war, that duty, loyalty, and comradeship, were not vague concepts, but shield, breastplate, and helmet of an individual's moral armour. With such men as examples, other men – ordinary men – rose from their trenches to advance against a fearsome enemy, stormed blood-soaked beaches swept by machine-guns, and steered their bows straight at the enemy's gun-muzzles. They all knew that they were probably about to die, but Scott had shown that death itself was not to be feared – just the fear of death. The strength of Evans, the gallantry of Oates, the determination of Bowers, the faith of Wilson, and the leadership of Scott, had failed to win the prize of the South Pole, and failed to bring them through their ordeal alive, but they had shown their countrymen how to fail and die with dignity and courage, so that others might achieve the victory.

BIBLIOGRAPHY

Books

Armitage, Albert B., *Cadet to Commodore* (Cassell & Company Ltd, London, New York, Toronto and Melbourne, 1925)

Burton, Robert, *Shackleton: The Antarctic and Endurance* (Headland, Robert *et al.*, London, 2000)

Carter, Robert R., *Searching for the Franklin Expedition, The Arctic Journal of Robert Randolph Carter* (The Naval Institute Press, Maryland, 1998)

Cherry-Garrard, Apsley, *The Worst Journey in the World* (Penguin Books Ltd, London, 1937)

Cyriax, Richard J., *Sir John Franklin's Last Expedition* (The Arctic Press, Plaistow & Sutton Coldfield, 1997)

Debenham, Frank, *In the Antarctic* (John Murray, London, 1938)

de Bray, Emile, *A Frenchman in Search of Franklin. De Bray's Arctic Journal, 1852-1854* (University of Toronto Press, 1992)

Evans, Adm Sir, E.R.G.E., *South with Scott* (Collins, London)

Fiennes, Ranulph, *Captain Scott* (Hodder & Stoughton, London, 2003)

Fisher, Margery and James, *Shackleton* (Barrie Books Ltd, London, 1957)

Guttridge, Leonard, *Icebound, The Jeannette Expedition's Quest for the North Pole* (Airlife Publishing Ltd, 1987)

Herbert, Wally, *Noose of Laurels, The Discovery of the North Pole* (Hodder & Stoughton, 1989)

Hooper, W.H., *Ten Months Among the Tents of the Tuski* (John Murray, London, 1853)

Hurley, Frank, *Shackleton's Argonauts* (Angus & Robertson, Sydney, London, Melbourne, Wellington, 1956)

Jones, A.E.G., *Henry Peter Pegler, Captain of the Foretop (1811-1848)* (Notes and Queries, December 1984)

Jones, A.E.G., *Polar Portraits, Collected Papers* (Caedmon of Whitby, 1992)

Jones, A.E.G., *A Miscellany* (A.E.G. Jones)

King, H.R.G., *The Antarctic* (Blandford Press Ltd, London, 1969)

Lamb, G.F., *Franklin: Happy Voyager, Being the Life and Death of Sir John Franklin* (Ernest Benn Ltd, London, 1956)

Lashly, William, *Under Scott's Command, Lashly's Antarctic Diaries* (Victor Gollancz Ltd, London, 1969)

Lloyd, Christopher, *Mr Barrow of the Admiralty, A Life of Sir John Barrow 1764-1848* (Collins, London, 1970)

Markham, R.Adm A.H., *The Great Frozen Sea* (Kegan Paul, Trench, Trubner & Co., Ltd, London, 1878)

Markham, Capt A.H., *Life of Sir John Franklin* (George Phillip & Son, 132 Fleet Street, London, 1891)

Markham, Sir Clemence, *Life of Admiral Sir Leopold McClintock* (John Murray, 1909)

Markham, Sir Clemence, *Arctic Obsession* (Bluntisham Books and the Erskine Press, 1986)

Markham, Sir Clemence R., *Antarctic Exploration*: A Plea for a National Expedition (The Royal Geographical Society, London, 1898)

McClintock, Adm Sir F.L., *The Voyage of the 'Fox' in Arctic Seas in Search of Franklin and his Companions* (John Murray, London, 1908)

Mills, Leif, *Frank Wild* (Caedmon of Whitby, 1999)

Mountevans, Adm Lord, *The Desolate Antarctic* (The Travel Book Club, London, 1949)

Nares, Capt RN, *The Official Report of the Recent Arctic Expedition* (John Murray, London, 1876)

Nares, Capt Sir G.S., *A Narrative of a Voyage to the Polar Sea During 1875-6 in HM Ships 'Alert' and 'Discovery'* (Sampson Low, Marston, Searle & Rivington, London, 1878)

Neatby, Leslie H., *The Search for Franklin* (M.G. Hurtig Ltd, Edmonton, Canada, 1970)

Osborn, Cdr Sherard (Edit), *The Discovery of the North-West Passage* (Charles E. Tuttle & Co. Rutland, Vermont & Tokyo, 1969)

Owen, Roderic, *The Fate of Franklin, The Life and Mysterious Death of the Most Heroic of Arctic Explorers* (Hutchinson of London, 1978)

Poulsom, Lt-Col N.W. and Myres, R., Adm. J.A.L., *British Polar Exploration and Research. A Historic and Medallic Record with Biographies, 1818-1999* (Savannah Publications, 2000)

Pound, Reginald, *Scott of the Antarctic* (World Books, London, 1968)

Preston, Diana, *A First Rate Tragedy, Captain Scott's Antarctic Expeditions* (Constable & Company Ltd, London, 1997)

Richards, Robert L., *Dr John Rae* (Caedmon of Whitby, 1985)

Savelle, James M., *Effects of Nineteenth Century European Exploration on the Development of the Netsilik Inuit Culture* (Canadian Arctic History, 1845-1859, National Museums of Canada, Ottawa, 1985)

Savours, Ann, *The Voyages of the Discovery* (Virgin Books, Virgin Publishing, 1992)
Scott, Capt Robert F., *The Voyage of the 'Discovery', Volumes I and II* (Smith, Elder & Co., London, 1905)

Seaver, George, *'Birdy' Bowers of the Antarctic* (John Murray, London, 1938)

Shackleton, Sir Ernest, *The Heart of the Antarctic* (William Heinemann, London, 1910)

Shackleton, Sir Ernest, *South* (William Heinemann, London, 1922)

Villarejo, Oscar, *Dr Kane's Voyage to the Polar Lands* (The University of Pennsylvania Press, 1965)

Wallace, Hugh N., *The Navy, The Company, and Richard King. British Exploration in the Canadian Arctic 1829-1860* (McGill-Queen's University Press, Montreal, 1980)

Wilson, Edward, *Diary of the Discovery Expedition to the Antarctic Regions 1901-1904* (Blandford Press Ltd, 1966)

Worsley, F.A., *The Great Antarctic Rescue* (Sphere Books Ltd, London, 1979)

Articles

Barr, William, 'Franklin in Siberia? Lieutenant Bedford Pim's Proposal to Search the Arctic Coast of Siberia, 1851-52' (Published in *Arctic*, Vol. 45, No. 1, March 1992)

Deacon, Margaret & Savours, Ann, 'Sir George Strong Nares (1831-1915) (Published in *Polar Record*, Vol. 18, No. 113, May 1976)

Erskine, Angus B., 'The Arctic Ship 'Fox' (Published in *Polar Record*, Vol. 33, No. 185, 1997)

Janes, Robert R., 'The Preservation and Ethnohistory of a Frozen Historic Site in the Canadian Arctic' (*Arctic*, Vol. 35, No. 3, September 1982)

Stone, Ian R., 'An Episode in the Franklin Search: The Prince Albert Expedition, 1850, Parts 1 and 2' (The *Polar Record*, Vol. 29, 1993)

Dickens, Charles, 'The Lost Arctic Voyagers' (Published in *Household Words*, November 1854)

Other

(Anonymous), *Arctic Awards and their Claimants* (T. Hatchard, London, 1856)

(Anonymous), 'Captain Austin's Arctic Expedition' (*The Nautical Magazine*, Vol. XIX, No. 7, July 1850)

Scott's Last Expedition, Volumes I and II (Smith, Elder & Co., London, 1913)

(Anonymous), *The Great Arctic Mystery* (Chapman & Hall, London, 1856)

The Dictionary of National Biography

The Geographical Magazine, June 1875

'The Life and Correspondence of Jane, Lady Franklin' (Misc.Don 447/1-2, Linconshire Archives)

Narrative of Sir John Richardson to the Admiralty Secretary (Admiralty Library Collection)

Narrative of Sir James Ross to the Admiralty Secretary (Admiralty Library Collection)

The Nautical Magazine:
   June 1850
   November 1851
   January 1852
   July 1852
   November 1852
   December 1852
   November 1853
   December 1853

Reports from Captain Kellett of HMS *Herald* and Commander Moore of *HM Sloop Plover* relative to their proceedings in the search for Sir John Franklin, by Bhering's Straits, November 22 1849 (Admiralty Library Papers)

Report of the Select Committee in Preserved Meats (Navy). (House of Commons, 3 May 1852)

Scientific Instructions for the Arctic Expedition, 1875, Suggested by the Arctic Committee of the Royal Society. (Her Majesty's Stationery Office, 1875)

The Search for Franklin – A Narrative of the American Expedition under Lieutenant Schwatka. (T. Nelson & Sons, London, 1888)

'The Search for Franklin (From the Private Journal of an Officer of the *Fox*)'. (*The Cornhill Magazine*, January 1860)

The Trans-Antarctic Expedition. Publicity leaflet published from the Expedition's offices at 4 New Burlington Street, London.

INDEX

If you are interested in purchasing other books published by Tempus,
or in case you have difficulty finding any Tempus books in your local bookshop,
you can also place orders directly through our website

www.tempus-publishing.com